NUMBER SEVEN

The Elma Dill Russell
Spencer Foundation Series

A JOURNEY THROUGH TEXAS

Barker Texas History Center Series, No. 2

A JOURNEY THROUGH TEXAS

Or, a Saddle-Trip on the Southwestern Frontier

FREDERICK LAW OLMSTED

Foreword by Larry McMurtry

University of Texas Press
Austin & London

Library of Congress Cataloging in Publication Data
Olmsted, Frederick Law, 1822–1903.
A journey through Texas.

(Barker Texas History Center series; no. 2)
Reprint of the 1857 ed. published by Dix, Edwards, New York.
Includes bibliographical references.
1. Texas—Description and travel. 2. Slavery in the United States—Texas.
3. Olmsted, Frederick Law, 1822–1903. I. Title. II. Series: Eugene C.
Barker Texas History Center. Barker Texas History Center series; no. 2.
F391.0512   1978   917.64   78-7028

ISBN 0-292-74007-7
ISBN 0-292-74008-5 pbk.

Foreword copyright © 1978 by the University of Texas Press

FOREWORD

Larry McMurtry

In December 1853, the Olmsted brothers—Frederick Law, then thirty-one years old, and John Hull, three years his junior—left Frederick's orderly but none too profitable Staten Island farm and set out for Texas. They proceeded comfortably enough, by rail and steamboat, over the Cumberland, down the Ohio and the Mississippi, and up the Red, disembarking, due to the dryness of the last stream, a few miles shy of the dusty little port of Natchitoches, Louisiana. There they purchased two horses and a mule named Mr. Brown and set off, as it were, into the teeth of the Texas winter.

Their journey westward soon left them thoroughly acquainted with bad food, drafty housing, wet and dry northers, and surly company; they experienced very little that could be described as comfortable until they fetched up at the small German emigrant community of New Braunfels, near San Antonio. The civility, the cleanliness, the neatly made beds, and the well-laid tables of New Braunfels reminded them happily of the little Bavarian inns they had visited during a walking tour of England, France, and Germany some years earlier—a venture that had resulted in *Walks and Talks of an American Farmer in England* (1852), Frederick's well-received first book. One consequence of that modest first success was that Frederick had been commissioned by Henry Raymond, the astute editor of the newly established *New York Daily Times* (after 1857, simply the *Times*), to travel through the southern slave states and contribute a series of letters, not merely upon slavery itself but upon the society that a slaveholding economy had produced. Frederick made this first trip in 1852 and 1853 and wrote so vividly and intelligently of what he found that Raymond was encouraged to send him off again.

While Frederick was thus launching a literary career, John Hull Olmsted was gallantly attempting to come to grips with the fact that he was a dying man. Like John Keats, whom he physically somewhat resembled,[1] John Hull Olmsted was tubercular; from 1851 on he sought in vain for a climate that might arrest the disease. Meanwhile, determined, if nothing else, to live while he was alive, he continued his medical studies, married an attractive and witty woman, Mary Perkins, and in the six years that remained to him fathered three children, the last born scarcely three months before his death.

When he decided to accompany his brother on the Texas trip, John Hull no doubt harbored the hope that the clean dry air of the prairies would work a miracle and keep him alive. Frederick, for his part, hoped to find on those same prairies something that might eventually improve the moral health of the republic: a place where the virtues of free-soil agriculture could fully assert themselves and thus demonstrate once and for all that slavery was as wasteful and inefficient as it was demoralizing. Stirred by the enthusiasm of Adolph Douai, the vigorous editor of the *San Antonio Zeitung*, Frederick continued for some years to promote a free-soil colony in West Texas, hoping to convince everyone by sheer weight of crop yield that slavery was detrimental to sound agricultural practice.

The Olmsteds stayed in central, south, and southeastern Texas for about four months. They had hoped to go on to California but were unable to raise a party of sufficient size to give them a fair chance of getting through the hostile Indians to the West. Disappointed in that regard, they luckily engaged a scout named John Woodland—Central Casting could have provided no more perfect Natty Bumppo—who guided them on a very pleasant excursion into northern Mexico. After that they started home, visiting Houston and Beaumont along the way and experiencing new miseries amid the mosquito-clouded bayous of Louisiana. Winter was well over by this time, and the humidity and oppressive heat did John Hull's lungs no good. He took a steamer to New Orleans and thence home, while Frederick rode north and returned by way of the "back country": Mississippi, Tennessee, Georgia, and North Carolina.

This trip and the one that preceded it yielded Frederick Law Olmsted three books: *A Journey in the Seaboard Slave States* (1856), *A Journey through Texas; or, a Saddle-Trip on the Southwestern Frontier* (1857), and *A Journey in the Back Country* (1860). Individually, none of the books was wildly successful, but a two-volume abridgment called *The Cotton Kingdom* (1861) had a good deal of influence, both at home and abroad. Though in some ways clumsier than the original volumes, thanks to some rather hasty updating, it still provides a very readable survey of antebellum society. The reader must be prepared to endure a good deal of proselytizing with regard to agricultural

1. See the photographs in *The Papers of Frederick Law Olmsted*, edited by Charles C. McLaughlin (Baltimore: Johns Hopkins Press, 1977), vol. 1.

method—a passion with Olmsted—but the overall picture is nonetheless more comprehensive than that given by other contemporary travelers: Charles Lyell, Fanny Kemble, Harriet Martineau, etc.

When the brothers returned east in 1854, it was soon clear that farming was from then on to be a theoretical rather than a practical passion with Frederick. In 1855 he moved to New York to pursue his literary career, leaving his brother to make what he could of the Staten Island farm. John Hull, in increasingly poor health, could make little of it, but he stuck with it gamely for two more years. Frederick, meanwhile, had joined the firm of Dix, Edwards, the publishers of the first two volumes of his trilogy. In 1856 the firm sent him to England to scout for literary properties, and when he left he deposited his journal, notes, and letters relating to the Texas trip with the ever amenable John Hull, who had agreed to work them up into a book. In his prefatory note to the book that eventually appeared, Frederick states that owing to the pressure of other business he had committed the writing to his brother with "free scope of expression and personality."

Laura Wood Roper, to whose masterful biography this foreword is indebted for the bulk of its facts, records that since John Hull had done most of the work on *Journey through Texas* it was agreed that he should have two-thirds of the royalties.[2] The fair-minded reader will be obliged, I think, to treat the book as a collaboration, though the exact degree of collaboration is a matter likely to remain unclear. The journal from which John Hull Olmsted worked is lost,[3] and our only means of judging how much "personality" and "expression" he contributed is by comparing the book with Frederick's letters to the *Times* or with the two volumes between which it is sandwiched.

In my view, *Journey through Texas* is easily the most engaging of the three books, though its appealing qualities are by no means all attributable to the light, humorous, and fanciful hand of John Hull Olmsted. In the main it is clearly Frederick's book; much of the reportage and all that is most editorial, analytical, or statistical are in the tone of the other two books, though it is certainly arguable that the middle book shows Frederick at his best. In *A Journey in the Seaboard Slave States* he was a bit perfervid—too eager on the one hand, too disappointed on the other; whereas, by the time he came to write *A Journey in the Back Country*, he seems more than a little fatigued, not merely by the memory of poor and inhospitable regions but by the necessarily repetitious nature of the kind of journalism he was producing.

2. *F. L. O.: A Biography of Frederick Law Olmsted* (Baltimore: Johns Hopkins Press, 1973).
3. *The Slave States*, a severely abridged version of the trilogy, edited by Harvey Wish (New York: Capricorn Books, 1959), p. 27.

Journey through Texas represents something of a golden mean. Frederick is at his mature and energetic best, and the narrative and analytic base he laid down is lightened just sufficiently by John Hull's softly ironic sense of humor and his occasionally happy turn of phrase. By this time, of course, Frederick was a seasoned journalist, with a forceful literary style. He had a good ear and was unflinchingly candid in reporting what he heard. He may not have had precisely an open mind, but he was a moderate man, quickly sympathetic and broadly curious. He basically disliked the South but, wherever he went, he responded both to accomplishment and to potential. The open prairies of central Texas appealed to the farmer in him, and also to the utopian. He saw there an opportunity for a society to develop which might yet escape the curse which lay on so much of the nation.

The Olmsted brothers were educated men, predisposed to aesthetic judgments and discriminations. Both had traveled abroad, and neither was loath to draw unfavorable comparisons. They liked good equipment, well-built houses, order, good design, good food, good farming, and good conversation. At first it seems that they will find none of the above in Texas, but once they get into the German settlements they are quickly soothed.

Nonetheless, strong negative reporting has a way of outweighing mild positives, and so vivid are their accounts of the squalor, brutality, flimsy housing, bad food, filth, and apathy met with in East Texas that descriptions of pleasanter times soon drift from one's memory. It is a shock, late in the book, to find Frederick speaking almost hyperbolically of the region between the Colorado and the Nueces:

> For sunny beauty of scenery and luxuriance of soil, it stands quite unsurpassed in my experience, and I believe no region of equal extent in the world can show equal attractions. It has certainly left such pictures in memory, as bring it first to mind as a field for emigration, when any motive suggests a change of my own residence.

The remark is to be found amid the more than one hundred pages of miscellaneous information that has been dumped at the end of the book, much of which was probably added for the direct purpose of attracting free-soil emigrants to the area.

In the bibliography he included in this material, Frederick lists some thirty-three books and articles about Texas; of these perhaps only two, John Bartlett's *Personal Narrative* (1854) and G. W. Kendall's *Santa Fe Expedition* (1844), can compete with *Journey through Texas* for the attention of today's reader. It is an intelligent, lively, readable book, packed with keen observation and lightened by a delicate strain of humor. The attention paid to the adventures and misadventures of their animals makes up for a good many tedious digressions on matters of high import, such as the cost per acre of improving land for quince stocks, peach trees, or sugar cane. Throughout the book there is an alternation, almost in the manner of Thackeray, of descriptive summary with dramatic scene. A great deal of attention is paid to food and to the interior decoration—or lack of it—of the various residences the brothers stayed in. Both brothers suffered bad food less willingly than they suffered fools—complaints about the monotony of the Texas diet are frequent. The rudeness of the planters and frontiersmen they encountered is strikingly rendered; in their coarseness, vehemence, and belligerence they remind one at times of the loud grotesques of Smollett.

The book is too long, mostly because of Frederick's endlessly patient efforts to explain why slavery results in bad agricultural practices. He could not resist attempting to spread the balm of rationality over an issue that had already scarred the body politic. He makes it clear that he regards slavery as morally reprehensible, but his concentration upon agricultural practice is at times so intense that he almost makes us feel that anything that is morally reprehensible will lead in the first instance to a misuse of agricultural opportunities.

Despite a few longueurs, and considerable repetition, *Journey through Texas* remains one of the most readable of nineteenth-century American travel books. Despite all the obstacles of climate and culture, the two young travelers were having a good time. They were not provincials, but neither were they jaded cosmopolites. The squalors of the scruffier plantations were annoying, but once they got to the prairies they found much to amuse, stimulate, and excite them. It was a new place, a wonderful country, and the sense it gave of freshness and almost limitless possibility is reflected in their reporting.

The book, of course, represents only a moment in the career of Frederick Law Olmsted, who went on to great achievement in a new and painstaking discipline. Because he did so much, it is worth emphasizing that part of his vivid and enduring picture of our frontier belongs to his less fortunate brother, John Hull Olmsted, who died in Nice the year the book was published.

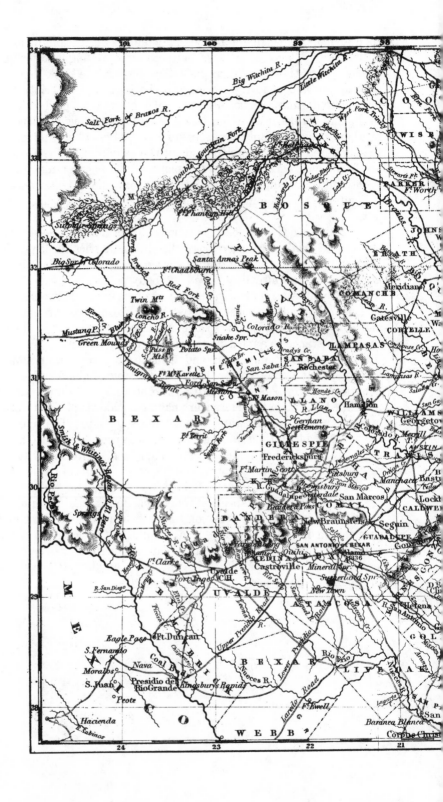

MAP

OF PART OF THE STATE OF

TEXAS.

Prepared by J. H. Colton & Co.
NEW YORK.

Richardson Co. sc

A

JOURNEY THROUGH TEXAS;

OR, A

SADDLE-TRIP ON THE SOUTHWESTERN FRONTIER:

WITH A

STATISTICAL APPENDIX.

BY

FREDERICK LAW OLMSTED,

AUTHOR OF "A JOURNEY IN THE SEABOARD SLAVE STATES,"
"WALKS AND TALKS OF AN AMERICAN FARMER IN ENGLAND," ETC., ETC.

NEW YORK:

DIX, EDWARDS & CO., 321 BROADWAY
LONDON: SAMPSON LOW, SON & CO.
EDINBURG: THOS. CONSTABLE & CO.
1857.

PREFACE.

THIS work is designed further to promote the mutual acquaintance of the North and South. The great extent and capacities of Texas, as well as its distinct position and history, have induced the author to devote to it a separate volume.

It has not been thought necessary to load the narrative with extended remarks and deductions upon the economical experience of the young State, but while the facts presented are suffered to speak for themselves, some of the more obvious conclusions to which their examination leads have been thrown into the form of a letter, for the reader's consideration.

Owing to the pressure of other occupations, the preparation of the volume from the author's journal has been committed, with free scope of expression and personality, to his brother, Dr. J. H. Olmsted, his companion upon the trip.

Note by the Editor.

The editor's motive for this journey was the hope of invigorating weakened lungs by the elastic power of a winter's saddle and tent-life. His present duty has been simply that of connecting, by a slender thread of reminiscence, the copious notes of facts placed in his hands, and in doing this he has drawn frankly upon memory for his own sensations. The lapse of two years may have breathed a little dullness on the pictures thus recalled, but it has served, also, to cool and harden any glow in the statements.

A sort of alter-egotism in the book was unavoidable, and some details that may seem rather trivial and spiritless have been preserved, because a traveler's own impressions depend so much on those unconsidered but characteristic trifles. The notes upon slavery in the volume are incidental, but the extraordinary effect upon federal policy produced by fluctuation in the local market, where ownership in forced labor is the principal investment, imparts to observations within these new limits a peculiar interest.

In an appendix will be found condensed tables of such statistics as are most useful for reference.

A LETTER TO A SOUTHERN FRIEND.

NEW YORK, *December 29th,* 1856.

MY DEAR FRIEND :—I regret that I cannot respond to the congratulatory, nor yet entirely to the conciliatory, expressions of your recent letter.

The character, and reputation of the nation, and with it the character, the social claims, and the principles, of every individual citizen, have been seriously compromised in the eyes of the civilized world, by recent transactions growing out of the unsettled state of our policy with regard to slavery-extension. The recent Presidential election decided nothing with respect to this, as you seem to suppose, because the vital question which really divides the country was not presented in its integrity by the party which triumphed. No person, therefore, claiming for himself a respectable and responsible position in society, can, with decency, it seems to me, when brought near the field of discussion, affect to be indifferent, or avoid a respectful expression of his own judgment upon the grave issues in debate. For instance, the extension of slavery into Texas, commenced, for good or evil, in our own day ; and when we of the North had the power and the constitutional right to prevent it. Our interest in its results cannot of course be deemed impertinent by its most jealous partisan. Offering to the public a volume of recent observations in Texas, I do not, therefore, see how I can, as you seem to suggest I should, avoid all discussion of slavery.

At the same time, I do not desire to engage in it, as I hardly need assure you, in a spirit at all inconsistent with a desirable friendship. Rather, in explaining the significance which, in my own mind, attaches to my narrative of facts, relative to the question upon which we have the misfortune to be divided in judgment, I shall hope to lessen, instead of aggravating, the causes of our difference.

Many of the comforts demanded by people in a moderate state of civilization are necessarily purchased at a greater cost, in a newly-settled region, than in the midst of a long-established community. We cannot expect to find a grist-mill, much less a baker's shop, still less a printing-office or a bookseller's shop, in an actual wilderness. The cost of good bread, therefore, or of intellectual sustenance, will be greater than where the constant demand to be expected from a numerous population has induced labor (or capital, which represents labor) to establish such conveniences.

For the same reason, the usual means of civilized education, both for young and for mature minds, will be procured with difficulty in the early days of any country. Consequently, though we may perceive some compensations, certain fallings-short from the standard of comfort and of character in older communities are inevitable.

The prosperity of a young country or state is to be measured by the rapidity with which these deficiencies are supplied, and the completeness with which the opportunity for profitable labor is retained.

An illustration will best enable me to explain how slavery prolongs, in a young community, the evils which properly belong only to a frontier. Let us suppose two recent immigrants, one in Texas, the other in the young free State of Iowa, to have both, at the same time, a considerable sum of money—say five thousand dollars—at disposal. Land has been previously purchased, a hasty dwelling of logs constructed, and ample crops for sustenance harvested. Each has found communication with his market interrupted during a portion of the year by floods;

each needs an ampler and better house; each desires to engage a larger part of his land in profitable production; each needs some agricultural machinery or implements; in the neighborhood of each, a church, a school, a grist-mill, and a branch railroad are proposed.

Each may be supposed to have previously obtained the necessary materials for his desired constructions: and to need immediately the services of a carpenter. The Texan, unable to hire one in the neighborhood, orders his agent in Houston or New Orleans to buy him one: when he arrives, he has cost not less than two of the five thousand dollars. The Iowan, in the same predicament, writes to a friend in the East or advertises in the newspapers, that he is ready to pay better wages than carpenters can get in the older settlements; and a young man, whose only capital is in his hands and his wits, glad to come where there is a glut of food and a dearth of labor, soon presents himself. To construct a causeway and a bridge, and to clear, fence, and break up the land he desires to bring into cultivation, the Texan will need three more slaves—and he gets them as before, thereby investing all his money. The Iowan has only to let his demand be known, or, at most, to advance a small sum to the public conveyances, and all the laborers he requires —independent, small capitalists of labor—gladly bring their only commodity to him and offer it as a loan, on his promise to pay a better interest, or wages, for it than Eastern capitalists are willing to do.

The Iowan next sends for the implements and machinery which will enable him to make the best use of the labor he has engaged. The Texan tries to get on another year without them, or employs such rude substitutes as his stupid, uninstructed, and uninterested slaves can readily make in his ill-furnished plantation work-shop. The Iowan is able to contribute liberally to aid in the construction of the church, the school-house, the mill, and the railroad. His laborers, appreciating the value of the reputation they may acquire for honesty, good judgment, skill and industry, do not need constant superintendence, and he is able to call on his neighbors and advise, encourage and stimulate them. Thus the church, the school, and the railroad are soon in operation, and with them is brought rapidly into play other social machinery, which makes much luxury common and cheap to all.

The Texan, if solicited to assist in similar enterprises, answers truly, that cotton is yet too low to permit him to invest money where it does not promise to be immediately and directly productive.

The Iowan may still have one or two thousand dollars, to be lent to merchants, mechanics, or manufacturers, who are disposed to establish themselves near him. With the aid of this capital, not only various minor conveniences are brought into the neighborhood, but useful information, scientific, agricultural, and political; and commodities, the use of which is educative of taste and the finer capacities of our nature, are attractively presented to the people.

The Texan mainly does without these things. He confines the imports of his plantation almost entirely to slaves, corn, bacon, salt, sugar, molasses, tobacco, clothing, medicine, hoes and plow-iron. Even if he had the same capital to spare, he would live in far less comfort than the Iowan, because of the want of local shops and efficient systems of public conveyance which cheapen the essentials of comfort for the latter.

You will, perhaps, say that I neglect to pay the Iowan laborers their wages. It is unnecessary that I should do so: those wages remain as capital to be used again for the benefit of the community in Iowa. Besides, the additional profit which has accrued to the farmer by reason of the more efficient tools and cattle he has acquired, the greater cheapness with which the railroad will transport his crops to be sold, the smaller subtractions from stock and crops he will have met with from the better employment of his neighbors, and the influence of the church and school upon them, will go far towards paying these debts.

The difficulty of obtaining a profitable return for labor, applied with the disadvantages which thus result from slavery, is such that all but the simplest, nearest, and quickest promises of profit are neglected in its direction. As a general, almost universal, rule, the Texan planter, at the beginning of any season, is in debt, and anxious to acquire money, or its equivalent, to meet his engagements. The quickest and surest method of getting it before the year ends, is to raise cotton—for cotton, almost alone, of all he can produce under these disadvantages, bears the cost of transportation to cash customers. He will rarely, as I have supposed, invest in a carpenter; he will rarely undertake the improvement of a road. He will content himself with his pioneer's log-cabin, and wait the pleasure of nature at the swamp and the ford. His whole income will be reinvested in field-hands.

He plants cotton largely—quite all that his laborers can cultivate properly. Generally, a certain force will cultivate more than it can pick, pack, and transport to public conveyance. Unwilling to lose the overplus, he obtains, upon credit again, another addition to his slave force. Thus the temptation constantly recurs, and constantly the labor is directed to the quickest and surest way of sustaining credit for more slaves.

After a certain period, as his capital in slaves increases, and his credit remains unimpaired, the dread of failure, and the temptation to accumulate capital become less, and he may begin to demand the present satisfaction of his tastes and appetites. Habit, however, will have given him a low standard of comfort, and a high standard of payment for it; and he will still be satisfied to dispense with many conveniences which have long before been acquired by the Iowan; and to pay a higher price for those he demands, than more recent, or less successful, immigrants to his vicinity can afford.

Thus he will have personally grown rich, perhaps; but few, if any, public advantages will have accrued from his expenditures. It is quite possible that, before he can arrive at that point of liberality in expenditure which the Iowan started with, the fertility of his soil will have been so greatly reduced that the results of labor upon it are no longer accumulative of profit, but simply enable him to sustain the mode of life to which he and his slaves are accustomed.

This occurs, I again remind you, not merely because labor is applied to the end of immediately realizing a return in slaves, but because it continues constantly to be applied without the advantage of efficient machinery, and the cheapest means of marketing its results; also, because the planter's mind, which, by a freer expenditure of capital at an early day, would have been informed and directed to a better method of agriculture, remains in ignorance of it, or locked against it by the prejudice of custom and habit.

I have described to you the real condition, and its historical rationale, of a majority of the better class of planters in Texas, as, after many favorable opportunities of acquaintance with them, I have apprehended it. My knowledge of Iowan proprietors, of similar capital, is not personal, but inferential and from report. It may be there are none such, but it makes little difference in the end whether the five thousand dollars to be expended is held by one proprietor, or divided among a number. It is so much capital disengaged.

I have made circumstantial inquiry of several persons who have resided both in Iowa and in Texas, and have ascertained, most distinctly, that the rapidity with which the discomforts of the frontier are overcome, the facility with which the most valuable conveniences, and the most important luxuries, moral, mental, and animal, of old communities, are reobtained, is astonishingly greater in the former than the latter.

Comparing Texas with New York, I can speak entirely from personal observation. I believe it is a low estimate, that every dollar of the nominal capital of the substantial farmers of New York represents an amount of the most truly valuable commodities of civilization, equal to five dollars in the nominal wealth of Texas planters. And this, notwithstanding that the climate of Texas has a great superiority over that of New York or Iowa. I think that the labor of one man in Texas will more easily produce adequate sustenance and shelter for a family and an ordinary farm-stock of working cattle, than that of two anywhere in the Free States.

And this, again, without regard to that quality of the climate which enables the Texan to share in the general monopoly of the South in the production of cotton—a quality so valuable that Texans sell scarcely anything out of the State but cotton, which they even find it profitable to exchange for corn raised in Ohio, and taxed with the expense of a great transportation, and several exchanges. Not that corn is produced with less labor in Ohio, but that cotton is produced with so much more profit in Texas. Corn, and every other valuable staple production of the soil of the Free States, except, perhaps, oats and potatoes, for which there are special substitutes, may be grown extensively, and with less expenditure of labor, in Texas. Nor did we—my medical companion and myself—have reason to retain the common opinion, after careful attention to the subject, that the health of white people, or their ability to labor, was less in the greater part of Texas than in the new Free States. We even saw much white and free labor applied to the culture of cotton with a facility and profit at least equal to that attending the labor of enslaved negroes, at the same distance from market.

All things considered, I believe that the prosperity of Texas, measured by the rapidity with which the inconveniences and discomforts, inevitable only in a wilderness or an uncivilized state of society, are removed, would have been ten times greater than it is, had it been, at the date of its annexation, thrown open, under otherwise equally favorable circumstances, to a free immigration, with a prohibition to slavery. I think that its export of cotton would have been greater than it now is; that its demand from, and contribution to, commerce would have been ten times what it now is; that it would possess ten times the length of railroad; ten times as many churches; ten times as many schools, and a hundred times as many school-children as it now has.

You may think it too soon to form a judgment of any value upon the prosperity of Texas, as measured by the other criterion I proposed—namely, "the completeness with which the opportunity for profitable labor is retained." But what do you say to the fact that, in the eastern counties, that spectacle so familiar and so melancholy in your own State, in all the older Slave States, is already not unfrequently seen by the traveler—an abandoned plantation of "worn-out" fields, with its little village of dwellings, now a home only for wolves and vultures?

This but indicates a large class of observations,* by which I hold myself justified in asserting that the natural elements of wealth in the soil of Texas will have been more exhausted in ten years, and with them the rewards offered by Providence to labor will have been more lessened than, without slavery, would have been the case in two hundred. Do not think that I use round numbers carelessly. After two hundred years' occupation of similar soils by a free-laboring community, I have seen no such evidences of waste as, in Texas, I have after ten years of slavery. And indications of the same kind I have observed, not isolated, but general, in every Slave State but two—which I have seen only in parts yet scarcely at all settled. Moreover, I have seen similar phenomena following slavery in other countries and in other climates.

It is not at all improbable, my good friend, that children of yours, in, perhaps, the tenth generation, will have to work, whatever may be their occupation, one hour a day more, during all their working lives, than they would have done but for this your policy of extending slavery over Texas, and thereby permanently

---

* Of this class, frequent notes on live stock will be found in the volume. The exception which Kentucky offers to all other Slave States, in this respect, is easily accounted for, and is clearly maintained by a great sacrifice of other sources of wealth, which sacrifice would be unnecessary, but for slavery.

liminishing the rightful profits of labor. Bread is to cost them more by the pound, cotton and wool stuffs more by the yard.

Will you say that no superficial observations of a passing stranger can shake your confidence in the great higher law of demand and supply? That slavery cannot be forced by any legislation to exist for an injurious period in any country or region where free labor would, on the whole, be more economical? That free labor, on the other hand, cannot be restrained? That the climate of Texas demands African laborers, and that Africans are incapable of persistent labor, unless they are controlled, directed, and forced by a superior will? There are a few facts mentioned in these pages which bear on both these points, and to which I will simply beg you to give a fair consideration. Especially, I would be glad to have you ponder the experience of the German colonists, of which, though the narration is influenced, perhaps, by an irresistible enthusiasm of admiration, the details have been carefully obtained and verified.

As to the needlessness of legal restrictions upon slavery where its introduction would be uneconomical, let me ask, do you consider public lotteries of money economical institutions? They exist in every civilized community wherein they are not prohibited by law. Gambling-houses, and places of traffic in stolen goods, you will hardly deem economical conveniences in any climate; yet laws are everywhere required to restrict their increase.

I consider that slavery is no less disastrous in its effects on industry—no less destructive to wealth. The laws and forces sustaining it, where it has been long established, may have become a temporary necessity, as poisons are to the life of some unfortunate invalids. Judge you of that. But laws intended to extend its field of improvidence are unjust, cruel, and oppressive. Revolutionary resistance to them by all men whose interest it is to have industry honestly paid, can only be wrong while likely to be unsuccessful.

There are two reasons, both of which, you have confessed to me, operate on your own mind, why, the power to hold slaves being secured, men employ them in preference to the much cheaper free labor, and why the vitality of slavery need be nowhere dependent on its mere economy as a labor system.

First: Slavery educates, or draws out, and strengthens, by example and exercise, to an inordinate degree, the natural lust of authority, common as an element of character in all mankind. To a degree, that is, which makes its satisfaction inconvenient and costly—costly of other means of comfort, not only to the individual, but to the community.

Thus, a man educated under the system will be disposed no longer than he is forced, by law or otherwise, to employ servants or laborers who may make demands upon him, and if those demands are refused, may in their turn legally refuse to obey him. He will prefer to accept much smaller profits, much greater inconveniences, than would a man otherwise educated, rather than submit to what he considers to be the insolence of a laborer, who maintains a greater self-respect, and demands a greater consideration for his personal dignity, than it is possible for a slave to do.*

Secondly: The power of exercising authority in this way is naturally overmuch coveted among you. It gives position and status in your society more than other wealth—(wealth being equivalent to power). It is fashionable with you to own slaves, as it is with the English to own land, with the Arabs,

---

* The apologetic style in which the Southern newspapers generally commented upon the homicide, by a member of Congress, educated in Alabama, of a servant in a hotel at Washington, last spring, affords a sad indication of the strength of this educational prejudice. In some cases no apology, but a distinct approval, of such a method of vindicating Southern habits of unmitigated authority was expressed. The Charleston *Standard* observed: " If white men accept the office of menials, it should be expected that they will do so with an apprehension of their relation to society, and the disposition quietly to encounter both the responsibilities and liabilities which the relation implies." The Alabama *Mail*, extending the scope of its demand to free soil, remarked : " It is getting time that waiters at the North were convinced that they are servants and not gentlemen in disguise. We hope this Herbert affair will teach them prudence."

horses; and as beads and vermilion have a value among the Indians which seems to us absurd, so, among you, has the power of commanding the service of slaves. Consequently you are willing to pay a price for it which, to one not educated as you have been, seems absurdly high. Nor are you more likely to dispense with slaves, when you have it in your power to possess them, than the Chinese with their fashion of the queue, Turks with their turban, or Englishmen with their hats.

We need no restrictions upon fashions like these, which are oppressive only to those who obey them. Such is not the case with the fashion of slavery.*

But still you may doubt if slavery can long remain where it is uneconomical; the influences I have mentioned might, you will reflect, induce a Southerner to continue to employ his slaves while he is able; but his ability to do so would soon be exhausted if the institution were really uneconomical; in a new country the opportunity of employing slaves would soon be lost, owing to the superior advantages those would have who employed the cheaper labor of freemen; in fact, capital would be rapidly exhausted in the effort to sustain the luxury of commanding slaves.

Such, precisely, is the case. How, then, does it continue? Do not be offended if I answer, by constantly borrowing and never paying its debts.

Look at any part of the United States where slavery has *predominated* for a historic period; compare its present aspect with that it bore when peopled only by "heathen salvages," and you

---

* It might be supposed that the distinct "mean white" class, characteristic of older communities in the Slave States, could hardly yet have been developed in a region where slavery itself has but just now been transplanted, and where the avenues of escape from it, and of better possibilities, are so open and inviting to all. But it appears that such a class is a necessary phenomenon attending slavery. The planter in Eastern Texas speaks with the same irritation of his poorer neighbors that he does elsewhere at the South, and says, "If there are hog-thieves anywhere, it is here." The existence of the classes, master and slave, implies the existence of a miserable intermediate class.

will see that the luxury of slaves, and what other luxury through their labor has therein been enjoyed, have been acquired at an immense cost beyond that of mere labor. You will see that what has been called the profit of slave labor has been obtained only by filching from the nation's capital—from that which the nation owes its posterity—many times the gross amount of all the production of that labor.*

Governor Adams, in a recent message to the legislature of South Carolina, intimates that, at ten cents a pound, English manufacturers are paying too little for the cotton this country sends them. I think twice that amount would be too little to recompense the country for the loss of capital at present involved in its production. I believe that, with free labor in Texas, unembarrassed by the inconveniences attending slavery, it could have been profitably exported at half that price.

You will still ask how slavery, laboring under such economical

---

* A respectable Southern critic has asked, if evidences of a spendthrift system of industry, similar to those described in the Slave States, might not have been found by one disposed to look for them, in the Free, and has quoted official testimony of a reduced production per acre of one of the crops cultivated in New York, as refuting my evidence of the desolating effects of slavery in the Seaboard States.

Waste of soil and injudicious application of labor is common in the agriculture of the North, but nowhere comparably with what is general at the South. Nowhere, in any broad agricultural district, does such waste appear to have taken place, without a present equivalent existing for it. Nowhere is the land, with what is attached to it, now less suitable and promising for the residence of a refined and civilized people, than it was before the operations, which have been attended with the alleged waste, were commenced.

I am mistaken if the same is true of Eastern Virginia and Carolina, or any other district where slavery has predominated for a historic period. The land, in these cases, is positively less capable of sustaining a dense civilized community, than it would be if no labor at all had ever been expended upon it. Had all its original elements of wealth remained intact, had it been hitherto entirely reserved from civilized occupation, it would have sold for more by the acre to-day, than it is now to be valued at with all the ameliorations and constructions which labor has effected upon it. Labor, in the case of Eastern Virginia, for two hundred years, by a community in which the controlling force has been the boasted Anglo-Saxon, the prevailing religion Christian and Protestant.

disadvantages, can take possession of any country, to the exclusion or serious inconvenience of free labor ?

Plainly, it may do so by fraud and violence—by disregard of the rights of citizens. I will not say that these are necessities of its existence, only that they are alleged to be so by those who have carried slavery into Texas, as well as by those who have sought to establish it in Kansas. These missionaries of the institution voluntarily make the declaration, and put it deliberately on record, that lawless violence and repudiation of state pledges must be permitted in order to maintain slavery in these regions. Whether with reason or not, the purpose to maintain slavery is constantly offered and received as a sufficient excuse for disregarding not merely personal rights under the Constitution, but the most solemn treaty-obligations with a foreign nation.*

When you demand of us to permit slavery in our territory, we know that you mean to take advantage of our permission, to

---

* Is not the general impression, that frequent deeds of lawless violence are a necessary and pardonable characteristic of our frontier community, based upon, and entirely sustained by, occurrences which are peculiar to the frontier of the Slave States ? Lynch law is not found a necessary preliminary to good government in Iowa and Minnesota. Tarring and feathering, mob executions, bowie-knife fracases, deadly family feuds, etc., etc., are characteristic only of communities, the controlling minds in which have been educated in the Slave States. No one looks with hope or anxiety for spontaneous popular invasions or filibustering occupations of Canada West by Minnesotans or Michiganians. Plundering parties of Maine backwoodsmen do not constantly menace the peaceful villages of Nova Scotia. We do not have periodical reports from Eastport, of piratical fleets preparing to invade Newfoundland. But last year, a large band of mounted Texan Free-Companions plundered and burned, in mere wantonness, a peaceful Mexican town on the Rio Grande ; four hundred United States troops listening to the shrieks of fleeing women, and looking on in indolence. This has passed without rebuke ; apparently with entire public and official indifference. It was looked upon as one of the necessary and pardonable occurrences of a frontier. Would this have been the case, if it had happened on the Northwestern frontier ? Is it not time the people of the free West were delivered from the vague reputation of bad temper, recklessness, and lawlessness, under which they suffer, and which, without doubt, greatly deters industrious and peacefully disposed persons from immigrating among them ?

forbid freedom of discussion, and freedom of election; to prevent an effective public educational system; to interrupt and annoy our commerce, to establish an irresponsible and illegal censorship of the press; and to subject our mails to humiliating surveillance.

And you ask—nay, you demand, and that with a threatening attitude—that we shall permit you to do all this; for what purpose?

Not because you need an extension of your field of labor. Governor Adams, in the message to which I have referred, alleges that the poverty and weakness of the South are chiefly due to its deficiency of laborers. To say that it has too few laborers is to say that it has too much territory. And that is true.

I learn from trustworthy and unprejudiced sources, that the gentlemen who have carried slaves to Kansas have not done so because they believe it to be the most promising field of labor for slaves open to them; they do not hesitate to admit it to be otherwise. But they have gone there as a chivalric duty to their class and to the South—that South to which alone their patriotism acknowledges a duty. If they succeed in once establishing slavery as a state institution, they have reason for thinking that Kansas will be thereafter avoided, as a plague country would be, by free labor. For, to say to an emigrating farmer, "Kansas is a slave state," is to tell him that if he goes thither he will have to pay a dear price for everything but land; for tools, for furniture, for stock; that he may have to dispense during his life—as may his children after him—with convenient churches, schools, mills, and all elaborate mechanical assistance to his labor. Thus they calculate—and this is their only motive —that two more senators may be soon added to the strength of slavery in the government. They are only wrong in forgetting that free laborers are no longer constrained, by a compact with them, to quietly permit this curse to be established in Kansas.

Danger from insurrection is supposed by some to be proportionate to density of population, and your demand is sometimes urged on the plea that an extension of the area subject to the waste of slavery is necessary to be made in order to avoid this calamity.

If one-third of the land included in the present Slave States be given up to the poor whites and the buffaloes, and the remainder be divided into plantations averaging a square mile in size, the present slave population must double in number before each of these plantations will be provided with a laboring force equal to five able-bodied men and women.

If the policy of thus dispersing capital and labor, withholding so much wealth as it does from the service of commerce, and involving so much unnecessary expenditure, be really persisted in, from a fear of a slave rebellion, I think we have a right to ask you, the gentlemen who own this hazardous property, to provide some less expensive means of meeting the danger with which it threatens you. For, where will this way of meeting it carry us? You are unsafe now: if safety is to be obtained by greater dispersion, how great must it be? In another generation you will require the continent, and the tide of white immigration will be returning to the old world. There is a great significance in the emigration driven, even now, from the Slave States, contrary to the normal inclination of immigration, which is always southward and outward, into the colder Free States, which already have more than twice their density of population.*

---

* The Census tables show that the Slave States have sent nearly six times as many of their population into the Free Territories as the Free States have sent into Slave Territories. Kentucky, alone, has sent into Free Territory 60,000 more than all the Free States have sent into Slave Territory. Virginia, alone, has sent 60,000 more into the Free Territory than all the Free States have sent into Slave Territory. North Carolina and Tennessee have sent several thousands more into the Free Territories than all the Free States have sent into Slave Territory. Maryland, with a total white population of 418,000, has sent more than half as many persons into the Free Territories as all the Free States together, with a total white population of 13,300,000, have sent into the Slave Territories — See *Putnam's Monthly*, December, 1856, p. 652.

But this is not the reason given by the most ardent and talented extensionists. Your favorite statistician, Mr. DeBow, agrees with the South Carolina professor, Drew, who, he says, has fully shown how "*utterly vain*" are the fears of those who apprehend danger from a great increase in the number of slaves.* So say many others, especially when arguing the military strength of the Slave States.

The only argument steadily and boldly urged in the South itself, is that slavery must be extended in order to preserve the equality of the South in the republic. It would be folly, your editors and orators constantly assure us, to think that the South will remain in association with the North, unless she can retain such an equality.

There can be no dishonor for 1,100,000 citizens (the number voting in the Slave States at the recent election) to have less power of control in the government of a republic than 2,900,000 (the number of Northern voting citizens). The alleged folly of permitting the greater number of citizens to obtain a power of controlling the federal government is founded solely in the rumor, that it is the purpose of those who oppose the extension of slavery to force an abolition of slavery where it exists under the sanction of the sovereign state governments.

I trust you are not one of those who credit this rumor. My acquaintance with the people of the North is extensive and varied. I know, so far as it is within the ability of a man to be informed of the purposes of other men, that this rumor is still, as Daniel Webster declared it to be twenty-five years ago, a wicked device of unprincipled politicians.† I lose respect for

---

* Resources of the South, etc., vol. ii., p. 233.

† In 1830, Daniel Webster said, in the Senate:

"I know full well that it is, and has been, the settled policy of some persons in the South, for years, to represent the people of the North as disposed to interfere with them in their own exclusive and peculiar concerns. This is a delicate and sensitive point in Southern feeling; and of late years, it has always been touched, and generally with effect, whenever the object has been to unite

gentlemen whom I find to have been imposed upon by it. There are men, who, it is constantly asserted, are notoriously leaders among those having this purpose, whom I have happened to meet often, under circumstances favorable to a free expression of their political views and intentions. I have heard from them never the slightest suggestion of a desire to interfere by force, or any action of the central government, with the constitutional rights of the state governments to maintain slavery.

Since the attempt to extend slavery in Kansas, by the repeal of our old compromise with you, I have heard one man express the conviction, to which others may be approaching, that we shall never have done with this constantly recurring agitation, till we place ourselves in an offensive position towards the South, threatening the root of the national nuisance. This man, however, was not one of those who are considered the special enemies of the South, nor a politician by profession, but an honest, direct-minded old farmer, who has heretofore been numbered among those the South chooses to deem its friends ; a man, too, who, as it happens, has seen the South, knows its condition, and maintains friendly communication with slaveholders.

This indicates, in my opinion, the only way in which the people of the North can be tempted to use the control they already actually possess, and by their numbers are justly entitled to, in the confederate government, in the unconstitutional and revolutionary manner these lying political speculators are so ready to anticipate.

The chief object of this false accusation, is to excite the ignorant masses of your own citizens to act, with blindly-zealous concert, in favor of measures to which, if honestly presented, they would be equally opposed with the intelligent people of the

the whole South against Northern men or Northern measures. This feeling, always carefully kept alive, and maintained at too intense a heat to admit discrimination or reflection, is a lever of great power in our political machine. It moves vast bodies, and gives to them one and the same direction. But it is without adequate cause; and the suspicion which exists is wholly groundless.''

North. Its danger is now made sufficiently obvious by the conspiracies, among the slaves, which, since the election, have been
discovered in Virginia, Kentucky, Tennessee, Mississippi, Arkansas, and Texas—perhaps elsewhere.

These are the first general and formidable insurrectionary
movements since 1820, when, as your rumor is, the machina-
tions of the abolitionists commenced. Many general and formidable insurrections are matters of history previous to 1820.
The improbability that the abolitionists have been engaged in
stimulating insurrections, between 1820 and the present time, is
apparent. When you consider that, in all the districts wherein
these conspiracies are now discovered, there have been large and
excited public meetings, harangued by loud-voiced speakers,
whose principal topic was the imminent danger of an interference
by Frémont, and the people of the North, in behalf of the slaves
against their masters—Frémont's name being already familiar in
their ears as that of a brave and noble man—remembering
this—how can you doubt whether the abolitionists, or your own
recklessly ambitious politicians, are most responsible for your
present danger?

The late message of President Pierce to Congress has been
distributed in the government publication and the newspapers by
hundreds of thousands in the Slave States, and has fallen directly
into the hands of half your house-servants, or may have been
given to any slave who purchases a plug of tobacco at a grocery. This message, or almost any of the speeches made by
Southern members in the debate upon it, which have, in like
manner, been freely scattered, will give the confident impression
to any man, not otherwise better informed, who reads it, or
hears it read or talked of, that a formidable proportion of the
white people of the North are determined " to effect a change in
the relative condition of the white and the black race in the
Slaveholding States;" that they are prepared to accomplish
this "through burning cities, and ravaged fields, and slaughtered
populations, and all that is terrible in foreign, complicated with

civil and servile war, devastation, and fratricidal carnage."* If he
have any disposition to obtain his liberty, it will at once be suggested to him that he and his fellows should be prepared to take
advantage of the suggestions thus made—the encouragement to
fight their way northward, thus published to them by a thoughtless Northern ally of their masters.   Is it the abolitionists or the
politicians you have most reason to fear?

Be assured, all attempts to extend slavery can only increase
the very danger which it is pretended they are made to avert.

In denying that a formidable number of the citizens of the Free
States are disposed to interfere between the slaves and the citizens in other States, I do not wish you to understand me to say
that there is not a large number of abolitionists among us: using
the word, as has lately become the custom, to mean those who
have formed a distinct judgment, that slavery is an evil,
the continuance of which it is proper, desirable, and possible
for you to more or less distinctly limit; who also think it
proper to express this opinion; who also think it their duty to
prevent those who hold the opinion that slavery is wholly a good
thing, desirable for indefinite perpetuation and extension, from
exercising the influence they endeavor to do, in our common
government, for the purpose of extending and perpetuating it.
I suppose about one-half of all the people of the Free States
are now distinctly and intelligently abolitionists, of this kind, and
nine-tenths of the remaining number are as yet simply too little
interested in the subject to have formed a judgment, by which
they can be reliably classed.   Out of a few localities, where
a commercial sympathy with planters is very direct, there is
no society in which an avowal of positive anti-abolition opinion
would not be considered eccentric.

Even of those voting at the late election for Mr. Buchanan,
among my acquaintance, more than half have expressed opinions
to me which would at once range them as abolitionists, and ex-

---

* Message of the President, December, 1856.

pose them to disagreeable treatment if uttered in Southern society. These voted as they did, not so much, I think, from fear that a division of the Union would result from Mr. Frémont's election, as because, being influential men in their party, and having been successful in obtaining the nomination of the candidate they deemed least dangerous of those advanced for the nomination, they felt bound in honor to sustain him.

Which way the progress of opinion tends, it is easy to see, and you need not trust my judgment. Examine the vote of the North in connection with statistics indicating the degree of intelligence and the means of transmitting and encouraging intelligence among—not the commercial or wealthy class, but—the general working people, and you will find Mr. Frémont's vote bears a remarkable correspondence to the advantage of any district or state in this particular. Now our means of improving education, of transmitting intelligence, and of stimulating reflection are very steadily increasing. The young men, attaining their majority in the next four years, will have enjoyed advantages, in these respects, superior to their predecessors. The effect of railroads, and cheaper postage—significantly resisted by those who are most violent partisans of the extension of slavery—and of cheaper books and newspapers, is, as to this question, almost all one way. It is our young men who are most sensitive to the insulting tone which the South thinks it proper to assume in all debates with those members of congress who are known to best represent the North. It is among those whose interest in public affairs is of recent date, that the old party terms of outcry are least expressive of evil.

It is not long since you yourself held in the highest respect and profoundest confidence as true citizens, such men as Chief Justice Parker and Judge Kent; Presidents Walker, Woolsey and King; James Hamilton, James S. Wadsworth, and John M. Read; Washington Irving, Longfellow and Bryant, and even Mr. Frémont—all now strongly sympathizing and openly coöperating with the party of the "abolitionists." There are many thousand young men who must still hold these honored names in as high respect as ever you did, who have lately acquired their first distinct political associations. Consider that, with these, the terms Abolitionist and Disunionist, Black Republican and Nigger-worshiper, must thus be hereafter irrevocably attached to names and characters once as familiar to the South as the North, and ever commanding, everywhere, the completest popular confidence, as the first gentlemen, the purest patriots, and the soundest thinkers in the land. Reflect, that at least nine out of ten of the clergy of every denomination, and of the lay-teachers, in the North, have been enrolled as " abolitionists," and probably a majority have thought it proper to publicly profess the faith now so denominated, and which the South has chosen to make the subject of the most violent, reckless, and relentless denunciation and persecution.

Do you think we shall go backward? Consider, that in those States which gave the only Northern majorities to Mr. Buchanan, an efficient public-school system has been a creation entirely of the last fifteen years : that in Southern Illinois and Indiana, where the vote against Mr. Fremont was heavier than elsewhere, the majority of living voters were born and lived in their early life, subject only to such educational advantages as existed—and exist—in the States of Virginia, North Carolina, Kentucky, and Tennessee. That the proportion of citizens who were educated in those States themselves, since schools became conveniently frequent, and newspapers and books a common luxury, will now very rapidly increase.

Very many other considerations might be adduced, if you do not believe that the policy of forcing an extension of slavery is necessary to the honor of the people of the South, and a duty to be performed without flinching, whatever sad consequences it may involve, why you should join me in pleading for its immediate and decisive abandonment.

I have said that already full one-half of the citizens of the North are decisively abolitionists in their convictions. You have

led them to consider the moral question involved in maintaining slavery where it is, by forcing them to think of the material profit or otherwise which will result to themselves and their children from carrying it where it is not, and their verdict is against you.*
I believe that, rather than be parties to its extension, rather than shift the responsibility of a decision upon those who are so unintelligent or uninformed as to be willing to settle in a territory where its prohibition is yet undecided—unless they are patriotic enough to go for the purpose of deciding it—they will accept anything else that you may place in the alternative. Be it disunion, be it war, foreign or domestic, it will not divert them from their purpose.

Any further extension or annexation of slavery, under whatever

---

* While the interest of the South in occupying a larger area of soil, is one that neither justice, generosity, friendship, nor self-interest would lead us to regard, the interest of the nation, *as a nation*, in my judgment, is strongly opposed to anything which unnecessarily deters the voluntary determination of independent laborers towards any unoccupied land. In fact, I believe that it is of far more consequence to apply the doctrine of free trade to labor than to anything else.

I have long been of the opinion that the proportion of capital nominally employed in agriculture in the Eastern Free States, though better there than in the Slave States, was far too great, as a matter of national economy.

Though I esteem the advantages of a tolerably complete social organization rather more than is usual, I consider that land has an exorbitantly high value, relatively to the reward of labor expended upon it, in New England, New York, New Jersey, and Pennsylvania. I could state interesting facts in the social condition of the agricultural, compared with other classes, to support this view. I suppose that in Kansas, and I am sure that in Western Texas, if slavery did not interfere, a laboring man with a small capital in stock and tools, would gain wealth as fast as he could in New England, if he were obliged to pay a rent one hundred per cent. higher on the value at which his land would be generally appraised.

If this is so, the interest of the merchant and the manufacturer equally with that of the laborer, enlists them to oppose the extension of slavery. Who can doubt for a moment that it does so, comparing the value to commerce of the demand of Virginia with Pennsylvania; of Kentucky with Ohio; of Missouri with Illinois, and of Texas with Iowa and Minnesota. Every laborer, who is given the opportunity to work in Iowa, may be depended upon to soon call upon Boston, New York, and Philadelphia, Lowell, Trenton, and Pittsburgh, for ten times as much as any slave who is carried to Texas.

pretense or covering it is attempted, will only be effected in contemptuous defiance of the people of the Free States.

I am, and I trust long to remain,

Your fellow-citizen, and friend,

FRED. LAW OLMSTED.

INDEX.

CHAPTER I.

ROUTE TO TEXAS.

CHAPTER II.

ROUTE ACROSS EASTERN TEXAS.

CHAPTER III.

ROUTE THROUGH WESTERN TEXAS.

CHAPTER IV.

A TRIP TO THE COAST.

CHAPTER V.

A TRIP OVER THE FRONTIER.

CHAPTER VI.

ALONG THE EASTERN COAST.

CHAPTER VII.

GENERAL CHARACTERISTICS.

CHAPTER VIII.

REGIONAL CHARACTERISTICS.

A JOURNEY THROUGH TEXAS.

CHAP. I.

ROUTE TO TEXAS.

SOUTHERN PHENOMENA.

In entering new precincts, the mind instinctively looks for salient incidents to fix its whereabouts and reduce or define its vague anticipations. Last evening's stroll in Baltimore, from the absence of any of the expected indications of a slave state, left a certain restlessness which two little incidents this morning speedily dissipated. On reaching the station, I was amused to observe that the superintendent was, overseer-like, bestride an active little horse, clattering here and there over the numerous rails, hurrying on passengers, and issuing from the saddle his curt orders to a gang of watchful locomotives.

And five minutes had not elapsed after we were off at a wave of his hand, before a Virginia gentleman by my side, after carelessly gauging, with a glance, the effort necessary to reach the hinged ventilator over the window of the seat opposite us, spat through it without a wink, at the sky. Such a feat in New England would have brought down the house. Here it failed to excite a thought even from the performer.

1

Here was rest for the mind. Scene, the South; bound West. It could be nowhere else. The dramatis personæ at once fell into place. The white baby drawing nourishment from a black mamma on the train; the tobacco wagons at the stations; the postillion driving; the outside chimneys and open-centre houses; the long stop toward noon at a railway country inn; the loafing nobles of poor whites, hanging about in search of enjoyment or a stray glass of whisky or an emotion; the black and yellow boys, shy of baggage, but on the alert for any bit of a lark with one another; the buxom, saucy, slipshod girls within, bursting with fat and fun from their dresses, unable to contain themselves even during the rude ceremonies of dinner; the bacon and sweet potatoes and corn-bread that made for most of the passengers the substantials of that meal; the open kitchen in the back-ground, and the unstudied equality of black and white that visibly reigned there: nothing of this was now a surprise.

BALTIMORE AND OHIO RAILROAD.

The Baltimore and Ohio Railroad runs for some eighty miles through a fine farming country, with its appropriate, somewhat tame, rural scenery. At Harper's Ferry, the Potomac hurries madly along high cliffs over a rocky bed, and the effect, as you emerge from a tunnel and come upon the river, is startling and fine. Jefferson pronounced it the finest scenery he had seen—but he was a Virginian. After this the road follows up the valley as far as Cumberland, coming upon new and wilder beauties at every bend of the stream. But a day in a railway car is, in the best surroundings, a tedious thing, and it is with great pleasure that the traveler, in the early evening, shakes the dust from his back, and partakes of a quietly-prolonged supper in the St. Nicholas, the gaudy but excellent new inn at

CUMBERLAND.

This Cumberland, whence comes so much winter-evening comfort to us of the North, has itself the aspect of a most comfortless place. The houses of its 3,000 inhabitants are scattered among and upon steep hills, and show little of the taste their picturesque situations suggest. There is a certain dinginess and a slow, fixed, finished look arising from absence of new constructions, that remind you, especially in the dim light of a November rainy day, of the small manufacturing towns of England. Judging from the tones we heard and the signs we saw in some parts of the town, some portion of its population seems to have come from Wales or the West of England, and to possess, legitimately, a slow-going propensity.

The mines, from which the chief supply of bituminous coal is drawn for the use of the Atlantic coast, lie ten miles from the town, and communicate with it and the world by a branch railway. The transportation of this material forms one of the chief items of the income of the B. and O. Railroad. The price of the coal, for which we in New York were paying nine dollars a tun, was in the town one dollar and a half; at the mines, unselected, half a dollar—a difference which, for my own part, I gladly pay.

Unattractive as is the town of Cumberland, it is not easily forgotten, from its romantic position. From the cultivated hills adjoining it, is seen a view which is, in its way, unsurpassed, and, but a few minutes' walk above it, is a wooded gorge, into which a road enters as into monstrous jaws, and, after sunset, the heart fairly quakes, spite of reason, to intrude, defiant of such scowls of nature.

OVER THE BLUE RIDGE.

From Cumberland the rails plunge into the wild Blue Ridge Mountains, and only by dint of the most admirable persistence in tunneling, jumping, squeezing, and winding, do they succeed in forming a path for the locomotive over to the great basin of the Ohio. Vast sums and incredible Southern pains have laid this third great social artery from the West, and New York, after all, receives the blood.

Rocks, forests, and streams, alone, for hours, meet the eye. The only stoppages are for wood and water, and the only way-passengers, laborers upon the road. The conquered solitude becomes monotonous. It is a pleasure to get through and see again the old monotony of cultivation.

Broader grow the valleys, wider and richer the fields, as you run down with the waters the Western slope. At length the fields are endless, and you are following upward a big and muddy stream which must be—and is, the OHIO. You have reached the great West. Here are the panting, top-heavy steamboats, surging up against wind and current. The train slips by them as if they were at anchor. Here are the flat-boats, coal laden from Pittsburgh, helpless as logs, drifting patiently down the tide. And here is

WHEELING.

A dark clouded day, a "first-class hotel" of the poorest sort, a day which began coldly by a dim candle four hours before sunrise, and ended beyond midnight, after ten hours' waiting on steamboat promises, are not conducive to the most cheering recollections of any town ; but the brightest day would not, I believe, relieve the bituminous dinginess, the noisiness, and straggling dirtiness of Wheeling. Its only ornament is the suspension bridge, which is as graceful in its sweep as it is vast in its design and its utility.

THE OHIO.

The stage of water in the river was luckily ample for first-class boats, and we embarked upon the *David L. White*, when at length she came, on her long way from Pittsburgh to New Orleans. She was a noble vessel, having on board every arrangement for comfortable travel, including a table of which the best hotel would not be ashamed. The passage to Cincinnati occupies thirty-six hours. From some conversational impressions, our anticipations as to enjoyment of scenery on the Ohio were small, and we were most agreeably disappointed to find the book that nature offered occupying us during all our daylight, to the exclusion of those paper-covered ones we had thought it necessary to provide. Primeval forests form the main feature, but so alternating with farms and villages as not to tire. Limestone-hills and ranges bluff frequently in bold wooded or rocky masses upon the river, terminating by abrupt turns the stately vistas of the longer reaches. For a first day, the rafts, " the flats," all the varieties of human river-life, are a constant attraction. The towns, almost without exception, are repulsively ugly and out of keeping with the tone of mind inspired by the river. Each has had its hopes, not yet quite abandoned, of becoming the great mart of the valley, and has built in accordant style its one or two tall brick city blocks, standing shabby-sided alone on the mud-slope to the bank, supported by a tavern, an old storehouse, and a few shanties. These mushroom cities mark only a night's camping-place of civilization.

The route, via Baltimore to Cincinnati, we found, on the whole, a very agreeable one. The time is somewhat longer than by the more northern routes; but the charming scenery and the greater quiet and comfort, amply repay the delay.

THE OHIO VINEYARDS.

Twenty miles above Cincinnati begin the vines. They occupy the hill-slopes at the river's edge, and near the city cover nearly the whole ground that can be seen under cultivation. They are grown as on the Rhine, attached to small stakes three or four feet high, and some three by six feet apart. What a pity the more graceful Italian mode of swinging long vine-branches from tree to tree, could not be adopted. But profit and beauty are, as often, here again at war. The principal cultivators are naturally Germans. For the most part the land is held by them in small parcels; but much is also rented for a fixed share of the crop. Only the large owners bottle their own crop. The grape juice is mostly sold to dealers who have invested in the necessary store-houses and apparatus. The principal dealer, as well as the largest landholder and grower of vines, is Nicholas Longworth. To his perseverance in prolonged experiments we are indebted for all this success in the production of native wine. It is pleasant to find now and then a case where the deserved fame and fortune have followed intelligent efforts of such a kind, before the hand that exerted them is laid low. The value of the wine crop in its present youth is little known.

In 1855, the crop about Cincinnati is estimated at $150,000.

There are about 1,500 acres of vines planted; 1,000 in full bearing, producing this year about 150 gallons only, to the acre. In 1853, the average crop was 650 gallons; the extreme yield 900 gallons to the acre. The acres planted in 1845, 350; in 1852, 1,200. Missouri and Illinois have also (1855) 1,100 acres planted. Mr. Longworth is said to have at the end of 1855, 300,000 bottles stored in his cellars; one-half bottled during the year. It will not be many years, I hope, before the famous hog crop will be of less value to this region in comparison. Let us pray for the day when honest wine and oil shall take the place of our barbarous whisky and hog-fat.

The approach to Cincinnati is announced by the appearance of villas, scattered on the hills that border the north side of the river, and by the concentration of human life and motion along the bank. But a moment after these indications attract your attention, the steamer rounds with a great sweep to the levee, and, before you appreciate your arrival, is pushing its nose among the crowd of boats, butting them unmercifully hither and thither in the effort for an inside place.

CINCINNATI.

From the edge of the stream rises the levee—a paved open hill of gentle inclination, allowing steamboats and carmen to carry on their usual relations at all stages of water. Then extends backward, on a gently-rising plateau, a square mile or two of brick blocks and hubbub. Then rise steeply the hills by which, in semicircle, the city is backed. At their base is a horrid debateable ground, neither bricks and mortar nor grass, but gaunt clay, before whose tenacity the city has paused, uncertain whether to " grade" or mount the obstinate barrier.

There is a prevalent superstition in Cincinnati that the hinder-most citizen will fall into the clutches of the devil. A wholesome fear of this dire fate, secret or acknowledged with more or less candor, actuates the whole population. A ceaseless energy per-vades the city and gives its tone to everything. A profound hurry is the marked characteristic of the place. I found it diffi-cult to take any repose or calm refreshment, so magnetic is the air. "Now then, sir!" everything seems to say. Men smoke and drink like locomotives at a relay-house. They seem to sleep only like tops, with brains in steady whirl. There is no pause in the tumultuous life of the streets. The only quiet thing I found was the residence of Mr. Longworth—a delicious bit of rural verdure, lying not far from the heart of the town, like a tender locket heaving on a blacksmith's breast.

What more need be said of Cincinnati? Bricks, hurry, and a muddy roar make up the whole impression. The atmosphere, at the time of our visit, was of damp coal smoke, chilly and dirty, almost like that of the same season in Birmingham. I was in-terested in inquiries about its climate, and learned that extreme variations of temperature were as common as upon the sea-board. That during one long season it was exposed to a fierce sun and a penetrating dust, and during another to piercing winds from the northwest. Snow falls abundantly, but seldom survives its day. On the whole, it was doubted if anxious lungs were better here than in New York. The environs, the purgatory of red clay once passed, are agreeable enough, even at this season, to be called charming—tasteful houses, standing on natural lawns among natural park-groups of oak, with river views and glimpses. The price of land for such places, within thirty or forty minutes' drive of town, was, I was told, $1,000 per acre; and, of all eligible land, within ten miles around, $200. Cheap soil cannot, therefore, be an inducement for settlers here. These are New York prices.

PORK.

Pork-packing in Cincinnati was, at the time of our visit, nearly at a stand-still, owing to the mild and damp weather unusual at the season. One establishment we found in partial operation. We entered an immense low-ceiled room and followed a vista of dead swine, upon their backs, their paws stretching mutely toward heaven. Walking down to the vanishing point, we found there a sort of human chopping-machine where the hogs were converted into commercial pork. A plank table, two men to lift and turn, two to wield the cleavers, were its component parts. No iron cog-wheels could work with more regular motion. Plump falls the hog upon the table, chop, chop; chop, chop; chop, chop, fall the cleavers. All is over. But, before you can say so, plump, chop, chop; chop, chop; chop, chop, sounds again. There is no pause for admiration. By a skilled sleight of hand, hams, shoulders, clear, mess, and prime fly off, each squarely cut to its own place, where attendants, aided by trucks and dumb-waiters, dispatch each to its separate destiny—the ham for Mexico, its loin for Bordeaux. Amazed beyond all expectation at the celerity, we took out our watches and counted thirty-five seconds, from the moment when one hog touched the table until the next occupied its place. The number of blows required I regret we did not count. The vast slaughter-yards we took occasion not to visit, satisfied at seeing the rivers of blood that flowed from them.

1*

TO LEXINGTON.

We left Cincinnati at daybreak of a cloudy November day, upon the box of the coach for Lexington, Ky. After waiting a long time for the mail and for certain dilatory passengers, we crossed the river upon a dirty little high pressure ferry-boat, and drove through the streets of Covington. This city, with its low and scattered buildings, has the aspect of a suburb, as in fact it is. It is spread loosely over a level piece of ground, and is quite lacking in the energy and thrift of its free-state neighbor. Whether its slowness be legitimately traced to its position upon the slave side of the river, as is commonly done; or only in principal part to the caprice of commerce, is not so sure. It is credible enough, that men of free energy in choosing their residence, should prefer free laws when other things are equal; but 200 miles further down the river, we find (as again at St. Louis) that things are not equal, and that the thrift and finery are upon the slave side. Leaving it behind, we roll swiftly out upon one of the few well-kept macadamized roads in America, and enter with exhilaration the gates of magnificent Kentucky.

THE WOODLAND PASTURES OF KENTUCKY.

Here spreads, for hundreds of miles before you, an immense natural park, planted, seeded to sward, drained, and kept up by invisible hands for the delight and service of man. Travel where you will for days, you find always the soft, smooth sod, shaded with oaks and beeches, noble in age and form, arranged in vistas and masses, stocked with herds, deer, and game. Man has squatted here and there over the fair heritage, but his shabby improvements have the air of poachers' huts amidst this luxuriant beauty of nature. It is landscape gardening on the largest scale. The eye cannot satiate itself in a whole day's swift panorama, so charmingly varied is the surface, and so perfect each new point of view. Midway of the route, the land is high and rougher in tone, and the richest beauty is only reached at the close of the day, when you bowl down into the very garden of the state—the private grounds, as it were, of the demesne. Here accumulation has been easy, and wealth appears in more suitable mansions, occupied by the lords of Durham and Ayrshire herds, as well as of a black feudal peasantry, unattached to the soil. There is hardly, I think, such another coach ride as this in the world, certainly none that has left a more delightful and ineffaceable impression on my mind.

THE ROAD.

Coach and teams were good, and we made excellent time. The weather was mild, and we were enabled to keep the box through the day. Our first driver, waked, probably, too early, was surly and monosyllabic. The second was gay, with a ringing falsetto, which occupied all his attention.

The third was a sensible, communicative fellow. He told us, among other things, that he had once driven over the road, eighty-four miles, during a high opposition, in seven hours, including all stops. This route is now done by railway, with great gain, no doubt, but also with what a loss! This free canter over the hills, exchanged for a sultry drag along the easiest grade. Where will our children find their enjoyment when everything gets itself done by steam?

PORK ON FOOT.

Our progress was much impeded by droves of hogs, grunting

their obstinate way towards Cincinnati and a market. Many of the droves were very extensive, filling the road from side to side for a long distance. Through this brute mass, our horses were obliged to wade slowly, assisted by lash and yells. Though the country was well wooded, and we passed through now and then a piece of forest, I venture to say we met as many hogs as trees in all the earlier part of the day. The bad (warm) weather was a subject of commiseration at every stopping place .

" CASH CLAY," FROM THE KENTUCKY POINT OF VIEW.

On the box with us were two Kentuckians, bound homewards— a farmer and a store-keeper, from the central part of the State. Many of the hogs, they told us, from the brand, belonged to Mr. Clay—Cassius—who buys them of farmers, and has them driven to market. He had made, they understood, $40,000 the previous year, in this business. " Well, he'll lose money this time," said one. " No," said the other, " he has sold them all, beforehand. They're all contracted for. He'll make another $40,000 this year, I shouldn't wonder. I know one man my- self who has paid him $2,000 to be let off from his engagement."

" Well, I aint sorry to have Cash Clay make money."

" Nor I either. If any man ought to make money, he had."

" Yes, he had that. He's a dam benevolent man, is Clay. There aint a more benevolent man in the state of Kentucky."

"No there aint, not in the world."

" He's a brave man. There aint no better man than Clay. I like a man that, when he's an abolitionist, frees his own nig- gers fust, and then aint afraid to talk to other folks."

" He's a whole man, if there ever was one. I don't like an

abolitionist, but by God I do like a man that aint afraid to say what he believes."

"I hate an abolitionist, but I do admire a Kentuckian that dares to stay in Kentucky and say he's an abolitionist if he is one."

"There aint many men, I reckon," said the driver, "that has got more friends than Cash Clay."

"They are good friends, too."

"He's got a good many enemies, too."

"So he has; but, I tell you, even his enemies like him."

"There's some of his enemies that don't like him much," said the farmer (a slaveholder).

"I reckon they'll let him alone after this, won't they."

"Well, I should think they'd got about enough of trying to fight him. There aint a braver man in Kentucky, and I guess everybody knows it now."

Afterwards at Lexington we heard Mr. C. spoken of in a similar tone of admiration for his courage and great force of character. He was considered an excellent farmer, of course on the subject of slavery "deluded" (with an expression of pity), and as to influence, "losing rapidly."

Our farmer, it appeared, was the owner of twenty negroes; for he mentioned that his whole family, including twenty black people, were laid up with erysipelas the previous year, and he had lost one of his best boys. Since then he had had dyspepsia horridly. "He wouldn't begrudge the likeliest nigger he had got to anybody who would cure him of dyspepsia." This started the store-keeper, who, thenceforward, could talk of little else than some "bitters" he had invented from a recipe "he had found in the dispensatory." After using it himself he had put it in circulation, and now had a regular labeled bottle, and had collected a set of certificates that would be a sure fortune to any man that had the capital to advertise. It appeared from the conversation that dyspepsia was a common complaint in Kentucky, as God knows it ought to be.

This "bitters" man was a rapid talker, and from the new and entire Westernism of his phrases was to us quite an original. I wish I could give, in his own language, a story he told of a "baär-fight," apropos of a chained cub we passed on the road. "By Godfrey," to his companion, "you ought not to have missed that." The hero of the tale, was a sorry cur of his own, who till that day had been looked upon as a spiritless thing of no account, but whose mission was revealed to him when his eyes fell on that baär. He came off the champion of the pack, leaving his tail in the pit, but a decorated and honored dog. The people came together, for twenty miles around, to see that baär-baiting, and the most respectable, sober old members of the church, became so excited as to hoot and howl like madmen, almost jumping over into the fight.

KENTUCKY FARMING.

The farms we passed on the road were generally small, and had a slovenly appearance that ill accorded with the scenery. Negro quarters, separate from the family dwelling, we saw scarcely anywhere. The labor appeared about equally divided between black and white. Sometimes we saw them at work together, but generally at separate tasks on the same farm. The main crop was everywhere Indian corn, which furnishes the food for man and beast, and the cash sales evidently of hogs and beef. Many of the farms had been a great while under cultivation. Large old orchards were frequent, now loaded with apples left, in many cases, to fall and rot, the season having been so abundant as to make them not worth transportation to market. I was much surprised, on considering the richness of the soil and the age of the farms, that the houses and barns were so thriftless and wretched in aspect. They were so, in fact, to one coming from the North; but on further experience they seemed, in recollection, quite neat and costly structures compared with the Southern average dwellings.

But a very small proportion of the land is cultivated or fenced, in spite of the general Western tendency towards a horizontal, rather than a perpendicular agriculture. Immense tracts lie unused, simply parts of our Great West.

CORN-BREAD BEGINS.—THE ROADSIDE.

We stopped for dinner at a small and unattractive village, and at an inn to which scarcely better terms could be applied. The meal was smoking on the table; but five minutes had hardly elapsed, when " Stage's ready," was shouted, and all the other passengers bolting their coffee, and handing their half dollars to the landlord, who stood eagerly in the door, fled precipitately to their seats. We held out a few moments longer, but yielded to repeated threats that the stage was off without us, and mounted to our places amid suppressed oaths on all sides.

At this dinner I made the first practical acquaintance with what shortly was to be the bane of my life, viz., corn-bread and bacon. I partook innocent and unsuspicious of these dishes, as they seemed to be the staple of the meal, without a thought that for the next six months I should actually see *nothing else.* Here, relieved by other meats and by excellent sweet potatoes baked and in *pone*, they disappeared in easy digestion.   Taken alone, with vile coffee, I may ask, with deep feeling, who is sufficient for these things?

At one of our stopping-places was a tame crow, hopping about in the most familiar way among the horses' heels.   When we were ready to start, the driver, taking the reins, said to it, " Now then, Charley; look out for yourself, we're going off."   The bird turned its wise head to one side, gave a sagacious wink with one of its bright bead eyes, as much as to say, " Do you look out for *yourself*, never mind me."

Near another we passed a husking bee—a circle of neighbors, tossing rapidly bright ears of corn into a central heap, with jokes and good cheer; near by, a group of idle boys looking on from a fence, and half-a-dozen horses tied around.   The whole a picturesque study, which, with the knowing crow added, I would like to have preserved on a better medium than one of the fading tablets of memory.

Saddles, it was easy to observe, were very much more used here than at the North, and I saw, not unfrequently, saddle-bags across them, which had been as traditional in my previous experience as the use of bucklers or bows.   Not long after, my legs grew to that familiarity with them as to be as much astonished to find themselves free from their pressure for a transient ride, as they now would have been to stride them for the first time.

LEXINGTON.

We had had glowing descriptions of Lexington, and expected much.   Had we come from the South we should have been charmed.   Coming from the East we were disappointed in the involuntary comparison.   Of all Southern towns there are scarce two that will compare with it for an agreeable residence. It is regular in its streets, with one long principal avenue, on which most of the business is done. The tone of building is more firm and quiet than that of most Western towns, and the public buildings are neat. There are well-supplied shops; many streets are agreeably shaded; but the impression is one of irre sistible dullness. It is the centre of no great trade, but is the focus of intelligence and society for Kentucky, which, however, is not concentrated in the town, but spread on its environs. These have undeniably a rare charm. The rolling woodland pastures come close upon the city, and on almost every knoll is a dwelling of cost and taste. Among these is

HENRY CLAY'S ASHLAND.

It was not without feeling that we could visit a spot haunted by a man who had loomed so high upon our boyhood. Nothing had been changed about the grounds or house. His old servant showed us such parts of the house as could be visited without intrusion, the portraits and the presents. The house was one of no great pretensions, and so badly built as to be already falling into decay. The grounds were simple and well retired behind masses of fine trees; the whole bearing the look of a calm and tasteful retreat. What a contrast life here, with the clash and passion, the unceasing and exciting labor of the capitol! As we left, we met Mr. James Clay, once chargé to Portugal, who purchased the homestead at his father's request. He struck us as a man of feeling and good sense, and spoke with regret of the necessity of rebuilding the house. He has since done this, and has suffered in consequence a bitter and personal newspaper controversy.

Lexington boasts a university, well attended, and ranking among the highest Western schools in its departments of Law and Medicine. Its means of ordinary education are also said to be of the best.

LEXINGTON AS A RESIDENCE.

With such advantages, social, atmospheric, educational, what residence more attractive for one who would fain lengthen out his summers and his days? Were it only free. In the social air there is something that whispers this. You cannot but listen. Discussion may be learned, witty, delightful, only—not free. Should you come to Lexington, leave your best thoughts behind. The theories you have most revolved, the results that are to you most certain, pack them close away, and give them no airing here. Your mind must stifle, if your body thrive. Apart from slavery, too, but here a product of it, there is that throughout the South, in the tone of these fine fellows, these otherwise true gentlemen, which is very repugnant—a devilish, undisguised, and recognised contempt for all humbler classes. It springs from their relations with slaves, " poor whites," and tradespeople, and is simply incurable. A loose and hearty blasphemy is also a weakness of theirs, but is on the whole far less repulsive. God is known to be forgiving, but slighted men and slaves hanker long for revenge. Lexington society, however, can, I believe, be said to have less of these faults so offensive to a Northern man, than any Southern city equally eligible in other respects.

But, besides the social objections, there are others of a different character. Malaria hangs over it, as over all the West, and whoever comes from the East runs double risk from its influences.

Labor, other than forced, and consequently, costly, slovenly, and requiring incessant supervision, is not to be had. The summer heats are tedious and severe, and the droughts so unmitigated as that sometimes the land is nearly baked to a depth of five feet, and the richest soil is no better than the poorest.

SLAVES IN FACTORIES

The population of Lexington is about 12,000. It is a market for hemp, and manufactures it in a rough way into bagging for cotton bales. One of these factories, worked by slaves, we visited. The labor was almost entirely done by hand, and very rudely. The plan of tasks was followed in the same way as in the tobacco factories at Richmond. By active working, a slave could earn himself $2 or $3 a week, besides doing his master's work. This sum he is always allowed to expend as he pleases. Thus, the stimulus of wages is applied behind the whip, of course the prime motor.

TOWARD LOUISVILLE.

From Lexington we went by rail to Frankfort and Louisville (94 miles; $3; 5 hours). The country passed over is, for many miles, of the same general character as that described north of Lexington—a rolling or gently-sloping surface, rich soil, woodland pastures,* herds, fine farms, and prominent houses. Then less-fertile and less-settled districts, elevated and thickly wooded with beech, ash, oak, and hickory. Land, we were told,

---

* Woodland pastures : a blue grass sod under oaks. The blue grass is indigenous, and is the same much prized with us for lawns. The oak is the burr oak, bearing a very large edible acorn, an excellent food for hogs. Its leaves are said to decay with great rapidity, so as to nourish, not destroy, the grass on which they fall. Throughout this region much attention has been naturally given to pure-bred stock. One man is owner of ten bulls and thirty cows, pure short-horns, of his own selection and importation.

of the better class, and improved, commanded $70 or $80 per acre ; near Lexington, $200. Its fertility was described as inexhaustible. One field was pointed out that had been cultivated in corn for sixty years, without interruption, and without manure. Its produce was still forty bushels to the acre, with meagre care. Of wheat, fifteen bushels was an average crop, though one farm had this year yielded thirty bushels without unusual pains.

On the train we found acquaintances, and had much animated conversation and advice upon our plans of travel. We could not help observing that the number of handsome persons in our car was unusual, and among the young Kentuckians we saw, were several as stalwart in form and manly in expression as any young men on whom my eyes have fallen.

SELF-DEFENSE.

A young man passing, with a pistol projecting from his pocket, some one called out with a laugh—" You'll lose your pistol, sir." This opened a little talk on weapons, in which it appeared that among young men a bowie-knife was a universal, and a pistol a not at all unusual, companion in Kentucky.

Frankfort has a remarkable situation on the Kentucky river, between its bank and a high bluff, which gives a threatening gloom to the back of the town. Though the capital of the state, it is but a small and unattractive place. Between it and Louisville the country is comparatively sterile and vacant—the country-houses are but cabins—and the villages small, and dirty, with no feature of external interest. The railway lies through a region in many places heavily wooded with beech, mingled with oak, hickory, sweet gum, and sugar maple. The mistletoe thrives here, selecting, when convenient, the boughs of the elm and the black locust. Near Louisville we saw the Kentucky coffee-tree, suggesting, at this season, our ailanthus.

BLACK CONVERSATION.

Near us in the railway car sat three mulattoes, quite at ease, and exciting no attention. Two of them were exceedingly white, and one looked so like an English friend of ours I should have hailed him passing in very early twilight. Their conversation, when audible, was ludicrously black, however. At a station one of them said, " I forgot to provide myself with cigors last night, so when I got up I hadn' got nothin' to smoke. I told Chloe and she jus' looked roun' on the floor, and ther' she found seven *stumps*."

" Good gracious Lord, you didn't smoke 'um, did you ?"

"Yes, I did that, and "—the rest was lost in uproarious guffaws. At another point the following queer passage reached us : " I'd rather belong to the meanest white man in Scott County, and have to get 200 lashes a-day, well laid on, with a raw hide ———"

FUGITIVE SLAVE LAW.

Here belongs, perhaps, a bit of Louisville conversation. We were passing on the river bank just as a flat, loaded with furniture, manned by a white and black crew, was shoved off for the other shore. A man near us shouted to the pilot, as the boat drifted off—" H——, remember, if any of them niggers, God damn 'em, tries to run, when you're over to the point, you've got a double-barrel fowling-piece loaded with buck."

" Yes, God damn 'em, I know it."

The negroes listened without remark or expression.

The general impression, from the negroes we saw in both city and country, is one of a painfully clumsy, slovenly, almost hope-less race. Intercourse with them, and dependence on them, as compulsory as is that of a master, would be, to a man of Northern habits, a despair.

LOUISVILLE.

Louisville has interminable ragged, nasty suburbs, and lacks edifices—in other respects it is a good specimen of a brisk and well-furnished city. Its business buildings are large and suitable, its dwellings, of the better class, neat, though rarely elegant, its shops gay and full, its streets regular and broad, its tone active, without the whirr of Cincinnati. It has great business, both as an entrepôt and as itself, a manufacturing producer. It owes its position to the will of nature, who stopped here, with rapids, the regular use of the river. Cincinnati, by the canal around them, has, however, almost free competition with it, and it has well stood its ground, showing some other than a temporary necessity for itself. It has grown with all a Western rapidity. In 1800, population, 600 ; 1820, 4,000 ; 1840, 21,000 ; 1850, about 50,000.

The hotel talk, while we stayed, was of little else than the Matt. Ward tragedy, and dire were the threats of summary punishment by the people, did the law fail in giving avenging justice.

DOWN THE OHIO.

Finding that the night exposure, by stage, would be too great to be voluntarily encountered at the season, we very reluctantly abandoned our plan of proceeding across the state to Nashville, by the way of the Mammoth Cave, and ordered our baggage to be sent on board the favorite steamer " Pike, No. ——," up for St. Louis. The promise of steamboat speed and comfort was too seductive, and the charms of river scenery, both on the Ohio and the Cumberland, had been glowingly painted for us.

Over a deep-rutted miry road, cut up by truck loads of cotton, sugar, and iron, we were driven two or three miles to Portland, once the rival, now the port and mean suburb, of Louisville. After only a few hours more or less, not days as we feared, beyond her advertised time, the fast mail boat Pike took her departure.

STEAMBOAT TIME.

It was a matter of luck, we found, that we were off so soon, and was so considered, with mutual congratulations, by passengers generally—other boats, advertised as positively to sail days before, lying quietly against the bank as we moved out. Just before we left, sitting on the guards, I heard the captain say, "Yes, I guess we might as well go off, I don't believe we'll get anything more. The agent told me to start out more than an hour ago; but I held on for the chance, you know." Shortly after this a man appeared in the distance running down the levee, with a carpet-bag, straight for us. The last bell had been rung with extra-terrible din, the gang-plank hauled aboard, and men were stationed at the hawsers to cast off. "Halloo, look at that chap," said the captain, "he's *hell-bent* on this boat now, aint he. I'll have to wait for that fellow, sure." Accordingly the plank was got out again, and the individual, who proved to be a deck passenger, walked on board.

Toward night of the same day, we were steaming down the river at a fine rate, when we suddenly made a shear to the right, and, after a long sweep, steamed some distance up the river, and gently laid our nose against the bank. The passengers all gathered to see the landing. Nothing was said, but, after a few minutes, the mate, who had been dressing, appeared, with a box of raisins under his arm, and walked up to a solitary house at some distance from the shore.   He was met at the door by an old gentleman and his wife, to whom he gave the box and a newspaper, and, after a moment's chat, he returned on board, gave the necessary orders, and we were soon on our way again.   Think of a huge "floating palace," of 600 tons, with 200 passengers on board, spending a quarter of an hour on such an errand!   But for thousands of miles here these steamers are the only means of communication, and every article, be it a newspaper or a thousand bales of cotton, must be delivered or dispatched in this one way.

The Pike proved herself all she claimed to be for safety and speed, laying up completely during a thick fog of the evening, and running rapidly where the way was clear.   Beds and table were good, of their kind, as was our general experience on Western boats.

THE RIVER BANKS.

New Albany, on the Indiana side of the river, nearly opposite Portland, appeared a place of great growth and energy.   From the hammering, we judged that its chief business was the production of machinery.   Along the shore are extensive ship-yards, for the perpetual creation of these short-lived high-pressure steamers. Below this, the only town of note is Evansville, which also has an encouraging and free-state look about it.   On the Kentucky side there is no village of consequence below Louisville.

Travelers usually make the observation in descending the Ohio, that the free side shows all the thrift and taste.   It is a customary joke to call their attention to this, and encourage them to dilate upon it when the boat's head has been turned around without their notice. And I cannot say with candor, that taking the whole distance, such was our own observation. The advantage, if any, is slight on the side of the free states. They certainly have more neat and numerous villages, and I judge more improved lands along the river bank; but the dwellings, not counting negro huts, appeared to us nearly on a par, and the farms, at a rough guess, of about equal value.

What is most striking everywhere, is the immensity of the wasted territory, rather than the beauty of the improved. The river banks seem, as you glide for hours through them, without seeing a house or a field, as if hardly yet rescued from the beasts and the savages, so little is the work done compared with that which remains to do. Near the mouth of the Ohio, this is still more striking, and on the Mississippi the impression is absolutely painful, so rich yet so entirely desolate and unused is the whole vast region. There is soil enough here, of the richest class, to feed and clothe, with its cotton and its corn, ten-fold our whole present population.

SMITHLAND—MOUTH OF THE CUMBERLAND.

At about 1 A. M., we found ourselves alone with a shivering boy, almost speechless with sleep, upon a wharf-boat, looking with regret on the fast-drifting lights of the Pike. Following, by a blurred lantern, his dubious guidance, we climbed a clay bank, and found ourselves shortly before our beds. At a first experience of a Western, viz., one-sheeted, bed, I was somewhat taken aback; and, determining not to abandon my hold on civilization sooner than necessary, I unconscionably caused the chambermaid, who was also the landlady, to be roused at this late hour, and had, amid much grumbling and tedium, my bed put in

2

a normal state.   Next morning I was happy to see that several panes had been put in the window in anticipation of our arrival, and some paper pasted about against the walls, but no provision for personal ablutions could be discerned, though as the curtainless window opened on a gallery, there was every opportunity for public inspection.   Descending in search of these unwonted articles, we discovered, by the sour looks we met, that we had caused a family indigestion by our night attack, and, suddenly concluding to adopt the customs of the country, we were shown to the common lavabo, and why not?   One rain bathes the just and the unjust, why not one wash-bowl?   Not twice in the next six months, away from cities or from residences we pitched for ourselves, did we find any other than this equal and democratic arrangement.

Smithland is—or was, for who knows what a Western year may bring forth—a thriving county seat, compcsed of about two taverns, one store, five houses and a wharf-boat.   Being Thanksgiving day, we dined in company with several of our fellow-citizens, wearing full-dress shirts, but no coats, on cornbread and pork, with sweet potatoes, and two pickles.

The prospect, in view of a long continuance of this life at Smithland, at the mouth of the Cumberland, being composed of the trees and bushes of the opposite shore, and of a long, flat reach of river, was not encouraging.   But, as good fortune would have it, we had scarcely began the melancholy digestion of our dinner, when the flat stern-wheel boat, David A. Tomkins, came in sight, and made direct for Smithland.   On ascertaining that she was actually bound for Nashville, with great eagerness we paid our first-class bill, and hurried our baggage on board, preferring rather, should delay occur, to contemplate for a

season the town, " as it appears from the river bank," to prolong-
ing our gaze at those bushes and the flat reach that lie before
the doors of Smithland, mouth of the Cumberland.

THE D. A. TOMKINS.

The boat was a good specimen of a very numerous class on
Western and Southern rivers. They are but scows in build, perfectly flat, with a pointed stem and a square stern. Behind is
the one wheel, moved by two small engines of the simplest and
cheapest construction. Drawing but a foot, more or less, of
water, they keep afloat in the lowest stages of the rivers. Their
freight, wood, machinery, boilers, hands and steerage passengers,
are all on the one flat deck just above the surface of the water.
Eight or ten feet above, supported by light stanchions, is laid
the floor used by passengers. The engines being, as generally
in Western boats, horizontal, this floor is laid out in one long
saloon eight or ten feet wide from the smoke-pipes, far forward,
which stretches to the stern. It is lined upon each side with
state-rooms, which open also out upon a narrow upper guard or
gallery. Perched above all this is the pilot-house, and a range
of state-rooms for the pilots and officers, popularly known as
" Texas." To this Texas, inveterate card-players retire on
Sundays, when custom forbids cards in the saloon. A few feet
of the saloon are cut off by folding doors for a ladies' cabin.
Forward of the saloon the upper deck extends around the
smoke-pipes, forming an open space, sheltered by the pilot-
deck, and used for baggage and open-air seats.

Such is the contrivance for making use of these natural
highways. And really admirable it is, spite of drawbacks, for its
purpose. Without it the West would have found it impossible

to be The West. Roads, in countries so sparsely settled, are impracticable. These craft paddle about, at some stage of water, to almost every man's door, bringing him foreign luxuries, and taking away his own productions; running at high water in every little creek, and at low water, taking, with great profit, the place of the useless steamers on the main streams.

Our captain promised we should be in Nashville the following day; but he should have added "water and weather permitting," for we had one hundred tedious hours to spend upon the narrow decks of the Tomkins. We were hardly fairly under way when we went foul of a snag, and broke, before we were clear, several buckets of our wheel. We ran on in a dilapidated state till near night, when the boat's head was put against the bank, and what timber was required was cut in the woods. Woods are common property here. With this and with planks kept on board for the purpose, the repairs were soon effected. With the twilight, however, came a thick fog down upon the river, and we remained, in consequence, tied quietly to a tree until late the next day, but a few miles from Smithland. The evening was something hard to pass; a fierce stove, a rattle of oaths and cards within, and the cold fog without. Luckily I had with me a Spanish grammar, in view of a probable Mexican journey, and to that I grimly applied myself with success. Our passengers were some twenty in number, mostly good-natured people from the neighboring country, fraternizing loudly with the officers of the boat, over their poker and brag. The ladies occupied themselves in sewing and rocking, keeping up a thin clatter of talk at their end of the cabin.

Early next day we passed a side-wheel steamer of a small class, upon a shoal, almost high and dry. She had been lying for a month where she was, all hands discharged, and the whole machine idle. We afterwards passed two or three others of a larger size, accidentally locked into the river by a fall of water. Our own craft, though drawing only fourteen inches, was within an ace of a similar predicament. After many times grounding, but always getting free after more or less delay, we were at length driven hard and fast by rapids upon a heap of rocks barely covered with water.

CRUTCHES AND SHOALS.

Then it was we learned the use of those singular spars which may always be seen standing on end against the forward deck, in any picture of a Western boat. They are, in fact, steamboat crutches. One of these, or the pair, if occasion require, is set upon the river-bottom, close to the boat's head, and a tackle led from its top to a ring in the deck. Then, by heaving on the windlass, the boat is lifted bodily off the ground. As soon as she swings free of bottom, steam is applied with fury, and forward she goes until the spar slips from its place, and lets her fall. Such was the amusement we had during the greater part of our Sunday on board. Finally, having secured, by going up and down the river, two wood-scows, and having got into them, lashed alongside, all our freight, having hobbled about here and there, looking for a wetter place, during many hours, we scratched over. The freight was soon restored, and the flat-boats sent adrift, to find their way home with the current, under the management, one, of an aged negro, the other of a boy and girl of tender years.

We were amused to notice of how little account the boat was considered, in comparison with the value of *time*. Whenever any part of the hull was in the way of these spars, axes were

applied without a thought, other than that of leaving hull enough
to keep afloat.   In fact, costing little, these steamers are used
with a perfect recklessness.   If wrecked, why, they have long
ago paid for themselves, and the machinery and furniture can almost always be saved.   This apparatus of stilts is used upon the
largest boats, and good stories are told of their persistence in
lifting themselves about, and forcing a passage over gravel banks,
whenever freights are higher than steamboats.   The " first boat
over " sometimes wins extravagant rewards.   When sugar, for
instance, goes up to $1 per pound in up-river towns, after a dry
season, a few hogsheads will almost pay for a cheap steamboat.

LIFE AND SCENERY ON THE CUMBERLAND.

The Cumberland, flowing, after its head branches unite, through
a comparatively level and limited district, though watering an
immense region, is but a small and quiet stream.   Its banks, so
far as navigation extends, are low, though frequently bluffs of
small height come jutting down to the river.   Ordinarily, the
trees of the rich bottom alone are to be seen overhanging the
placid surface.   For miles, almost for hours, there is not a break
in the line of dripping branches.   Monotony is immediate.   But
it is not without suffering this that a traveler can receive true
and fixed impressions.   You turn again and again from listlessly
gazing at the perspective of bushes, to the listless conversation
of the passengers, and turn back again.   Making a landing, or
stopping to wood-up, become excitements that make you spring
from your berth or your book.   Two sounds remain still very
vividly in my ears in thinking of this sail—the unceasing
" Choosh, choosh; choosh, choosh," of the steam, driven out into
the air, after doing its work; and the " shove her up! shove her

up!" of the officer of the deck, urging the firemen to their work. The first of these sounds is of course constantly heard upon high-pressure boats, and is part and parcel of Western scenery. Of a calm day it rings for miles along, announcing the boat's approach. On board, the sound is not as annoying as might be expected. Carried high, in wide-mouthed pipes, it is partly dulled, and, once under way, is but a slow rhythmic accompaniment to the progress, which, in so monotoned a panorama, becomes not unpleasant.

Turkeys, buzzards, and ducks make up the animated nature of the scenery. The ducks clatter along the surface, before the boat as it approaches, refusing to leave the river, and accumulating in number as they advance, until all take refuge in the first reedy shelter offered by a flat shore.

The buzzards, hovering, keen-eyed, in air, swoop here and there towards whatever attracts their notice, or loiter idly and gracefully along, following the boat's motion with scarce a play of the wing, as if disdaining its fussy speed.

The turkeys sit stupidly in the trees, or fly in small or large flocks across the stream. We counted more than ninety in one frightened throng. One of them was brought down by a rifle-shot from the pilot-house, but fell into the woods. The boat stopped to pick him up, but the bank proving difficult, we went on without so pleasant a supper dish.

It is a matter of surprise to meet so few farms along the banks of such a stream. But it is the common surprise of the West. Everything almost, but land, is wanting everywhere. Except a small quantity of tobacco, hardly anything else than corn is here cultivated. The iron works along the river make a large market for bread-stuffs, i. e., corn-bread stuffs. The farms are carried on by slave labor on a moderate scale.   The farmers, not working themselves, are generally addicted to sporting, and to an easy view of life.   The spots chosen for cultivation, so far as can be seen from the river, are those where the land comes high to the bank, affording a convenient landing.   A consider-able item of revenue is the furnishing of wood to passing steam-ers—much black muscle paying thus its interest.   The wood is piled in ranks along the bank, or sometimes a flat is loaded ready for steamers to take in tow, so that no time may be lost in waiting.   We saw the usual picturesque evening wooding-up scenes to great advantage here.   An iron grating, filled with blazing chips of rich pine, is set upon the boat's guard, or upon the bank.   A red glare is thus thrown over the forest, the water, the boat, and the busy group of men, running, like bees, from shore to boat.   A few minutes of mad labor suffice to cover the boat's spare deck-room—the torch is quenched, and, with a jerk of the bell, the steamer moves off into the darkness.

IRON WORKS.—NEGRO WAGES AND LABOR.

Near the course of the Cumberland are several furnaces and iron mines.   Their supply of fuel is drawn from the river forests, and near them wood-land sells at $5 per acre.   Improved land is roughly estimated at $20.   Lime is found adjoining the ore. One of these establishments employs a capital of $700,000, and *owns* 700 negroes.   In most of them the hands are hired.   For common labor, negroes are almost exclusively used.   " Because white men don't like the work, and won't do it unless they are compelled to.   You can't depend on 'em.   You can't drive 'em like you can a nigger."   Foreign laborers are sometimes used; but, though they do very well at first, soon " get off the notion."

Wages, we were informed by a flat-boatman, were from forty cents to one dollar per day, with board. White men don't hire by the year; too much like a nigger. The furnaces pay $200 a year wages, and, for hands at all skilled, $250. A gentleman on board, however, tells me he hires his boys in preference to farmers at $120 a year (clothed and M.D.'d), because it is safer. They are less subject to accidents; they do not work so fiercely and wear themselves out, and are less likely to fall into bad habits. The negroes themselves much prefer the furnaces, because, though the work is far more severe, "there is more life," and they can get money in plenty by overwork, as in the factories. The mate tells us that, for the same reason, negroes much prefer being hired to boats. They then get "Sunday money" for work on Sunday, and pick up little sums in various other ways, working on other boats, or helping, if firemen, the deck hands in port; doing extra work out of their watch; taking care of horses, luggage, etc.

It is not unusual for the slave to buy his time of his owner at a fixed price, and to hire himself on the river. The money thus acquired they, of course, spend as pleases themselves. Much of it they drink. The black deck hands we have observed calling for drinks at the bar several times in an evening. " It's the kind of life niggers like," says the mate. " They'll have almost nothing to do maybe for a day or two, and then have to work like the devil, perhaps all night, if the boat gets aground or has a big lot of freight to come on at a landing. They just make a frolic of it. White men don't like to work so, but it just suits niggers. They go to singing, and work as if they were half crazy." Steamboat food also pleases them much better than their farm allowance.

2*

In the river villages are some tobacco factories, in which negroes are alone employed. In cotton factories only whites, because negroes cannot be trusted to take care of machinery, and negro women's capacity for labor in the field makes their wages higher than white women's.

LIVE FREIGHT.

One evening we were hailed in the darkness to come in and take some freight aboard. It proved to be a negro woman *which* her master wished to send to Nashville. Putting her on board, he demanded a bill of lading. The captain declined to sign it. " Then I can't send her." " Very well. I'll be dam'd if ever I sign a bill of lading for that sort of property. She might choose to jump overboard. Shove off. Go ahead." "What boat is that?" "The D. A. Tomkins." "Are you from Cincinnati?" "Yes, damn you."

A friend told us of a singular scene of which he was once witness at Louisville. A large gang of negroes, *in irons*, had been brought on board a boat, bound down the river. The captain coming on board saw them, and was so seized with indignation that he swore he would never carry a slave on his boat, and ordered the whole gang, their master, and his baggage, to be hustled out upon the levee. It was no sooner said than done, to the great astonishment of the bystanders, who, however, were awed by his impetuous anger, and made no demonstration.

As we lay quiet one evening in the fog, we heard and listened long to the happy wordless song of the negroes gathered at fire-light work, probably corn-husking, on some neighboring plantation. The sound had all the rich and mellow ring of pure physical contentment, and did one good to hear it. Like the nightingale, the performers seemed to love their own song, and to wait for its far off echo. It was long before we discovered that this was artificial, and came in response from the next plantation. No doubt, had one the tender and ubiquitous ear of a fairy, he might hear, of a fine evening, this black melody, mingled with the whippoorwills' notes, all the way from Carolina to Kansas, resounding, as the moon went up, from river to river.

NASHVILLE.

It was with very great pleasure that we left the woods behind us, and emerged into the cultivated district surrounding Nashville. On a narrow boat, the berths and table must be correspondingly restricted, and four days of such confinement prove a great fatigue. After an amount of excited shrieking on the part of our steam-whistle, in quite inverse proportion to our real importance, we opened the town, and in a few minutes lay beneath its noble suspension bridge, resting our crazy head upon its levee. Two negroes with carriages had answered our tremendous calls, two with hand-barrows soon joined them, and we were very shortly in lodgings in the heart of the town.

The approach by the river, at a low stage of water, is anything but striking. The streets are, as usual, regular—some of them broad—but the aspect of the place, as a whole, is quite uninviting. The brick, made from adjacent clay, are of a sombre hue, and give, with many neglected frame houses, a dull character to a first impression; in fact, though there are some retired residences of taste in the town, there is little that calls out admiration from an Eastern man.* It is our misfortune that all the

---

* The mansions of palatial magnitude and splendor, mentioned in Lippincott's late Gazetteer, we did not see.

towns of the Republic are alike, or differ in scarcely anything else than in natural position or wealth. Our federal union has been also architectural. Nashville has, however, one rare national ornament, a capitol, which is all it pretends to be or need to be.

The whole city is on high ground; but this stands at its head, and has a noble prominence. It is built of smooth-cut blue limestone, both within and without, and no stucco, sham paint, nor even wood-work, is anywhere admitted. Ornamenting its chambers are columns of a very beautiful native porphyry, fine white grains in a chocolate ground. Better laws must surely come from so firm and fit a senate house.

Like Lexington, Nashville stands in the centre of a rich district, for which it is a focus of trade and influence. Being also the state capital, and its chief town in point of size, it holds its most distinguished and cultivated society. In its vicinity are some large and well-administered estates, whose management puts to shame the average bungling agriculture of the state. The railroad to Chatanooga, connecting with the seaboard towns, was just completed at the time of our visit, and gave promise of renewing the vigorous youth and growth of the town. Perhaps the demands and condition of its society are best illustrated by one fact, which may be said to speak volumes—the city has a bookstore (Mr. Berry's), which is thought to contain a better collection of recent literature, on sale, than is to be found elsewhere in the United States. Certainly its shelves have the appearance of being more variously filled than any accessible to dollars and cents in New York, and furnished us everything we could ask at a moment's notice.

The population of the town, in 1853, was estimated at 18,000. It is a speaking fact that a state so large should show a capital so small. Nor, except Memphis, its port, which has 10,000, is there any other town worth mentioning in the state. Servile labor must be unskilled labor, and unskilled labor must be dispersed over land, and cannot support the concentrated life nor amass the capital of cities.

RETURN TO THE OHIO.

After a day or two of cordial personal intercourse, we left Nashville, by water, for New Orleans. Taking a light-draught passenger-steamer down the Cumberland, we met with no delay, other than that usual at the time of starting. The boat was advertised for ten o'clock. Wishing to make an excursion, we went on board at two, and stated our plans to the captain. He had no objection to our excursion, but his boat was going off *instantly*, and we must hurry our baggage on board if we wished to go in her. We did so, and then sat five hours in that dismalest of all delays, the waiting to be off.

We passed Smithland the second morning, and shortly after reached Paducah, at the mouth of the Tennessee, a much jauntier place than its neighbor. By good luck, a first-class New Orleans steamer rounded to the wharf-boat just as we arrived, and with hardly a moment's delay we were installed in one of her capacious state-rooms.

THE SULTANA.

The Sultana was an immense vessel, drawing nine feet, and having an interminably long saloon. Loaded to the full, her guards, even at rest, were on the exact level of the water, and the least curve in her course, or movement of her living load, sent one of them entirely under. Like the greater number of Western boats I had the fortune to travel upon, some part of her machinery was

" out of order." In this case one of the wheels was injured and must be very gently used. Carrying the mails, and making many landings, this proved a serious detention, and we were more than six days in making the passage from Cairo to New Orleans, which may be made in little over two.

Little could be added, within the same space, to the steamboat comfort of the Sultana. Ample and well-ventilated state-rooms, trained and ready servants, a substantial as well as showy table; at the head of all, officers of dignity and civility. A pleasant relic of French river dominion is the furnishing of red and white wines for public use at dinner. A second table provides for the higher employés of the boat and for passengers who have found themselves *de trop* at the first. A third is set for white servants and children, and a fourth for blacks. Among the last, several ladies made their appearance, in whom, only when thus pointed out, could you observe any slight indication of colored ancestry. No wise man, therefore, should fall blind in love, on board these steamers, till this fourth table has been carefully examined.

THE MISSISSIPPI.

In a voyage so long you forget the attitude of expectation usual on a steamboat, and adapt your habits to the new kind of life. It is not, after all, very different from life at a watering-place. Day after day you sit down to the same table with the same company, changing slightly its faces as guests come and go. You meet the same persons in your walks upon the galleries and in evening conversation. New acquaintances are picked up and welcomed to more or less of intimacy. Groups form common interests, and from groups cliques and social envies. The life, especially in the tame Mississippi scenery, is monotonous; but

is barely long enough to get tedious, and the monotony is
of a kind you are not sorry to experience once in a lifetime.
With long sleeps, necessitated by nocturnal interruptions from
landings and woodings, long meals, long up and down walks, and
long conversations, duly interlarded with letters and books, time
passes, and space. With the Southern passengers, books are a
small resource, *cards* fill every vacuum. Several times we were
expostulated with, and by several persons inquiries were made,
with deep curiosity, as to how the deuce we possibly managed to
pass our time, always refusing to join in a game of poker, which
was the only comprehensible method of steaming along. The
card parties, begun after tea, frequently broke up only at dawn
of day, and loud and vehement disputes, as to this or that, occupied not only the players, but, per force, the adjacent sleepers.
Much money was lost and won with more or less gaiety or
bitterness, and whatever pigeons were on board were duly plucked
and left to shiver.

Nothing can be less striking than the river scenery after the
first great impression of solemn magnitude is dulled. Before
and behind are eight or ten miles of seething turbid water; on
each side is half a mile of the same, bounded by a sand or mud
bank, overhung by the forest. The eye finds nowhere any
salience. Steamers, flats, rafts, wood-yards and villages (almost
synonymous), now and then a little rise of land charted as a
"bluff," a large snag, a cut-off, where the river has charged
through an opposing peninsula—such are the incidents that
serve to mark the hours; in the days they are forgotten, and, as
at sea, you mark only the weather and the progress.

Moving constantly southward, you find each day pleasant
tokens of a milder zone. First come the scathed leaves still

clinging to the cotton-woods.   Then the green willows and pop-
lars, and the cotton-wood unharmed.   Then magnolias and cotton fields show themselves, and you dispense after dinner with
your overcoat.   Then Spanish moss—soon in such masses as to
gray the forest green.   Then cypress swamps, the live oak and
the palmetto along the shore, preluding but little the roses, jessamines, and golden oranges, the waving brightness of the cane-
fields, and the drifting clouds from the sugar works.

Human life along the Mississippi is indescribably insignificant.
To use a popular expression, it is "literally nowhere."   The
villages having large names upon the map are really but a
shanty or two, and when found will hardly serve to make a
note on.   Even Chuzzlewit's descriptions might pass as not far
from accurate.   I had heard some ludicrous accounts of Cairo,
for instance, at the mouth of the Ohio, but was fairly shocked
with amusement to see it in all sober detail composed of item,
one house, leaning every way, uncertain of the softest spot to
fall; item, one shanty, labeled "Telegraph office;" item, four
flat-boats, high and dry, labeled "boarding," "milk," etc.;
item, four ditto, afloat, labeled "Post-office," "milk," etc.
Compared with such a *town* as this, our craft, with its vast population and regal splendor, should rank a great metropolis.   Most
of these places find it as necessary to show their name upon the
spot as upon the map, and display large permanent signs toward
the river, as

ORATORIO LANDING.

Sometimes other attractions are added in large letters, as

NORTHERN TERMINUS, MOBILE, OHIO R. R.—5,000 MEN WANTED.

And will be "wanted" a long time, I fear.   The Mississippi valley, in fact, with all its 16,000 miles of uninterrupted steamboat

navigation, is a great wilderness of unexplored fertility, into which a few men have crept like ants into a pantry. We give it a vast importance in our thoughts, but it is an entirely prospective one. Has the reader ever thought to compare, for example, the twelve or fourteen hundred miles of river between St. Louis or Louisville and New Orleans with the one hundred and fifty that flow between Troy and Albany and New York? If not, a little footing up of figures from the last census will surprise him:

	Pop.		Pop.
Louisville	43.194	Albany and Troy	78,548
St. Louis	77.860	Poughkeepsie	13,944
Memphis	8.841	Hudson	6,286
Vicksburg	3.678	Catskill	5,454
Natches	4,434	Newburg	11,415
Baton Rouge	5,347		
		Hudson River Towns.	115,647
Mississipppi Towns:		Add New York	750,000
With St. Louis	100.160		
With Louisville	85.494	Total about	860,000
Add New Orleans	120.000		
		Distance	150 miles
Total about	220.000		
Distance	1,400 m's		

The Western region, including these as its principal towns, sends sixteen senators to Congress. The Eastern towns together send not one; form, that is, less than half the population of one state. Is not the noise made within the Republic also in inverse proportion?

Who would not rather own his ten acres on the Hudson than the two hundred or five hundred considered of equal value on the Mississippi?

We had few opportunities of going on shore at our many landings. Carrying a large supply of coal out of the Ohio, it was only on the last day or two that we made long stops for wood. Twice we stopped at cotton plantations. On both, the hands were at work picking. One, in Mississippi, where we had time to visit the negro quarters, we found to be an outlying plantation without a residence. There were a dozen or twenty cheap white-washed board cottages, in a long straight row, with out windows, raised three feet from the ground upon log stilts. Each served for two families, having a common central chimney and one entrance. At the door of some were bits of log as a step, at many nothing at all. In the centre, the overseer's cottage, larger than the rest, and planted in a garden. About the others all was bare or dirty uninclosed space. In one of the cottages was an old woman cooking the dinner of mush and bacon. She directed us to the field, where we found all the women at work, picking. The men were getting wood from the swamp. The picking went on with a rapid and sullen motion, one gang carrying the cotton to the gin-house in huge baskets. All wore tight Scotch bonnets. The cotton plants, seven feet high, stood eighteen inches apart in rows six feet apart.

Near Fort Adams we noticed tomato and melon vines still untouched by frost. And there we heard with reluctant ears that yellow fever was lingering, and that the proprietor of an adjoining plantation had died the night before. The number of victims in New Orleans had been terrible during the summer, and though the city was now reported safe, it was not without a sense of relief that we shivered in our berths through the night before our arrival, and saw, at daylight, by the ice on our decks, that the frost long prayed for had come with us, as we swept to the centre of the thronged crescent that had been for days our half-dreaded goal.

CHAP. II.

ROUTE ACROSS EASTERN TEXAS.

ROUTES INTO TEXAS.

TEXAS has but two avenues of approach—the Gulf and Red River. Travelers for the Gulf counties and the West enter by the sea, for all other parts of Texas, by the river. The roads leading into the state through Louisiana, south of Natchitoches, are scarcely used, except by residents along them and herdsmen bringing cattle to the New Orleans market. The ferries across the numerous rivers and bayous are so costly and ill tended, the roads so wet and bad, and the distance from steam-conveyance to any vigorous part of the state so very great, that the current is entirely diverted from this region.

The travel by Red River has three centres, Natchitoches, Shrieveport, and Fulton. Immigrants enter now chiefly by the two last. To Shrieveport come the wagons from Alabama and Mississippi, to Fulton those from Arkansas and Tennessee.

The Gulf steamers touch at but two ports, Galveston and Indianola; and as cotton and all produce, on its way out to the world, must pass through the same points, these five places may be strictly called the five gates of Texas.

For our purposes Natchitoches was deemed the best rendezvous, and there, on the 15th December, we were to join our friend B., a volunteer companion.

ALEXANDRIA.—RED RIVER.

Leaving New Orleans by steamboat at dusk, we entered Red River at dinner-time next day, and the second morning reached Alexandria. At low water there are here falls, which prevent further navigation. For the transfer of our passengers and freight we were detained all day, with the usual lies about time. The village is every bit a Southern one—all the houses being one story in height, and having an open verandah before them, like the English towns in the West Indies. It contains, usually, about 1,000 inhabitants, but this summer had been entirely depopulated by the yellow fever. Of 300 who remained, 120, we were told, died. Most of the runaway citizens had returned, when we passed, though the last case of fever was still in uncertain progress.

Passing the rapids on our way to the boat above, we saw the explosion of the first of M. Maillefert's rock blasts under water. His undertaking, since, if I am not misinformed, successfully carried out, was to open a navigable passage through the rocks that form the rapids. The jet of water shot suddenly high in air was very beautiful. The boat above, when reached, we found the most diminutive specimen we had met with. In her saloon were but twelve berths, and, as there were some forty or fifty of us, it may be imagined we spent an unenviable night. The table was most barbarous in quality and even totally insufficient in quantity. We were right glad, the following afternoon, to make our escape at Grand Ecore, a village of eight or ten houses upon the bluff where the river divides, and, at this stage of water, the port of Natchitoches. The old channel was now quite dry. Three or four miles' drive along it was necessary to take us to the town.

OUR MOUNT.

We spent several days in Natchitoches purchasing horses and completing the preparations for our vagrant life in Texas. Finding little that was eligible in the horse-market, and hoping to do better further on, B. left us for San Augustine, by public conveyance, with our combined plunder. After patient trials we contented ourselves with two animals, that proved a capital choice. I beg to make the reader acquainted.

"MR. BROWN," our mule; a stout, dun-colored, short-legged, cheerful son of a donkey, but himself very much of a gentleman. We could not have done better. Having decided that a pack mule would be the most free and easy way of carrying our impediments, we selected "Mr. B." from a Missouri drove passing through the town, and appointed him to that office. Receiving his first ration simultaneously with the notice of his appointment, he manifested much satisfaction, and from first to last, until his honorable discharge, we had mutually no serious occasion for any other feeling. He was endowed with the hereditary bigotry of his race, but while in our service was always, if not by hook then by crook, amenable to reason. When gentle persuasives failed, those of a higher potency were exhibited, and always with effect. Though subjected sometimes to real neglect, and sometimes even to contemptuous expressions (for which, I trust, this, should it meet his eye, may be considered a cordial apology), he was never heard to give utterance to a complaint or vent to an oath. He traveled with us some two thousand rough miles, kept well up, in spite of the brevity of his legs, with the rest, never winced at any load we had the heart to put upon him, came in fresh and active at the end, and, finally, sold for as much as we gave for him. A saddle, saddle-bags, and the doctor, were temporarily put upon his back until the pack was overtaken.

F. chose a sturdy but gay little roan "creole pony," who also proved to have all the virtues of his class. These ponies are a tough, active race, descended and deteriorated from good Spanish and Norman blood, running at large almost wild upon the prairies of Southwestern Louisiana. Our little individual had been the property of a physician now dead of fever, and we found him an animal of excellent temper and endurance, full of boyish life and eagerness, warm in his friendships with man and beast, intelligent, playful, and courageous. Once on friendly terms with such a comrade, he is like an old family negro, you are loth and half-ashamed to offer him for sale at last, and little "Nack," as he was called, endeared himself to all of us to that degree, that tears stood in our eyes, as well as his, when we were forced to part.

A RED RIVER PLANTATION.

Thus mounted, we made one mild day of our stay at Natchitoches, an experimental trip of some ten or fifteen miles out and back, at the invitation of a hospitable planter, whose acquaintance we had made at the hotel. We started in good season, but were not long in losing our way and getting upon obscure roads through the woods. The planter's residence we did not find, but our day's experience is worth a note.

We rode on from ten o'clock till three, without seeing a house, except a deserted cabin, or meeting a human being. We then came upon a ferry across a small stream or "bayou," near which was a collection of cabins. We asked the old negro who tended the ferry if we could get something to eat anywhere in

"Have you had a physician to see that child?" asked the doctor, drawing back his chair.

She had not.

"Will you come to me, my dear?"

The child came to him, he felt its pulse and patted its hot forehead, looked down its throat, and leaned his ear on its chest.

" Are you a doctor, sir?"

" Yes, madam."

"Got some fever, hasn't it?"

" Yes."

" Not near so much as't had last night."

" Have you done anything for it?"

" Well, there was a gentleman here; he told me sweet ile and sugar would be good for it, and I gave it a good deal of that: made it sick, it did. I thought, perhaps, that would do it good."

"Yes. You have had something like this in your family before, haven't you? You don't seem much alarmed."

" Oh yes, sir; that ar one (pointing to the frowzy girl, whose name was Angelina) had it two or three times—onst most as bad as this. All my children have had it. Is she bad, doctor?"

"Yes. I should say this was a very serious thing."

" Have you any medicine in the house?" he asked, after the woman had returned from a journey to the kitchen. She opened a drawer of the bureau, half full of patent medicines and some common drugs. " There's a whole heap o' truck in thar. I don't know what it all is. Whatever you want, just help yourself. I can't read writin; you must pick it out."

Such as were available were taken out and given to the mother, with directions about administering them, which she promised to obey. " But the first and most important thing for you to do is

the neighborhood. He replied that his master sometimes took in travelers, and we had better call and try if the mistress wouldn't let us have some dinner.

The house was a small square log cabin, with a broad open shed or piazza in front, and a chimney, made of sticks and mud, leaning against one end. A smaller detached cabin, twenty feet in the rear, was used for a kitchen. A cistern under a roof, and collecting water from three roofs, stood between. The water from the bayou was not fit to drink, nor is the water of the Red River, or of any springs in this region. The people depend entirely on cisterns for drinking water. It's very little white folks need, however—milk, claret, and whisky being the more common beverages.

About the house was a large yard, in which were two or three China trees, and two splendid evergreen Cherokee roses; half a dozen hounds; several negro babies; turkeys and chickens, and a pet sow, teaching a fine litter of pigs how to root and wallow. Three hundred yards from the house was a gin-house and stable, and in the interval between were two rows of comfortable negro cabins. Between the house and the cabins was a large post, on which was a bell to call the negroes. A rack for fastening horses stood near it. On the bell-post and on each of the rack-posts were nailed the antlers of a buck, as well as on a large oak-tree near by. On the logs of the kitchen a fresh deer-skin was drying. On the railing of the piazza lay a Mexican saddle with immense wooden stirrups. The house had but one door and no window, nor was there a pane of glass on the plantation.

Entering the house, we found it to contain but a single room, about twenty feet by sixteen. Of this space one quarter was occupied by a bed—a great four-poster, with the curtains open, made up in the French style, with a strong furniture-calico day-coverlid. A smaller camp bed stood beside it. These two articles of furniture nearly filled the house on one side the door. At the other end was a great log fire-place, with a fine fire. The outer door was left constantly open to admit the light. On one side the fire, next the door, was a table; a kind of dresser, with crockery, and a bureau stood on the other side, and there were two deer-skin seated chairs and one (Connecticut made) rocking-chair.

A bold-faced, but otherwise good enough-looking woman, of a youngish middle-age, was ironing a shirt on the table. We stated our circumstances, and asked if we could get some dinner from her. She reckoned we could, she said, if we'd wait till she was done ironing. So we waited, taking seats by the fire, and examining the literature and knick-knacks on the mantel-piece. These consisted of three Natchitoches *Chronicles*, a Patent Office Agricultural Report, Christie's *Galvanic Almanac*, a Bible, *The Pirate of the Gulf*, a powder-horn, the sheath of a bowie-knife, a whip-lash, and a tobacco-pipe.

Three of the hounds, a negro child, and a white child, had followed us to the door of the cabin, three chickens had entered before us, a cat and kittens were asleep in the corner of the fire-place. By the time we had finished reading the queer advertisements in French of runaway negroes in the *Chronicle*, two of the hounds and the black child had retired, and a tan-colored hound, very lean, and badly crippled in one leg, had entered and stood asking permission with his tail to come to the fire-place. The white child, a frowzy girl of ten, came towards us. I turned and asked her name. She knitted her brows, but made no verbal reply. I turned my chair towards her, and asked her

to come to me. She hung her head for an instant, then turned, ran to the hound and struck him a hard blow in the chops. The hound quailed. She struck him again, and he turned half around, then she began with her feet, and kicked him out, taking herself after him.

At length the woman finished her ironing, and went to the kitchen, whence quickly returning, she placed upon the table a plate of cold, salt, fat pork; a cup of what to both eye and tongue seemed lard, but which she termed butter; a plate of very stale, dry, flaky, micaceous corn-bread; a jug of molasses, and a pitcher of milk.

" Well, now it's ready, if you'll eat it," she said, turning to us. " Best we've got. Sit up. Take some butter;" and she sat down in the rocker at one end of the table. We took seats at the other end.

" Jupiter! what's the matter with this child?" A little white child that had crawled up into the gallery, and now to my side —flushed face, and wheezing like a high-pressure steamboat.

" Got the croup, I reckon," answered the woman. " Take some 'lasses."

The child crawled into the room. With the aid of a hand it stood up and walked round to its mother.

" How long has it been going on that way?" asked we.

" Well, it's been going on some days, now, and keeps getting worse. 'Twas right bad last night, in the night. I reckoned I should lose it, one spell."

We were quite faint with hunger when we rode up, but didn' eat much of the corn-cake and pork. The woman and the high pressure child sat still and watched us, and we sat still and d our best, making much of the milk.

3

to shut the door and make up the fire, and put the child to bed and try to keep this wind off her."

" Lord! sir, you can't keep *her* in bed—she's too wild."

" Well, you must put some more clothes on her. Wrap her up, and try to keep her warm. The very best thing you can do for her is to give her a warm bath. Have you not got a washing tub?"

" Oh! yes, sir, I can do that. She'll go to bed pretty early —she's used to going between sundown and dark."

" Well, give her the warm bath, then, and if she get worse send for a physician immediately. You must be very careful of her, madam."

We walked to the stable, and as the horses had not finished eating their corn, I lounged about the quarters, and talked with the negro.

There was not a single soul in the quarters or in sight of the house except ourselves, the woman and her children, and the old negro. The negro women must have taken their sucklings with them, if they had any, to the field where they were at work.

The old man said they had " ten or eleven field hands, such as they was," and his master would sell sixty to seventy bags of cotton: besides which they made all the corn and pork they wanted, and something over, and raised some cattle.

Sixty bales of cotton would be worth three thousand dollars. Last year, the negro said, their crop was larger still. The expenses of the family (not very heavy, if our dinner was an in-dication) and of the negroes would probably be defrayed by the swine and corn crop, and the profits should have been, in two years, full six thousand dollars. What do people living in this style do with so much money? They buy *more negroes* and enlarge their plantations.

But it must be remembered that they were having the first use
of a very fine alluvial soil, and were subject to floods and fevers.
The yellow fever or cholera another year might kill half their
negroes, or a flood of the Red River (such as occurred August,
1849, and October, 1851) destroy their whole crop, and so use
up several years' profits.

A slate hung in the piazza, with the names of all the cotton-
pickers, and the quantity picked the last picking day by each, thus :
Gorge, 152 ; David, 130 ; Polly, 98 ; Hanna, 96 ; Little Gorge,
52, etc.   The whole number of hands mentioned on the slate
was fourteen.   Probably there were over twenty slaves, big and
little, on the plantation.

When our horses were ready, we paid the negro for taking
care of them, and I went in and asked the woman what I might
pay her for what we had eaten.

" What !" she asked, looking in my face as if angry.

I feared she was offended by my offering money for her hospitality, and put the question again as delicately as I could.   She
continued her sullen gaze at me for a moment, and then answered as if the words had been bullied out of her by a Tombs
lawyer,

" Dollar, I reckon."

" What !" thought I, but handed her the silver.

Riding out at the bars let down for us by the old negro, we
wondered if the child would be living twenty-four hours later,
and if it survived, what its moral chances were.   Poor, we
thought.   Five miles from a neighbor; ten, probably, from a
Louisiana* school ; hound-pups and negroes for playmates.

---

* The State Superintendent lately recommended that two out of three of the
Directors of Common Schools in Louisiana should be required to know how

We found our way back to the town only late in the evening. We had ridden most of the day over heavily-timbered, nearly flat, rich bottom land. It is of very great fertility; but, being subject to overflow, is not very attractive in spite of its proximity to a market.

THE ROAD BEFORE US.

Natchitoches was the terminus of the old Spanish trail from Monterey, Chihuahua, and Sante Fé, by San Antonio, to the States, and, as such, had a considerable military and commercial importance. This trail we were to follow, with slight deviations to the Rio Grande.

We set out with some difficulty, amusing rather to by-standers than to ourselves, owing to the numerous holds upon civilization we were reluctant to let go. Having bequeathed to the servants everything we thought we could spare to lighten our load, our saddles were still so encumbered that we could scarcely find room for the most important articles, viz., ourselves. Besides the bursting saddle-bags, both pommel and cantle, rising high in Mexican fashion, were hung with blankets, overcoats, ammunition-pouches, lunch-bags, et cetera. Once astride in all this lumber it was no small game that was inducement to dismount, and as to a free trot or a canter, with loose guns hammering our thighs, and everything else our knees and the horses flanks, it was not to be thought of except in dire extremity. However, a few days' experience made all right, and by means of a leather holder, attaching the gun closely to the pommel, and by tight packing and buckling generally, we shortly found ourselves very

to read and write; and mentioned that in one parish, instead of the signature, the *mark* of twelve different directors was affixed to a teacher's certificate.

good Texans in the matter of equestrianism, and had the full freedom of the road and the prairie.   But steady horseback travel can by no means be prosecuted in the rapid and lively style of a morning ride.   Consideration for your horse as well as for yourself soon reduces it to a jogging caravan life, which, unless in capital company or stimulating scenery, gets, like other uniform modes of travel, laborious and dull.

A word as to the saddles for such a trip.   They should be chosen to fit the horse rather than the rider, consequently should be bought after the horse, and of course in Texas.   We had had varying advice about taking English or Mexican saddles, but the Texan, a cross of the two, is far the best for the purpose.   As used in Texas, it is frequently an open tree, with no covering whatever, two wooden pads lying flat upon the muscles of the back, and fitting them as closely as possible, joined by an upright back and high pommel, leaving an open space of free air over the spine.   A blanket, smoothly folded, is always placed under it in lieu of pad, which serves in camp for a manger, when corn is to be had, and for a wrap at night.   Before and behind are long deer-skin thongs, far better than straps and buckles.   An extra blanket hangs by these, swinging loose like a saddle-cloth. With a well-fitting saddle of this kind, galls can almost always be escaped, especially if pains be taken to uncover, wash, and rub dry the heated back at every opportunity.

It was with great satisfaction that we found ourselves of a crisp December morning fairly en route, with all preliminaries, from steamboats to buckles, at last, accomplished.

Five minutes' ride took us deep into the pines.   Natchitoches, and with it all the tumult and bother of social civilization, had disappeared.   Under the pines and beyond them was a new, calm, free life, upon which we entered with a glow of enthusiasm, which, however, hardly sufficed to light up a whole day of pine shadow, and many times afterwards glimmered very dull ovei days on days of cold corn-bread and cheerless winter prairies.

PINEY WOOD TRAVEL.

For two days, as far as the boundary of Texas, we rode through these pines over a sandy surface, having little rise and fall, watered here and there by small creeks and ponds, within reach of whose overflow, present or past, stand deciduous trees, such as, principally, oaks and cotton-woods, in a firmer and richer soil. Wherever the road crosses or approaches these spots, there is or has been usually a plantation.

The road could hardly be called a road. It was only a way where people had passed along before. Each man had taken such a path as suited him, turning aside to avoid, on high ground, the sand, on low ground, the mud. We chose, generally, the untrodden elastic pavement of pine leaves, at a little distance from the main track.

EMIGRANT TRAINS.

We overtook, several times in the course of each day, the slow emigrant trains, for which this road, though less frequented than years ago, is still a chief thoroughfare. Inexorable destiny it seems that drags or drives on, always Westward, these toil-worn people. Several families were frequently moving together, coming from the same district, or chance met and joined, for company, on the long road from Alabama, Georgia, or the Carolinas. Before you come upon them you hear, ringing through the woods, the fierce cries and blows with which they urge on their jaded cattle. Then the stragglers appear, lean dogs or fainting negroes, ragged and spiritless. An old granny, hauling on, by the hand, a weak boy—too old to ride and too young to keep up. An old man, heavily loaded, with a rifle. Then the white covers of the wagons, jerking up and down as they mount over a root or plunge into a rut, disappearing, one after another, where the road descends. Then the active and cheery prime negroes, not yet exhausted, with a joke and a suggestion about tobacco. Then the black pickininnies, staring, in a confused heap, out at the back of the wagon, more and more of their eyes to be made out among the table legs and bedding as you get near ; behind them, further in, the old people and young mothers, whose turn it is to ride. As you get by, the white mother and babies, and the tall, frequently ill-humored master, on horseback, or walking with his gun, urging up the black driver and his oxen. As a scout ahead is a brother, or an intelligent slave, with the best gun, on the look-out for a deer or a turkey. We passed in the day perhaps one hundred persons attached to these trains, prob-ably an unusual number; but the immigration this year had been retarded and condensed by the fear of yellow fever, the last case of which, at Natchitoches, had indeed begun only the night before our arrival. Our chances of danger were considered small, however, as the hard frosts had already come. One of these trains was made up of three large wagons, loaded with furniture, babies, and invalids, two or three light wagons, and a gang of twenty able field hands. They travel ten or fifteen miles a day, stopping wherever night overtakes them. The masters are plainly dressed, often in home-spun, keeping their eyes about them, noticing the soil, sometimes making a remark on the crops by the roadside; but, generally, dogged, surly, and silent. The women are silent, too, frequently walking, to relieve the teams, and weary, haggard, mud be-draggled, forlorn, and disconsolate, yet hopeful and careful. The negroes, mud-incrusted, wrapped in old blankets or gunny-bags, suffering from cold, plod on, aim- less, hopeless, thoughtless, more indifferent than the oxen to all about them.

A YELLOW GENTLEMAN.

At noon, when we had stopped in the woods for a lunch, at a roadside fire, left well piled for the next comer, as is the pleasant custom, by some one in advance, a handsome mulatto young man rode up, and bowing, joined us at this open hearth. He proved a pleasant fellow, genial and quite intelligent. He accepted a share of our eatables, and told us he had been sent back to look for a lost dog. "His master, and a little boy, and two nigger women, and another yellow fellow, were on ahead." When we had finished, he said—" Perhaps youm (you and he) 'll wait a spell longer."

" Yes."

" Well, then, I'll go along, my master 'll be looking for me," and he rode off, lifting his hat like a Parisian.

ROAD TALK.

Stopping at a cabin for a few minutes, I was left alone. As I rode out a man on the road joined me, with

" How d'ye do?"

" Good morning."

" Going into Texas?'

" Yes. To Austin."

" Yes. Come from Alabama?"

" No: from New York."

" Come through Nakitosh?"

3*

" Yes."

" Get that horse in Natchitoches?"

" Yes."

" What did ye have to give for him?"

" Sixty dollars."

" What do ye reckon I had to give for this one?"

" I haven't the least idea.   How far is it to Fort Jesup?"

" You going to Fort Jesup to-night?"

" I expect to."

" You'll have to ride a dam smart hickory."

" How far is it?"

" Fourteen miles, and long ones.   That's a smart little horse. Mine can't trot so fast."

" I see he can't."   (He was on a canter.)   " But I am a little in haste."

" I got a right smart saddle and bridle 'long o' this one. What do ye think I gin for him?"

" I can't imagine."

" Well, I gin $20, saddle and bridle, too, less 'n two months ago."

" What's the matter with him?"

" Damnation laziness, that's what's the matter with him. Can't make him go, only by spurring him all the time.   Can't make him trot by no matter of whippin'; you take his skin off he won't trot.   Do you ever drink anything?"

" Not very often."

" Will you drink now?"

" No, I thank you."

" What kind of a piece is that in that case?"

" A short rifle."

" Will she shoot good ?"

" Yes."

" Well, you're too much for me."

" What ?"

" You're too much for me, you are. I can't keep along with you no further. Good-by."

After a while we came up with our noon friend, the yellow boy. " Well, you've overtook me again," said he. " Do you ever drink ? Take some whisky," offering the jug.

LAND LOCATING.

His master, riding near, was from Mississippi, going to " locate land" in Texas, and had no particular point in view. Most emigrants make a first excursion alone, to look at the country, and having selected a spot to suit them return and bring out their families the following season. The country is so little settled, that it is not difficult to find land in desirable neighborhoods, the title to which is still vested in the state, and immigrants usually purchase " land warrants," or " head rights," giving a title to a certain number of acres of the public domain, and choose, i. e., " locate," the particular spot for themselves.

COTTON HAULING.

We met, in course of the day, numerous cotton wagons, two or three sometimes together, drawn by three or four pair of mules or oxen, going slowly on toward Natchitoches or Grand Ecore, each managed by its negro driver. The load is commonly five bales (of 400 pounds each), and the cotton comes in this tedious way, over execrable roads, distances of 100 and even 150 miles. It is usually hauled from the eastern tier of Texan counties to the Sabine; but this year there had been no rise of water in the rivers, and from all this region it must be carried to Red River. The distance from the Sabine is here about fifty miles, and the cost of this transportation about one cent a pound; the freight from Grand Ecore to New Orleans from one to one and a quarter cents. If hauled 150 miles in this way, as we were told, the profit remaining, after paying the charges of transportation and commission, all amounting to about five cents, must be exceedingly small in ordinary years.

At night we met three or four of these teams half-mired in a swamp, distant some quarter of a mile one from another, and cheering themselves in the dark with prolonged and musical " yohoi's," sent ringing through the woods. We got through this with considerable perplexity ourselves, and were very glad to see the light of the cabin where we had been recommended to stop.

THE ENTERTAINMENT FOR MAN AND BEAST.

This was "Mrs. Stokers'," about half way to the Sabine. We were received cordially, every house here expecting to do inn-duty, but were allowed to strip and take care of our own horses, the people by no means expecting to do landlord's duty, but taking guests on sufferance. The house was a double log cabin—two log erections, that is, joined by one long roof, leaving an open space between. A gallery, extending across the whole front, serves for a pleasant sitting-room in summer, and for a toilet-room at all seasons. A bright fire was very welcome. Supper, consisting of pork, fresh and salt, cold corn-bread, and boiled sweet potatoes, was served in a little lean-to behind the house. After disposing of this we were shown to our room, the other cabin, where we whiled away our evening, studying, by the light of the great fire, a book of bear stories, and conversing with the young man of the family, and a third guest. The room was open to the rafters, and had been built up only as high as the top of the door upon the gallery side, leaving a huge open triangle to the roof, through which the wind rushed at us with a fierce swoop, both while we were sitting at the fire and after we retreated to bed. Owing to this we slept little, and having had a salt supper, lay very thirsty upon the deep feather bed. About four o'clock an old negro came in to light the fire. Asking him for water, we heard him breaking the ice for it outside. When we washed in the piazza the water was thick with frost, crusty, and half inclined not to be used as a fluid at all.

After a breakfast, similar in all respects to the supper, we saddled and rode on again. The horses had had a dozen ears of corn, night and morning, with an allowance of fodder (maize leaves). For this the charge was $1 25 each person. This is a fair sample of roadside stopping-places in Western Louisiana and Texas. The meals are absolutely invariable, save that fresh pork and sweet potatoes are frequently wanting. There is always, too, the black decoction of the South called coffee, than which it is often difficult to imagine any beverage more revolting. The bread is made of corn-meal, stirred with water and salt, and baked in a kettle covered with coals. The corn for breakfast is frequently unhusked at sunrise. A negro, whose business it is, shells and grinds it in a hand-mill for the cook. Should there be any of the loaf left after breakfast, it is given to the traveler, if he wish, with a bit of pork, for a noon-"snack," with no further charge. He is conscious, though, in that case, that he is robbing the hounds, always eagerly waiting, and should none remain, none can be had without a new resort to the crib. Wheat bread, if I am not mistaken, we met with but twice, out of Austin, in our whole journey across the state.

WORN-OUT LAND.

The country was very similar to that passed over the day before, with perhaps rather more of the cultivable loan. A good part of the land had, at some time, been cleared, but much was already turned over to the "old-field pines," some of them even fifteen years or more. In fact, a larger area had been abandoned, we thought, than remained under cultivation. With the land many cabins have, of course, also been deserted, giving the road a desolate air. If you ask, where are the people that once occupied these, the universal reply is, "gone to Texas."

THE PEOPLE.

The plantations occur, perhaps, at an average distance of three or four miles. Most of the remaining inhabitants live chiefly, to appearances, by fleecing emigrants. Every shanty sells spirits and takes in travelers. Every plantation has its sign, offering provender for sale, generally curiously worded or spelled, as "Corn Heare." We passed through but one village, which consisted of six dwellings. The families obtained their livelihood by the following occupations: one by shoeing the horses of emigrants; one by repairing the wheels of their wagons; one by selling them groceries. The smallest cabin contained a physician. It was not larger than a good-sized medicine chest, but had the biggest sign. The others advertised "corn and fodder." The prices charged for any article sold or service performed were enormous; full one hundred per cent. over those of New Orleans.

We took our pork and corn-bread, at noon, in the house of an old gentleman of a pious fox-hunting turn. He was so old a settler, he said, as to have moved *out* of Texas at the time it was ceded to Spain, and he was still sore on the point, as if he had been swindled by some party in the transaction. His table was richly supplied with Methodist publications, and he gave us a very pressing invitation to stop and have a hunt.

In course of the day we passed a small sugar apparatus—a battery of four kettles. We were told that it was not uncommon for plantations about here to grow enough sugar for home-use.

SPANISH REMAINS.

We met Spaniards once or twice on the road, and the population of this district is thought to be one half of Spanish origin. They have no houses on the road, however, but live in little hamlets in the forest, or in cabins contiguous to each other, about a pond. They make no progress in acquiring capital of their own, but engage in hunting and fishing, or in herding cattle for larger proprietors of the land. For this business they seem to have an hereditary adaptation, far excelling negroes of equal experience.

THE PROGRESS OF DILAPIDATION.

The number of cattle raised here is now comparatively small, most of the old herd proprietors having moved on to pastures new in Western Texas. The cane, which is a natural growth of most good soils at the South, is killed if closely fed upon. The blue-joint grass (not the blue-grass of Kentucky) takes its place, and is also indigenous upon a poorer class of soils in this region. This is also good food for cattle, but is killed in turn if closely pastured. The ground then becomes bare or covered with shrubs, and the "range" is destroyed. The better class of soils here bear tolerable crops of cotton, but are by no means of value equal to the Red River bottoms or the new soils of any part of Texas. The country is, therefore, here in similar condition to that of the Eastern Slave States. The improvements which the inhabitants have succeeded in making in the way of clearing the forest, fencing and tilling the land, building dwellings, barns, and machinery, making roads and bridges, and introducing the institutions of civilization, not compensating in value the deterioration in the productiveness of the soil. The exhausted land reverts to wilderness.

OUR OLD FRONTIER.

Shortly after noon rain began to fall from the chilly clouds that had been threatening us, and sleet and snow were soon driving in our faces. Our animals were disposed to flinch, but we were disposed to sleep in Texas, and pushed on across the Sabine. We found use for all our wraps, and when we reached the ferry-house our Mackintoshes were like a coat of mail with the stiff ice, and trees and fields were covered. In the broad river bottom we noticed many aquatic birds, and the browsing line under the dense mass of trees was almost as clean cut as that of Bushy Park. The river, at its low stage, was only three or four rods across. The old negro who ferried us over, told us he had taken many a man to the other side, before annexation, who had ridden his horse hard to get beyond the jurisdiction of the states.

THE FIRST HOUSE IN TEXAS.

If we were unfortunate in this stormy entrance into Texas, we were very fortunate in the good quarters we lighted upon. The ferry has long been known as Gaines's ferry, but is now the property of Mr. Strather, an adjacent planter, originally from Mississippi, but a settler of long standing. His log-house had two stories, and being the first we had met having glass windows, and the second, I think, with any windows at all, takes high rank for comfort on the road. At supper we had capital mallard-ducks from the river, as well as the usual Texan diet.

'We were detained by the severity of the weather during the following day, and were well entertained with huntsman's stories of snakes, game, and crack shots. Mr. S. himself is the best shot in the county. A rival, who had once a match against him for two thousand dollars, called the day before the trial, and paid five hundred dollars to withdraw. He brought out his rifle for us, and placed a bullet, at one hundred and twenty yards, plump in the spot agreed upon. His piece is an old Kentucky rifle, weighing fourteen pounds, barrel forty-four inches in length, and throwing a ball weighing forty-four to the pound.

A guest, who came in, helped us to pass the day by exciting our anticipations of the West, and by his free and good advice. He confirmed stories we had heard of the danger to slavery in the West by the fraternizing of the blacks with the Mexicans. They helped them in all their bad habits, married them, stole a living from them, and ran them off every day to Mexico. This man had driven stages or herded cattle in every state of the Union, and had a notion that he liked the people and the state of Alabama better than any other. A man would get on faster, he thought, in Iowa, than anywhere else. He had been stage-driver in Illinois during the cold winter of 1851–2, and had driven a whole day when the mercury was at its furthest below zero, but had never suffered so much from cold as on his present trip, during a norther on a Western prairie. He was now returning from Alexandria, where he had taken a small drove of horses. He cautioned us, in traveling, always to see our horses fed with our own eyes, and to hang around them till they had made sure of a tolerable allowance, and never to leave anything portable within sight of a negro. A stray blanket was a sure loss.

Mr. S. has two plantations, both on upland, but one under the care of an overseer, some miles from the river. The soil he considers excellent. He averaged, last year, seven and a half bales to the hand; this year, four and a half bales. The usual crop of corn here is thirty bushels (shelled) to the acre.

Hearing him curse the neighboring poor people for stealing hogs, we inquired if thieves were as troublesome here as in the older countries. "If there ever were any hog-thieves anywhere," said he, "it's here." In fact, no slave country, new or old, is free from this exasperating pest of poor whites. In his neighborhood were several who ostensibly had a little patch of land to attend to, but who really, he said, derived their whole lazy subsistence from their richer neighbors' hog droves.

SLAVE LIFE.

The negro-quarters here, scattered irregularly about the house, were of the worst description, though as good as local custom requires. They are but a rough inclosure of logs, ten feet square, without windows, covered by slabs of hewn-wood four feet long. The great chinks are stopped with whatever has come to hand—a wad of cotton here, and a corn-shuck there. The suffering from cold within them in such weather as we experienced, must be great.   The day before, we had seen a young black girl, of twelve or fourteen years, sitting on a pile of logs before a house we passed, in a driving sleet, having for her only garment a short chemise.   It is impossible to say whether such *shiftlessness* was the fault of the master or of the girl.   Probably of both, and a part of the peculiar southern and southwestern system of "get along," till it comes better weather.

THE RED LAND DISTRICT.

The storm continuing a third day, we rode through it twenty-five miles further to San Augustine.   For some distance the country remains as in Louisiana.   Then the pines gradually disappear, and a heavy clay soil, stained by an oxide of iron to a uniform brick red, begins.   It makes most disagreeable roads, sticking close, and giving an indelible stain to every article that touches it.   This tract is known as the Red Lands of Eastern Texas.

On a plantation not far from the river, we learned they had made eight bales to the hand.   Mentioning it, afterwards, to a man who knew the place, he said they had planted earlier than their neighbors, and worked night and day, and he believed had lied, besides.   They had sent cotton both by Galveston and by Grand Ecore, and had found the cost the same, about $8 per bale of 500 lbs.

We called at a plantation offered for sale.   It was described in the hand-bills as having a fine house.   We found it a cabin without windows.   The proprietor said he had made ten bales to the hand, and would sell with all the improvements, a new gin-house, press, etc., for $6 per acre.

The roadside, though free from the gloom of pines, did not

cheer up, the number of deserted wrecks of plantations not at all diminishing. The occupied cabins were no better than before. We had entered our promised land; but the oil and honey of gladness and peace were nowhere visible. The people we met were the most sturdily inquisitive I ever saw. Nothing staggered them, and we found our account in making a clean breast of it as soon as they approached.

We rode through the shire-town, Milam, without noticing it. Its buildings, all told, are six in number.

We passed several immigrant trains in motion, in spite of the weather. Their aspect was truly pitiful. Splashed with a new coating of red mud, dripping, and staggering, beating still the bones of their long worn-out cattle, they floundered helplessly on.

SAN AUGUSTINE.

San Augustine made no very charming impression as we entered, nor did we find any striking improvement on longer acquaintance. It is a town of perhaps fifty or sixty houses, and half a dozen shops. Most of the last front upon a central square acre of neglected mud. The dwellings are clap-boarded, and of much higher class than the plantation dwellings. As to the people, a resident told us there was but one man in the town that was not in the constant habit of getting drunk, and that this gentleman relaxed his Puritanic severity during our stay in view of the fact that Christmas came but once that year.

A TEXAN FÊTE.

Late on Christmas eve, we were invited to the window by our landlady, to see the pleasant local custom of The Christmas Serenade. A band of pleasant spirits started from the square, blowing tin horns, and beating tin pans, and visited in succession every house in the village, kicking in doors, and pulling down fences, until every male member of the family had appeared, with appropriate instruments, and joined the merry party. They then marched to the square, and ended the ceremony with a centupled tin row. In this touching commemoration, as strangers, we were not urged to participate.

MANNERS.

A gentleman of the neighborhood, addicted, as we knew, to a partiality towards a Rip Van Winkle, tavern-lounging style of living, told us he was himself regarded by many of his neighbors with an evil eye, on account of his " stuck up" deportment, and his habit of minding too strictly his own business. He had been candidate for Representative, and had, he thought, probably been defeated on this ground, as he was sure his politics were right.

Not far from the village stands an edifice, which, having three stories and sashed windows, at once attracted our attention. On inquiry, we learned a story, curiously illustrative of Texan and human life. It appeared that two universities were chartered for San Augustine, the one under the protection of the Methodists, the other of the Presbyterians. The country being feebly settled, the supply of students was short, and great was the consequent rivalry between the institutions. The neighboring people took sides upon the subject so earnestly, that, one fine day, the president of the Presbyterian University was shot down in the street. After this, both dwindled, and seeing death by starvation staring them in the face, they made an arrangement by which both were taken under charge of the *Fraternity of*

Masons. The buildings are now used under the style of " The Masonic Institute," the one for boys, the other for girls. The boys occupy only their third story, and the two lower stories are falling to ludicrous decay—the boarding dropping off, and the windows on all sides dashed in.

The Mexican 'habitations of which San Augustine was once composed, have all disappeared. We could not find even a trace of them.

At San Augustine we rejoined our friend B., who had, in fact, arrived but a few minutes before us. He had come on foot nearly all the distance from Natchitoches, out of compassion for the poor teams that should have dragged him, and had suffered extremes of cold and wet dismals. Our friend was a Northern man, but an old original Texan settler, ranger, and campaigner; a trader in Central and Northern Mexico; a volunteer in the Mexican war, and, withal, a Californian. A man of such large experience and familiarity with practical details in matters we were quite unversed in, it was a rare good fortune to fall in with. But we were not long in discovering that prejudices creep in with experience, and that simple common sense goes a great way, too.

PACKING THE MULE.

We had set out intending, should no circumstance prevent, to spend near a year in the saddle, partly in Mexico, and a great part in Indian country, hundreds of miles from any resources but our own. We accordingly provided ourselves, before leaving home, with the best equipment we could devise for the purpose, and to carry the necessary weight with the most freedom we chose a pack mule.

Few things gave us more pleasure, for more reasons than one, than the complete success of the pack-apparatus we had had the hardihood to have made and to bring with us from New York. B., when he saw it, was almost convulsed with laughter and contempt. We should have half Texas hooting at our heels! There was no occasion to pay our bill, we should never get out of the inn-yard with that concern. A real " aparejo," with a Mexican muleteer to put it on, was the only contrivance that could be ever used for packing. Our affair, even if it did not topple over at the first step, would cut the mule to the bone in ten miles slow walk! During our few days' stay at San Augustine, we heard so much of this foreboding as to be fairly tired of the name of "aparejo," and to have ourselves a considerable misgiving as to the result.

But we had read Ward's account of the Mexican "aparejo," and of his substitution for it of the English pack-saddle, and we stood firm, insisting that our contraption should have at least a fair trial.

The affair that excited so much amusement and discussion was a simple pack-saddle, to which we had attached iron hooks, for a couple of wicker hampers. It is composed of two wooden pads joined by four straight horns, like those of a saw-horse, riveted at the crossings, and projecting above, so as to give a convenient hitching place for any stray bit of rope. Along the crotches of these horns we laid our tent, made up in a compact roll; into the hampers we stowed our household gods, and, buckling a long leather girth over all, there we were.

On starting, B. entirely refused to take lunch-materials, knowing that we should shortly return to buy a wagon for our hampers or their contents. But nothing happened. The mule walked off with as much unconcern as if he had been trained to carry hampers from his birth. At noon, becoming hungry, we stopped at a cabin for dinner. During the meal Mr. Brown excited us by lying down and attempting to *roll*. However, no damage was done; for, finding a hamper well girthed down on whichever side he turned, he became content to sit quietly and await our pleasure.

Dreadful, as night approached, were the anticipations on B.'s part, of the inhuman spectacle he was about to show us on removing the saddle. When the hampers had been lowered he fairly groaned as we unbuckled the girths. We ourselves were not without fear. But not a hair was started. After a roll the mule was as gay as a kitten, and the spot heated by the saddle in ten minutes could not be found.

For a day or two it was to-morrow, oh! to-morrow. But when day after day passed, and the mule still continued sound in case and in excellent spirits, B., like a gentleman, gave in, and acknowledged that it beat all. Still, on the point of the " aparejo," he would not yield, maintaining, that though this might do well enough for a jaunt, the " aparejo" was the only reliable thing for a long pull. Now, the " aparejo" consists, in brief, of a leather sack of hay, and five or six fathoms of rope. With these tools, the reader may imagine how tedious and torturous a process is the roping on of the loose boxes or bags that contain a traveler's *things*.

In short, our saddle and hampers worked admirably, and can, in all respects, be recommended for a similar service.

ADDITIONS TO THE COMPANY.

We found as much difficulty in obtaining suitable horses in San Augustine as at Natchitoches, and were some days in making choice. Finally, B. made purchase of an old gray, afflicted with an osseous structure which had long outgrown its hide, but otherwise serving well enough for temporary use. Being an animal of experience, he knew enough not to waste his remaining substance in useless steps, and never budged a leg except under positive orders. He answered, however, for a start for a "trade," and after a few days was left to ruminate upon the prairie, and a spunky young mustang took his place in the caravan.

A chestnut mare was the last acquisition—a lithe, shapely thing, with a keen volatile eye, a fine ear, and open nostril. I found no friendship in her face, nor did she ever yield to the last, one single smile to my tender advances. Restless, anxious, overdone from the start, her nerves were too large for her dainty muscle, and she was quite unfit for steady travel.

She could out-walk, out-trot, out-run any of her companions, at their utmost effort, by three to two, with the most natural ease. She never declined any work whatever, but, frequently, all consolation, and, what was more annoying, all food. Such treatment as travelers could give she felt beneath her, and took from the first the position of a high-bred girl who had seen better days. When I suggested, sometimes, a run over the prairie, she was off like a hawk at the slightest pressure of the legs, and we were flying mad out of sight in an instant. Such sports, however, she disdained to enjoy with me, though fairly sobbing after them with repressed excitement, turning a flashing eye toward mine, as much as to ask, "Is that the creature to carry saddle-bags?"

OUR EXPERIENCE WITH ARMS.

For arms, expecting to rely much on them for provision as
4

well as defense, we selected a Sharp's rifle, a double fowling-piece, Colt's navy revolvers, and sheathed hunting knives. In this we found we had not gone wrong, every expert who inquired into the matter highly approving our choice, and our own experience for us clinching the matter. The Sharp, in sure hands (not ours), threw its ounce ball as exactly, though far deeper, into its mark, at one thousand three hundred yards, as a Kentucky rifle its small ball at one hundred. For force, we can testify to its ball passing through a four-inch white oak fence-post; and for distance, to constantly striking a piece of water a mile and a quarter distant, with the ordinary purchased cartridge. By the inventor it can be loaded and fired eighteen times in a minute; by us, at a single trial, without practice, nine times. Ours was the Government pattern—a short carbine, of light weight, and conveniently arranged for horseback use. Its barrel had been browned, a box made in the stock, and a ramrod added, to which a cleaning brush could be attached. Its cost in this shape was forty dollars. We were furnished with moulds for both conical and round balls, as when cartridges fail it may be loaded at the muzzle with the ramrod, in the ordinary way. It was also fitted with Maynard's primer, a self-capping apparatus, which, however, we found so unreliable as to be useless in practice. The capsule never failed to fix itself in position, but frequently did not explode. Nothing about the piece during our trip gave way or got out of order.

Two barrels full of buck-shot make a trustier dose, perhaps, than any single ball for a squad of Indians, when within range, or even in unpracticed hands for wary venison; but the combination of the two with Colt's, makes, I believe, for a traveling party, the strongest means of protection yet known.

Of the Colt's we cannot speak in too high terms. Though subjected for six or eight months to rough use, exposed to damp grass, and to all the ordinary neglects and accidents of camp travel, not once did a ball fail to answer the finger. Nothing got out of order, nothing required care; not once, though carried at random, in coat-pocket or belt, or tied thumping at the pummel, was there an accidental discharge. In short, they simply gave us perfect satisfaction, being all they claimed to be. Before taking them from home we gave them a trial alongside every rival we could hear of, and we had with us an unpatented imitation, but for practical purposes one Colt we found worth a dozen of all others. Such was the testimony of every old hunter and ranger we met. There are probably in Texas about as many revolvers as male adults, and I doubt if there are one hundred in the state of any other make. For ourselves, as I said, we found them perfect. After a little practice we could very surely chop off a snake's head from the saddle at any reasonable distance, and across a fixed rest could hit an object of the size of a man at ordinary rifle range. One of our pistols was one day submerged in a bog for some minutes, but on trial, though dripping wet, not a single barrel missed fire. A border weapon, so reliable in every sense, would give brute courage to even a dyspeptic tailor.

OFF AGAIN.

December 26.—Thus fully equipped, far beyond what the tame event justified, we sallied forth from the inn-gate at San Augustine amid the cheers of the servants and of two small black boys who had watched with open eyes all our proceedings. Fanny, the mare, took naturally the lead, followed by B. leading the mule by his halter, and Nack brought up the rear. The mule, however, soon found the halter an annoyance, and pulling it away, walked on at his own gait. Seldom afterwards did he give us any trouble in guiding him. At first the mare must lead the way, but soon he consented to go himself in advance, and be driven whithersoever we would. When he loitered, the point of a ramrod was thrust into his flank, a stimulus of which he soon learned to have a peculiar dread. He was sometimes extremely reluctant to pass a well-filled, satisfactory-looking corn-crib, and in towns showed a strong propensity to turn down lanes, and to force a passage into spaces between buildings which were too narrow for his hampers, but on such occasions his long halter was attached, by a turn or two, to the strong pommel of the mare's saddle, and by dint of dragging before and poking behind he was forced onwards. In going through wood he always gauged very exactly the width of his load, frequently declining to venture where we thought he could pass, and going a circuitous course upon his own hook.

THE COUNTRY.

We rode, during the day, eighteen miles, through a somewhat more pleasing country. The houses were less rude, the negro-huts more comfortable, the plantations altogether neater, than those we had passed before. We noticed one group of magnolias and a few willow or swamp oaks (*quercus phellos*), whose leaves are long and narrow, like those of the willow, and remain green through the greater part of the winter. The principal wood was oak, mingled here and there with chestnut. We stopped for the night at a remarkably comfortable house, but could look out, as usual, at the stars between the logs. There being but one bed, B. lay upon the floor, with his feet to the fire.

PIETY IN NEGROES.

The host was an intelligent man, and had a supply of books upon the mantel. Speaking about the preferences of negroes for certain religious sects, he said they were not particularly religious about here any way. They generally joined the church which their master attended, if he attended any. Otherwise, that which was nearest.

B. told of an old negro, near Victoria, the only Baptist of the neighborhood. He always "stuck up for his own faith," and was ready with a reason for it. "You kin read, now, keant you?"

"Yes."

"Well, I s'pose you've read de Bible, haint you?"

"Yes."

"You've read about John de Baptis', haint you?"

"Yes."

"Well, you never read 'bout any *John de Methodis'*, did you? You see I has de Bible on my side, den."

"DONE GONE."

Our host called out, "Boy, why don't you get me those things?"

"I *done* got 'em, sar," replied the boy.

At San Augustine, the morning previous, the children of the house were running about, wishing the lodgers a merry Christmas *for a dime*. One of them came to me a second time, but seeing her mistake, shouted out, "Oh! you done give me Christmas gift."

"Done gone," for "gone" is an ordinary expression.

Other modes of speech that strike a Northern man at almost any part of the South are—

The use of "Ho!"—"Ho! John!" when we should call out simply, "John."

"Far" and "bar," for fair, bear, etc.

The constant use of "no account"—such a man, dog, or shower is of "no account"—for, worth little.

"Sure" and "I wonder," as replies.

"Christ," as an expletive, like "Sacristie."

"Yellow fellow," for a mulatto. (Why yellow *fellow*, but black *man ?*)

"Ill," for "vicious."   "Is your dog ill?"

"Miss Jane," by the negroes to the mistress after marriage.

Constantly execrable grammar—"I never sawed," "I have saw." This by the lazy, schoolless, young men and women.

NACOGDOCHES.

December 27.—A similar country. At two, P. M., reached Nacogdoches, a considerable town. Near it the soil changes to sand, bearing pines. The houses along the road, at the entrance to the village, stand in gardens, and are neatly painted—the first exterior sign of cultivation of mind since Red River. The town is compact, the houses framed and boarded. One or two old Mexican stone buildings remain, and, like the Aztec structures in more Southern cities, have been put to the uses of the invading race. One of them, fronting, with an arcade, on the square, is converted into a bar-room. About Nacogdoches there are many Mexicans still living. Two or three of them, wrapped in blankets and *serapes*, we saw leaning against posts, and looking on in grand decay. They preserve their exclusiveness, their priests and their own customs, intermarrying, except accidents, only among themselves, and are considered here as harmless vagabonds.

As we entered the town, we overtook one of them, a young lad of a delicate brunette complexion and a soft, attractive eye, mounted on a donkey, carrying a bunch of ducks and a turkey across his saddle. B. hailed him at once in Spanish, and bought a brace of his ducks for two dimes. For the turkey he asked four bits (50 cents). He could speak no English; the fowl he had shot upon the creek.

The streets were full of people, and our arrival caused a sharp use of eyes and tongues. We were at once pronounced Californians, and accepted, of course, the designation. Our fit-out was examined in detail, as to prices and excellence, and, for the most part, highly approved. The pack, not lacking now the prestige of actual performance, was pronounced a touch beyond anything they had seen.

When we inquired the occasion of-the concourse, we were told they were " having a march." It was a joint celebration of Masons, Odd Fellows, and Sons of Temperance. The first we had the pleasure of seeing. There were about fifty men in black, with various insignia of sashes and aprons. After forming behind a house, two and two, they marched out upon the square, at the word of command, " the precession will forward." A tall negro with a violin struck up a jig with much dignity, and the officers in command displayed their swords to the best advantage by using them as walking sticks. After perambulating the square, the body entered the court-house, the floor of which had been strewn to a depth of six inches with saw-dust, converted thus into a vast spittoon.

SUPPLIES.

In this town of 500 inhabitants, we found there was no flour. At San Augustine we had inquired in vain at all the stores for refined sugar. Not satisfied with some blankets that were shown us, we were politely recommended by the shop-keeper to try other stores. At each of the other stores we were told they had none, the only blankets in town we should find at ——'s, naming the one we had just quitted. The same thing occurred with several other articles.

We provided ourselves with a couple of tin kettles, a frying-pan, and a small axe, preparatory to camp-life, which we were determined to begin at once.

At night we reached a creek (streamlet) among the pines, five miles beyond Nacogdoches, and there made our first camp. Pitching our tent in the deepening twilight, at a first trial we met with some blundering difficulties. B. looked on with an experienced smile, while we made our arrangements as snug as time permitted, saying nothing, but busying himself with picking and cooking the ducks. After supper, rolling himself in his blanket, he disappeared for the night, with his feet to the fire, disdaining the canvas curtains. For ourselves, we lay quietly awake till morning dawned, numb with cold, and perhaps having a little secret excitement at the novel bed-chamber.

On drawing our curtains, we found water already hot, and B. hugging his knees over the fire. We cooked a kettle of choco-late, picked the duck bones, in default of better picking, and went on our way.

THE ANGELINA.

The soil continued sandy, and the timber pine, during the early part of the day; afterwards, oaks and black-jack, a black-barked, short, gnarly oakling (*quercus ferruginea*). The soil of the creek-bottoms bears good cotton, and on the edge of the Angelina bottoms we saw a very heavy crop. The Angelina ferry is reached by a rude causeway, with bridges at intervals, some two or three miles in length, the only structure of the kind we saw in the state, though there is hardly a stream where it is not more or less needed. By a levee, these bottoms might probably be made very valuable.

CAMP DIET.

We camped some twenty-five miles from Nacogdoches (Cherokee Co.). Finding nothing else, after foraging the neighborhood, than a few small and watery sweet-potatoes, we had recourse to our own stores, and made trial of Borden's meat biscuit, a preparation which won high encomiums at the London Exhibition. After preparing a substantial dish of it, according to directions, we all tried it once, then turned unanimously to the watery potatoes. Once afterwards on the journey we tried again, with no better luck, then left all we had purchased to the birds. It may answer to support life, no doubt, where even corn-meal is not to be had, but I should decidedly undergo a very near approach to the traveler's last bourne, before having recourse to it, if that we had were an ordinary specimen.

Next morning, after renewed efforts, we procured a few eggs. While eating them, we observed that Mr. Brown was missing. He had been turned loose, with the idea that he would not stray far from his companions, to augment the bulk of his rations by browsing upon dead leaves and shrubs. F. went in search of him. He soon met a stranger, who asked, in reply to inquiries, " Was it a large mule ?—Did he have a lariat ?—Shod ?—Shoes

4*

worn ?"   " It was a large dun mule, you could not mistake it."
" Oh, I have not seen your mule, but I saw the trail back yonder."   He was at last found some four miles down a by-road,
whither he had followed a party of people returning from a ball.
Among their animals were two young colts, towards which mules
are said to have a peculiar tenderness.   On seeing F., probably
recollecting something hamperish in his face, the mule made off
into a swamp.   After a long chase he was captured, having his
lariat inextricably entangled in a vine, which was cut into small
pieces to free him.

THE NECHES.—WORN-OUT PLANTATIONS.

Crossed the Neches into Houston County.   This day's ride
and the next were through a very poor country, clay or sand soil,
bearing short oaks and black-jack.   We passed one small meadow,
or prairie, covered with coarse grass.   Deserted plantations
appeared again in greater numbers than the occupied.   One farm,
near which we stopped, was worked by eight field hands.   The
crop had been fifty bales; small, owing to a dry season.   The
corn had been exceedingly poor.   The hands, we noticed, came
in from the fields after eight o'clock.

The deserted houses, B. said, were built before the date of
Texan Independence.   After Annexation the owners had moved
on to better lands in the West.   One house he pointed out as
having been the residence of one of a band of pirates who occupied the country thirty or forty years ago.   They had all been
gradually killed.

During the day we met two men on horseback, one upon
wheels, and passed one emigrant family.   This was all the motion
upon the principal road of the district.

The following is a note of expenses during twenty-four hours. It will give a concise idea of our fare.

1 bbl. corn (in the husk), - - - -	$1 00
12 bundles corn-fodder, - - - -	75
Corn-bread, - - - - -	10
Bacon, - - - - - - -	05
Eggs, - - - - - - -	03
Chocolate (from our own stores), - -	20
	$2 13

Horses, 44 cents each; Men, 12½ cents each.

The chocolate being soon exhausted, and not to be replaced, and eggs being a rare luxury, our private necessary expenses may be put down at five cents each per diem. To live upon this sum would, for some patients, be a capital prescription; for others it is only a sour and aggravating discomfort.

The Neches is here about three rods in width. Were it not for overhanging timber, it would be, at high water, a navigable stream; as it is, keel-boats sometimes come up as far as the ferry where we crossed. Like all the eastern rivers of Texas it is thick with mud. The Colorado is the first stream that runs clear. West of it each becomes more limpid as you progress. The water of the Medina, twenty miles beyond San Antonio, is as pure and transparent at the ford as the finest plate-glass. This beauty of the West is not the least of those that have caused such a desertion of Eastern settlements.

A SUNDAY IN CAMP.—ALIMENTARY SUBSTANCES.

The second day's camp was a few miles beyond the town of Crockett—the shire-town of Houston County. Not being able to find corn for our horses, we returned to the village for it.

We obtained what we wanted for a day's rest, which we proposed for Sunday, the following day, and loaded it into our emptied hampers. We then looked about the town for current provisions for ourselves. We were rejoiced to find a German baker, but damped by finding he had only molasses-cakes and candies for sale. There was no flour in the town, except the little of which he made his cakes. He was from Hamburgh, and though he found a tolerable sale, to emigrants principally, he was very tired of Crockett, and intended to move to San Antonio among his countrymen. He offered us coffee, and said he had had beer, but on Christmas-day a mass of people called on him; he had "treated" them all, and they had finished his supply.

We inquired at seven stores, and at the two inns, for butter, flour, or wheat-bread, and fresh meat. There was none in town. One inn-keeper offered us salt-beef, the only meat, except pork, in town. At the stores we found crackers, worth in New York 6 cents a pound, sold here at 20 cents; poor raisins, 30 cents; Manilla rope, half-inch, 30 cents a pound. When butter was to be had it came in firkins from New York, although an excellent grazing country is near the town.

SUNDAY HABITS.

We got some work done at a saddler's. He told us he didn't do work on Sundays, but he would try to finish this in the evening, and would leave it at the next store for us. The stores, he said, were all open, and made their best sales on Sunday. It was usual in this part of the country. We asked if there were a church in the town?

"Yes."

"Of what denomination?"

"Oh, none in particular.   They let anybody preach that comes along."

BLACK TEMPERANCE.

Returning with our corn, we overheard the following negro conversation:

"Wher' you gwine to-morrow?"

"To ———'s."

"Ken you get whisky ther?"

"Yes."

"Good rye-whisky?"

"Yes."

"What do they ask for it?"

"A dollar and a half a gallon.   I don't want no whisky dat costs less 'n a dollar and a half a gallon.   I'd rather hev it then your common rot-gut fur a dime.   I don't want to buy no whisky fur less 'n a dollar and a half a gallon."

"Well, I du.   I'd like it was a picayune a gallon, I would."

January 1, 1854.—Our Sunday camp was in a sheltered spot, where fuel abounded.   The tent faced a huge hollow log, against which we built, before going to bed, an enormous fire of logs, piled six or eight feet high.   The blaze shot high in air, and illumined the whole neighborhood.   But ice formed, notwithstanding, in water standing at the mouth of the tent, and we passed another very chilly night.   We had anticipated that cold would be the greatest enemy to comfort, and had made every provision for encountering it.   We put on at night extra underclothing, an overcoat, a Guernsey shirt, two hunting-shirts, and even Canada leggins.   But through all this, and a triple thickness of blanket, and through an india rubber carpet, the cold of the ground penetrated and benumbed us.   The thermometer stood, at 10 P. M., at 38 deg. (Fahrenheit); at 8 A. M., at 36 deg.; at 12 M., Jan. 1st, in the tent, on which the sun was pouring, at 80 deg.; at 8 P. M., at 44 deg.

After feeding the horses, F. went with the rifle in search of something for ourselves, but returned, having seen nothing. B., going with dimes, had better luck. He brought at last a hoe-cake and half a dozen eggs, from a neighboring cabin. A rough omelette was speedily constructed and demolished.

At this camp we were annoyed by hogs, beyond all description. At almost every camp we were surrounded by them; but here they seemed perfectly frantic and delirious with hunger. They ran directly through the fire, and even carried off a chicken which B., on a second excursion, had been able to procure, after it was dressed and spitted. While the horses were feeding, it required the constant attendance of two of us to keep them at bay ; and even then they secured more than half the corn. Fanny was so shocked and disturbed as to refuse all food. For some minutes the fiercest of them would resist even a clubbing, eating and squealing on through the blows. These animals proved, indeed, throughout Texas, a disgusting annoyance, though after procuring an excellent dog, a day or two after, we were rid of the worst of it.

We occupied our day in writing and reading (for in our luxuriously capacious hampers was a compact little library of diamond editions), and in making, sailor-like, repairs to such articles as were already giving way under the continued wear and tear of travel.

A ROASTED BROAD-AXE.

Two pleasant incidents occurred :

A negro, who had been prowling about us for some time, suddenly came up and said :—

"Genlumun, whar's that log ?"

"What log ?"

"Why, that ar log whar I lef' my broad-axe."

We had seen no broad-axe.

"Well, I lef' my axe right here day afore yesterday, in de holler of a log. Yes, sar, dis am de very spot. Dat ar's whar I was cutting."

Sure enough, on poking in our ashes, we found something like an axe, which we offered him. As it was red hot, he declined taking it, and commenced, in a whining tone, to describe how new it was, how he had put it all sharp in our big log, and how he should have to pay for it, cause his massa never would believe that it had done gone got burned up.

As we had, in fact, had the use of the wooden helve, we determined that we were bound in equity to pay for it, and sent him off with the cooled axe, a box of *Borden's biscuit*, and a dollar, laughing on the other side of his mouth.

A WINDFALL.

Not long after this, while strolling with the gun, I came upon traces of fresh blood, and following them, *found* a fine fat wild turkey upon the ground. It had evidently been shot within an hour or two, and had had time to fly and run thus far from the sportsman before dropping.

This was a waif at any time not to be despised, and in the actual state of our larder, a real piece of good fortune. Keeping for awhile my own counsel, I carried it proudly into camp, where its arrival was welcomed with profuse congratulations.

Two hours thereafter, we were feeling decidedly happier men.

A FAMILY SERVANT.

At the cabin where our hoe-cake was purchased, a negro man was the sole servant. He had been away, he said, all night, to see his wife, and came home at four o'clock to grind the corn, and bake it for the family's breakfast. The women of the family did no house work. The planter raised only corn and hogs. These were the hogs whose acquaintance we had made.

Life there was certainly cheap. This one negro, supposing them to be squatters, was the only investment, except a few days' work once in a lifetime, in cutting and piling together the logs that composed their residence. A little corn and bacon, sold now and then to travelers, furnished the necessary coffee and tobacco ; nature and the negro did all the rest.

THE DAY OF REST.

An emigrant party from Alabama passed, having fifty negroes, and 100 head of cattle, sheep, etc., going to the Brazos, to settle. " Oh, my God! How tired I am," I heard an old negro woman exclaim. A man of powerful frame answered, " I feel like as tho' I couldn't lift my legs much longer." This was about twelve o'clock.

Near us, within sound, were two negroes all day splitting rails —Sunday and New Year's day.

POST-OFFICE DEPARTMENT.

At evening F. rode into town to mail our letters. One was a package of notes, on letter sheets, in a large envelope. Wishing to prepay it he asked, " What is the postage on this, sir ?"

"How many sheets are there?"

"Oh, twelve or fourteen."   The postmaster commenced tearing off one end of the envelope.

"Stop.   Don't open it."

"It'll save putting it in a way-bill.   I suppose I've no right to charge only one cent?"

"Yes, three cents per half ounce.   It must be weighed."

His scales were "broke down," but it was finally weighed after a fashion, paid roundly, and put in a bag, unmarked.

THE FIRST PRAIRIE.

Jan. 2.—We came to-day upon the first prairie of any extent, and shortly after crossed Trinity River.   After having been shut in during so many days by dreary winter forests, we were quite exhilarated at coming out upon an open country and a distant view.   During the whole day's ride the soil improved, and the country grew more attractive.   Small prairies alternated agreeably with post-oak woods.   The post-oak (*quercus obtusiloba*) forms a very prominent feature in Texas scenery and impressions.   It is a somewhat small broad-leaved oak of symmetrical shape, and appears wherever the soil is light and sandy, in a very regular open forest growth.   It stands in islands in the large prairies or frequently borders on open prairie through a large tract.   The roads, where practicable, prefer the post-oak, for summer shade and dry and uniform footing.   It is seldom cleared for cultivating the soil; but in the West, where timber is scarce, an island of post-oak adds very much to the value of a tract for sale, furnishing materials for cabin and fences.

TRINITY RIVER NAVIGATION.

We came upon the Trinity at a bluff, and found the ferryman absent. His wife and a little son attempted to ferry us over, but the boat was unprovided with oars, and though we all helped as well as we could, with poles and bits of board, we were several times swept down the river, and obliged to drag the boat back to the point of starting. After long labor we succeeded in reaching the opposite bank.

The Trinity here is, at this low water stage, about three rods wide, muddy, and running with some rapidity.

It is considered the best navigable stream of Texas; but this winter there had been no rise, and no navigation for six months. It was still at low water when we crossed it on our return, four months later. At high water it is navigable as high as the Three Forks above, or some 300 miles from its mouth. But none of the Texan rivers can be said to be permanently navigable, as is evident, when this is called the best of them. The Brazos is broader, but more rapid and dangerous. In good seasons, boats reach points from one to two hundred miles from its mouth. The Colorado is said to be navigable for 200 miles, or as far as Austin ; but is so only for the smallest class of boats, and that so seldom, and with so much danger, that, practically, all freight is hauled to and from the coast by mules and oxen : in fact, cotton is hauled on wagons, from all parts of the state, to Houston, Indianola, or Red River, unless its owners are content to leave it an indefinite period upon the nearest river-bank, subject to the vague chances of a *rise*.

TRINITY BOTTOM LANDS.

On landing on the west side of the Trinity, we entered a rich bottom, even in winter, of an almost tropical aspect. The road had been cut through a cane-brake, itself a sort of Brobdignag grass. Immense trees, of a great variety of kinds, interlaced their branches and reeled with their own rank growth. Many vines, especially huge grape-vines, ran hanging from tree to tree, adding to the luxuriant confusion. Spanish moss clung thick everywhere, supplying the shadows of a winter foliage.

These bottom lands bordering the Trinity are among the richest of rich Texas. They are not considered equal, in degree of fatness, to some parts of the Brazos, Colorado, and Guadalupe bottoms, but are thought to have compensation in reliability for steady cropping. The open coast-prairie grazing districts extend to within a short distance of where we crossed. Above are some fine planting counties, and high up, in the region of the Forks of the Trinity, are lands equally suitable to cotton, wheat, and corn, which were universally described to us as, for Southern settlers, the most promising part of the state.

We made our camp on the edge of the bottom, and for safety against our dirty persecutors, the hogs, pitched our tent *within* a large hog-yard, putting up the bars to exclude them. The trees within had been sparingly cut, and we easily found tent-poles and fuel at hand.

SALE OF LANDS AND HANDS.

The plantation on which we were intruding had just been sold, we learned, at two dollars per acre. There were seven hundred acres, and the buildings, with a new gin-house, worth nearly one thousand dollars, were included in the price. With the land were sold eight prime field hands. A quarter of the land was probably subject to overflow, and the limits extended over some unproductive upland.

When field hands are sold in this way with the land, the family servants, who have usually been selected from the field hands, must be detached to follow the fortunes of the seller. When, on the other hand, the land is sold simply, the whole body of slaves move away, leaving frequently wives and children on neighboring plantations. Such a cause of separation must be exceedingly common among the restless, almost nomadic, small proprietors of the South.

But the very word "sale," applied to a slave, implies this cruelty, leaving, of course, the creature's whole happiness to his owner's discretion and humanity.

As if to give the lie to our reflections, however, the rascals here appeared to be particularly jolly, perhaps adopting Mark Tapley's good principles. They were astir half the night, talking, joking, and singing loud and merrily.

This plantation had made this year seven bales to the hand. The water for the house, we noticed, was brought upon heads a quarter of a mile, from a rain-pool, in which an old negress was washing.

LEON COUNTY.

January 3.—From the Trinity to Centreville—county town of Leon County. At some fork in the indistinct road we have gone wrong, and are to the northward of the regular course. During the first part of the day we went over small, level, wet prairies, irregularly skirted by heavy timber, with occasional isolated clumps and scattered bushes. Most of the prairies have been burned over. Both yesterday and to-day we have been surrounded by the glare of fires at night. The grass is coarse and reedy, and exceedingly dry. Our road was little better than a cow-track, and once we followed a worn cattle-path for some two or three miles, and were obliged to follow it back again.

After a few miles began post-oak, which changed to black-jack, and for the remainder of the day the country was as forbidding as a moor. We shot a few quails, which are very common, and saw, several times, turkeys and wild geese. During the day we passed but one house and one still saw-mill, in a narrow belt of pine. At night, rain threatening our canvas, we took shingle shelter in preference, in the

CENTREVILLE HOTEL.

The hotel was only a log cabin, and we suffered, as usual, from drafts of cold air. Our animals, however, were well sheltered.

Mentioning to the host our annoyance from hogs, he offered us a perfect protection in the shape of a sturdy bull-terrier. After examining her, we added her to our company. She was made up of muscle, compactly put together behind a pair of frightful jaws, and had a general aspect which struck awe into small Mexicans and negroes wherever she appeared. Hogs cared little for her eye; but at the word of command she would spring upon them like a hungry lion, and rout a whole herd.

"Judy" (this was her sonorous name) manifested some reluctance to join our party, and was, consequently, tied by a stout cord to the mule, and hung by the neck until she—came.

She tried, from time to time, the experiment of going an independent route upon the opposite side of stumps and trees, with the result of being suddenly arrested, and quickly reappearing upon the other side, with the loss of much temper and some nose. She also manifested much disgust by yelps at the mud-puddles through which she was dragged without regard to delicacy. Finally, toward night of her first day's journey, having become much entangled in the mule's legs and her own, by some Providence, the cord parted, and she suddenly became the object of the tenderest epithets and sundry remnants of corn-bread, on which, not knowing what else to do, she came along, and frankly gave allegiance to her new masters. She suffered much from fatigue, and in process of time wore her feet to the bone, but by great care, which she certainly deserved, she accompanied us not only through Western Texas, but even accomplished, on foot, the whole distance back to Richmond, Va. Her tired bones have now found a last rest upon Staten Island.

Our host was even more than commonly inquisitive, while we happened to be in the humor of brevity. Finally, as we were leaving, he asked us directly, what we were about. We must excuse him, but his curiosity was so strong, and he knew he should have a thousand people asking him. We told him some of us were traveling for health. He had reckoned that was it. Well, we had taken the right way. He had left the height of luxury in New Orleans on that account himself, and had had perfect health in Texas.

There was much very rich land about here, he said, in the creek bottoms. We had passed one field white with excellent cotton, entirely unpicked. This, he informed us, was often the case. The crop was so great that the hands that had sown the seed were unable to reap. Ten bales to the hand were sometimes made.

ACROSS THE BRAZOS.

Through further experiences of this sort of travel it is useless to ask the reader's company in detail of days.

Until we reached Austin, the people, in cultivation of character and style of life, were as uniform as their pork and corn diet. The features of the country became gradually more attractive. Near the Navasoto we rejoined the regular San Antonio road, and came out upon large open prairies with long and heavy skirts of timber, and this description applies to the whole region as far as the Colorado, the prairies, as you proceed westward, growing more and more extensive, and the proportion of wooded land smaller.

We crossed the Brazos at the old Mexican post of Tenoxtitlan, but saw no traces of ruins near the ferry. The Brazos bottoms were here some six miles in width, with a soil of the greatest fertility.

SADDLE AND TENT LIFE.

Our days' rides were short, usually from twelve to twenty miles only, which is about the common distance, we found, in steady travel. We soon reduced the art of camping to a habit, and learned to go through the motions with mechanical precision, and the least possible fatigue.

As the shadows grow long we intimate to one another that it is time to be choosing a camp ground, and near the first house at which we can obtain corn, select a sheltered spot, where fuel and water are at hand. Saddles off and hampers—the horses are left free, save Fanny, who is tied for a nucleus. The mule instantly is down, and reappears with his four feet in the air, giving loud grunts of satisfaction. A tree, overhanging a smooth slope, is taken for the back-rope of the tent, the hampers, saddles, and arms placed by it. The tent is unrolled and hoisted to the tree, a pole is cut for its other end, the long tent-rope carried over it and made fast to a bush or a peg, and when the corners are pegged out by the flat iron pegs attached, our night quarters are ready, and our traps already under it, secure from dew. One of us, meanwhile, has collected fuel and lighted a fire, brought water and set it heating. Then there is a journey for corn, and a task to husk it. The horses are caught and offered their supper, each on his own blanket, as manger. They bite it from the ear, taking, now and then, especially the mule, some of the husks, as salad. By this time it is nearly dark, and we hastily collect fuel for the night, thinking, rather dolefully, what we may have for supper. If nothing have been shot or bought there is only the hot corn-meal, engaged at the cabin with the corn, to be sent for. This we discuss with some rancor and a cup of coffee. Then comes a ramble out into the vague, nominally for logs of fire-wood, but partly for romance. A little way from the fire-light glower indistinct old giants all about; sticks crack under the feet, the horses start and peer wildly, with stretched ears, after you; who knows what wild-cat, wolf, or vagabond nigger may be watching to spring upon you if you go further from the light. Then, leaning upon your elbow, you lounge awhile upon the confines of combustion, toasting your various fronts, and never getting warmed through. Then a candle and a book or pencil in the tent, hooded in blankets. Then a piling on of logs for a parting and enduring fire, and your weary bones, covered with everything available, stretch themselves, from a saddle-bag, out towards the blaze, and—the chilly daylight.

VENISON.

The following evening, beyond Centreville, we stopped at a small cabin, on a hill, in the edge of a prairie, which was occupied by the families of two herdsmen. They could not lodge us.

Could they provide us corn for our horses? They rather grumblingly consented to do so; the man who measured it out (and gave short measure, too,) muttering that "they had to most slave themselves for travelers." Perhaps the woman would oblige us by making a pone or two of corn-bread? She supposed she must accommodate us. And, perhaps, they might have some meat? Yes, they had some venison and turkeys that they had shot that day. We should be glad to have a small slice of venison, if they could spare it. Yes, they would let us have some venison.

Instead of a small slice of venison, the man cut off a whole haunch and threw it into our corn-sack. For this the charge was only twenty-five cents. The pone was twenty-five cents and the corn one dollar per bushel. We went to the nearest wood and camped for the night.

THE PRAIRIES.

In the morning we at first rode through the rich alluvial border of a creek, dark with the rank luxuriance of a semi-tropical vegetation; great trees, with many reclining trunks springing together from the ground, their limbs intricately interlaced with vines; grotesque cactus and dwarf palm, with dark, glossy evergreen shrubs, and thickets of verdant cane hedging in our bridle-path; the sunshine but feebly penetrating through the thick, waving canopy of dark gray moss which everywhere hung above our heads.

5

Soon after fording the creek, we ascended a steep hill, the forest still continuing, till, reaching the brow, we came out suddenly, as if a curtain had risen, upon a broad prairie, reaching, in swells like the ocean after a great storm, to the horizon before us; a thick screen of wood edging it in the distance on the left, and an open grove of low, branching oaks breaking irregularly upon it, with spurs and scattered single trees, to the right. Our path, turning before us, continued along this broken edge, crossing capes and islands of the grove, and bays of the prairie. Horses and gray and red cattle dotted the waving brown surface, and in one of these bays, to our right, were six deer unconcernedly browsing. As we approached, however, they stopped, and raised high their heads, sniffing the air, and after a few moments' debate, slowly and undecidedly, often stopping to look again, they walked into cover.

After two miles' ride along the woodland border, the prairie opened fair in the course before us, and our trail led directly across it. The waving surface soon became regular, like the swell of the ocean after the subsidence of a gale which has blown long from the same direction. Very grand in vastness and simplicity were these waves. Four of them would cover a mile, and yet as we ascended one after another, the contour of the next would appear dark against the sky, following Hogarth's line of beauty and of grace with mathematical exactness. Vertically, the line of the swell bent before us, and on the left we saw in the hollow of the wave, or as its crest was there depressed, the far away skirt of the dark wood; on the right, only the remote line of the prairie swelling against the horizon. Here were red and black clouds of distant fires. The sky was nearly covered with gusty, gray clouds, with the clearest blue seen through them.

The night had been unusually mild, and the forenoon was becoming sultry.

THE FIRST NORTHER.

Once again we came to the brow of the swell; but instead of the usual grassy surface before us, the ground was dead black—the grass having been lately burned off. The fire must have been intense; for the whole surface of the ground appeared charred and black as ink. The air had been perfectly calm; but as we arrived near the next summit there was suddenly a puff of wind from the westward, bringing with it the scent of burning hay; and in less than thirty seconds, another puff, chill as if the door of a vault had been opened at our side; a minute more, it was a keen but not severe cold northerly wind. In five minutes we had all got our overcoats on, and were bending against it in our saddles. The change in temperature was not very great (12° in 12 minutes,) but was singularly rapid; in fact, instantaneous—from rather uncomfortably warm to rather uncomfortably cool.

" Is this a norther?" asked we.

" I shouldn't wonder," said B.

It was our first experience.

Steadily the gale rose, and the cold increased during the day. And all day long we rode on, sometimes in the low, dark, and comparatively calm and mild " bottom lands," sometimes in the shelter of post-oak groves, but mainly across the high, broad, bleak, upland prairies. At sunset, we had seen no house for an hour or two, and were fearing that we should have to find a harbor in some sheltered spot, where we could stay our tent against the blast, and let our horses go unfed. As we came to the top of one of the prairie swells, we saw, about half a mile to the right of the road, a point of woodland, and a little beyond it, on a hill-top, was a house.   We turned off, and with some difficulty made our way across the gullies between the hills, and approached the house.   It proved to be deserted; but beyond it, on the top of the next and highest hill, there was another.   We rode to it, and inquired if we could obtain corn for our horses, and shelter and food for ourselves.   The proprietor " supposed we might," and our horses were led away, not to a stable, but to a pen or yard, on the windward side of the hill.   We strapped blankets upon them, and left them before their corn, to weather it as they could, and betook ourselves to the house.

A GRAZIER'S FARM.

It was a log cabin, of one room, fourteen feet by fourteen, with another small room in a " lean-to" of boards on the windward side.   There was no window, but there were three doors, and openings between the logs in all quarters.   The door of the " lean-to" was barricaded, but this erection was very open ; and as the inner door, from sagging on its wooden hinges, could not be closed at all, the norther had nearly free course through the cabin.   A strong fire was roaring in the great chimney at the end of the room, and we all clustered closely around it, " the woman" alone passing through our semicircle, as she prepared the " pone" and " fry," and coffee for supper.

Our host seemed a man of thirty, and had lived in Texas through all the " trouble times."   His father had moved his family here when Texas was still Mexican territory ; and for years of the young man's life, Indians were guarded against and hunted just as wolves now are by the shepherd.   They had always held their ground against them, however, and had constantly increased in wealth, but had retired for a few weeks before the Mexican invasion. His father had no property when he came here, but the wagon and horses, and the few household effects he brought with him. " Now," said the son, " he raises fifty bales of cotton"—equivalent to informing us that he owned twenty or thirty negroes, and his income was from two to three thousand dollars a year. The young man himself owned probably many hundred acres of the prairie and woodland range about him, and a large herd of cattle. He did not fancy taking care of a plantation. It was too much trouble. He was a regular Texan, he boasted, and was not going to slave himself looking after niggers. Any man who had been brought up in Texas, he said, could live as well as he wanted to, without working more than one month in the year. For about a month in the year he had to work hard, driving his cattle into the pen, and roping and marking the calves ; this was always done in a kind of frolic in the spring—the neighboring herdsmen assisting each other. During the rest of the year he hadn't anything to do. When he felt like it he got on to a horse and rode around, and looked after his cattle ; but that wasn't work, he said—'twas only play. He raised a little corn ; sometimes he got more than he needed, and sometimes not as much ; he didn't care whether it was enough or not—he could always buy meal, only bought meal wasn't so sweet as that was which they ground fresh in their own steel mill. When he wanted to buy anything, he could always sell some cattle and raise the money ; it did not take much to supply them with all they wanted.

This was very evident. The room was, as I said, fourteen feet square, with battens of split boards tacked on between the broader openings of the logs. Above, it was open to the rafters, and in many places the sky could be seen between the shingles of the roof. A rough board box, three feet square, with a shelf in it, contained the crockery-ware of the establishment; another similar box held the store of meal, coffee, sugar, and salt, a log crib at the horse-pen held the corn, from which the meal was daily ground, and a log smoke or store-house contained the store of pork. A canopy-bed filled one quarter of the room; a cradle, four chairs seated with untanned deer-hide, a table, a skillet or bake-kettle, a coffee-kettle, a frying-pan, and a rifle laid across two wooden pegs on the chimney, with a string of patches, powder-horn, pouch, and hunting- knife, completed the furniture of the house. We all sat with hats and overcoats on, and the woman cooked in bonnet and shawl. As I sat in the chimney-corner I could put both my hands out, one laid on the other, between the stones of the fire-place and the logs of the wall.

A pallet of quilts and blankets was spread for us in the lean-to, just between the two doors. We slept in all our clothes, including overcoats, hats, and boots, and covered entirely with blankets. At seven in the morning, when we threw them off, the mercury in the thermometer in our saddle-bags, which we had used for a pillow, stood at 25 deg. Fahrenheit.

We contrived to make cloaks and hoods from our blankets, and after going through with the fry, coffee and pone again, and paying one dollar each for the entertainment of ourselves and horses, we continued our journey.

The norther was stronger and the cold greater than the day before; but as we took it on our quarter in the course we were going during most of the day, we did not suffer.

HARBOR IN AN INN.

Late in the same evening we reached the town of Caldwell,

the "seat of justice" of Burleson County. We were obliged to leave our horses in a stable, made up of a roof, in which was a loft for the storage of provender, set upon posts, without side-boarding, so that the norther met with no obstruction. It was filled with horses, and ours alone were blanketed for the night. The mangers were very shallow and narrow, and as the corn was fed on the cob, a considerable proportion of it was thrown out by the horses in their efforts to detach the edible portion. With laudable economy, our landlord had twenty-five or thirty pigs running at large in the stable, to prevent this overflow from being wasted.

The hotel building was an unusually large and fine one ; the principal room had glass windows. Several panes of these were, however, broken, and the outside door could not be closed from without ; and when closed, was generally pried open with a pocket-knife by those who wished to go out. A great part of the time it was left open. Supper was served in another room, in which there was no fire, and the outside door was left open for the convenience of the servants in passing to and from the kitchen, which, as usual here at large houses, was in a detached building. Supper was, however, eaten with such rapidity that nothing had time to freeze on the table.

TEXAN CONVERSATION.

There were six Texans, planters and herdsmen, who had made harbor at the inn for the norther, two German shop-keepers and a young lawyer, who were boarders, besides our party of three, who had to be seated before the fire during " the evening." We kept coats and hats on, and gained as much warmth, from the friendly manner in which we drew together, as possible. After ascertaining, by a not at all impertinent or inconsiderate method of inquiry, where we were from, which way we were going, what we thought of the country, what we thought of the weather, and what were the capacities and the cost of our fire-arms, we were considered as initiated members of the crowd, and "the conversation became general."

One of the gentlemen asked me if I had seen " this new instrument."

" What instrument ?"

" This *grand boojer.*"

" I never heard of it before ; what is it ?"

" I don't know, only that." He pointed to a large poster on the wall, advertising " *L. Gilbert's celebrated patent* GRAND, BOUDOIR *and square piano-fortes.*"   I mention the circumstance as a caution to printers on the choice of words for the use of their emphatic type.

" Sam Houston and his eccentricities" formed a very interesting topic of conversation. Nearly every person present had seen the worthy senator in some ridiculous and not very honorable position, and there was much laughter at his expense. As he seemed to be held in very little respect, we inquired if he were not popular in Texas.   He had many warm old friends, they said, and always made himself popular with new acquaintances, but the greater part of the old fighting Texans hated and despised him.

ABOUT NIGGERS.

But the most interesting subject to Northerners which was talked of, was brought up by two gentlemen speaking of the house where they spent the previous night.   " The man made a white boy, fourteen or fifteen years old, get up and go out in the norther for wood, when there was a great, strong nigger fellow lying on the floor, doing nothing. God! I had an appetite to give him a hundred, right there."

" Why, you wouldn't go out into the norther, yourself, would you, if you were not forced to ?" inquired one, laughingly.

" I wouldn't have a nigger in my house that I was afraid to set to work at anything I wanted him to do at any time. They'd hired him out to go to a new place next Thursday, and they were afraid if they didn't treat him well, he'd run away. If I couldn't break a nigger of running away, I wouldn't have him any how."

" I can tell you how you can break a nigger of running away, certain," said another. " There was an old fellow I used to know in Georgia, that always cured his so. If a nigger ran away, when he caught him, he would bind his knee over a log, and fasten him so he couldn't stir ; then he'd take a pair of pincers and pull one of his toe-nails out by the roots; and tell him that if he ever run away again, he would pull out two of them, and if he run away again after that, he told them he'd pull out four of them, and so on, doubling each time. He never had to do it more than twice—it always cured them."

One of the company then said that he was at the present time in pursuit of a negro. He had bought him of a connection of his in Mississippi; he told him when he bought him that he was a great runaway. He had run away from him three times, and always when they caught him he was trying to *get back to Illinois;* that was the reason he sold him. " He offered him to me cheap," he continued, " and I bought him because he was a first-rate nigger, and I thought perhaps I could break him of running away by bringing him down to this new country. I expect he's

5*

making for Mexico, now.   I am a-most sure I saw his tracks on
the road about twelve miles back, where he was a-coming on this
way.   Night before last I engaged with a man who's got some
first-rate nigger dogs to meet me here to-night ; but I suppose the
cold keeps him back."   He then asked us to look out for him as
we went on west, and gave us a minute description of him that
we might recognize him.   He was " a real black nigger," and
carried off a double-barreled gun with him.   Another man, who
was going on by another road westward, offered to look for
him that way, and to advertise him.   Would he be likely to
defend himself with the gun if he should try to secure him, he
asked.   The owner said he had no doubt he would.   He was as
humble a nigger when he was at work as ever he had seen ; but
he was a mighty resolute nigger—there was no man had more
resolution.   " Couldn't I induce him to let me take the gun by
pretending I wanted to look at it, or something ?   I'd talk to
him simple ; make as if I was a stranger, and ask him about the
road, and so on, and finally ask him what he had got for a gun,
and to let me look at it."   The owner didn't believe he'd
let go of the gun ; he was a " nigger of sense—as much
sense as a white man ; he was not one of your kinkey-headed
niggers."   The chances of catching him were discussed.   Some
thought they were good, and some that the owner might almost
as well give it up, he'd got such a start.   It was three hundred
miles to the Mexican frontier, and he'd have to make fires to cook
the game he would kill, and could travel only at night ; but then
every nigger or Mexican he could find would help him, and if he
had so much sense, he'd manage to find out his way pretty
straight, and yet not have white folks see him.

SHEEP AND PRICES.

We had observed sheep not far from Caldwell for the first time. They were in a large flock of some four or five hundred, overlooked by a black boy on horseback, attended by two hounds. We were told that the wool from this flock had been sold in the neighborhood at twenty-seven cents per pound, and that the flock had averaged four pounds to the fleece.

There had been a "hiring" of negroes at the County House the week before. Eight or ten were hired out at from $175 to $250 per annum—the hirer contracting to feed them well and to provide two substantial suits of clothing and shoes.

The price of beef at Caldwell was two cents per pound; pork, five cents; corn-fed ditto, six cents.

MANNERS AND THE WEATHER.

We slept in a large upper room, in a company of five, with a broken window at the head of our bed, and another at our side, offering a short cut to the norther across our heads.

We were greatly amused to see one of our bed-room companions gravely *spit* in the candle before jumping into bed, explaining to some one who made a remark, that he always did so, it gave him time to see what he was about before it went out.

The next morning the ground was covered with sleet, and the gale still continued (a pretty steady close-reefing breeze) during the day.

We wished to have a horse shod. The blacksmith, who was a white man, we found in his shop, cleaning a fowling-piece. It was too d——d cold to work, he said, and he was going to shoot some geese; he, at length, at our urgent request, consented to earn a dollar; but, after getting on his apron, he found that we had lost a shoe, and took it off again, refusing to make a shoe while this d——d norther lasted, for any man. As he had no shoes ready made, he absolutely turned us out of the shop, and obliged us to go seventy-five miles further, a great part of the way over a pebbly road, by which the beast lost three shoes before he could be shod.

This respect for the norther is by no means singular here. The publication of the week's newspaper in Bastrop was interrupted by the norther, the editor mentioning, as a sufficient reason for the irregularity, the fact that his printing-office was in the north part of the house.

We continued our journey during the day in spite of the increased chilliness of the air, occasioned by the icy surface with which the sleet of the night had clothed the prairies, without any discomfort, until we were obliged again to enter one of these prairie houses. During the next night it fell calm, and the cold, as measured by the contraction of the mercury, was greater than at any time before. But the sun rose clear the next day and by noon, the weather was mild and agreeable as in the fairest October day in New York.

During the continuance of the norther, the sky was constantly covered with dense gray clouds, the wind varied from N.N.E. to N.W., and was also of variable force. Our thermometrical observations were as follows:

Jan. 5th, 10.30 A.M. - - 67° | 2 P.M. - - - - - - 47°
"   10.42 "   - - 55° | 4 " - - - - - - 42°
6 P.M. - - - - - 40°
Jan. 6th, 7.30 A.M. - - - - - 25°

It continued at about this point during the following two days, when it fell (Jan. 8th, 7.30 A.M.) to 21°.

THE COLORADO.

Two more days' ride took us to Austin. We struck the Colorado at Bastrop—a village of considerable size and promise, situated on the left river bank, and at the edge of an isolated patch of *pine timber*, from which nearly all the pine lumber used in Western Texas is taken.

The Colorado is the first of the clear water streams. Its still, limpid, blue-green surface appeared very charming, as the ferryman slowly pulled us over. Its width was here some four or five rods. Owing to obstructions and to its irregularities of depth, it can scarcely be called navigable, though cotton is sometimes rafted down or floated in flats, and steamboats ascend in very high water.

The "bottom" was here narrow, the surface rising rapidly to open prairie or post-oak. Along the edge of the overflowed bottom are some large and well-cultivated plantations. It was at one of these we first noticed the practice of extending fences over the road, compelling mail-coaches and travelers to seek out a new path wherever it suits them. The law in Texas permits this with very loose restrictions.

The scenery along the river is agreeable, with a pleasant alternation of gently-sloping prairies and wooded creek bottoms. Here and there, particularly near Bastrop, is a good house and a rich and well-cultivated plantation. Much of the soil is of the heavy black character known as " hog-wallow parara," the prairie surface being marked with a constant succession of depressions, miry in wet weather and disagreeable enough in dry, from the continual rise and fall, and consequent pitching motion, of wagon or horse. The road upon the sward was very indistinct, and we followed some wagon tracks, at twilight, two hours out of our way, reaching the ferry below Austin at nine o'clock in the evening. After some search, we found the ferry-house, but no one was stirring. After not a little thumping at the door, the ferry-man appeared, with—

"What's the matter?"

"Nothing in particular; we want to cross the ferry."

"I thought somebody must be sick; trav'lin' at this time o' night."

"Is it so extraordinary to cross the ferry in the evening?"

"Yes, sir, a very extraordinary thing, indeed."

AUSTIN.

Austin has a fine situation upon the left bank of the Colorado. Had it not been the capital of the state, and a sort of bourne to which we had looked forward for a temporary rest, it would still have struck us as the pleasantest place we had seen in Texas. It reminds one somewhat of Washington; Washington, *en petit*, seen through a reversed glass. The Capitol—a really imposing building of soft cream limestone, nearly completed at the time of our visit, and already occupied—stands prominent upon a hill, towards which, nearly all the town rises. From it a broad avenue stretches to the river, lined by the principal buildings and stores. These are of various materials and styles, from quarried stone to the logs of the first settlers. Off the avenue, are scatered cottages and one or two pretty dwellings. They are altogether smaller in number and meaner in appearance than a stranger would anticipate. The capital was fixed, in fact, upon a thinly-settled frontier, at a point the speculative, rather than the actual, centre of the state. There is one little church, with a pretty German turret, another of stone is in process of erection, and a

Governor's mansion is to be built. There is a very remarkable number of drinking and gambling shops, but not one book-store A druggist, who keeps a small stock of books, sold us, at one dollar, giving his word that its cost was seventy-five cents to him self, a copy of "Eagle Pass" (one of Putnam's Semi-Monthly Li brary), the price of which, elsewhere, is forty cents. The popu lation, at the census of 1850, was 629; the estimate, when we were there, 3,000; a large one, we thought. The country around the town is rolling and picturesque, with many agreeable views of distant hills and a pleasant sprinkling of wood over prairie slopes.

HOTELS.

We had reckoned upon getting some change of diet when we reached the capital of the state, and upon having good materials not utterly spoiled, by carelessness, ignorance, or nastiness, in cooking. We reckoned without our host.

We arrived in a norther, and were shown, at the hotel to which we had been recommended, into an exceedingly dirty room, in which two of us slept with another gentleman, who informed us that it was the best room in the house. The outside door, opening upon the ground, had no latch, and during the night it was blown open by the norther, and after we had made two in-effectual attempts to barricade it, was kept open till morning. Before daylight, a boy came in and threw down an armful of wood by the fire-place. He appeared again, an hour or two afterwards, and made a fire. When the breakfast-bell rung, we all turned out in haste, though our boots were gone and there was no water. At this moment, as we were reluctantly pulling on our clothing, a negro woman burst into the room, leaving the door open, and laid a towel on the wash-table. "Here!" we

cried, as she ran to the door again; " bring us some water, and
have our boots brought back." She stood half outside the door,
and shaking her finger at us in a weird manner, replied : " Haant
got no time, master—got fires to make and ebery ting ;" and she
vanished.

When finally we got to breakfast, and had offered us—but I
will not again mention the three articles—only the " fry" had
been changed for the worse before it was fried—we naturally began to talk of changing our quarters and trying another of the
hotels. Then up spoke a dark, sad man at our side—" You
can't do better than stay here ; I have tried both the others, and
I came here yesterday because the one I was at was *too dirty!*"
And the man said this, with that leopard-skin pattern of a table-
cloth, before him, with those grimy tools in his hands, and with
the hostler in his frock, smelling strongly of the stable, just handing him the (No. 3). Never did we see any wholesome food on
that table. It was a succession of burnt flesh of swine and bulls,
decaying vegetables, and sour and mouldy farinaceous glues, all
pervaded with rancid butter. After a few days, we got a
private room, and then, buying wheat-bread of a German baker,
and other provisions of grocers, cooked what was necessary for
ourselves, thus really coming back to caravansarism.

We met at Austin many cultivated, agreeable and talented
persons ; among them gentlemen whose manner of thinking on
certain subjects, on which their opinions differed much from my
own, greatly gratified me. With regard to slavery, for instance,
these gentlemen, I doubt not, honestly and confidently believe
the institution to be a beneficial one ; gradually and surely making the negroes a civilized and a Christian people, and paying its
way (perhaps with handsome dividends) to the capitalists who

are the stockholders; that all the cruelty, or most of it, is a necessary part of the process, necessary at least in the present constitution of property and of society. The determination and calculation to make another Slave State of Lower California, which was openly expressed in their circle, did not seem to them, therefore, anything at all to be regretted or disapproved of. If it would be profitable, it would be benevolent, they were confident.

The only thing they feared was the injury to business which might occur if it should be made the occasion for another sectional excitement. This would be fanatical and deplorable.

I fear there is some appearance of irony in what I have written. I did not intend it. I sincerely have a very deep respect for the men who think and express their thoughts in this simple manner. They are men of real benevolence and great talent; but it does seem to me circumstances have given a singular twist to their minds. No doubt they can see just such idiosyncrasies in Northern minds.

But it was a pleasure to meet men, again, with whom such subjects could be looked upon from their moral side.

LEGISLATURE.

We visited, several times, the Texas Legislature in session, and have seldom been more impressed with respect for the working of Democratic institutions.

I have seen several similar bodies at the North; the Federal Congress; and the Parliament of Great Britain, in both its branches, on occasions of great moment; but none of them commanded my involuntary respect for their simple manly dignity and trustworthiness for the duties that engaged them, more than the General Assembly of Texas. There was honest eloquence displayed at every opportunity for its use, and business was carried on with great rapidity, but with complete parliamentary regularity, and all desirable gentlemanly decorum.   One gentleman, in a state of intoxication, attempted to address the house (but that happens elsewhere), and he was quietly persuaded to retire.

THE MATERIALS OF LIVING.

The cost of living at Austin is extraordinarily high.   Subjoined is a list of prices of building materials, etc., and of articles of household use, as sold at retail :

Pine lumber is carted from Bastrop, thirty miles.   Boards are sold at $4 50 to $5 a hundred feet.   Brick, poorly made in the vicinity, are sold at the kilns at $10 per M.   The town stands upon a ledge of very soft limestone, which is worked almost as easily as wood.   It is frequently used for building—I did not learn at what cost.

Wages of negroes are higher than I have known them anywhere else, notwithstanding some German competition in the labor market.   The Germans complained that the labor in building the State Capitol was advertised to be contracted for to the lowest bidder.   Many Germans came with offers, but were underbid by negro owners.   After the Germans had all left town again, these gentlemen threw up their contracts, and new contracts were made with them at advanced prices.   A lot of the negroes engaged as laborers on the Capitol, only one of them a poor mechanic, were lately hired for the year at $280 each, the hirer to clothe and board them, etc.; field hands in the country, $190, clothes, etc.   A negro cook, the poorest possible, I was told was paid $60 a month at the hotel.   Another I heard of hired at $600 a year.   I saw a very pretty girl, twelve years old, who had been bought for $600. A first-rate white journeyman mechanic commanded $50 a month and found.

Rents—very high. A smithy, 30 by 20 feet, of brick, one story high, rented for $50 a month. A log shanty, the poorest a mechanic could think of living in, $10 a month.

Rails, for fencing on plantations, $5 per hundred. Iron, bar, 8c.; nail, 9c.; shoe, 10c.; cast-steel, 30c.; horse-shoeing, 75c. a shoe; charcoal, 25c. a bushel; mineral coal, none to be had; wood for fuel, knotty oak, $3 a cord; washing, $1 per dozen.

There were thousands of cattle pasturing within sight of the town; but milk sold by contract, for the season, at $12\frac{1}{2}$c. a quart, and at retail at 15c. to 20c. Butter—Goshen, 40c.; country fresh, 50c.

Flour, $15 a barrel; bread, of inferior flour, by German bakers, 8c. per lb.; corn, 50c. per bushel; sweet potatoes, 50c. to 75c. a bushel; eggs, 25c. per dozen; crackers, 15c. per lb.; sugar, crushed, $18\frac{3}{4}$c. per lb.; "Star" (New York) candles, 40c. per lb.; apples, inferior, 75c. per dozen; beef, fresh, $3\frac{1}{2}$c. per lb.; pork, do., 6c.; bacon, sides, 18c.; hams, 20c. to 25c. per lb.

Rope, Manilla half-inch line, 40c. per lb. Harness leather (such as is bought in New York at 20c.), 40c. per lb.

Freight is wagoned by mules and oxen from both Houston and Indianola, but principally from the latter place.

AN EASTERN PLANTER.

Before leaving Eastern Texas behind us, I must add a random note or two, the precise dates of which it would have been uncivil to indicate.

We stopped one night at the house of a planter, now twenty years settled in Eastern Texas. He was a man of some education and natural intelligence, and had, he told us, an income, from the labor of his slaves, of some $4,000. His residence was one of the largest houses we had seen in Texas. It had a second story, two wings and a long gallery. Its windows had been once glazed, but now, out of eighty panes that originally filled the lower windows, thirty only remained unbroken. Not a door in the house had been ever furnished with a latch or even a string; when they were closed, it was necessary to *claw* or to ask some one inside to push open. (Yet we happened to hear a neighbor expressing serious admiration of the way these doors fitted.) The furniture was of the rudest description.

One of the family had just had a hemorrhage of the lungs; while we were at supper, this person sat between the big fireplace and an open outside door, having a window, too, at his side, in which only three panes remained. A norther was blowing, and ice forming upon the gallery outside. Next day, at breakfast, the invalid was unable to appear on account of a " bad turn."

On our supper-table was nothing else than the eternal fry, pone and coffee. Butter, of dreadful odor, was here added by exception. Wheat flour they never used. It was " too much trouble."

We were waited upon by two negro girls, dressed in short-waisted, twilled-cotton gowns, once white, now looking as though they had been drawn through a stove-pipe in spring. The water for the family was brought in tubs upon the heads of these two girls, from a creek, a quarter of a mile distant, this occupation filling nearly all their time.

This gentleman had thirty or forty negroes, and two legitimate sons. One was an idle young man. The other was already, at eight years old, a swearing, tobacco-chewing young bully and ruffian. We heard him whipping his puppy behind the house, and swearing between the blows, his father and mother being at hand. His tone was an evident imitation of his father's mode of dealing with his slaves.

"I've got an account to settle with you; I've let you go about long enough; I'll teach you who's your master; there, go now, God damn you, but 1 havn't got through with you yet."

"You stop that cursing," said his father, at length, "it isn't right for little boys to curse."

"What do *you* do when you get mad?" replied the boy; "reckon you cuss some; so now you'd better shut up."

We repeatedly heard men curse white women and children in this style, without the least provocation.

LITERATURE.

In the whole journey through Eastern Texas, we did not see one of the inhabitants look into a newspaper or a book, although we spent days in houses where men were lounging about the fire without occupation. One evening I took up a paper which had been lying unopened upon the table of the inn where we were staying, and smiled to see how painfully news items dribbled into the Texas country papers, the loss of the tug-boat "Ajax," which occurred before we left New York, being here just given as the loss of the "splended steamer Ocax."

A man who sat near said—

"Reckon you've read a good deal, hain't you?"

"Oh, yes; why?"

"Reckoned you had."

"Why?"

"You look as though you liked to read. Well, it's a good thing. S'pose you take a pleasure in reading, don't you?"

"That depends, of course, on what I have to read. I suppose everybody likes to read when they find anything interesting to them, don't they?"

"No; it's damn tiresome to some folks, I reckon, any how, 'less you've got the habit of it. Well, it's a good thing; you can pass away your time so."

FOREIGN RELATIONS.

The sort of interest taken in foreign affairs is well enough illustrated by the views of a gentleman of property in Eastern Texas, who was sitting with us one night, " spitting in the fire," and talking about cotton. Bad luck he had had—only four bales to the hand; couldn't account for it—bad luck; and next year he didn't reckon nothing else but that there would be a general war in Europe, and then he'd be in a pretty fix, with cotton down to four cents a pound. Curse those Turks! If he thought there would be a general war, he would take every d——d nigger he'd got right down to New Orleans, and sell them for what they'd bring. They'd never be so high again as they were now, and if there should come a general war they wouldn't be worth half so much next year. There always were some infernal rascals somewhere in the world trying to prevent an honest man from getting a living. Oh, if they got to fighting, he hoped they'd eat each other up. They just ought to be, all of them—Turks, and Russians, and Prussians, and Dutchmen, and Frenchmen—just be put in a bag together, and slung into hell. That's what he'd do with them.

We afterwards noted a contrast when a German cotton-farmer, beyond the Colorado, expressed to us, apropos to the same probable depreciation of prices of the next year, the greatest *fear* lest the sovereigns should not permit a general war to take place, with its chances for the peoples.   There are some hearts that swim above prices.   God bless them.

BLACK HOUSEKEEPING.

Remarking, one day, at the house of a woman who was brought up at the North, that there was much more comfort at her house than any we had previously stopped at, she told us that the only reason that the people didn't have any comfort here was, that they wouldn't *take any trouble* to get anything. Anything that their negroes could make they would eat; but they would take no pains to instruct them, or to get anything that didn't grow on the plantation.   A neighbor of hers owned fifty cows, she supposed, but very rarely had any milk and scarcely ever any butter, simply because his people were too lazy to milk or churn, and he wouldn't take the trouble to make them.

This woman entirely sustained the assertion that Northern people, when they come to the South, have less feeling for the negroes than Southerners themselves usually have.   We asked her (she lived in a village) whether she hired or owned her servants.   They owned them all, she said.   When they first came to Texas they hired servants, but it was very troublesome; they would take no interest in anything; and she couldn't get along with them.   Then very often their owners, on some pretext (ill-treatment, perhaps), would take them away.   Then they bought negroes.   It was very expensive: a good negro girl cost seven or eight hundred dollars, and that, we must know, was a great deal of money to be laid out in a thing that might lie right down the next day and die. They were not much better either than the hired servants.

Folks up North talked about how badly the negroes were treated; she wished they could see how much work her girls did. She had four of them, and she knew they didn't do half so much work as one good Dutch girl such as she used to have at the North. Oh! the negroes were the laziest things in creation; there was no knowing how much trouble they gave to look after them. Up to the North, if a girl went out into the garden for anything, when she came back she would clean her feet, but these nigger girls will stump right in and track mud all over the house. What do they care? They'd just as lief clean the mud after themselves as anything else—*their time isn't any value to themselves.* What do they care for the trouble it gives you? Not a bit. And you may scold 'em and whip 'em—you never can break 'em into better habits.

I asked what were servants' wages when they were hired out to do housework? They were paid seven or eight dollars a month; sometimes ten. She didn't use to pay her girl at the North but four dollars, and she knew she would do more work than any six of the niggers, and not give half so much trouble as one. But you couldn't get any other help here but niggers. Northern folks talk about abolishing Slavery, but there wouldn't be any use in that; that would be ridiculous, unless you could some way get rid of the niggers. Why, they'd murder us all in our beds—that's what they'd do. Why, over to Fannin, there was a negro woman that killed her mistress with an axe, and her two little ones. The people just flocked together, and hung her right up on the spot; they ought to have piled some wood round her, and burned her to death; that would have been a good lesson to the rest. We afterwards heard her scolding one of her girls; the girl made some exculpatory reply, and getting the best of the argument, the mistress angrily told her if she said another word she would have two hundred lashes given her. She came in and remarked that if she hadn't felt so nervous she would have given that girl a good whipping herself; these niggers are so saucy, it's very *trying* to one who has to take care of them.

Servants are, it is true, " a trial," in all lands, ages, and nations. But note the fatal reason this woman frankly gives for the inevitable delinquencies of slave-servants, " Their time isn't any value to themselves !"

The women of Eastern Texas seemed to us, in general, far superior to their lords. They have, at least, the tender hearts and some of the gentle delicacy that your " true Texan" lacks, whether mistresses of slaves or only of their own frying-pan, They are overworked, however, as soon as married, and care gives them thin faces, sallow complexions, and expressions either sad or sour.

A NORTHERN SETTLER.

Another night we spent at the house of a man who came here, when a boy, from the North. His father was a mechanic, and had emigrated to Texas just before the war of Independence. He joined the army, and his son had been brought up— rather had grown up—Southern fashion—with no training to regular industry. He had learned no trade. What need? His father received some thousand acres of land in payment of his services. The son earned some money for himself by driving a team; bought cattle, took a wife, and a house, and now had
6

been settled six years, with a young family.   He had nothing to do but look after his cattle, go to the nearest town and buy meal and coffee occasionally, and sell a few oxen when the bill was sent in.   His house was more comfortless than nine-tenths of the stables of the North.   There were several windows, some of which were boarded over, some had wooden shutters, and some were entirely open.   The doors were closed with difficulty. We could see the stars, as we lay in bed, through the openings of the roof; and on all sides, in the walls of the room, one's arm might be thrust out.   Yet that night the mercury fell below twenty-five degrees of our Fahrenheit thermometer.   There was the standard food and beverage, placed before us night and morning.   We asked if there was much game near him?   There were a great many deer.   He saw them every day.   Did he shoot many?   He never shot any; 'twas too much trouble to hunt them.   When he wanted "fresh," 'twas easier to go out and stick a hog (the very words he used).   He had just corn enough to give our horses one feed—there was none left for the morning.   His own horses could live well enough through the winter on the prairie.   He made pets of his children, but was cross and unjust to his wife, who might have been pretty, and was affectionate.   He was without care—thoughtless, content, with an unoccupied mind.   He took no newspaper—he read nothing.   There was, indeed, a pile of old books which his father had brought from the North, but they seemed to be all of the Tract Society sort, and the dust had been undisturbed upon them, it might have been, for many years.

This man did have the wit to say he believed he should have been better off now if he had remained at the North.   Think of the probabilities—the son of a master mechanic, with a considerable capital.   Educate him where you please, in any country not subject to the influence of slavery, how different would have been his disposition, how much higher and more like those of a reasonable being, would have been his hopes, aims, and life.

SLAVERY WITH A WILL.

We were several times struck, in Eastern Texas, with a peculiarity in the tone of the relation between master and slave. Elsewhere at the South, slavery had seemed to be accepted generally, as a natural, hereditary, established state of things, and the right and wrong of it, or the how of it, never to be discussed or thought of any more than that of feudal tenures elsewhere.   But in Texas, the state of war in which slavery arises, seems to continue in undertone to the present..

" Damn 'em, give 'em hell," frequent expressions of the ruder planters towards their negroes, appeared to be used as if with a meaning—a threat to make their life infernal if they do not submit abjectly and constantly.   There seemed to be the consciousness of a wrong relation and a determination to face conscience down, and continue it; to work up the " damned niggers," with a sole eye to selfish profit, cash down, in this world. As to " treasures in Heaven," their life is a constant sneer at the belief in them.

TEXAS AS IT USED TO BE.

I will add no further details upon the moral and social aspect of Eastern Texas.   Cheap as such privileges may be considered, old Texans express, in speaking of them, great admiration and satisfaction.   Society has certainly made a great advance there in becoming even what it is.   The present generation has, peculiarly, but the faults founded upon laziness.   The past, if we may believe report, had something worse. In fact, in the rapid settlement of the country, many an adventurer crossed the border, spurred by a love of life or liberty, forfeited at home, rather than drawn by the love of adventure or of rich soil. Probably a more reckless and vicious crew was seldom gathered than that which peopled some parts of Eastern Texas at the time of its first resistance to the Mexican government.

"G. T. T.," (gone to Texas,) was the slang appendage, within the reader's recollection, to every man's name who had disappeared before the discovery of some rascality. Did a man emigrate thither, every one was on the watch for the discreditable reason to turn up.

Mr. Dewees, in his naive "Letters from Texas," thus describes (1831):

"It would amuse you very much, could you hear the manner in which people of this new country address each other. It is nothing uncommon of us to inquire of a man why he ran away from the States! but few persons feel insulted by such a question. They generally answer for some crime or other which they have committed; if they deny having committed any crime, or say they did not run away, they are generally looked upon rather suspiciously. Those who come into the country at the present time, frequently tell us rough, ragged, old settlers, who have worn out our clothes and our constitutions in the service of the country, that they have a great deal of wealth in the States which they are going after, as soon as they can find a situation to suit them. But we, not relishing this would-be aristocracy, generally manage to play some good joke upon them in return.

"One day, there were quite a number of these aristocrats, who seemed to think themselves better than those who were worn out by toil and hardships, seated at the dinner table, in a sort of tavern kept by a man named William Pettis, or Buck Pettis, as he was always called at San Felipe ; these persons were boasting largely of their wealth, their land, their negroes, the ships they had at sea, etc. There was at the table an old man by the name of Macfarlane, a don't care sort of a fellow, who had married a Mexican wife, and was living on the Brazos when we first came to the country. He listened to them quietly for a while, at length he could restrain himself no longer. ' Well, gentlemen,' he said, ' I, too, once commenced telling that I had left a large property in the States, and, in fact, gentlemen, I told the story so often, that at length I really believed it true, and eventually started to go for it. Well, I traveled on very happily till I reached the Sabine river which separates this country from the United States. On its bank I paused, and now for the first time, began to ask myself seriously, What am I doing ? Why am I here ? I have no property in the States, and if I had, if I cross the river, 'tis at the risk of my life; for I was obliged to flee to this country to escape the punishment of the laws. I had better return, and live in safety as I have done. I did so, gentlemen, and since then have been contented without telling of the wealth I left in the States.' The relation of this story so exasperated these for whose benefit it was told, that they fell upon the old gentleman, and would have done him injury, had it not been for the interference of his friends. This, however, put a stop to long yarns."

If your life, in those times, an old settler told us, would be of the slightest use to any one, you might be sure he would take it, and it was safe only as you were in constant readiness to defend it. Horses and wives were of as little account as umbrellas in more advanced States. Everybody appropriated everything that suited him, running his own risk of a penalty. Justice descended into the body of Judge Lynch, sleeping when he slept, and when he woke hewing down right and left for exercise and pastime.

Out of this has come, with as much rapidity as could be expected, by a process of gradual fermentation and admixture, the present society.

LAW AND GOSPEL.

We picked up one incident oddly illustrating the transition state :

We were speaking of the probability of a further annexation of Mexican territory, with a road companion, upon a prairie near the Brazos. He was an old ranger, had made one of the Mier expedition, and had the fortune to draw a white bean on the occasion of the decimation. He had afterwards spent two years in Mexico, as prisoner.

" Mexico !" said he, " what the hell do we want of it? It isn't worth a cuss. The people are as bigoted and ignorant as the devil's grandchildren. They haven't even the capacities of my black boy. Why, they're most as black as niggers any way, and ten times as treacherous. How would you like to be tried by a jury of Mexicans ? You see it an't like it was with Texas. You go any further into Mexico with your surveyor's chains, and you'll get Mexicans along with your territory ; and a dam'd lot of 'em, too. What are you going to do with 'em? You can't drive 'em out, because there an't nowhere to drive 'em. No, *sir !* There they've got to stay, and it'll be fifty year before you can outvote 'em. Well, they'll elect the judges, or they'll elect the

legislature, and that'll appoint their judges—same thing. And
their judges an't a going to disqualify them, you may be dam
sure of that. But how many of 'em would pass muster for a
jury ? The whole of 'em ought to be disqualified. Just think
of going before a jury of them. How could they understand
evidence ? They don't know the first difference between right
and wrong, any way."

We asked an explanation of the "disqualifying." It appeared that the Texan county courts had the power to disqualify
citizens from serving upon juries for bad moral character, gross
ignorance, or mental incapacity. In further explanation, he
gave us the incident :

The decision as to moral character, of course, rests with the
judges. A few years ago, it happened that the bench in ———
County was filled entirely by ministers of the gospel, and men
of bigoted piety. The court, during a night session, ruled
that no man should be considered as of good moral character,
who was known to have drunk spirits, to have played a game of
cards, or to have used profane language. Accordingly, the
whole population of the county was incapacitated, except a few
leading church members in good and regular standing. And
though every one was glad to be rid of jury-duty, in general,
no one liked to be classed in this way as unfit for it, and the indignation rose nearly to open riot. However, the matter was
passed by, and nothing done until the following election, when
the tables were turned by rigorously excluding all church members from the court.

The reader who has not been there, may think our social experience of this part of the state peculiar and exceptional. I
can only say that we traveled on an average not more than

fourteen miles a day, and so must have stopped at almost every tenth or fifteenth house on the chief emigrant and mail-road of the state. I have given our impressions as we received them, and the only advantage they now have over his own, is in the the strength which the reiteration of day after day gives over that of page after page. Had we entered Texas by the sea, stopped at the chief towns and the frequented hotels, traveled by public conveyances, and delivered letters to prominent and hospitable individuals, upon rich old coast plantations, our notes of the East might have had, perhaps, a more rosy tone.

CHAP. III.

ROUTE THROUGH WESTERN TEXAS.

OVER THE COLORADO.

AFTER spending a pleasant week in Austin, we crossed the Colorado, into, distinctively, Western Texas.

The river is here too a blue green in color, and we enjoyed again the beauty of its placid surface and transparent depths, as the "flat" slowly rippled its way to the further bank. Its width is about a hundred yards. Not far from the ferry is a floating mill, erected by an enterprising German, similar to those that have so quaint an effect, moored in platoons by the towns upon the Rhine, the wheel slowly paddled by the current. Owing to the danger from the sudden freshets to which the stream is liable, and from the rafts of broken timber which come sweeping down, it was considered a doubtful speculation. The wooded bottom is narrow, and we soon came upon high prairies.

THE WESTERN PRAIRIES.

The impression as we emerged, strengthened by a warm, calm atmosphere, was very charming. The live-oaks, standing alone or in picturesque groups near and far upon the clean sward, which rolled in long waves that took, on their various slopes,

6*

bright light or half shadows from the afternoon sun, contributed mainly to an effect which was very new and striking, though still natural, like a happy new melody. We stopped, and, from the trunk of a superb old tree, preserved a sketched outline of its low gnarled limbs, and of the scene beyond them.

Had we known that this was the first one of a thousand similar scenes, that were now to charm us day after day, we should have, perhaps, spared ourselves the pains. We were, in fact, just entering a vast region, of which live-oak prairies are the characteristic. It extends throughout the greater part of Western Texas, as far as the small streams near San Antonio, beyond which the dwarf mesquit and its congeners are found. The live-oak is almost the only tree away from the river bottoms, and everywhere gives the marked features to the landscape.

The live-oaks are often short, and even stunted in growth, lacking the rich vigor and full foliage of those further east. Occasionally, a tree is met with, which has escaped its share of injury from prairie burnings and northers, and has grown into a symmetrical and glorious beauty. But such are comparatively rare. Most of them are meagerly furnished with leaves, and as the leaf, in shape, size, and hue, has a general similarity to that of the olive, the distant effect is strikingly similar. As far West as beyond the Guadalupe, they are thickly hung with the gray Spanish moss, whose weird color, and slow, pendulous motions, harmonize peculiarly with the tone of the tree itself, especially where, upon the round, rocky, mountain ledges, its distorted roots cling, disputing a scant nourishment with the stunted grass.

A MULE LESSON.

At the end of an afternoon's ride, mostly over bare prairies, we reached Manchac Spring. A lucky accident compelled us to stop at the house we found there, and for once we were obliged to confess that quarters within were better than any canvas we could have set up without. B. had quitted us at Bastrop to re-join us at San Antonio. In passing through the thin wood upon the banks of a branch we started a covey of quails, and hitching Fanny, I went after broiled birds for supper. Mr. Brown was not much disposed to go on without the mare, and F. was dis-posed to give him a lesson in single driving for future con-venience. A sort of pitched tournament or ramrod-skrimmage ensued, in which the persevering activity of Nack and F. were pitted against the tortuous and obstinate movements of the loaded mule. F. finally came off victor; but in the rapid coun-ter-marchings the horns of the pack-saddle came into violent contact with a low branch of live-oak, and the saddle gave way at one of its joints. For repairs more time would be necessary than we could spare from the labors of camping.

A WELL-ORDERED PLANTATION.

We found a plantation that would have done no discredit to Virginia. The house was large and well constructed, standing in a thick grove, separated from the prairie by a strong worm-fence. Adjacent, within, was the spring, which deserved its pro-minence of mention upon the maps. It had been tastefully grot-toed with heavy limestone rocks, now water-stained and mossy, and the pure stream came gurgling up, in impetuous gallons, to pour itself in a bright current out upon the prairie. The foun-tains of Italy were what came to mind, and " Fontana de Manci-occo" would have secured a more natural name.

Everything about the house was orderly and neat. The pro-prietor came out to receive us, and issued orders about the horses, which we felt, from their quiet tone, would be obeyed, without our supervision. When we were ushered into a snug supper-room and found a clean table set with wheat-bread, ham, tea, and preserved fruits, waited on by tidy and ready girls, we could scarce think we had not got beyond the bounds of Texas. We were, in fact, quit, for some time to come, of the lazy poverty of Eastern Texas.

AGRARIAN IDEAS.

There were two or three travelers besides ourselves. The conversation ran upon the Germans, through whose settlements one, a Jerseyman, had just passed. The " Dutch" he had seen at the North, he said, were very different from those of this country. There, they were honest and industrious, and minded their business. Here, they didn't appear to have any business. They were thieves and loafers, and nothing better than a " set of regular damn'd agrarians." All joined in these denunciations, which appeared to afford them relief, though founded, so far as they could show us, on mere prejudice. The master of the house was not backward, and intimated that he refused them fire and water as outlaws and barbarians, whenever he had the opportunity. "Agrarianism," a strange charge for such a country and place, we reflected, probably meant free-laborism and abolitionism, but did not push investigations.

APPROACH TO THE GERMANS.

On entering Texas we had been so ignorant as not to know that there were larger settlements of Germans there than in any other Southern State. We had met about the usual number of German traders in the Eastern towns, and once had heard that there were a large number settled at San Antonio. At Bastrop.

at a watchmaker's shop, I had seen, with surprise, a *German newspaper*, the *San Antonio Zeitung* of the week previous, and found that it contained more news of matters of general interest than all the American Texan papers I had come across since entering the state.

In Austin, we learned from Governor Pease and other acquaintances familiar with our route, that we should reach, in a day or two, the German settlements, and pass through, in fact, a German village of considerable size—Neu Braunfels. We inquired with a good deal of interest as to the condition and social relations of the Germans, and learned, from the same sources, that the great part of them were exceedingly poor, but that, as a body, they were thriving. As to slavery, as fast as they acquired property, they followed the customs of the country and purchased slaves, like other white people, even Northern men, who invariably conquered their prejudices when they came here to settle and found their practical inconvenience. However, no one could give us any precise information about the Germans, and we had not the least idea that they were so numerous, and had so important a position in Western Texas, until we reached them, a day or two after this.

AGRICULTURAL.

Our host was a man of accurate information in agricultural matters. He told us he was now (January 14) beginning to plough for his spring crops. Corn is planted usually in the middle of February. He planted cotton in May, and even in June, as there was no danger of its not maturing here as in the Eastern and Northern cotton states, and its growth is more rapid, if not exposed when young to checks from cold. This is much later than is customary; but the time varies, with the amount and the period of rain of each season.   Corn, he told us, was killed here if touched by frost after it is sprouted.

The prairie is broken by huge ploughs, drawn by six yoke of oxen, turning a sod thirty-two inches wide and four inches deep. He thought it better policy to use a smaller plough, drawn by two or three yoke of oxen, and in breaking fresh prairie to turn a shallow furrow.   The old sod, when turned deep under, rots much more slowly, and remains a long time an impediment to cultivation.   These great ploughs have two clumsy wheels attached, and once set in furrow need no other guidance.   His own had a mould-board the hinder part of which was made of iron-rods, for lightness and strength.   It acted like a coarse screen, and was said to answer well.*

THE GROUND AND ATMOSPHERE.

Leaving Manchac Spring, our road led us across a bleak open prairie, on whose rolls stood no house, and scarce a tree, for fifteen miles.   At our right, to the north, was a range of distant

---

* At this house, where everything was extremely neat, and where we had silver cups for drinking, there was no other water-closet than the back of a bush or the broad prairie—an indication of a queerly Texan incompleteness in cultivation of manners.

From something a German gentleman afterwards told us, it would appear that water-closets are of recent introduction in Texas. He had lived some time in the town of S——, then quite a large settlement, before he had time to erect one of those little social necessaries. Though the first to do so, he had no idea that it was a matter of interest to any other person than himself; but no sooner did it appear, than he was assailed for *indecency*, and before he well knew on what account, his edifice was torn down and dragged away by a nocturnal mob. He shortly rebuilt it. It again disappeared on the sly. Nothing daunted, he caused a third to be put up, and as the thing was founded on a real want in human nature, it *took*, and two or three others appeared. Nothing further occurred until the following Christmas, when the whole number in the town, now twelve or fifteen, were found drawn up in a line upon the public square.

hills, from which orchards of live-oak occasionally stretched to within a moderate distance of us.

While riding slowly, we saw some white objects on a hill before us. We could not make them out distinctly, and resorted to the spy-glass. "Sheep," said one. "Cattle," said the other. As we rode on, we slowly approached. "Yes, sheep," said one. "Decidedly not sheep," said the other. Suddenly, one of the objects raises a long neck and head. "Llamas—or alpacas." "More like birds, I think." Then all the objects raise heads, and begin to walk away, upon two legs. "What! ostriches? Yes, ostriches, or something unknown to my eye." We were now within four or five hundred yards of them. Suddenly, they raised wings, stretched out their necks, and ran over the prairie, but presently left ground, and flew away. They were very large white birds, with black-edged wings, and very long necks and legs. They must have been a species of crane, very much magnified by a refraction of the atmosphere.

MESQUIT GRASS.

A great change occurred here in the prairie grass—we had reached the *mesquit grass*, of which we had heard much throughout Eastern Texas. The grass of the Eastern prairies is coarse and sedgy, like that of rank, moist, outlying spots in New England. Where not burned, it lay, killed by the frost, in a thick, matted bed upon the ground. Our animals showed no disposition to eat it. This mesquit they eat eagerly as soon as we came upon it, as if it were an old acquaintance. It is a fine, short grass, growing with great vigor and beauty over the Western prairies. It is usually found in very thick tufts and patches, interspersed with other grasses, but in the San Antonio river district covers the whole surface. It is extremely nutritious and palatable to cattle, horses, and sheep, and has the very great advantage of preserving its sweetness, to a certain degree, through the winter. The usual frosts, perhaps owing to the closeness of its growth, do not kill it to the ground, the lower parts of its leaves and stem retaining a slight verdure, unless burned over, until new leaves shoot out in spring. It is this which gives the prairies of Western Texas their great superiority, as a pasture ground, over those of the central and eastern parts of the state, and mark it as forever a pastoral country, whatever, in other respects, be its future.

SAN MARCOS.

At noon we forded the Blanco, the principal branch of the San Marcos river, a bright, clear, rapid stream.

In its bottoms and those of the San Marcos (which rises from a single spring a few miles west) are said to lie the best lands of Texas. Ward mentions that, as long ago as 1804, the banks of the main stream were selected for a Spanish colony, on account of their surpassing fertility. I have never seen a district whose soil seemed to me so rich. It was like a fine garden compost, in which black vegetable mould, clay, and lime had been equally mixed. The few cotton fields we passed were still white. Not more than half the product seemed to have been picked.

The difficulty, however, which will go far to prevent this from becoming a great enslaved planting country, was again brought to our notice by complaints of the loss of negroes, who were supposed to have fled to Mexico. Another difficulty which the planter has here to encounter, is the scarcity of timber, and of all materials suitable to fencing purposes. Very strong and high fences are required to resist the charges of the half wild cattle and horses of the prairies. Wire fences are sometimes used, but are expensive, if well made, and very few planters have the patience or enterprise to make trial of hedges.

We were told that two bales and a half of cotton had been sometimes picked here from an acre. Owing to the freedom of the new soil from weeds, much less labor is required than in old settled countries. One hand is said to be able to tend twenty acres of corn and ten of cotton. If the ground have been well prepared corn requires but two ploughings after planting, and will yield, one year with another, fifty bushels to the acre. It is admitted that, to take care of thirty acres, a hand must be hard worked; but it is said to be often done. In Virginia, ten acres of corn per hand is considered a good allowance.

San Marcos was a town of about three shabby houses. Beyond it our road approached closely the hill-range, which is made up of spurs coming down from mountains North. They are well wooded with cedar and live-oak. With such a shelter from the northers and such a soil, it is no wonder that the settlers are numerous. We passed a house perhaps every mile, beyond San Marcos, and, in general, they were of a better character than we had seen anywhere before, unless in the neighborhood of Bastrop or Austin. The workmanship applied to farming and the crops resulting, appeared to have been also much better.

We pitched our tent at night in a live-oak grove, by the side of a deep pure spring, at the mouth of a wooded ravine closed by rugged hills toward the north. Behind us were the continuous wooded heights, with a thick screen of cedars; before us, very beautiful prairies, rolling off far to the southward, with the smooth grassed surface, varied here and there by herds of cattle, and little belts, mottes and groups of live-oak. The cactus,

growing rank, tortuous, and grotesquely hideous, and the " yucca,"
or " Spanish bayonet," here a low clump of sharp-pointed stiff,
tusk-like leaves, indicated our gradual approach to Mexico.

The night was oppressively warm. After breakfast a sudden
black cloud rose in the North, and with incredible swiftness and
a frightful roar spread over the heavens. The cattle came running headlong for the cover, and we hurried everything under
the tent, expecting a deluge of rain. It was only wind—a norther. An immense change took place at once in the temperature,
the thermometer indicating a fall of 15° in fifteen minutes, and
the furious wind gave a cutting effect, which was most severe.
The following were the temperatures observed:

Jan. 16. 9.52 A.M.	- - 72° Ther.	Jan.16. 10.39 A.M.	- - 51° Ther.
" 9.54 "	- - 70° "	" 11.27 "	- - 47° "
" 9.56 "	- - 68° "	" 12.00 "	- - 45° "
" 9.58 "	- - 66° "	" 9.30 P.M.	- - 39° "
" 10.00 "	- - 64° "	Jan.17. 10.30 A.M.	- - 39° "
" 10.02 "	- - 62° "	" 1.00 P.M.	- - 49° "
" 10.06 "	- - 58° "	" 3.15 "	- - 57° "
" 10.10 "	- - 56° "	" 5.00 "	- - 57° "
" 10.16 "	- - 54½° "	" 9.30 "	- - 48° "

A NEIGHBOR OF THE GERMANS.

We had applied for corn at a house not far from camp. The
family were at supper.

" I wished," said I, " to inquire if I could get some corn of
you ?"

" I reckon you might."

" I won't trouble you to leave your supper."

" No trouble."

Out comes the proprietor, leaving a strong negro to wait upon
the table. He was a young man, but had been settled for seve-

ral years at this place.   He informed us that we should be among
the German settlers in the first hour of our next day's ride.   We
anxiously made inquiries to ascertain what his *experience* had
been with regard to the character of the Germans; for we had
obtained, from the short intercourse we had enjoyed with this
people in their native land, such a kind regard for them that we
were yet unwilling to trust the fairness of the judgment of them,
which the American Texans seemed to have formed.   We were
immediately surprised and gratified by his answers.   He seemed
to have had no reason at all to think of them as bad neighbors, but
as extremely useful and valuable ones.   Their mechanics worked
cheaply, steadily and excellently.   Their teamsters frequently
camped within twenty rods of his house; he had no complaints
to make of them at all.   They had been very honest and trustworthy in their dealings with him.

" But I understand," said I, " that they are in a rather
wretched condition, and are hardly able to get their living in this
country."

" Why, the most of them seem to be very poor people," said
he, " but they are getting along very well, I should think, for
poor folks ; they are every year improving about their houses
and building new houses which are more comfortable than the
old ones, and they work their little pieces of land first-rate.   I
reckon those that had a good deal of money when they came
out, have a good many of them got poor.   You see they did
not come here expecting to do anything to make money by, but
because they thought they could live a good deal cheaper here
than in the old country.   Well, they don't know how to give up
their old habits, and they think they must have their wine to
drink, and so on, as they have been used to ; and it used to cost

them a dime a bottle, they say, there, and here it costs four bits, and I reckon a good many have got poor that way. But the people that came here poor must be getting along very well—at any rate they say so, and it looks so."

"I am told that they buy negroes as fast as they get money enough to be able to."

Yes, he reckoned they did. How many of them owned negroes, that he knew? He couldn't tell. Were there a hundred? Oh, no. Were there ten? No, not more than five. And I supposed he knew some hundreds of them? Yes, he knew more than a thousand, he thought, that did not own slaves.

GERMAN FARMS.

The country, next morning, continued the same in all respects as that of the day before. The first German settlers we saw, we knew at once. They lived in little log cabins, and had inclosures of ten acres of land about them. The cabins were very simple and cheap habitations, but there were many little conveniences about them, and a care to secure comfort in small ways evident, that was very agreeable to notice. So, also, the greater variety of the crops which had been grown upon their allotments, and the more clean and complete tillage they had received contrasted favorably with the patches of corn-stubble, overgrown with crab-grass, which are usually the only gardens to be seen adjoining the cabins of the poor whites and slaves. The people themselves were also to be seen, men, women, and children, busy at some work, and yet not so busy but that they could give a pleasant and respectful greeting to the passing traveler.

A few miles further on, we passed several much more comfortable houses, boarded over, and a good deal like the smaller class of farm-houses in New England, but some of them having exterior plaster-work, or brick, laid up between the timbers, instead of boards nailed over them. About these were larger inclosures, from which extensive crops of corn had been taken; and it caused us a sensation to see a number of parallelograms of COTTON—FREE-LABOR COTTON. These were not often of more than an acre in extent. Most of them looked as if they had been judiciously cultivated, and had yielded a fine crop, differing, however, from that we had noticed on the plantations the day before, in this circumstance—the picking had been entirely completed, and that with care and exactness, so that none of the cotton, which the labor of cultivation had produced, had been left to waste. The cotton-stalks stood rather more closely, and were of less extraordinary size, but much more even or regular in their growth than on the plantations.

A FREE-MINDED BUTCHER.

We were entering the valley of the Guadalupe river, which is of the same general character as that of the San Marcos, and had passed a small brown house with a turret and cross upon it, which we learned was a Lutheran church, when we were overtaken by a good-natured butcher, who lived in Neu-Braunfels, whence he had ridden out early in the morning to kill and dress the hogs of one of the large farmers. He had finished his job, and was returning.

He had been in this country eight years. He liked it very much; he did not wish to go back to Germany; he much preferred to remain here. The Germans, generally, were doing well, and were contented. They had had a hard time at first, but they were all doing well now—getting rich. He knew but one German who had bought a slave; they did not think well of slavery; they thought it better that all men should be free; besides, the negroes would not work so well as the Germans. They were improving their condition very rapidly, especially within the last two years. It was sickly on the coast, but here it was very healthy. He had been as well here as he was in Germany—never had been ill. There were Catholics and Protestants among them; as for himself, he was no friend to priests, whether Catholic or Protestant. He had had enough of them in Germany. They could not tell him anything new, and he never went to any church.

We forded, under his guidance, the Guadalupe, and after climbing its high bank, found ourselves upon the level plateau between the prairie hills and the river on which Neu-Braunfels is situated. We had still nearly a mile to ride before entering the town, and in this distance met eight or ten large wagons, each drawn by three or four pairs of mules, or five or six yokes of oxen, each carrying under its neck a brass bell. They were all driven by Germans, somewhat uncouthly but warmly and neatly dressed; all smoking and all good-humored, giving us "good morning" as we met. Noticing the strength of the wagons, I observed that they were made by Germans, probably.

"Yes," said the butcher, "the Germans make better wagons than the Americans; the Americans buy a great many of them. *There are seven wagon-manufactories in Braunfels.*"

NEU-BRAUNFELS.

The main street of the town, which we soon entered upon, was very wide—three times as wide, in effect, as Broadway in New York. The houses, with which it was thickly lined on each side

for a mile, were small, low cottages, of no pretensions to ele-
gance, yet generally looking neat and comfortable. Many were
furnished with verandahs and gardens, and the greater part were
either stuccoed or painted. There were many workshops of
mechanics and small stores, with signs oftener in English than
in German; and bare-headed women, and men in caps and short
jackets, with pendent pipes, were everywhere seen at work.

AN EVENING FAR FROM TEXAS.

We had no acquaintance in the village, and no means of introduction, but, in hopes that we might better satisfy ourselves
of the condition of the people, we agreed to stop at an inn and
get dinner, instead of eating a cold snack in the saddle, without
stopping at noon, as was our custom. "Here," said the butcher,
" is my shop—indicating a small house, at the door of which hung
dressed meat and beef sausages—and if you are going to stop,
I will recommend you to my neighbor, there, Mr. Schmitz." It
was a small cottage of a single story, having the roof extended so
as to form a verandah, with a sign swinging before it, " Guadalupe Hotel, J. Schmitz."

I never in my life, except, perhaps, in awakening from a
dream, met with such a sudden and complete transfer of associations. Instead of loose boarded or hewn log walls, with crevices
stuffed with rags or daubed with mortar, which we have been
accustomed to see during the last month, on staving in a door,
where we have found any to open; instead, even, of four
bare, cheerless sides of whitewashed plaster, which we have
found twice or thrice only in a more aristocratic American residence, we were—in short, we were in Germany.

There was nothing wanting; there was nothing too much, for

one of those delightful little inns which the pedestrian who has tramped through the Rhine land will ever remember gratefully. A long room, extending across the whole front of the cottage, the walls pink, with stenciled panels, and scroll ornaments in crimson, and with neatly-framed and glazed pretty lithographic prints hanging on all sides; a long, thick, dark oak table, with rounded ends, oak benches at its sides ; chiseled oak chairs; a sofa, covered with cheap pink calico, with a small vine pattern ; a stove in the corner; a little mahogany cupboard in another corner, with pitcher and glasses upon it; a smoky atmosphere; and finally, four thick-bearded men, from whom the smoke proceeds, who all bow and say " Good morning," as we lift our hats in the doorway.

The landlady enters; she does not readily understand us, and one of the smokers rises immediately to assist us. Dinner we shall have immediately, and she spreads the white cloth at an end of the table, before she leaves the room, and in two minutes' time, by which we have got off our coats and warmed our hands at the stove, we are asked to sit down. An excellent soup is set before us, and in succession there follow two courses of meat, neither of them pork, and neither of them fried, two dishes of vegetables, salad, compote of peaches, coffee with milk, wheat bread from the loaf, and beautiful and sweet butter—not only such butter as I have never tasted south of the Potomac before, but such as I have been told a hundred times it was impossible to make in a southern climate. What is the secret? I suppose it is extreme cleanliness, beginning far back of where cleanliness usually begins at the South, and careful and thorough *working*.

We then spent an hour in conversation with the gentlemen who were in the room. They were all educated, cultivated, well-bred, respectful, kind. and affable men. All were natives of Germany, and had been living several years in Texas. Some of them were travelers, their homes being in other German settlements ; some of them had resided long at Braunfels.

It was so very agreeable to meet such men again, and the account they gave of the Germans in Texas was so interesting and gratifying, that we were unwilling to immediately continue our journey, We went out to look at our horses ; a man in cap and jacket was rubbing their legs—the first time they had received such attention in Texas, except from ourselves, or by special and costly arrangement with a negro. They were pushing their noses into racks filled with fine mesquit hay—the first they had had in Texas. They seemed to look at us imploringly. We ought to spend the night. But there is evidently no sleeping-room for us in the little inn. They must be full. But then we could sleep with more comfort on the floor here, probably, than we have been accustomed to of late. We concluded to ask if they could accommodate us for the night. Yes, with pleasure—would we be pleased to look at the room they could afford us? Doubtless in the cock-loft. No, it was in another little cottage in the rear. A little room it proved, with blue walls again, and oak furniture ; two beds, one of them would be for each of us—the first time we had been offered the luxury of sleeping alone in Texas ; two large windows with curtains, and evergreen roses trained over them on the outside—not a pane of glass missing or broken—the first sleeping-room we have had in Texas where this was the case ; a sofa ; a bureau, on which were a complete set of the *Conversations Lexicon ;* Kendall's Santa Fé Expedition ; a statuette in porcelain ; plants in pots ; a brass study lamp ; a large ewer and basin for washing, and a couple of tow-

7

els of thick stuff, full a yard and a quarter long. O, yes, it will do for us admirably ; we will spend the night.

In the afternoon, we called upon the German Protestant clergyman, who received us kindly, and, though speaking little English, was very ready to give all the information he could about his people, and the Germans in Texas generally. We visited some of the workshops, and called on a merchant to ascertain the quality and amount of the cotton grown by the Germans in the neighborhood. At supper, we met a dozen or more intelligent people, and spent the later evening, with several others, at the residence of one of our accidental inn acquaintances.

I will simply remark here, that the facts learned from these gentlemen, confirmed the simple good accounts of the butcher.

As I was returning to the inn, about ten o'clock, I stopped for a few moments at the gate of one of the little cottages, to listen to some of the best singing I have heard for a long time, several parts being sustained by very sweet and well-trained voices.

In the day time, I saw in the public street, at no great distance from a school-house, a tame doe, with a band on its neck, to distinguish it from the wild deer, lest it should be shot by sportsmen. It was exceedingly beautiful, and so tame that it allowed me to approach, and licked my hand. In what Texan town, through which we have passed before, could this have occurred.

In the morning we found that our horses had been bedded, for the first time in Texas.

As we rode out of town, it was delightful to meet again troops of children, with satchels and knapsacks of books, and little kettles of dinner, all with ruddy, cheerful faces, the girls especially so, with their hair braided neatly, and without caps or bonnets, smiling and saluting us—" *guten morgen*"—as we met. Nothing so pleasant as that in Texas before, hardly in the South.

Such was our first encounter with the Germans in Texas. Chance afterwards threw us in the way of seeing much more of them; but I have preferred to preserve the order of time and give now simply these first notes, that the reader who follows us may receive our succession of impressions.

THE SAN ANTONIO ROAD.

We had hardly left the town, which is straggling thickly to the westward and merges, by degrees, its town-lots into ten-acre homesteads and small farms, when one of our table companions came up on the road behind us, also on his way to San Antonio. He joined us, by our invitation, and though we found some difficulty in mutual comprehension, added much to our pleasure and information.

The distance to San Antonio, by the shortest road, is about thirty miles. The old road follows up a creek bottom, and houses, sheltered by live-oaks, stand thick along it, each in the centre of a little farm, having a broad open range of pasture before it. We left these and the hills beyond them, to the right, and went in a straight course out upon the open prairies. The grass had, in many places, been recently burned, giving the country a desolated surface of dead black monotony.

The trees were live-oaks and even these very rare. The ground-swells were long, and so equal in height and similar in form, as to bring to mind a tedious sea voyage, where you go plodding on, slow hour after slow hour, without raising a single object to attract the eye.

At noon we crossed the Cibolo (pronounced by Texans "Sewilla"), a creek which has the freak of here and there disappearing in its course for miles, leaving its bed dry, except during freshets. Here were several settlements, almost the only ones on the day's route. Not very far away, however, are, in several places, Germans, who have built neat stone houses out upon the prairie away from any running water, depending entirely upon wells.

Seven miles from San Antonio we passed the Salado, another smaller creek, and shortly after, rising a hill, saw the domes and white clustered dwellings of San Antonio below us. We stopped and gazed long on the sunny scene.

The city is closely-built and prominent, and lies basking on the edge of a vast plain, through which the river winds slowly off beyond where the eye can reach. To the east are gentle slopes toward it; to the north a long gradual sweep upward to the mountain country, which comes down within five or six miles; to the south and west, the open prairies, extending almost level to the coast, a hundred and fifty miles away.

There is little wood to be seen in this broad landscape. Along the course of the river a thin edging appears, especially around the head of the stream, a short ride above the city. Elsewhere, there is only limitless grass and thorny bushes.

These last, making *chapparal*, we saw as we went further on, for the first time. A few specimens of *mesquit (algarobbia glandulosa)* had been pointed out to us; but here the ground shortly became thickly covered with it. This shrub forms one of the prominent features of Texas, west of San Antonio. It is a short thin tree of the locust tribe, whose branches are thick set with thorns, and bears, except in this respect, a close resemblance to a straggling, neglected peach-tree. Mixed with other shrubs of a like prickly nature, as an undergrowth, it frequently forms, over acres together, an impenetrable mass. When the tree is old, its trunk and roots make an excellent fire-wood; but for other purposes it is almost useless, owing to its bent and tortuous fibre. A great value is said to lie in its gum, which, if properly secured, has been pronounced equal to gum-arabic in utility.

By a wall of these thorns the road is soon closed in. Almost all the roads of entrance are thus lined, and so the city bristles like the porcupine, with a natural defense. Reaching the level, we shortly came upon the first house, which had pushed out and conquered a bit of the chapparal. Its neighbor was opposite, and soon the street closed in.

The singular composite character of the town is palpable at the entrance. For five minutes the houses were evidently German, of fresh square-cut blocks of creamy-white limestone, mostly of a single story and humble proportions, but neat, and thoroughly roofed and finished. Some were furnished with the luxuries of little bow-windows, balconies, or galleries.

From these we enter the square of the Alamo. This is all Mexican. Windowless cabins of stakes, plastered with mud and roofed with river-grass, or "tula;" or low, windowless, but better thatched, houses of adobes (gray, unburnt bricks), with groups of brown idlers lounging at their doors.

The principal part of the town lies within a sweep of the river upon the other side. We descend to the bridge, which is close down upon the water, as the river, owing to its peculiar source, never varies in height or temperature. We irresistibly stop to examine it, we are so struck with its beauty. It is of a rich blue and pure as crystal, flowing rapidly but noiselessly over pebbles and between reedy banks. One could lean for hours over the bridge-rail.

From the bridge we enter Commerce street, the narrow principal thoroughfare, and here are American houses, and the triple nationalities break out into the most amusing display, till we reach the main plaza. The sauntering Mexicans prevail on the pavements, but the bearded Germans and the sallow Yankees furnish their proportion. The signs are German by all odds, and perhaps the houses, trim-built, with pink window-blinds. The American dwellings stand back, with galleries and jalousies and a garden picket-fence against the walk, or rise, next door, in three-story brick to respectable city fronts. The Mexican buildings are stronger than those we saw before, but still of all sorts, and now put to all sorts of new uses. They are all low, of adobe or stone, washed blue and yellow, with flat roofs close down upon their single story. Windows have been knocked in their blank walls, letting the sun into their dismal vaults, and most of them are stored with dry goods and groceries, which overflow around the door. Around the plaza are American hotels, and new glass-fronted stores, alternating with sturdy battlemented Spanish walls, and confronted by the dirty, grim, old stuccoed stone cathedral, whose cracked bell is now clunking for vespers, in a tone that bids us no welcome, as more of the intruding race who have caused all this progress, on which its traditions, like its imperturbable dome, frown down.

SAN ANTONIO.

We have no city, except, perhaps, New Orleans, that can vie, in point of the picturesque interest that attaches to odd and antiquated foreignness, with San Antonio. Its jumble of races, costumes, languages and buildings; its religious ruins, holding to an antiquity, for us, indistinct enough to breed an unaccustomed solemnity; its remote, isolated, outposted situation, and the vague conviction that it is the first of a new class of conquered cities into whose decaying streets our rattling life is to be infused, combine with the heroic touches in its history to enliven and satisfy your traveler's curiosity.

Not suspecting the leisure we were to have to examine it at our ease, we set out to receive its impressions while we had the opportunity.

After drawing, at the Post-office window, our personal share of the dear income of happiness divided by that department, we strolled, by moonlight, about the streets. They are laid out with tolerable regularity, parallel with the sides of the main plaza, and are pretty distinctly shared among the nations that use them. On the plaza and the busiest streets, a surprising number of old Mexican buildings are converted, by trowel, paint-brush, and gaudy carpentry, into drinking-places, always labeled " Exchange," and conducted on the New Orleans model. About these loitered a set of customers, sometimes rough, sometimes affecting an " exquisite" dress, by no means attracting to a nearer acquaintance with themselves or their haunts. Here and there was a restaurant of a quieter look, where the traditions of Paris are preserved under difficulties by the exiled Gaul.

The doors of the cabins of the real natives stood open wide, if indeed they exist at all, and many were the family pictures of jollity or sleepy comfort they displayed to us as we sauntered curious about. The favorite dress appeared to be a dishabille, and a free-and-easy, loloppy sort of life generally, seemed to have been adopted as possessing, on the whole, the greatest advantages for a reasonable being. The larger part of each family appeared to be made up of black-eyed, olive girls, full of animation of

tongue and glance, but sunk in a soft embonpoint, which added
a somewhat extreme good-nature to their charms. Their dresses
seemed lazily reluctant to cover their plump persons, and their
attitudes were always expressive of the influences of a Southern
sun upon national manners. The matrons, dark and wrinkled,
formed a strong contrast to their daughters, though, here and
there, a fine cast of feature, and a figure erect with dignity, attracted the eye. The men lounged in roundabouts and cigaritos,
as was to be expected, and, in fact, the whole picture lacked nothing that is Mexican.

Daylight walks about the town yielded little more to curiosity.
The contrast of nationalities remained the chief interest. The
local business is considerable, but carried on without subdivision
of occupation. Each of a dozen stores offers all the articles
you may ask for. A druggist or two, a saddler or two, a watchmaker and a gunsmith ply almost the only distinct trades. The
country supplied from this centre is extensive, but very thinly
settled. The capital owned here is quite large. The principal
accumulations date from the Mexican war, when no small part
of the many millions expended by Government were disbursed
here in payment to contractors. Some prime cuts were secured
by residents, and no small portion of the lesser pickings remained in their hands. Since then the town has been well-to-do,
and consequently accumulates a greater population than its position in other respects would justify.

The traffic, open and illicit, across the frontier with interior
Mexico, has some importance and returns some bulky bags of
silver. All the principal merchants have their agencies on the
Rio Grande, and throw in goods, and haul out dollars, as opportunity serves. The transportation of their goods forms the

principal support of the Mexican population. It is this trade, probably, which accounts for the large stocks which are kept, and the large transactions that result, beyond the strength of most similar towns.

All goods are brought from Matagorda Bay, a distance of 150 miles, by ox-teams, moving with prodigious slowness and irregularity. In a favorable season, the freight-price is one-and-a-quarter cents per lb., from Lavacca. Prices are extremely high, and subject to great variations, depending upon the actual supply, and the state of the roads.

Cash is sometimes extremely scarce in the town. The Mexican dollars are sent forward to a good market. Government brings its army-stores direct from the coast. But some hay, corn, and other supplies, are contracted for in the region, and from this source, and from the leavings of casual travelers, and new emigrants, the hard money for circulation is derived. Investments at present are mostly in lands. There are no home-exports of the least account. Pecan-nuts, and a little coarse wool, are almost the only items of the catalogue. The wealth and steady growth of the town depend almost entirely upon the rapid settlement of the adjacent country.

A scanty congregation attends the services of the battered old cathedral. The Protestant church attendance can almost be counted upon the fingers. Sunday is pretty rigidly devoted to rest, though most of the stores are open to all practical purposes, and the exchanges keep up a brisk distribution of stimulants. The Germans and Mexicans have their dances. The Americans resort to fast horses for their principal recreation.

We noticed, upon a ruined wall, the remains of a placard, which illustrates at the same time a Yankee shrewdness in devot-

7*

ing a day to grief, without actual loss of time, and the social manners of the people :

"RESOLUTIONS *on the death of* THE HON. DANIEL WEBSTER."

"Be it resolved by the Board of Aldermen of the city of San Antonio, in Common Council assembled, that, by the death of the late Daniel Webster, the people are plunged in mourning, and in testimonial of our grief, we sincerely join with other cities and towns of our country in requesting a suspension of labor, and the closing of all places of business, on SUNDAY, *the* 10*th inst.*, from 10 o'clock A. M. to 4 o'clock P. M., and that all the flags in the city be displayed at half-mast, and minute guns fired through the day."

The town of San Antonio was founded in 1730 by a colony of twelve families of pure Spanish blood, from the Canary islands. The names of the settlers are perpetuated to this day, by existing families, which have descended from each, such as Garcia, Flores, Navarro, Garza, Yturri, Rodriquez. The original mission and fort of San Antonio de Valero dates from 1715, when Spain established her occupancy of Texas.

THE MISSIONS.

Not far from the city, along the river, are these celebrated religious establishments. They are of a similar character to the many scattered here and there over the plains of Northern Mexico and California, and bear a solid testimony to the strangely patient courage and zeal of the old Spanish fathers. They pushed off alone into the heart of a savage and unknown country, converted the cruel brutes that occupied it, not only to nominal Christianity, but to actual hard labor, and persuaded and compelled them to construct these ponderous but rudely splendid edifices, serving, at the same time, for the glory of the faith, and for the defense of the faithful.*

* Good drawings of two of these missions may be seen in Bartlett's "Personal Narrative.

The Alamo was one of the earliest of these establishments. It is now within the town, and in extent, probably, a mere wreck of its former grandeur. It consists of a few irregular stuccoed buildings, huddled against the old church, in a large court surrounded by a rude wall; the whole used as an arsenal by the U. S. quartermaster. The church-door opens on the square, and is meagerly decorated by stucco mouldings, all hacked and battered in the battles it has seen. Since the heroic defense of Travis and his handful of men, in '36, it has been a monument, not so much to faith as to courage.

The Mission of Concepcion is not far from the town, upon the left of the river. Further down are three others, San Juan, San José, and La Espada. On one of them is said to have been visible, not long ago, the date, " 1725." They are in different stages of decay, but all are real ruins, beyond any connection with the present—weird remains out of the silent past.

They are of various magnificence, but all upon a common model, and of the same materials—rough blocks of limestone, cemented with a strong gray stucco. Each has its church, its convent, or celled house for the fathers, and its farm-buildings, arranged around a large court, entered only at a single point. Surrounding each was a large farm, irrigated at a great outlay of labor by aqueducts from the river.

The decorations of the doors and windows may be still examined. They are of stucco, and are rude heads of saints, and mouldings, usually without grace, corresponding to those described as at present occupying similar positions in Mexican churches. One of the missions is a complete ruin, the others afford shelter to Mexican occupants, who ply their trades, and herd their cattle and sheep in the old cells and courts. Many is the picturesque sketch offered to the pencil by such intrusion upon falling dome, tower, and cloister.

THE ENVIRONS.

The system of aqueducts, for artificial irrigation, extends for many miles around San Antonio, and affords some justification for the Mexican tradition, that the town, not long ago, contained a very much larger population. Most of these lived by agriculture, returning at evening to a crowded home in the city. These water-courses still retain their old Spanish name, "acequias." A large part of them are abandoned, but in the immediate neighborhood of the city they are still in use, so that every garden-patch may be flowed at will.

In the outskirts of the town are many good residences, recently erected by Americans. They are mostly of the creamy limestone, which is found in abundance near by. It is of a very agreeable shade, readily sawed and cut, sufficiently durable, and can be procured at a moderate cost. When the grounds around them shall have been put in correspondence with the style of these houses, they will make enviable homes.

THE SAN ANTONIO SPRING.

There are, besides the missions, several pleasant points for excursions in the neighborhood, particularly those to the San Antonio and San Pedro Springs. The latter is a wooded spot of great beauty, but a mile or two from the town, and boasts a restaurant and beer-garden beyond its natural attractions. The San Antonio Spring may be classed as of the first water among the gems of the natural world. The whole river gushes up in one sparkling burst from the earth. It has all the beautiful accompaniments of a smaller spring, moss, pebbles, seclusion, sparkling sunbeams, and dense overhanging luxuriant foliage. The effect is overpowering. It is beyond your possible conceptions of a spring. You cannot believe your eyes, and almost shrink from sudden metamorphosis by invaded nymphdom.

BATHING.

The temperature of the river is of just that agreeable elevation that makes you loth to leave a bath, and the color is the ideal blue. Few cities have such a luxury. It remains throughout the year without perceptible change of temperature, and never varies in height or volume. The streets are laid out in such a way that a great number of houses have a garden extending to the bank, and so a bathing-house, which is in constant use. The Mexicans seem half the time about the water. Their plump women, especially, are excellent swimmers, and fond of displaying their luxurious buoyancy. The fall of the river is such as to furnish abundant water-power, which is now used but for a single corn-mill. Several springs add their current to its volume above the town, and that from the San Pedro below. It unites, near the Gulf, with the Guadalupe, and empties into Espiritu Santo Bay, watering a rich, and, as yet, but little-settled country.

The soil, in the neighborhood of the city, is heavy, and sometimes mixed with drifts of limestone pebbles, and deposits of shell, but is everywhere black, and appears of inexhaustible fertility, if well cultivated and supplied with moisture. The market-gardens, belonging to Germans, which we saw later in the season, are most luxuriant. The prices of milk, butter, and vegetables are very high, and the gains of the small German market-farmers must be rapidly accumulating.

TOWN LIFE.

The street-life of San Antonio is more varied than might be supposed. Hardly a day passes without some noise.   If there be no personal affray to arouse talk, there is some Government train to be seen, with its hundred of mules, on its way from the coast to a fort above ; or a Mexican ox-train from the coast, with an interesting supply of ice, or flour, or matches, or of whatever the shops find themselves short. A Government express clatters off, or news arrives from some exposed outpost, or from New Mexico.   An Indian in his finery appears on a shaggy horse, in search of blankets, powder, and ball.   Or at the least, a stage-coach with the "States," or the Austin, mail, rolls into the plaza and discharges its load of passengers and newspapers.

The street affrays are numerous and characteristic.   I have seen, for a year or more, a San Antonio weekly, and hardly a number fails to have its fight or its murder.   More often than otherwise, the parties meet upon the plaza by chance, and each, on catching sight of his enemy, draws a revolver, and fires away. As the actors are under more or less excitement, their aim is not apt to be of the most careful and sure, consequently it is, not seldom, the passers-by who suffer.   Sometimes it is a young man at a quiet dinner in a restaurant, who receives a ball in the head ; sometimes an old negro woman, returning from market, who gets winged.   After disposing of all their lead, the parties close, to try their steel, but as this species of metallic amusement is less popular, they generally contrive to be separated ("Hold me ! Hold me !") by friends before the wounds are mortal. If neither is seriously injured, they are brought to drink together on the following day, and the town waits for the next excitement.

Where borderers and idle soldiers are hanging about drinking-places, and where different races mingle on unequal terms, assassinations must be expected. Murders, from avarice or revenge, are common here. Most are charged upon the Mexicans, whose passionate motives are not rare, and to whom escape over the border is easiest and most natural.

The town amusements of a less exciting character are not many. There is a permanent company of Mexican mountebanks, who give performances of agility and buffoonery two or three times a week, parading, before night, in their spangled tights with drum and trombone through the principal streets. They draw a crowd of whatever little Mexicans can get adrift, and this attracts a few sellers of whisky, *tortillas,* and *tamaules* (corn slap-jacks and hashed meat in corn-shucks), all by the light of torches making a ruddily picturesque evening group.

The more grave Americans are served with tragedy by a thin local company, who are death on horrors and despair, long rapiers, and well oiled hair, and for lack of a better place to flirt with passing officers, the city belles may sometimes be seen looking on. The national background of peanuts and yells, is not, of course, wanting.

A day or two after our arrival, there was the hanging of a Mexican. The whole population left the town to see. Family parties, including the grandmother and the little negroes, came from all the plantations and farms within reach, and little ones were held up high to get their share of warning. The Mexicans looked on imperturbable.

San Antonio, excluding Galveston,* is much the largest city

---

* The two towns have nearly kept pace in growth. The yellow fever, it is said, has now given San Antonio the advantage.

of Texas. After the Revolution, it was half deserted by its Mexican population, who did not care to come under Anglo-Saxon rule. Since then its growth has been rapid and steady. At the census of 1850, it numbered 3,500; in 1853, its population was 6,000; and in 1856, it is estimated at 10,500. Of these, about 4,000 are Mexicans, 3,000 Germans, and 3,500 Americans. The money-capital is in the hands of the Americans, as well as the officers and the Government. Most of the mechanics and the smaller shopkeepers are German. The Mexicans appear to have almost no other business than that of carting goods. Almost the entire transportation of the country is carried on by them, with oxen and two-wheeled carts. Some of them have small shops, for the supply of their own countrymen, and some live upon the produce of farms and cattle-ranches owned in the neighborhood. Their livelihood is, for the most part, exceedingly meagre, made up chiefly of corn and beans.

THE MEXICANS IN TEXAS.

We had, before we left, opportunities of visiting familiarly many of the Mexican dwellings. I have described their externals. Within, we found usually a single room, open to the roof and invariably having a floor of beaten clay a few inches below the level of the street. There was little furniture—huge beds being the universal pièce de résistance. These were used by day as sofa and table. Sometimes there were chairs and a table besides; but frequently only a bench, with a few earthen utensils for cooking, which is carried on outside. A dog or a cat appears on or under the bed, or on the clothes-chest, a saint on the wall, and frequently a game-cock fastened in a corner, supplied with dishes of corn and water.

We were invariably received with the most gracious and beaming politeness and dignity. Their manner towards one another is engaging, and that of children and parents most affectionate. This we always noticed in evening walks and in the groups about the doors, which were often singing in chorus—the attitudes expressive of confident affection. In one house, we were introduced to an old lady who was supposed by her grandchildren to be over one hundred years old. She had come from Mexico, in a rough cart, to make them a visit. Her face was strikingly Indian in feature, her hair, snow white, flowing thick over the shoulders, contrasting strongly with the olive skin. The complexion of the girls is clear, and sometimes fair, usually a blushing olive. The variety of feature and color is very striking, and is naturally referred to three sources—the old Spanish, the Creole Mexican, and the Indian, with sometimes a suspicion of Anglo-Saxon or Teuton. The hair is coarse, but glossy, and very luxuriant; the eye, deep, dark, liquid, and well set. Their modesty, though real, we heard, was not proof against a long courtship of flattering attentions and rich presents. The constancy of the married women was made very light of, not that their favors were purchasable, but that they are sometimes seized by a strong penchant for some other than their lord. There was testimony of this in the various shades and features of their children; in fact we thought the number of babies of European hair and feature exceeded the native olive in number. We noticed, in a group of Mexican and negro women, when an indelicate occurrence took place, that the former turned away in annoyed modesty, while the latter laughed broadly. Their constitutions, in general, are feeble, and very many of both sexes, we were informed, suffered from scrofulous disease. Nevertheless, with good stimulus, the men make admirable laborers.

The common dress was loose and slight, not to say slatternly. It was frequently but a chemise, as low as possible in the neck, sometimes even lower, with a calico petticoat. On holidays they dress in expensive finery, paying special attention to the shoes, of white satin, made by a native artist.

The houses of the rich differ little from those of the poor, and the difference in their style of living must be small, owing to the want of education and of all ambition. The majority are classed as laborers. Their wages are small, usually, upon farms near San Antonio, $6 or $8 a month, with corn and beans. That of the teamsters is in proportion to their energy. On being paid off, they hurry to their family and all come out in their best to spend the earnings, frequently quite at a loss for what to exchange them. They make excellent drovers and shepherds, and in work like this, with which they are acquainted, are reliable and adroit. A horse-drover, just from the Rio Grande, with whom we conversed, called them untiring and faithful at their work, but untrustworthy in character. To his guide, he paid $24 a month, to his " right bower," $15, and to his " left bower," $12 a month.

Their tools are of the rudest sort. The old Mexican wheel of hewn blocks of wood is still constantly in use, though supplanted, to some extent, by Yankee wheels, sent in pairs from New York. The carts are always hewn of heavy wood, and are covered with white cotton, stretched over hoops. In these they live, on the road, as independently as in their own house. The cattle are yoked by the horns, with raw-hide thongs, of which they make a great use.

They consort freely with the negroes, making no distinction from pride of race. A few, of old Spanish blood, have purchased negro servants, but most of them regard slavery with abhorrence.

The Mexicans were treated for a while after annexation like a conquered people. Ignorant of their rights, and of the new language, they allowed themselves to be imposed upon by the new comers, who seized their lands and property without shadow of claim, and drove hundreds of them homeless across the Rio Grande. They now, as they get gradually better informed, come straggling back, and often their claims give rise to litigation, usually settled by a compromise.

A friend told us, that, wishing, when he built, to square a corner of his lot, after making diligent inquiry he was unable to hear of any owner for the adjoining piece. He took the responsibility, and moved his fence over it. Not long after, he was waited upon by a Mexican woman, in a towering passion. He carried her to a Spanish acquaintance, and explained the transaction. She was immediately appeased, told him he was welcome to the land, and has since been on the most neighborly terms, calling him always her " amigo."

Most adult Mexicans are voters by the organic law ; but few take measures to make use of the right. Should they do so, they might probably, in San Antonio, have elected a government of their own. Such a step would be followed, however, by a summary revolution. They are regarded by slaveholders with great contempt and suspicion, for their intimacy with slaves, and their competition with plantation labor.

Americans, in speaking of them, constantly distinguish themselves as " white folks." I once heard a new comer informing another American, that he had seen a Mexican with a revolver.

"I shouldn't think they ought to be allowed to carry fire-arms. It might be dangerous." "It would be difficult to prevent it," the other replied; "Oh, they think themselves just as good as white men."

From several counties they have been driven out altogether. At Austin, in the spring of 1853, a meeting was held, at which the citizens resolved, on the plea that Mexicans were *horse-thieves*, that they must quit the county. About twenty families were thus driven from their homes, and dispersed over the western counties. Deprived of their means of livelihood, and rendered furious by such wholesale injustice, it is no wonder if they should take to the very crimes with which they are charged.

A similar occurrence took place at Seguin, in 1854; and in 1855, a few families, who had returned to Austin, were again driven out.

Even at San Antonio, there had been talk of such a razzia. A Mexican, caught in an attempt to steal a horse, had been hung by a Lynching party, on the spot, for an example. His friends happened to be numerous, and were much excited, threatening violence in return. Under pretext of subduing an intended riot, the sheriff issued a call for an armed posse of 500 men, with the idea of dispersing and driving from the neighborhood a large part of the Mexican population. But the Germans, who include among them the great majority of young men suitable for such duty, did not volunteer as had been expected, and the scheme was abandoned. They were of the opinion, one of them said to me, that this was not the right and republican way. If the laws were justly and energetically administered, no other remedy would be needed. One of them, who lived on the Medina, in the vicinity of the place of the occurrence, told us he had no complaint to make of the Mexicans; they never stole his property, or troubled him in any way.

The following is the most reliable estimate I can obtain of the actual Mexican population in Texas, (1856):—

San Antonio	. . . .	4,000
Bexar Co.	. . . .	2,000
Uvalde Co.	. . . .	1,000
Laredo .	. . . .	1,500
El Paso, with Presidio	. . .	8,500
Lower Rio Grande Counties	. .	3,000
Goliad and Nueces Counties	. .	1,000
Other parts of State .	.	1,000
Floating, say	. . . .	3,000
		25,000

A PAUSE.

We had made it our first business, on arriving at San Antonio, to find what company was to be had for our Mexican trip, and we were somewhat dismayed, on delivering our letters, to find that communication with Mexico was thought to be infrequent and precarious. Merchants dispatched goods occasionally to different points on the Rio Grande; now and then a Government express, or an officer with escort, left for our military stations there; a post-rider, once a week, crossed the desert beyond the Nueces, riding rapidly and sleeping on the ground. But traveling parties, such as we had thought to join, for the interior cities of Mexico, were almost unheard of: in fact, in the unsettled state of political affairs in that crazy Republic, it was considered highly dangerous for a party to travel there, whose numbers did not enable them, not only to stand nightly guard, but to resist, if necessary, organized attacks upon the road.

A train for Chihuahua, via El Paso, was just about leaving, which, if we wished to go in that direction, would afford us ample protection. We rode a mile or two out of town to the spot where it was encamped. It was commanded, we found, by Julius Froebel, who escaped, by so slender a thread, the republican martyrdom which his companion, Robert Blum, actually suffered in Vienna, and whose scientific contributions to the natural and human history of the central parts of the continent, have now and then appeared in the *New York Tribune*. The train was a very large one, and equipped in the best style. There were twenty-six wagons, drawn by 260 mules, with experienced drivers, forage and provisions, besides professional hunters, to obtain fresh meat where possible. Mr. Froebel, however, gave such an account of the slowness and tedium of the travel-life of such a trip as quite discouraged us, especially as the train was to leave within twelve hours. We were fortunate, the event proved, in not having joined it, as, though it reached its destination quite safely, it was detained for *some months*, in camp at the frontier, near El Paso, while custom-house difficulties were being arranged.

After a day or two, our friend B. announced that a change in his business affairs at the north would compel him to ask a discharge from his enlistment, which we unwillingly granted. This more completely blocked our wheels, and threw us quite upon chance for our route and our company. We made inquiries on all sides without success. The officer in command of the station here could give us no promise of company, within a short time, even to the Rio Grande. We consulted many old border travelers, who strongly dissuaded us from attempting the trip by ourselves. Finally, among the boarders at a German inn, we heard of a scientific gentleman, living at Braunfels, who was about to make the trip to the city of Mexico, and resolved on returning there to offer ourselves as companions.

On entering San Antonio, our fellow-traveler had taken us with him to this German inn, the more willingly on our part, as we retained a vivid impression of the contrast between the hotel at Neu-Braunfels and every other hotel we had seen in Texas. We had been extremely interested in what we had seen of the Germans, too, and were glad of an excuse to see more of them. We found a miserable old Mexican house, and close quarters enough for sleeping, but most pleasant company, a hearty, hospitable, unremitting kindness, and a table which, with its refreshing salads and variety of vegetables, was like returning spring to our salt and husky palates. At each meal we met some twenty boarders, mostly clerks or men in business, but with a sprinkling of professional men, and, from first to last, gentlemen in manner, and full of such information as we wanted. We cannot too strongly recommend a quiet traveler to follow our example.

By their advice we called upon the editor of their German newspaper, who received us most politely, and was able, not only to give us the name of the gentleman who was intending to go to Mexico, but to give us a more accurate idea of the numbers and position of the Germans in Texas than we had before obtained.

A NORTHER.

The day before we left San Antonio was cold and foggy. The following morning was warm but still foggy, making our ride, with a light wind behind us, exceedingly oppressive. We threw off our coats, and soon stripped off vest and cravat; but this, we found, was not enough, and we were obliged to stop to take off our flannel. Our horses were reeking with sweat. At two o'clock the thermometer, in a cool, shady spot, stood at 79°, and the sky was nearly clear. We were very tired and thirsty, and one of us suggested that this was the very country and the very weather for mirage. It was not long after we saw the edge of the horizon rising in the flickering heat, and groups of trees standing free in the air, as an island or a point stretches off into the sky of a hot day on the sea-coast. Then the trees connected themselves with the land below upon each side, and we saw a beautiful lake, the water rippling in the sunlight. It grew wider and longer, and shortly was like the open sea, with a rich and shady shore, extending up, at intervals, like bays and rivers, into the land. Soon the lakes were common here and there about us, calm of surface, trees with heavy foliage bending over their banks to rest in the water. Had we not been prepared, by a knowledge of the country, we should have been strongly tempted to ride towards some of them for a drink of cool water.

Later in the day, the air became clearer, and a pleasant breeze played upon our backs. The mirage gradually disappeared, and we lost it in descending a swell of the prairie. It was near sunset, with a dull cloud bank in the north. We were still suffering with the heat, when one of us said—

"See this before us, what is it, fog again or smoke?"

"A prairie fire, I think," said the other.

"Probably it is ; but what is this on the hill close by, this is fog, surely? It must be a norther coming. Yes, it is a norther; listen to that roar! We must get our clothing on or we shall be chilled through."

First, a chilly whiff, then a puff, the grass bends flat, and, bang, it is upon us—a blast that would have taken a top-gallant sail smack out of the bolt-ropes, and cold as if blowing across a sea of ice. We galloped to the nearest ravine, and hurried on all the clothing we could muster. Fortunately, though our baggage was left behind, we had taken a supply, having strapped blankets, Guernsey shirts, and Canada leggins, behind our saddles.

At nine o'clock, the thermometer stood at thirty-three degrees, and, at seven next morning, at twenty-one degrees. A thermometer hanging in Neu-Braunfels showed a fall of sixty degrees in seven hours.

These northers upon the open prairies are exceedingly trying. The fierce wind that accompanies such a sudden change gives them triple effect, especially as they often interrupt warm, relaxing weather. Teamsters, herdsmen, and travelers, caught out far from habitations, not unfrequently perish, and very great suffering is caused to animals. Cattle instinctively make for the nearest shelter of trees; but, on the open prairies of the coast, they fall by thousands before a freezing rain, which is sometimes added.

The northers continue from one to three days, growing milder at the close, and occur once or twice a week during the winter months. But a tight house and a blazing fire make one quite independent of them, and such we found in the German inn.

NEU-BRAUNFELS.—THE ORPHANS.

Our naturalist, we were told, lived adjacent to the Orphan Asylum at Neu-Wied, a hamlet some three miles from the town.

Thither, after breakfast, next day, we went, with a note of introduction, on foot, and briskly, for it was too cold to ride.

The Orphan Asylum, as we approached it, had the appearance of being a small American farm-house, with a German rear erection of brick laid up in a timber frame-work. A large live-oak sheltered the stoop, but the whole establishment was very rough,

8

with a common rail-fence about it, and not the least indication of fashionable philanthropy. As we entered a large, dark, unpainted hall, a man came forward from an inner room, who, from his dress, might have been taken for a day-laborer. It was the gentleman, however, whom we wished to see—a courteous and cultivated professor.

It was a holiday, and he had been engaged in preparing some botanical specimens, but immediately left them to ferry us over the Guadalupe, which ran through his grounds, the probable traveler residing beyond.

Leaving the house, we passed through a garden in the rear where he showed us little plots of wheat from Egypt, Algiers, Arabia, and St. Helena, which he was growing to ascertain which was best adapted to the climate. Wheat-growing, of any sort, is a novelty here, but the Germans are not satisfied with corn, nor are they willing to pay for the transportation of flour from Ohio, like the Anglo-Americans. There has been, therefore, considerable wheat grown among them, and that with satisfactory success.

From the garden, we passed into a grove, where, in a circular opening of the trees, a rude theatre had been formed, which was used by musical parties from Neu-Braunfels, and as a school or lecture-room in summer.

Not finding the gentleman of whom we were in search, we returned to the professor's house, and spent there, at his invitation, a delightful day.

He had come to this country in 1839. In the steerage of his ship there were about forty Norwegians with their families. They suffered much hardship, and he assisted and comforted them as much as was in his power. They were very grateful.

and before reaching New York they unanimously requested him to continue with them as their pastor, and assist them in forming their settlement at the West. While the ship was detained at Quarantine, he went to the city with the captain to make arrangements for their necessary stay in the city. Returning to Staten Island, he found the ship had gone up, and the ferry-boat had discontinued running for the night. It was not till late the next day that he succeeded in finding the ship at her wharf in New York, and then all the Norwegians had departed. He spent several days searching for them, but saw none of them until nearly two years afterwards. He was then in a crowd at Milwaukie, when his arm was suddenly seized with both hands by a little boy, who sprung up to kiss him, crying, "Oh! papa E.! oh, papa E.!" It was one of the children of the steerage.

He went with the boy to his father's house, who told him that some persons came on board the ship, while they were still at Quarantine, and represented that they had been engaged by some of their countrymen to advise and assist the emigrants. They were accordingly taken to a boarding-house as soon as the ship reached New York, and during the evening they were induced to purchase a considerable tract of land by the counsel of their disinterested friends, who also furnished them with cheap tickets to carry them through to Milwaukie by a steamboat that was to start the next morning. They had thus been led to leave the city almost immediately ; but the lands they had purchased, and, in part, paid for, they never found. The deeds they had received were forgeries.

From Wisconsin he had come to Texas, and joining the first company of the settlers who established Neu-Braunfels, became their pastor. The following year several thousand were landed upon the coast, and, unprovided with food or shelter, perished like sheep. Slowly, droves of them found their way into Neu-Braunfels, haggard and almost dying, having lost all family affection or fellow-feeling in intense despairing personal suffering. Many children came whose parents had died, and he found them starving upon the river bank. He could not bear the sight, but collected sixty of them, and went to work upon this farm with them. He had no means of his own, but took what he could find belonging to the children, and has since sustained them. Working with his wife and the children in the field he has managed to raise corn and keep them alive, until now, in better times, they are mostly distributed as helps in various homes. Eighteen are with him still, all calling him papa. He had obtained from the Legislature an incorporation for a University at Braunfels, and himself, as yet, sole Professor, had given a classical education to a few pay scholars.

The whole narrative was exceedingly interesting, as we heard it at our simple farm-house dinner—the Professor, with his horny hands, and with his much-patched coat, telling us of his own noble conduct in the simplest manner, but sometimes glowing and flushing with a superb home eloquence.

HISTORY OF THE GERMAN SETTLEMENTS.

The most accurate and full published account of these German settlements is the report of a lecture, by FREDERICK KAPP, upon the Germans in Texas, in the *New York Tribune* of January 20, 1855. From this, and from our notes of oral statements on the spot, I will concisely give the story. The experiment was a most interesting one; that of using associated capital for the transportation and settlement of emigrants on a large scale; in fact, the removal, in organized bodies, of the poor of an old country to the virgin soil of a new.

In the year 1842, among many schemes evolved in Germany by the social stir of the time, and patronized by certain princes, from motives of policy, was one of real promise. It was an association, of which Count Castel was the head, for the diminution of pauperism by the organized assistance and protection of emigrants. At this time, annexation being already almost a certainty, speculators, who represented the owners of large tracts of Texas land, appeared in Germany, with glowing accounts of their cheapness and richness. They succeeded in gaining the attention of this association, whose leaders were pleased with the isolated situation, as offering a more tangible and durable connection with their emigrants, and opening a new source of wealth and possible power. A German dependency or new Teutonic nation might result. Palmerston, it is said, encouraged the idea,* the Texan political leaders then coquetting with an English Protectorate, to induce more rapid advances on the part of the United States.

In 1843, an agent of the association, Count Waldeck, visited Texas, but effected nothing else than to secure himself a slave plantation, not far from the coast. He was dismissed. The following year the association commenced active operations. It

---

* According to the work of Mr. SIEMERING upon the Germans in Texas, now in the hands of the publisher, this encouragement went so far as to take the form of a contract between the Verein and the British Government. By it the former agreed to place 10,000 families in Texas ; the latter to furnish armed protection to the colony. A new market with indefinite capacities ; a new source of cotton ; opposition to slavery and to the extension of the area of the United States ; such were the sufficient motives for England. Prince Leiningen was the half-brother of the Queen of England. Prince Solms was an intimate friend of Prince Albert, with whom he was educated at Bonn. Copies of the correspondence still exist.

obtained, under the title of the MAINZER ADELS VEREIN, a charter from the Duke of Nassau, who assumed the protectorate. It had the Prince of Leiningen as president; Count Castel as director; Prince Frederick of Prussia, the Duke of Coburg-Gotha, and some thirty other princes and nobles as associated members. A plan, inviting emigrants, was published, offering each adult, subscribing $120, a free passage and forty acres of land; a family, subscribing $240, a free passage and eighty acres. The association undertook to provide log-houses, stock, and tools at fair prices, and to construct public buildings and roads for the settlements.

Prince Solms, of Braunfels, was appointed General Commissioner and proceeded to Texas. Had he procured from the State Legislature a direct grant of land for the colony, as he might have done, all would have been well. But, most unfortunately, the association were induced, without sufficient examination, to buy a grant of the previous year. It was held by Fisher and Miller, and the tract was described by them as a second paradise. In reality, it lay in the heart of a savage country, hundreds of miles beyond the remotest settlement, between the Upper Colorado and the great desert plains, a region, to this day, almost uninhabited. This wretched mistake was the ruin of the whole enterprise. The association lost its money and its character, and carried many emigrants only to beggary and a miserable death.

In the course of the year, 180 subscribers were obtained, who landed with their families in the autumn upon the coast of Texas, and marched towards their promised lands, with Prince Solms at their head. Finding the whole country a wilderness, and being harassed by the attacks of Indians, on reaching the union of the Comal with the Guadalupe, they became disheartened, and there Prince Solms, following the good advice of a naturalist of the company, Mr. Lindheimer, encamped, and laid out the present town of Neu-Braunfels.

This settlement, receiving aid from home, while it was needed, was a success, in spite of the Prince, who appears to have been an amiable fool, aping, among the log-cabins, the nonsense of mediæval courts. In the course of a year he was laughed out of the country.

He was succeeded by C. Von Meusebach, who proved at least much better adapted to the work.

Had he not been reduced to inaction by home routine, and a want of funds, the misery that followed might, perhaps, have been prevented.*

In course of the next year, 1845, more than 2,000 families joined the association. The capital which had been sufficient for its first effort was totally inadequate to an undertaking of this magnitude. These poor people sailed from Germany, in the fall of this year, and were landed in the winter and early spring, on the flat coast of the Gulf, to the number of 5,200. Annexation had now taken place, and the war with Mexico was beginning. The country had been stripped of provisions, and of the means of transportation, by the army. Neither food nor shelter had been provided by the association. The consequences may be imagined. The detail is too horrible. The mass remained for

---

* It is here difficult to sift various statements to an exact appreciation.—A new company (at Bieberich) subsequently bought out the Verein, but Mr. Martin, their agent in Texas, has never entered possession, having been forced into the law by Spies, the successor of Meusebach. In 1855, the original Fisher makes his re-appearance, with a scheme for " scaling " both claims, and securing what remains. This speculation nowise affects the actual colonists.

months encamped in sand-holes, huts, or tents : the only food procurable was beef.   The summer heats bred pestilence.

The world has hardly record of such suffering.   Human na ture could not endure it.   Human beings became brutes.   " Your child is dying."   " What do I care?"   Old parents were hurried into the ground before the breath of life had left them.   The Americans who saw the stragglers, thought a new race of savages was come.   Haggard and desperate, they roved inland by twos and threes, beyond all law or religion.   Many of the survivors reached the German settlements; many settled as laborers in American towns.   With some of them, Meusebach founded an-other town—Fredericksburg—higher up than Braunfels.   He also explored the Fisher grant, and converted the surrounding Indians, from enemies, into good-natured associates.

" It is but justice," says Mr. Kapp, " to throw the light of truth upon all this misery.   The members of the association, although well-meaning, did not understand what they were about to do.   They fancied that their *high protection*, alone, was suffi-cient to make all right.   They had not the remotest idea of the toil and hardship of settling a new country.   They permitted themselves to be humbugged by speculators and adventurers; they entered into ruinous bargains, and had not even funds enough to take the smallest number of those, whom they had induced to join them, to the place of settlement.   When money was most wanted, they failed to send it, either from mistrust or neglect. To perform the obligation imposed by the agreement with Fisher, they induced the emigration to Texas by the most enchanting and exaggerated statements.   The least that even the less san-guine ones expected, was, to find parrots rocking on the boughs, and monkeys playing on the palm-trees."

This condemnation seems to fall justly.

Such was the unhappy beginning. But the wretchedness is already forgotten. Things soon mended. The soil, climate, and the other realities found, were genial and good, if not Elysian. Now, after seven years, I do not know a prettier picture of contented prosperity than we witnessed at Neu-Braunfels. A satisfied smile, in fact, beamed on almost every German face we saw in Texas.

PRESENT APPEARANCES.

Of the general appearance of Neu-Braunfels I gave some notion in describing the route to San Antonio. We now took pains to obtain some definite facts with regard to its condition. The dwellings in general are small and humble in appearance, but weather-tight, and, generally, provided with galleries or verandahs, and with glazed casement windows. In the latter respect, they have the advantage over most houses we have seen in Texas, and, I have no doubt, the average comforts of life within are much greater than among the Anglo-Americans, generally, in the state.

The citizens are, however, nearly all men of very small capital. Of the original settlers scarcely any now remain, and their houses and lands are occupied by more recent emigrants. Those who have left have made enough money during their residence to enable them to buy farms or cattle-ranches in the mountains, to which they have removed.

Half the men now residing in Neu-Braunfels and its vicinity, are probably agricultural laborers, or farmers, who themselves follow the plough. The majority of the latter do not, I think, own more than ten acres of land each. Within the town itself,

8*

there are of master-mechanics, at least, the following numbers, nearly all of whom employ several workmen:

Carpenters and Builders	20
Wagon-makers	7
Blacksmiths	8
Gun and Locksmiths	2
Coppersmiths	1
Tinsmiths	2
Machinists	1
Saddlers	3
Shoemakers	6
Turners	2
ʻTailors	5
Button and Fringe-makers . . .	1
Tanners	3
Butchers	3
Bakers	4

There are four grist-mills, and a couple of New-England men are building a sash and blind factory, and propose erecting a cotton factory.

A weekly newspaper is published—the *Neu-Braunfels Zeitung*. It is a paper of much higher character than most of the German American papers, edited by the naturalist, Lindheimer.

There are ten or twelve stores and small tradesmen's shops, two or three apothecaries, and as many physicians, lawyers, and clergymen. I do not think there is another town in the slave states in which the proportion to the whole population of mechanics, or of persons employed in the exercise of their own discretion in productive occupations, is one-quarter as large as in Neu-Braunfels, unless it be some other in which the Germans are the predominating race.

There are several organizations among the people which indicate an excellent spirit of social improvement: an Agricultural

Society, a Mechanics' Institute, a Harmonic Society, a Society for Political Debates, and a "Turners'" Society. A horticultural club has expended $1,200 in one year in introducing trees and plants.

These associations are the evidence of an active intellectual life, and desire for knowledge and improvement among the masses of the people, like that which distinguishes the New-Englanders, and which is unknown wherever slavery degrades labor. Will this spirit resist the progress of slavery westward, or must it be gradually lost as the community in which it now exists becomes familiar with slavery?

In Neu-Braunfels and the surrounding German hamlets, there are five free schools for elementary education, one exclusive Roman Catholic school, a town free school of higher grade, and a private classical school. In *all* of these schools English is taught with German. The teacher of the higher department of the central town school is paid four hundred dollars a year; that of the primary department (a female), two hundred dollars.

The following were the prices current at the time of my visit: Maize, 35 cents a bushel; meal, 45 cents; wheat, none in market; flour, extra St. Louis, $12; soda crackers, 20 cents; beef, fresh, retail for households, 3 cents per pound; pork, 7 cents; bacon, sides, 15 cents; hams, sugar-cured, 20 cents; fowls, 25 cents each; turkeys, 50 cents; ditto, wild, 25 cents; ducks, 20 cents; venison, a whole deer, $1, a quarter, 20 cents, or about 1 cent a pound; mutton, 7 cents; sweet potatoes, 50 cents per bushel.

There are here two items which New York farmers will hardly credit when placed in connection. Maize, 35 cents a bushel; pork, 7 cents a pound; and, still more remarkable, hams, 20 cents! In New York, I suppose, corn was fully double that price, and pork no higher.

Pine boards, 50 cents a foot; cedar, 40 cents; bar iron, 8 to 9 cents per pound; nails, $8 per keg. These articles are brought in wagons from the coast, about one hundred and fifty miles. Transportation by teams (owned and driven altogether by Germans), usually one cent a pound from the coast. Stone and brick clay, lime, sand and water-power can be conveniently and cheaply obtained.

Money here, as everywhere else in Western Texas, is very scarce, and may be always loaned on perfectly trustworthy securities, at fifteen per cent. and upwards. The law of Texas makes all above eight per cent. usurious. Master-mechanics, with whom I conversed, informed me that they had no lack of work, but that it was difficult to get payment in money.

Journeymen (late emigrants and rough hands) informed me that they were paid wages, $15 a month and upward, and found. Farm-laborers, $8 to $15, and found. Domestics (females), $5 to $8. It is very difficult to obtain the latter, and still more difficult to keep them, as but few girls emigrate in proportion to the men, and they generally obtain situations for life within a few weeks after their arrival. This state of things is likely to continue for a long time, and, as the Germans grow wealthy and luxurious, will, undoubtedly, lead to their occasionally purchasing slaves to relieve themselves from the annoyance of constant changes in their household.

In Neu-Braunfels and the immediate vicinity are living about three thousand Germans.* The Anglo-American population

* Since our notes, the adjacent farming county has increased its population at the expense of the town. The county-population is now estimated at 5,000, the town, 2,000.

of the place does not exceed twenty. Just out of the town a wealthy planter has settled, who holds one hundred negroes. He also owns a mill and water-power, and a good deal of real estate. Another American, living in the town, owns a negro girl, and one negro girl is hired by one of the Germans as a domestic. There are no other negroes in town. The blacks of the plantation, we were told, had acquired the power of speaking German in an extremely short time after their arrival.

Sunday was observed more thoroughly as a day of rest from labor than we had seen in any town of Texas. The stores, except one kept by a New-Englander, were closed during the day. The people who appeared in the streets were well dressed, quiet, and orderly. We saw no drunkenness. In the evening there were amusements, among them a ball, which the Lutheran pastor was expected to attend.

The health of the town is good. For several years there has been no epidemic illness. The greater part of those of whom I made inquiry assured me their health had been better here than in Germany.*

The Lutheran clergyman informed us that he had registered but seven deaths, during the year, among his congregation. The pastoral record during the early years of the settlement tells a pathetic story. It is as follows:

	Deaths.	Births.		Deaths.	Births.
1845 . .	27	9	1847 . .	71	35
1846 . .	304	34	1848 . .	19	75

About one-half the people, if I am not mistaken, are nominal Catholics.

---

* Some particulars of the summer temperature will be found in the Appendix.

FREE COTTON.

In the town, each house has its garden-plot, and over the neighborhood are scattered hundreds of small farms. Owing to the low price of corn, most of these had been cultivated, partly, in cotton during the year before our visit.* The result was a total crop of eight hundred bales, which, at Galveston, brought from one to two cents a pound more than that produced by slaves, owing to the more careful handling of white and personally interested labor; but the expense of hauling cotton to the coast prevents any large profits at this distance. A railroad or a local manufactory must precede any extensive cultivation of cotton, while corn, which requires much less labor, can find a market at a fair price. With water-power and hands upon the spot, it certainly seems an unnatural waste of labor to carry the staple to Massachusetts to be spun, but such, for want of local capital, is now the course of trade.

In spite of the common assertion, that only blacks can endure the heat of southern labor, the production of cotton, by whites alone, is by no means rare. There are very many, both of those who work their own small cotton farms and of those who work with their few negroes, day after day in the field. Corn cultivation, for year after year, is the common work of the less vagabond of the poor whites. But there is hardly in the South another as striking an instance of pure free-labor upon cotton-fields, as this of the Germans. Their cotton goes in one body to market, entirely separate from the great mass exported, and from their peculiar style of settlement, it may be even considered as

* For the two succeeding years, corn has returned to its old price of $1 and upwards. At this price cotton cannot compete with it, consequently its cultivation has been temporarily abandoned.

the product of one large plantation, worked by white hands, and divided into well-marked annual tasks.

These 800 bales, therefore, though but a drop in the bucket to the whole crop, are a very substantial evidence of the possibilities of not only white, but of well-regulated free-labor in the South.

KENDALL'S RANCH.

We had the pleasure of spending an evening at Neu-Braunfels with Mr. G. W. KENDALL, of the *New Orleans Picayune*, who has a sheep-ranch five or six miles north of the town. Upon it he has a good stock of mares, some cattle, and a large flock of sheep, under charge of an imported Scotch shepherd. Owing to some mismanagement, in cold weather, his first experiences were not very favorable. Now the farm was in a fair way to be extremely profitable. He uses no negroes, but hires all extra labor done by Germans from the town. In talking over our plans with him we found no particular encouragement toward entering Mexico. We should find the distance, he said, everywhere, at least twice as far as it was reported. The scenery was composed of desert plains and cactus, and once a day, perhaps, of a stone wall, in addition. We should wear out about one horse a week, and would be robbed each day of something we had, until we should reach Mexico without a sou in our pockets, and without one rag with which we started. Certain circumstances in his first visit to Mexico, we thought, however, might have given him a permanently unfavorable impression.

A GERMAN CABIN.

Our naturalist, we found, had but vague Mexican intentions. We returned to San Antonio, by way of Seguin. Setting out late from the latter place, we were benighted on the road, and took shelter at a cabin, which we found occupied by two German settlers. Their house and life are worth describing, from its contrast, if nothing else, with the home of the native poor white further East.

There were, a man and his wife, with a son, and another single man, who came from Germany four years ago. They landed at Lavacca, and came directly to the interior, at Neu-Braunfels. For the first year the bachelor hired himself to a farmer; the second he had been employed in a grocery in San Antonio. The other, who was a shoemaker in Germany, worked at his trade. The two then combined their capital, most of it made during these two years, and purchased, about a year since, the cabin they lived in, 100 acres of land, and some cattle. The land was worth about $2 an acre, but they ranged their cattle over as much of the adjoining prairie as they chose. The soil was extremely fertile, and the pasturage rank and nutritious. They had raised last summer a large supply of corn for themselves and their stock, together with a good store of various vegetables. Their stock of cattle had been carefully watched, and, with the natural increase, now exceeded twenty head. They had sold butter, eggs, shoes, and stockings, and purchased two mares, now heavy with colt. They had taken up the rotten wooden floor of the American, preferring to it a hard earthen floor. They had repaired the roof, and, with a stucco, which they formed by mixing grass with a calcareous clay, had made tight and smooth walls inside and out, doing all the work with their own hands. The house was small, but tight and comparatively comfortable. They had put glass sashes into the windows, and had made new doors, swinging easily on their hinges, and furnished with wooden latches

The house was not comfortable enough for them, however, and they told us that next year, or as soon as they had got certain fences made, and land broken up, they were going to build a new house, at another point on their land where there were some trees. It would not cost them anything to make it, they said, because they could cut all the wood on their own land, and they could do all the work themselves in the winter.

They were in a very solitary situation—fifteen miles from any village, but with two other German settlers and an American plantation within three miles. They were well satisfied with the country.

"And you are glad you left Germany?" I asked the young man.

"O, yes; very glad: a thousand times better here."

"You can have more comfort here?"

"Oh, no; not so much. It is hard for a young man, he can have so little pleasure. These American gentlemen, here in Texas, they do not know any pleasure. When they come together sometime, what do they? They can only sit all round the fire and *speet!* Why, then they drink some whisky; or may be they play cards, or they make great row. They have no pleasure as in Germany."

"Why, then, do you like it better to be here?"

"Because here I am free. In Germany I cannot say at all how I shall be governed. They govern the people with soldiers. They tried to make me a soldier, too, but I run away."

"In Germany, too, I suppose, you had to work very hard."

"Oh, we work harder here; but, by-and-by, when we get fixed, then we will not have to work hard then, it will be very easy. In three years I go back to Germany. I left a sweet-

heart there. I marry her and come back and have here my
home."

"But they will arrest you because you ran away and did not
serve as a soldier."

"Ah, no; for then I shall be *a citizen!*"

"Did you give notice, when you first arrived, of your intention, then?"

"Oh, yes."

"Do most of the Germans do so?"

"Those that have good sense—all."

We were surprised to hear how well the son of the shoemaker,
a boy of fourteen, spoke English, and asked where he learned it?
"At school in Neu-Braunfels." He had attended school, where
he had been taught English, while his father lived there during
two years. This year he had not been at school, because they
had too much work to do in their new place; but next winter
they would send him to an American academy—boarding-school
—where, he said, he thought he should learn very fast; but it
would be very costly; two dollars a month for the lowest class
and four dollars for the uppermost.

All of them were well dressed, but the woman was a pattern
of neatness. As she cooked our supper it seemed as if she had
been "made up" for a model housewife. She had a fine, healthy,
kind German face, and was so good-natured and so desirous to
make us comfortable, and so easily amused and gratified herself,
that when we left we parted from a friend.

The house was supplied with about the same amount of large
furniture as an American's—bedsteads, and chests, and cupboards
—but there were fifty little conveniences to be used in cooking,
or for other purposes, here, which are wanting there. For sup-

per we had wheat and Indian bread, buttermilk and eggs. At breakfast, besides the same articles, there were also *pfannekuchen,* something between a pancake and an omelette, eaten with butter and sugar. The sugar was refined, and the butter yellow and sweet. " How can you make such butter?" we asked, in astonishment. "Oh, ho! it is only the American ladies are too lazy; they not work enough their butter. They give us fifty cent a pound for our butter in San Antone! yes, fifty cent! but we want to eat good butter, too." Such was the fact. At the house of the American herdsman I described in Eastern Texas, who owned probably one hundred cows, there was no milk or butter —it was too much trouble. A friend told me that he had spent a fortnight at the house of an American here who owned five hundred cows, without tasting milk or butter; not because the family did not like these luxuries, but because *it was too much trouble.* The German had a cow driven into a pen to be milked at daylight. His wife milked her herself. The American owned a number of negroes. The German was happy in the possession of freedom, undebilitated by mastership or slaveship.

Or is it, as they say, the climate? and will the German, in his turn, after a few years, be debilitated so by it and labor only under the influence of fear or of excited passion? I do not believe it.

THE GERMANS IN THE MOUNTAINS.

Finding still no company for Mexico at San Antonio, we gladly accepted an invitation from the German editor, Dr. Douai, to accompany him on a few days' excursion, he was about making, into the mountains to the northward.

There are certain persons with whom acquaintance ripens rapidly. Our companion, we found, was one of these. We listened to some details of a varied and stormy life, in learning what brought him here, and were not long in falling into discussions that ran through deep water, and demanded all our skill in navigation.

Our horses took advantage of our absence to stray into unknown parts, and for some hours after we started, we traveled loosely over the prairies, only keeping their heads toward the north.   Night, however, found us on the Cibolo, and near a settlement, where we secured quarters for the night.

Five or six miles from San Antonio, the prairies rise, in gentle slopes, into hills, which become steeper and nearer one another as you travel further.   In thirty miles, the valleys have become very narrow, and the hills and mountains rugged with projecting strata of limestone.   These strata are very peculiar, and are said to be characteristic of the inland region all the way to Missouri.   They are of the thickness of building stones, and lying horizontally, they give the hills the appearance of artificial structures, so that a conical hill leaves very much the impression of a crumbling, overgrown pyramid.   The soil is black, but has been washed from the square edges.   Wherever it exists, grass grows, even over the summits of the mountains, if they be not bare rocks.   In the smaller valleys, particularly the following day, we found ourselves in real Sonora scenery.   The stunted live-oaks were rarely to be seen, besides grass, there were only large cacti, yuccas, and agaves, scattered over the arid rocky elevations.

In the larger valleys, were groves of post-oak, and along the principal water-courses, timber of various kinds, and some good bottom-land, as on the Cibolo, at the road-crossing, where a town called Börne had been laid out, and a few houses built.   But the natural use of the country was, palpably, for grazing, and that, sheep-grazing.   We could hardly refrain from expecting, on each bleak hill, to startle a black-faced flock, and see a plaided, silent, long-legged shepherd appear on the scene.

A NEW SETTLER.

The family whose hospitality we sought, were newly arrived German farmers. They had reached Texas in the fall, and had been settled here but about two months.

Their house, although built merely for temporary occupancy, until they could spare time and money for one more comfortable, was a very convenient long, narrow log cabin, with two rooms, each having a sleeping loft over it, two halls, or rooms open at the ends, and a corn-crib. The cooking was done outside, by a camp-fire, but with utensils brought from Germany, and peculiarly adapted to it. A considerable stock of furniture was stored in the halls, yet in the boxes in which it had been imported. The walls of the two rooms had been made tight with clay, the doors were furnished with latches. (No man who has traveled much on the frontier will look upon these indications as trivial.) Our supper was served to us on china, on a clean table-cloth, in one of these rooms, skillfully and nicely. A sofa, occupying one side of the room, had evidently been made by the women of the family after the building of the cabin. On the walls there were hnng a very excellent old line engraving of a painting in the Dresden gallery, two lithographs, and a pencil sketch, all glazed, and framed in oak.

The family consisted of several middle-aged and elderly people, a young man, a young lady, and four very sweet, flaxen-haired children. They were all very neatly dressed, the head-dresses of the females being especially becoming and tidy. They were courteous and affable, and the tones of voice were amiable and musical.

Our conversation with them was naturally left pretty much to our German companion. He went, however, after supper, to call on one of the neighbors. An hour or two later, as I returned to the house, after looking to our horses, one of the elder women spoke to me in German. I could not understand, and she called to the young lady, who came before me, and bowing in a very formal manner, addressed me in these words : " Sire, will you to bed now go, or will you for rest wait?" I replied that I would at once go to bed, if she pleased. She bowed and walked before me till opposite the open door of the second tight room, in which a candle had been placed, and pointing to it, said : " There, Sire." There were three single beds in our sleeping-room, all extremely clean, and we were provided with washing apparatus, and other bed-chamber luxuries very unusually found, even in the " best hotels," in the Southwest. The walls of the room, too, were adorned with some good engravings, and some paintings of religious subjects, of ordinary merit.

The head of this family had been a tradesman in a small town in Bavaria, where, also, he had owned a little farm. He had evidently been able to live there with considerable comfort. He could not, however, see any way in which he might provide for his family, so that he could leave them without great anxiety at his death. But now, if this farm should be divided among his children, all of them could, by honest labor, be sure of obtaining, come the worst, sufficient food, and raiment, and shelter, and in no case would they be dependent on the favor or kindness of public functionaries for the privilege of laboring for their living.

" Only one thing," said the mother, " we regret. It is that our children, who have so well commenced their education in Germany, cannot here continue it."

SISTERDALE.

Next day our road took us over a rugged ridge to the valley of the Guadalupe. From the summit was a wide and magnificent view of misty hills and wooded streams. We were crossing a little creek beyond, when two horsemen, in red shirts and slouched hats, came over the hill upon us at a hand gallop. They no sooner saw us, than they reined up with a shout, and gave our companion a hearty grasp of the hand. They were two men of Sisterdale, in search of stray cattle.

Sisterdale is a settlement of eight or ten farms, about forty miles from San Antonio, upon the Guadalupe, at the junction of the Sister creeks and the crossing of the Fredericksburg road. The farmers are all men of education, and have chosen their residences, the first by chance, the latter by choice, within social distance of one another. Up and down the Guadalupe, within long walking range, are a dozen or twenty more, single men, living in huts or caves, earning a tough livelihood chiefly by splitting shingles. They are of the same stamp, but of less social disposition, disheartened, or tired of circumstances, a sort of political hermits, who have retired into the woods, and live with one companion, or in complete solitude.

The gentlemen we met were two of these singular settlers; one of them, the schoolmaster, a Berlin student; the other a Baron, over whose Texan "domain" we were actually passing. He took us to his castle, which was near by. It was a new log-house. The family occupied a lean-to in the rear, as the roof was not quite finished. Here we were presented to the lady, who received us with cordial politeness, holding up, in commendation of the climate, a bouncing baby, seven days old, weighing, she said, three times as much as babies at home.

During a luncheon of bread and broth, we were interrupted by the clatter of hoofs. On looking out, we found a dozen men on horseback, partly Americans, from the next settlement. They were on their way to the Dale, to attend a Justice's Court. Draining our cups we joined the cavalcade.

A few minutes brought us to the judge's house, a double log-cabin, upon a romantic rocky bluff of the Guadalupe. He came out to receive us, and after converting his dining-room into a temporary court-room, for the reception of the legal arrival, resumed his long pipe, and gave us a special reception in his own apartment. We had interrupted him at work at notes upon a meteorological table, and availed ourselves of his judicial absence to look over his observations, and to make notes of such as interested us. They will be found in the Appendix.

Court over, our host rejoined us. The case had been one of great simplicity, requiring a few words only, to fix the value of a dog which had been shot and to reconcile all parties. This function of a peacemaker, we found, was one that was a habitual blessing to the neighborhood, with the judge—a certain largeness in his nature sufficing to quell all expressions of ill-feeling and put an end to silly discords.

He was partly bald, but seemed to have an imperturbable and happy good-nature that gave him eternal youth. A genial cultivation beamed from his face. He had been a man of marked attainments at home (an intimate associate with Humboldt and a friend of Goethe's Bettina), and kept up here a warm love for nature. His house was the very picture of good-nature, science, and back-woods. Romances and philosophies were piled in heaps in a corner of the logs. A dozen guns and rifles, and a Madonna, in oil, after Murillo, filled a blank on the wall. Deer-skins covered the bed, clothes hung about upon antlers, snake-skins were stretched to dry upon the bedstead, barometer, whisky, powder-horns, and specimens of Saxony wool, occupied the table.*

The dinner was Texan, of corn-bread and frijoles, with coffee, served in tin cups, but the salt was Attic, and the talk was worthy of golden goblets.

We passed, as may be imagined, a rarely pleasant day. A stroll to the Guadalupe showed us the corn-field and the sheep—a small flock of the finest Saxony. They had been selected with care, had arrived safely, and had now been, for two or three years, shifting for themselves. They had thriven well, but the flock of twelve had not much increased, owing to the depredations of panthers and Indians. A German shepherd had been shot by Indians in the early days of the settlement, and it was afterwards impossible to give, to so small a flock, the constant attention they needed. They had been, however, very profitable for their numbers, from the constant demand for thorough-bred bucks.

THE UPPER GUADALUPE.

The Guadalupe was even more beautiful here than below, quick and perfectly transparent. I have rarely seen any resort of wood-nymphs more perfect than the bower of cypress branches and vines that overhang the mouth of the Sister creek at the ford near the house. You want a silent canoe to penetrate it; yet would be loth to desecrate its deep beauty. The water of both

---

* OTTO VON BEHR has since gone to heaven. About a year after our visit to the Dale he went to Germany to spend a few months, and on his return was seized with an illness, at sea, which terminated fatally, after his ship had entered the Mississippi. A touching notice of his life and death appeared in a number of the *San Antonio Zeitung* of March, 1855. His loss, out of such a settlement, it may be conceived, is irreparable.

9

streams has a delicate, cool, blue-green color; the rocky banks are clean and inviting ; the cypresses rise superbly from the very edge, like ornamental columns. We found, while shooting in the river bottoms, some real monarchs of this species—(*c. disticha*). One of them, which had fallen, was at least fourteen feet in diameter. Its heart, as is frequently the case, was unsound. It is one of the most common trees along the creeks of this region. The wood is similar to that of the pine, but less valuable for the purposes of the lumberman. The trunks of the older trees rise branchless to a great height, having a bark remarkably clean and bright, and a foliage feeble and quivering, like that of the larch.

In the afternoon, several neighbors had dropped in, and there was some pleasant dispute as to what roof should offer us shelter. We were, finally, carried off by Mr. T., whose farm lies uppermost on the Guadalupe. A somewhat circuitous route thither led us to a high hill, from which we saw the valley to great advantage. The farm lies in a bend of the river, and has an agreeable proportion of timber and of rich meadow. The house, of logs, is large, warm, and substantial.

The evening's talk ran upon the principles of government, and kept us late. Mr. T. had been a member of the Frankfort Parliament. He had arrived in this country with little else available than a hopeful energy, but with this capital had become, in a few years, what, in Texas, was considered a wealthy man, owning large tracts of land, and able to live freely upon his rents.

FARMING IN THE DALE.

We rode with him, next day, over the Dale. The land is much broken, but well wooded and drained. In each little valley are one or more small prairies adapted to cultivation, and the hills are thickly covered with grass. It is here not the mesquit, but a taller and coarser leaf, rich in summer but affording poor nourishment in winter. Cattle, however, manage to find their own subsistence through the year, browsing, during the cold, in the river bottoms, where there is always some verdure as well as protection from the wind. The soil for cultivation is excellent. The principal crop is corn, the yield being thirty to sixty bushels, from what would be considered at the North a very small outlay of labor. Wheat has been introduced with such success as to induce the settlers to send for harvesting and thrashing-machines. The crop this year had been bad, owing to dry weather. One of the greatest sources of profit is from droves of hogs, which increase with remarkable rapidity, and pick their living from the roots and nuts of the river bottoms. The distribution of a few ears of corn at night brings them all every day to the crib. Tobacco is cultivated by the settlers for their own use, but none has yet been prepared for market.

A WELL-CULTIVATED SETTLEMENT.

We called upon several of the settlers. The first house was a surprise—a neat, stuccoed, Swiss cottage, almost the only thing of the kind we had seen in Texas. Its proprietor came from the plough to welcome us—literally, a free laborer. We found within, a thousand evidences of taste such as the exterior led us to expect. Another short ride took us to a large stuccoed log-house, near the bank of one of the Sister creeks. Here lives a professor who divides his time between his farm and his library. The delicious brook water has been turned to account by him for the cure of disease, and his house is thrown open to patients. To any friend of mine who has faith in pure

air and pure water, and is obliged to run from a Northern winter, I cannot recommend a pleasanter spot to pass his exile than
this.

Evening found us in the largest house of the settlement, and a
furious norther suddenly rising, combined with the attractive reception we met to compel us to stay two days without moving.

Mr. D., our host, was a man of unusually large education,
and, having passed some years at school in England, spoke English in perfection. Before the Revolution he had controlled an
estate on which the taxes were $10,000. He had become a
popular leader, and was placed at the head of the temporary
government of his Duchy. When the reaction came, all was
swept away, and, exiling himself, he came to settle here. Now,
working with his own hands in the Texan backwoods, he finds
life not less pleasant than before.

His house stands upon a prominence, which commands the
beautiful valley in both directions. His fields are just below.
He had this year cultivated sixty acres, and with the help of the
forenoons of his two sons, of fourteen and fifteen, who are at
school the rest of the day, had produced 2,500 bushels of corn,
besides some cotton, wheat, and tobacco. These sons were as
fine pictures of youthful yeomen as can be imagined—tall, erect,
well knit, with intelligent countenances, spirited, ingenuous, gentle and manly. In speaking of his present circumstances, he
simply regretted that he could not give them all the advantages
of education that he had himself had. But he added that he
would much rather educate them to be independent and self-re-
liant, able and willing to live by their own labor, than to have
them ever feel themselves dependent on the favor of others. If
he could secure them, here, minds free from prejudice, which

would entirely disregard the conclusions of others in their own study of right and truth, and spirits which would sustain their individual conclusions without a thought of the consequences, he should be only thankful to the circumstances that exiled him.

Our supper was furnished by the boys, in the shape of a fat turkey from the river bottoms. This one made eighty-five that had been shot by them during the winter. Among other feats of theirs at the gun, we were told of two adventures with panthers. Made aware, at dusk, one night, by the dogs, that something unusual was around the house, the two boys started with their guns to see what it might be. Light enough was left to show them a panther, who retreated, and, pressed by the dogs, took to a tree in the bottoms. He was ensconced in the branches of a cotton-wood that hung obliquely over the stream. It was too dark to see his exact position, and taking places upon the bent trunk, to prevent his descent, the boys agreed to keep guard till the moon rose. But they were tired with work, and daylight found them both asleep where they were—the panther missing! He had either walked over their bodies or dropped into the river.

On the other occasion, the boys were alone with their mother, Mr. D. having gone on a two or three days' excursion. They were awakened in the night by a stir about the out-houses. There had been signs of a panther about the hog-yard for several days, and they sprang out as they were, seizing their guns, in the hope of putting an end to the marauds. The night was pitchy dark, and stealing cautiously along, they came suddenly upon an enormous panther, within a few yards of the door. The panther gave one bound into a tree, probably more startled than themselves. He was quite invisible, and perfectly still. One of the boys thought of a lantern, and, running back, found his mother already up and alarmed.   "A lantern," he shouted, in a furious whisper, and ran back to the tree. The mother appeared with the lantern at the door, and came, in her night-dress, to the tree. What would she have thought at court, five years before, of holding a lantern, to shoot a panther? She held it high. Both boys took slow aim at the glaring eye-balls, which alone were visible above them. One pulled; the gun snapped. A quick jerk of the eye-balls gave warning of a spring, when a ball from the other rifle brought the panther dead to their feet. It proved, by daylight, the largest that had been known in the settlement, measuring nine feet from nose to tip of tail, and weighing, by estimate, 250 lbs.

After supper, there were numerous accessions of neighbors, and we passed a merry and most interesting evening. There was waltzing, to the tones of a fine piano, and music of the highest sort, classic and patriotic. The principal concerted pieces of Don Giovanni were given, and all parts well sustained. After the ladies had retired, the men had over the whole stock of student-songs, until all were young again. No city of fatherland, we thought, could show a better or more cheerful evening company. One of the party said to me: "I think, if one or two of the German tyrants I could mention, could look in upon us now, they would display some chagrin at our enjoyment, for there is hardly a gentleman in this company whom they have not condemned to death, or to imprisonment for life."

In exile, but free, these men make the most of life.

I have never before so highly appreciated the value of a well-educated mind, as in observing how they were lifted above the mere accident of life. Laboring like slaves, (I have seen them working side by side, in adjoining fields,) their wealth gone; deprived of the enjoyment of art, and, in a great degree, of literature; removed from their friends, and their great hopeful designs so sadly prostrated, " their mind to them a kingdom is," in which they find exhaustless resources of enjoyment.   I have been assured, I doubt not, with sincerity, by several of them, that never in Europe had they had so much satisfaction—so much intellectual enjoyment of life, as here.   With the opportunity permitted them, and the ability to use it, of living independently by their own labor—with that social and political freedom for themselves which they wished to gain for all their countrymen, they have within them means of happiness that wealth and princely power alone can never command.

But how much of their cheerfulness, I thought, may arise from having gained, during this otherwise losing struggle to themselves, the certain consciousness of being courageously loyal to their intellectual determinations—their private convictions of right, justice, and truth.

Truly, it has seemed to me, there may be a higher virtue than mere resignation, and our times may breed men as worthy of reverence as the martyrs of past ages.

What had not these men lost—voluntarily resigned—that mean, and depraved, and wicked souls are most devout to gain. And for what ?   For the good of their fellow men—for their convictions of truth and justice.   Under orders of their conscience.   In faithfulness to their intellect.   And they have failed in every earthly purpose, but are not cast down—are not unhappy.   What shall we think of those from whom life was also taken—-who as cheerfully and bravely gave their life also ?

I was looking, in a room here, at some portraits of gentlemen and ladies. "Those are some of my relatives that remain in Germany." "And who are these?" I asked, pointing to a collection, on the opposite wall, of lithograph and crayon-sketched heads. "These are some of my friends. That one—and that one—and that one—have been shot; that one—and that one—are in prison for life; that one—poor fellow—is in Siberia; and that one—he has been made to suffer more than all the others, I am afraid."

I once, when in Germany, met an American clergyman, who, I have since seen, has been sent to Asia, to teach the Hindoos Christianity. He was good enough to inform me, that all the German Republicans were mischievous, cut-throat infidels, who well deserved to be shot, hung, and imprisoned for life; and that I very much wronged those who were doing this for them, in some feelings I was expressing. He had dined, only the day before, with several of the higher classes, with a number of Prussian and Austrian officers, and he never met with more gentlemanly and kind-hearted men. When I mentioned the fact, that one of these officers had, a few days before, knocked down upon the pavement, with a blow of his fist, an aged laboring man, for coming, guiltlessly, into the street with red stockings, he presumed that he had thought it his duty to do so; harsh measures had to be used to support the laws, when the people were so exceedingly depraved. He did not alter very much my feelings about the circumstance, and I confess that a few days with these refugees in Texas has been worth more to me than many sermons.

AROUND FREDERICKSBURG.

Amid such hospitality of such men, the time we had intended to devote to an examination of Fredericksburg and the country north of it, slipped by, and we were compelled to return to San Antonio without seeing it. The village, we learned, was quite similar in character to Neu-Braunfels, but on a much smaller scale, containing about 700 inhabitants, who are chiefly Catholics. The country around them, although not equal to that below, was good, very fertile along the creek and river bottoms, and afforded excellent pasturage. Following the Llano and San Saba, downwards, the land becomes richer and better wooded, and the region of the Upper Colorado was described to us as being one of the finest parts of the state. This district, now Llano and San Saba Counties, has since been much taken up by emigrants, principally planters, who have located, as much as possible, with reference to the proposed line of the Pacific Railroad. The outposted settlers here, however, are still much exposed to attacks of Indians. Fredericksburg itself has grown rapidly during the last year or two. The population of the town is now 1,200; all Germans. The adjacent country has also become closely settled.

From Fredericksburg starts the upper road to El Paso. It is called forty miles shorter than the lower road, but as water is scarce, it is less used.

Mr. Bartlett, the Boundary Commissioner, followed this route. Of this vicinity, he says: "The soil continues of good quality, until the San Saba is reached. From that, to the north fork of Brady's Creek, it is not so good. The grass is generally light to the latter place, with less wood and water, though enough for parties traveling." We then reach "the great table-land of Texas, where there is little rain and a poor soil."

The furthermost German settlements now reach the San Saba. The extreme settlements of the northern part of the state are near the clear fork of the Brazos, at Fort Belknap, where there is an
9*

Indian reservation of forty leagues, and enough American settlers to have formed the new County of Young. These outposts are connected by a road, now in considerable use, which passes by Forts McKavett, Chadbourne, and Phantom Hill. A line of settlements will soon follow, and the Indians will then be confined to the great desert plains, which can furnish them with little game, and, probably, no cultivated food. Starvation will compel submission or emigration, and this great district will become open to peaceable occupation.

UP-COUNTRY FARMING.

In the month of March, after our return from the coast, we made a second excursion to the mountains, by ourselves, partly to pass away idle time, partly to renew the pleasant intercourse of our first visit, partly in order to learn more definitely, for our own benefit, what were the prospects for a northern man who should fix on this point for a future home, in case he should be driven to a milder climate. Western Texas had charmed us; and of all Western Texas the Upper Guadalupe seemed, all things considered, the most attractive point. I know of no other spot in a Southern state where white agricultural laborers can be hired, than the German neighborhoods of Texas; in fact, no other spot where the relative advantages of white or slave labor can be even discussed in peace. From a thorough examination of Southern agriculture, we had become convinced that slave-labor is everywhere uneconomical and cruel, and, to a man of Northern habits, to the last degree, an irritating annoyance, which, when choosing for a lifetime, he should not voluntarily inflict upon himself. Here new and old emigrants can be hired in all capacities, as in Michigan or Iowa.

Within the German neighborhood, the mountains presented the principal advantage of being free from the malarious diseases of the lower country. Not one of the inhabitants of Sisterdale had had intermittent fever, or had known one day's sickness since their settlement. The elevated country, also, offered purer water, a more invigorating winter, and a cooler and more steady breeze during the long summer. The dry hillside furnished the best range for sheep, and if the position were chosen not too far from the edge of the great mesquit prairies, no pasture in the world could rival this for cattle. The cultivable soil was adapted to wheat—an indispensable luxury. The social privileges, if deficient in some respects, such as access to good public schools, were certainly superior to most back-woods, or even agricultural residences. San Antonio, except the principal port, the most populous and well-stocked town of Texas, would be within a day's ride. Within visiting-reach would be Europeans, of broad cultivation and genial hospitality.

One of the gentlemen of Sisterdale gave us his own reasons for his choice of a residence, and they will not be inappropriate here. He was not an exile, and had even been offered office under the reactionary government after the events of 1848. But he had taken active part on the side of liberal progress, and, well aware that the aristocratic government, once finding itself firmly reëstablished, would not forget its enemies, he determined to look for a home in America while he had the opportunity. He set out with the intention of traveling rapidly over the whole country, and afterwards examining more carefully such points as had attracted him. He landed at Boston. The town pleased him, but the farms were too cold and sterile. With the country around New York he had been delighted, and for a pleasant residence

only he should have chosen Staten Island or Rockland County
over any other position in America ; but he was determined to
engage in agriculture, and could not persuade himself, after investigation, that the sales from a farm here would pay even the
interest on its cost.   The scenery of Vermont and Champlain
was very beautiful, but the long winter too forbidding.   Next he
was induced to stop in Michigan ; but, on examination, he found
two objections : the rich land was low and, unhealthy ; the high
land was gravelly, and with gravel he had previously had experience enough.   With Illinois he was better pleased, as an agricultural country, than any he had seen at the North, particularly
with the high lands along the Mississippi, at no great distance
from St. Louis.   He then traveled through most of the Southern
states, liking extremely their sunny luxuriance.   The hospitali-
ties of Louisiana, and the Creole life there, he had enjoyed vastly,
perhaps from its contrast with his own nature, and would have
been tempted to settle there, but he had become, as he traveled,
disgusted with slave-labor, and the impossibility of using any
other was evident.   He then rode through Texas.   On reaching
the Germans he was so thoroughly delighted with the situation
that he abandoned any further search, and, making a purchase
of a large tract in the mountains, returned at once for his family.
He remains entirely satisfied that his choice was just.

His farm had, for profit, fully equaled his expectations.   I
have mentioned with how little labor he had secured 2,500 bushels
of corn, upon sixty acres of ground.   The price, unfortunately,
this year, had never been known to be so low.   It was worth, on
the spot, but twenty-five cents per bushel.   But none was sold
at this price, and in March we had the pleasure of paying eighty
cents per bushel for what we purchased for the use of our animals

in the neighborhood, and, not long after, the price reached and remained at one dollar. But a new farm demands a great outlay for the first preparation of the land, for the residence and the stock, and readily absorbs, for some years, all the cash it can produce.

Land, in this neighborhood, was generally held in tracts of from 600 to 2,000 acres. In the mountains but one-fifth to one-third of this would be handsomely-lying surface suitable for the plough. The price of land varied, of course, in proportion. Tracts of 1,000 acres, well watered, and containing one-quarter good land, were valued at about $2 per acre ; in 1856, probably, $2 50. Most of those upon the Upper Guadalupe have a front upon the river. For a stock or sheep-farm but few acres are necessary. Forty acres would probably suffice for all desirable purposes, such as preventing a disagreeable contiguity and preserving a convenient outlet to " the range" or great public pasture, as well as for growing sufficient grain and vegetable food for the family and work-horses. The following are the statistical results of our inquiries :

COST OF A STOCK AND SHEEP-FARM.

Land—1,000 acres, at $2 50, - - - -	$2,500
House and furniture, - - - - -	750
Fencing and breaking 50 acres, by contract, -	500
Horses, working oxen, and tools, - - -	350
Stock-cattle 200, at $9 per head, - - -	1,800
Sheep, say 650 Illinois ewes, at $4, - - -	2,600
Improved bucks, - - - - - -	500
	$9,000

ANNUAL PRODUCTION.

23 cows, at $20, - - - - - -	$460	
23 steers, at $20, - - - - - -	460--	$920

Lambs, say 600 improved, at $4 00, -   -   - 2,400
Wool, say 1,300 lbs., at   25,   -   - 325— 2,725
                                                        ———$3,645

Deduct wages, { 2 farmers,   -   -   -   - $360
              { 2 shepherds, -   -   -   - 360— $720
  "   interest on stock, etc., $5,500, at 8
          per cent., -   -   -   -   -   -   440
                                                   ——— 1,160

          Clear returns, -   -   -   -   -   - $2,485
(The *farm*, say $3,500, will pay 8 per cent. in increased value.)

COST OF A COTTON PLANTATION.

Land—1,000 acres, at $2 50, -   -   -   - $2,500
House and furniture,   -   -   -   -   -   600
Fencing and ploughing 70 acres, by contract, -   700
Gin, press mules, harness, and tools, -   -   -   800
Slaves—2 prime hands, $1,000,   -   -   - 2,000
  "   4 half hands, $600, (breeding women) - 2,400

                                              $9,000

ANNUAL PRODUCTION.

At 3 bales per hand, 450 lbs. each, 5,400 lbs., at 6 cents, -   - $324
  "   "   "   "   at 8 cents, -   - 432
At 4 bales "   "   7,200 lbs., at 6 cents, -   - 432
  "   "   "   "   at 8 cents, -   - 576
At 5 bales "   "   9,000 lbs., at 6 cents, -   - 540
  "   "   "   "   at 8 cents, -   - 720

    The average,   -   -   -   -   -   -   -   - $522
    Increase in negroes, 7 per cent.,   -   -   -   -   - 308

                                                      $830
    Deduct clothing and expenses, $150,
      "   interest on capital, at 8 per cent., $720   -   - 870

              Loss, -   -   -   -   -   -   - $40

I have added a similar estimate for a cotton plantation of the same capital. The contrast is very strongly in favor of the farm. The plantation barely pays its eight per cent., at five bales per hand, netting six cents at the press. The farm, losing eight per cent. of lambs and twenty-five per cent. of calves, pays thirty per cent.

It is difficult to fix an average price for cotton. Where land can yet be bought at $2 50 per acre, it is probable that the freight and charges on cotton hauled to the coast would destroy all profit. To be within profitable reach of market, the planter must pay $5 to $10 per acre for a suitable tract of 1,000 acres. This would essentially interfere with the necessary investment in labor.

In this comparison each is supposed to have average luck. Each is understood to provide subsistence, for the first season, for the family and laborers, and afterwards is supposed to obtain the same from the soil, which he finds previously prepared for operations by contract. In practice, a plantation is very often compelled to import both corn and pork, while, from the field cultivated by the farm workmen, with some help from the shepherds, there should be a surplus of corn, beans, and pork for sale.

The following presents the same comparison on a large scale. So extensive a capital has, perhaps, never been applied to sheep-husbandry in this country, but in Mexico far larger farms exist, and such are probably destined to be established in Texas, along the edge of the great Western plains. The same capital invested in a cotton plantation is not rare at the South. I have been told that there are, in one county (Adams), in Mississippi, five men who make over five thousand bales each.

SHEEP ON A LARGE SCALE.

Land—1,000 acres, at $2, - - - -	$2,000
House and furniture, - - - - -	4,000
Fencing and ploughing, by contract, - -	2,000
Tools, horses, wagons, - - - - -	1,500
24,125 Northern sheep, at $4, - - -	96,500
Improved bucks, - - - - - -	14,000
Capital outlay, - - - - -	$120,000

ANNUAL PRODUCTION.

40,000 lbs. wool, at 25 cents, - - - -	- $10,000	
18,000 lambs (25 per cent. lost), at $4, - -	- 72,000	
		$82,000
Deduct wages, 100 Mexican shepherds, at $180,	- $18,000	
" 10 head " 500,	- 5,000	
" 1 bailiff, - - 1,400,	- 1,400	
" 14 farm hands, - 200,	- 2,800	
" 1 farm foreman, - 500,	- 500	
Deduct interest on $115,000, at 8 per cent., - -	9,200	
		36,900
Clear returns, - - - - - -		$45,100

COTTON ON A LARGE SCALE.

Land—2,000 acres, bottom, at $8 50, - -	$17,000
50 prime field hands, at $1,000, - - -	50,000
50 half hands, at - 600, - - -	30,000
50 quarter hands, at - 300, - - -	15,000
House and furniture, - - - - -	4,000
Quarters and overseers' houses, - - -	2,000
Mules and tools, - - - - - -	2,000
Capital outlay, - - - - -	$120,000

ANNUAL PRODUCTION.

At 4 bales per hand, of 450 lbs., 158,400 lbs., at 8 cents, -	$12,672
Increase of slaves, at 5 per cent., $4,750 - - - -	4,750
	$17,422

Deduct annual expenses, - - - - - - $1,000
"   interest on $120,000, at 8 per cent., - - 9,600
                                              10,600

Clear returns,   - - - - - - $6,822

THE COMANCHE SPRING ROAD.

On this second excursion to the mountains, we took the old, now disused, Fredericksburg road, which passes by Comanche spring. We saw but one house after leaving San Antonio till we reached the spring. This was a small stone building, in the centre of a farm, some four miles from the city. A solitary Mexican, who was hoeing corn, directed us on our way. The old road-marks were grown over with grass, and quite indistinct. At Comanche spring, we found a German stock-farmer, with a considerable establishment. The spring gushes from the rocks of a hillside, furnishing a great abundance of clear water. It was covered with a roof, and flowed into large limestone tanks, for what purpose we did not learn. The road had hitherto followed a long, narrow valley, through steep hills, which furnished excellent pasture, but no land for agriculture. We here struck to the right, across the dry bed of the Cibolo, attempting to follow a road which should bring us obliquely to the Guadalupe, some ten miles below Sisterdale. But we soon lost the trail, and at night were obliged to camp without water. In the morning we procured water from a pool in the bed of the Cibolo, whose general course we had followed at no great distance, and then set out by compass toward the northwest, across the grassy hills. Taking the first entering valley that offered in that direction, we left the Cibolo bottom, which is broad and fertile, but wanting in wood and water, and, continually ascending where the best ground offered, found ourselves, after a good deal of labor, upon a rocky ridge that overlooked the Guadalupe. The surface was agitated in steep waves as far as the eye could reach, and with its broken lights and its silvery ribbon of water, winding many miles away, made a rich and effective, though wild, landscape. We marked one of the few settlements in sight, and, after scrambling down a mass of broken rock, found ourselves at the head of a valley which opened directly towards it. On our way down we saw many deer, but were always warily seen by them first.

FORDING THE GUADALUPE.

At last we reached a trail, coming from the southeast, which entered the bed of the Guadalupe, at the foot of the valley, and passed on the opposite side to a house—the settlement we had seen from above. The water appeared deep and swift, and the trail on the opposite bank rose some distance below. The entrance seemed to be by a perpendicular jump of some ten feet, and not one of our animals would approach it. We fell to shouting for directions, and soon a man came from a corn-field, and indicated across the roar a private entrance through a mud-hole. Fanny, as the tallest and most agile, was detailed to explore the depth of water. But she was also the most excitable, and, after nearly breaking her legs among stumps and decaying branches in the deep mud-hole, was very unwilling to breast the furious clear stream. At length, by patient urgency, and step by step, she advanced, staggering with the force of the current, and slipping upon the smooth boulders of the bottom, wetting me to the thighs. In the centre she fell, and, recovering herself, turned her head to the current, and refused to budge, standing, yet on the very point of swimming, apparently poised to a nicety between the contending forces of buoyancy, gravity, and the impulse of the torrent, and ready to yield to the strongest at the slightest movement. From one side, I was recommended, by signs, to come on, from the other to come back. The position became disagreeable and chilly, not to say ridiculous. So, when the mare had somewhat recovered her breath, shaking my feet clear of the stirrups, I gave her the spurs with such cruelty as I was capable of using. The cool suspense was soon terminated by a full cold bath, for after a momentary stagger and plunge, over we rolled, helter-skelter, puffing, sneezing, kicking, and striking out among one another generally. Luckily, the mare's head was towards the further bank, and partly dragged by the bridle, and partly scrambling and swimming, on my own hook, I soon emerged without losing hold of the mare or my temper. Not wishing to have my exertion go for nothing, I procured a stout bag of corn at the house, and, on a second trial, crossed without difficulty. The additional weight, perhaps, secured us a better foothold. If so, the idea should have occurred to us of carrying over the others, puss-back, for the long legs of the mare would certainly have reached and held bottom had she been well ballasted from above. As it was, it was useless to think of getting over dry on the short pegs of Mr. Brown and the pony, and, after drying the wet clothing and distributing the corn among our four-footed companions, we proceeded upon a trail which led up the right bank. After some six miles it also took to the river. As it was now near dusk, and I was indifferently disposed for so active a hydropathic course as that to which an attempt to follow up the examination into the depth and current-force here might have led, we camped upon the bank.

A WANDERING JOURNEYMAN.

We had not been long at rest before we were joined by a short, active German, with a pack, who inquired of us the direction to San Antonio. It appeared he was a German mechanic, who had recently arrived in Texas, and hearing that there was a German settlement without a blacksmith in the mountains, had set out to walk there, and offer his services in exchange for a plot of land where he might raise food for his family. He had lost his way, and had wandered all day along the river, swimming it twice with his clothes upon his head. He had left his wife sick, and had already been out two days longer than he anticipated, and was only anxious to return. We indicated the shortest practicable route across the hills, but, as the sun was setting, advised him to share the hospitality of our tent, and start again in the morning. This he accepted, setting himself at once at work to get wood from the bottom, and helping us through the preparation and the demolition of the supper like an adept, adding a private pone of corn-bread from his pack. From his story, it appeared he had been a traveling apprentice, and had found himself in Pesth on the outbreak of the Revolution in Hungary. He was ordered home to Saxony, and, traveling slowly, had reached Munich at the close of the war, where he was allowed to remain. There he married, and when his time was finished, became an emigrant. In the morning he was off before sunrise, heading for Comanche spring.

CURRIE'S CREEK.

Before we were ready to start, next day, a negro came to the opposite side of the ford, who told us it was easy and safe. We found it so, but too deep for our hampers. We were obliged to unpack them, and carry the contents in successive trips of the mare. Not far beyond the thick wood of the bottom of the north side, we came upon Currie's Creek, and found an American settler, with some negroes. He is owner of an adjacent saw-mill, rented and managed by a German, who appeared a man of education, and, we learned, was one of the exiles who had re-treated to the Guadalupe. At the last freshet, the whole roof of the mill, which is on high ground, and has its power from the creek, was covered by the back-water of the river. The chief wood sawed is cypress, and all lumber finds a ready market.

Our road followed Currie's Creek, a pleasant brook, bordered by meadows, here and there interrupted by ledges of rock, ex-tending from the hills, and walling the roadside with stunted live-oak and cedar. We stopped, a few miles on, near three or four families of American farmers, new settlers, still engaged in finish-ing their houses. The rocky hills here extend in bluffs to the Guadalupe; the creek bottom is wide, and covered with trees, across whose tops we looked from the dry terrace on which we camped.

Going on next day, we gradually mounted the ridge which sheds the water of the creek, and, from the highest point of the road, ascended a little peak not far off. The view was even wider than that on the other side the Guadalupe. The whole upper valley now lay before us, with those of the two Sister creeks and a wild array of tumbled hills to the north. The valleys appeared densely wooded, with here and there a green and fertile prairie. With the glass we could distinguish three houses in the dale, and behind us the settlements we had left three hours before. A dwarf live-oak reached even these sum-mits, with the cactus and the aloes. A coarse, thin grass cover-

ed all the soil.   We were again much struck with the artificial
look of the near hills, and several times in walking stopped,
thinking we had discovered old mason work in the blocks of apparently hewn stone we climbed over.

As we descended, we found thicker grass, and abundant
springs, guaranteeing its verdure through the summer.   There
could not be better range for sheep.   For other purposes it is of
no value.

We met here the first snake of the season, a bright, glistening
fellow, basking upon a ledge.   We interrupted his siesta with a
pistol-ball, as he seemed to us an ugly customer, measuring some
seven feet in length, but we were afterwards familiar with his
species, which is quite harmless to anything else than eggs, for
which they have an irresistible hankering.

VENISON AT LAST.

On one of the grassy slopes we came upon a deer.   He had
not seen us; venison was certain.   Dismounting quietly, we led
the horses a few rods back, the ground covering them.   Then
creeping directly up, as the wind favored, in the cover of a patch
of bushes, I saw the deer still unalarmed, and within easy rifle-
range.   Now, it is necessary to confess, that down to this time,
we had not eaten one morsel of venison of our own shooting.
Many times before, after long preliminaries, I had got within
what I supposed was fair " Sharp" range, and had blazed away
without result, until I began to have a certain distrust of " Sharp."
It might do very well, as I knew, at a target, but seemed to be
less reliable, for some reason, on the open prairie.   But here
there was no occasion for long range, the deer was within almost
pistol-shot.   A barrel of buck might have been a trifle safer, but
as there certainly could be no mistake now, Sharp should have

the credit. I drew a fine bead upon a well-defined spot behind the left shoulder, thinking of how the venison should be packed, and the pleasure we should have, should any of the friends in the Dale visit our camp, in offering them a tender steak, as if it were a matter of course for us to be never without wild meat, and—but it seemed too much like a butcher, dashing in the ribs of the innocent brute, cropping the tender grass just there, all guileless and unsuspicious. However, there was no denying the advantages to mankind. I raised the muzzle again to place, and taking a second cool and deliberate aim, (I would have staked anything on winning at a target) pulled. Crack! Putting my hand to my knife, I stepped forward, to put an end to any brief misery I had created, when I saw my venison going at a spanking rate, down the mountain, a stiff white tail, derisively hoisted, like the colors of a runaway prize, behind him. The Doctor, who had lain looking on with some envy, was already mounted, and driving the mule down the road, in speechless contempt. Quickly breeching another cartridge, I sent a spiteful ball after the flying tail, by this time a mile away, and not waiting to see if it caught the spindle-legged rascal, resumed my seat in the saddle, and a rear position on the road, just beyond conversational distance, having, probably, some idea of the feelings of a centaur when he rejoins his companions with his tail between his legs.

A FIGHT WITH A PRAIRIE FIRE.

On reaching the dale, we crossed the creek, and selected our camping ground on a narrow slope of prairie, near the foot of a rocky spur of the mountains. One stream ran parallel with the hillside, at about two hundred yards distance.

We halted at a spot where three or four large live-oaks, growing at the foot of the hill, threw a shade upon the grass. Having staked the horses out to graze, we proceeded to make our camp. I unrolled the tent, and cut stakes to set it up, while the Doctor began to burn the grass off a small circle of the ground, that we might have a place to cook our supper upon, without danger of setting fire to the prairie at large. There was a strong southerly wind blowing; the grass had not been at all fed down, and was the thickest and heaviest we had anywhere seen, and perfectly dead and dry. Just as the fire was touched to the grass, there came an unusually violent gust, and in a moment it was burning furiously. He immediately attempted to smother it, and fearing that it would get beyond his control, called to me to assist him. I caught up a corn sack, and in half a minute was at his side, but the fire had already spread several feet, and when we tried to prevent its progress to leeward, we were almost immediately so suffocated by heat and smoke from flames to windward, that we were obliged to come back. In another moment the fire was *leaping* along the top of the grass before the wind, and we saw that in this direction it was master of the prairie.

The fire extended itself in an ellipse, slowly to windward, rapidly across the wind, furiously before it. Our first care was to prevent its reaching our tent, ammunition, and camp-stores, which were to windward. The only artillery we could make use of was our corn-sacks; striking hard with these upon the flame at any particular point, it would be blown out and smothered, and the progress of the fire at that point prevented, until it was again reached by the flame from the side.

Starting together, we extinguished the flame at the extreme windward point to which it had reached, and then proceeding from each other each way, we continued to put it out, and to restrict its sidewise progress within two diverging diagonal lines. From the live-oaks, at the foot of the steep hill, there extended along its base, for a hundred yards or more, a thick growth of brushwood. Following up the fire industriously in this direction, I soon had arrested its windward progress until it had reached the coppice, within which, as its only fuel was a few dry leaves and dead sticks, I was glad to perceive it extended very slowly. I therefore joined the Doctor, who was in a similar manner following it up on the right. Finding one of us could, with certainty, prevent its extending to windward, we hastened its advance laterally by drawing it along with a burning wisp, as fast as we could, and still keep it within our control, until we reached the bank of the creek. There was then no danger of its reaching the camp until it had burned around the coppice, and advanced to windward beyond the live-oaks.

Before us there were now several acres of black, smoking, ground, beyond which the flames and white smoke still roared frightfully, and entirely obscured the view. Running around the live-oaks, and along the side of the hill, to the left, to see what the progress might be in that direction, we found that there were several irregularly parallel coppices and outcrops of rock, which interrupted and divided the advance of the fire, so that, although when it reached a steep slope of thick grass it swept over it with flashing rapidity, its movement up the hill was, on the whole, comparatively slow.

I continued running along the hillside, above the fire, to observe how far it had reached directly to leeward, and what was before it in that direction. We were very fearful of the damage that might be done to the settlers by our carelessness, there being

10

the liability, not only of the destruction of their remaining winter pasture, but also that their fences, and even their cabins and
fodder-stacks and cattle, might be consumed by the fire driving
so furiously before the wind. I found there was a curve to the
left, in the course of the creek, and of the hill, and, at about a
quarter of a mile beyond the camp, came to a small gully or
ravine which ran straight down the hillside, and across the prairie at its foot, to the creek. The sides of this gully, which was
about ten feet deep and twenty feet across on the top, were thinly
covered, to the foot of the steep hill, with trees and brushwood,
and it occurred to me that it might be possible to stop the progress of the flame as it came down its windward side, where it
crossed the prairie below, and then to put it out as it came irregularly and divided through the bushes.

The van of the fire had already arrived at the bushy part of
the gully, and the two wings were coming up, as I have described,
in elliptic sweeps—one upon the prairie, the other upon the steep
hillside. I arrived at the foot of the bushes, in the gully, just as
the right wing of the fire upon the prairie began to pass them.
There was, fortunately, a slight shift of the wind to the right of
the fire at this moment, occasioned, probably, by the fire itself,
so that its advance down the side of the gully was rather sidewise
to the wind, and I could crawl on my knees close under, and
beat it back with my sack. The grass was stronger and taller
than usual at this point, and some dead bushes retained the fire,
so that I had much difficulty in smothering it, and was obliged
repeatedly to return; nevertheless I succeeded in breaking the
line, and continued advancing and increasing the length of the
gap faster than the flame came up on the right to the gully.
Finally, I reached the creek again, and effectually prevented the

further advance of the fire here by touching off some long rushy bogs in the edge of the water, and then putting it out with my wet sack to the leeward of these also. A triangle of the prairie was thus left burning on the edge of the creek, but was surrounded by water and burned ground, so that its communication with the prairie beyond was entirely cut off.

The sun had gone down, and it had grown dark before I had accomplished this, and the wind had considerably moderated, as well as changed its direction. I returned up the hill on the burned ground, and found the fire had been successfully withstood by the bushes in the gully, and the flames were advancing among them only at intervals and slowly. Wherever they appeared, I easily succeeded in smothering them. Thus the enemy, which had before been charging in column, with resistless force, upon the smooth prairie, was able only to move in a long line, irregular and broken by the scattered masses of brushwood and the ledges, up the hill, and its right upon the gully, and its left upon the coppice and live-oaks of our camp.

Advancing upon the fire in its rear, and running through the flame, I found the Doctor, taking advantage of the lull of the wind, setting fire to the grass to the windward of the main line, and constantly smothering it and preventing its progress to leeward, so that when the flame, charging only to windward, met the other, it would have cut off its fuel and thus arrest it. He was then moving up and across the hill, always advancing diagonally upon the main fire, and destroying all the grass before it, between the scattered copses of brushwood. I went to the left of the line and there pursued the same tactics, advancing upwards and sidewise upon the hillside, setting fire to the grass to windward of me, and allowing none to burn to leeward. After about two hours of this labor we met, and though the fire was still burning with a great roar around a large circle below us, we had the satisfaction of knowing that we had entirely surrounded it and cut off its supplies, and restricted its damages to a matter of small consequence. If it had reached the prairie beyond the gully or over the hill, it might have extended to Canada or California for all we could do.

There is something peculiarly exciting in combatting with a fierce fire. It calls out the energies and the strength of a man like actual war. We had been hotly engaged for more than three hours, and it may be imagined we returned to our tent, after patrolling together our whole outer lines, greatly exulting and fatigued. Our wounds were mainly for the good of the trade of shoemakers and tailors, and the singeing our heads received somewhat postponed our poll-tax payment to the hair-cutters. The landscape was still brightly illuminated by the central fire on the hillside, and we amused ourselves with each other's appearance, our faces, red with heat, being painted in a very bizarre fashion, like Indian warriors', with streaks and spots, and clouds of soot and coal.

Having got up our tent and washed, and changed our drenched clothing, and made a pot of coffee, and watered our horses, and given them corn, we brought out our blankets and lay down in the edge of the standing grass, and waited still an hour, that we might be sure all was safe for the night, before we went to sleep. And as the flames grew less, and the smoke-cloud slowly vanished, and the big, red moon came up swelling like a balloon on the other side of the dale, and the ants came crawling up our legs, and the first musquito of the season came singing in our ears, we reflected on the immense destruction of insect life that such fires must occasion, and recalled, in the leisure of imagination, some of the scenic effects of the flame and smoke hurrying up the face of the hill, that had passed with but momentary perception while we were in the heat of our exertions.

"The fear of the damage it might do the settlers," said the Doctor, "did not make me feel the culpability of starting the fire, nearly as much as seeing the ants crowding away from it upon the stones in the edge of the water, when we had carried it down to the creek, and afterwards, when I noticed the tumultuous excitement of a wren, that probably had a nest in the bushes."

The grandest and most remarkable picture that had painted itself on my memory, had presented itself at the time when I came up the hill in the rear of the fire. The ground under me, and above the level of the eyes before me, was black as the darkness of the darkest night. I could see nothing, and knew not on what I should place my foot. I stretched out my hands before my face, to defend me from anything that might stand in my way, and I could not see my hands. I particularly noticed this, and it seemed to me I was groping in a sea of darkness, when just over me there was an atmosphere of light. My eyes, looking upward, were dazzled. The tide of fire was moving on, in one grand, clean sweep, and, through the waving flames and the turbid surge of hurrying sparks and lurid smoke, I saw, in distinct brightness, the ragged edges of the protruding rocks, and of the rough bark of old trunks and branches of dwarf-oaks, and the young leaf-points of the bushes, in their springing life, against the dim red dusk of the general grassy slope—and, further up, the outline of the hill itself against the dark, distant sky.

TO SAN ANTONIO.—QUI VIVE.

We spent a week in this camp, visiting and visited by the settlers, examining tracts of land, and collecting such agricultural information as we could; the general results of which have been tabled above. We then rode over the rocky hills again, and followed the Comanche Spring road to San Antonio. During the last night's camp, some miles below the Spring, we were disturbed by some noise in the night. Going out, we could discover nothing but the growling dog; the horses were feeding quietly at their stakes. Shortly after, we heard what might be a smothered foot-fall, but after a more thorough search, returned to our blankets again. While we were building the fire, after morning dawned, a well-armed party came up, consisting of an American, with two negroes, and a small pack of hounds. The negroes crouched at the fire.

"Mornin', gentlemen," said the white man.

"Good morning, sir."

"Travlin'?"

"Yes."

"Well. I swaar you came near not travlin' much further, last night."

"How so?"

"Well, you see, I've lost my horses since a week ago, and bein' as how a new settler, I couldn't very well afford to do without 'em. Late last night, I heerd bells around, so I went and roused out two of my niggers, and told 'em to see if that wan't our horses ranging back again. Well, they went out, and by and by came back almighty skeered, a sayin' they'd follerd 'em by the bells over the hills this way, and had come into a Mexican camp before they knew it. Well, I knew as no honest

Mexicans could have any good business over here, and I just put on my boots, and told 'em to call the rest, and get the dogs, and I got the guns, and we set out to see who ye was. So when we got here, I kinder scooted roun' to see what I could, and I tell you I didn't like the looks o' ye. I told part of 'em to go down the road round the hill, and I went up with the rest that way, and when we got covered up with the hill we made a fire and lay round till daylight, keepin' watch of ye. Tell ye what, if ye'd budged much, you'd have got some buck-shot in your stomachs, you may bet on that. Them's likely animals you've got there."

"Yes, sir."

"Well, I'll go 'long. Han't seen a pair of gray horses, have ye, with a bay mare with 'em?"

Moral: (For prairie travelers,) Never mind what's stirring, lie quiet in your blankets.

GAME.

A good deal of large game is still found in these hills, though it is disappearing before the rapid settlement of the country. As an evidence of its past abundance, we were told that a gentleman, who resided at Comanche Spring, undertook to make, a few years since, a collection of the skins of Texan wild animals for a Prussian cabinet. He employed a German carpenter of the vicinity, for nine months, to hunt for him, and during this period the man delivered to him 11,000 lbs. of wild meat. There was still, at a spot near Currie's Creek, a man who made his livelihood by hunting. He kept a pack of trained hounds, and had killed sixty bears in the course of two years. During the last year, he had devoted himself to bee-hunting, and had sold two hundred dollars' worth of honey and wax. Mr. Vogt, a herdsman on the Cibolo, told us that wild cattle were still to be seen on the ridge between the Cibolo and the Medina. They frequently associate with his herds, and almost every year he shoots two or three of them. He describes them as of various colors, small, and very active, and the bulls as of a savage ferocity.

We passed, on the Salado, a second flock of five or six of the immense white cranes (I suppose *grus Americana*), mentioned previously. We did our best to get one in hand, but found them exceedingly shy, even of Sharp's rifle.

"HEAPS" OF BEARS.

While in the mountains, the settlers told us, with fresh excitement, the story of a great bear-hunt, which had but recently come off. The hero was one of the German hermits, named P——, a famous sportsman. Not long before, he had had a "personal difficulty" with a bear, in which, after the animal had drawn his fire, he closed with the hunter, now armed only with a knife, upon a rocky ledge, and attempted either to throw him over the precipice, or to force him, in pure vengeance, to roll down the steep with himself. Almost crushed with the hug, P., with his one free hand, had succeeded in giving the bear seven deep stabs, and left him dead upon the verge.

On the last occasion, he had wounded a bear, who took to his heels, and disappeared in a pile of rocks. Following with all his speed, P. found a hole, down which the bear seemed to have dropped. Convinced that his shot had been fatal, yet unable to enter the cavity, he pried a large stone over the mouth, and went for assistance. His hut-companion returned with him, and they at first attempted to smoke the bear out. Not succeeding in this, they battered the edges of the aperture till it was large enough to enter. Then, held by the heel, P. went on his hands in search of his booty. After some not very pleasant groping, he found the carcass, and, attaching a rope, it was hauled out, a magnificent he-bear, worth a good deal in cash, and much more in glory. But while half-smothered in the cave, he had heard an indistinct growl, at no great distance, which indicated that more fun was to be had, if properly applied for. It was a hazardous experiment, but one that exactly suited P.'s humor, to enter, and have a hand-to-hand fight in the dark with the growler, whoever he was.

Arming himself with a freshly capped and cocked Colt, and placing a knife between his teeth, he crept cautiously in again. The passage shortly became narrow, and he soon reached a turn which he could only pass feet foremost. Retreating a bit, he turned himself, and pushed on. On clearing the obstacle, he found himself free, and heard now close before him, the steady breathing of a bear. It was a darkness of Erebus, but hit or miss he resolved to have a shot. Aiming, deliberately, at the sound, he fired two barrels, then took himself out as fast as hands and knees would carry him. But no stir followed, and it was impossible to tell the result.

Piling the rocks again over the aperture, the two returned to their hut, manufactured torches of wax from a bee-tree, and calling a neighbor or two to see the sport, went again to the den. Armed now with a torch, P. forced himself to where he had been before, and saw his bear lying dead. It was dragged out.

After a congratulatory and recuperative draught of whisky all round, P. resolved on further explorations. He found, beyond the scene of his last adventure, a narrow cleft in the rocks. He had hardly squeezed himself into this, when he suddenly found his hand in contact with a third bear—*dead*. It had probably

10*

been smothered by their smoke.   This, too, was got out amid an excitement that made the woods ring with echoes.

But if three bears had been found, that was no reason why there should not be more beyond.   Creeping down again to the cleft, he squeezed in, head foremost, as before.   He had not progressed far, when he was met with a savage roar, and the glare of a pair of mad eyes in motion directly before him.   He attempted to fall back to recover himself, but one of the neighbors, who had made up his mind to have a finger in the pie, was close behind, and prevented, by his entangled body, any quick retreat; so aiming hurriedly between the eyes, he fired.   Before his excited senses had recovered from the reverberated din and smoke, he saw the eyes again in a different place, this time fixed in a steady gaze.   He fired again.   The echoes over, nothing more was to be seen or heard.   Advancing cautiously once more, he came upon *two warm carcasses, both shot between the eyes.*   Here was the end of the cave.   He had killed the whole of the Bruin family.

Imagine the cheers, when the *five bears* were carried by his neighbors, on poles, into the settlement, P. striding modestly at the rear.   A three days' feast of bears'-meat and whisky was proclaimed and celebrated, and P., if he do not, like old Put., find his way into history, will at least live long in local tradition.

CHAP. IV.

A TRIP TO THE COAST.

WE left San Antonio on the 14th of February for an excursion to the coast. The road lies, for some miles, through mesquit chapparal, which extends much further from the town than on the Austin road. It is sparse, however, and good grass grows beneath it. The Mexican inhabitants make use of these great commons, driving in their cows every night.

A MULE SPIRT.

Our week in the mountains Mr. Brown had spent in corn-fed idleness at the inn-stables. On resuming the hampers, he eyed them wickedly, as if he were more than half inclined to resist, and, when we reached the crossing of the Cibolo, with a snort of fat defiance, he suddenly declared his independence, and tearing his lariat from our hands, set off to display his claims to the original freedom of his ancestors. Throwing his ears and his heels straight out behind him, he made first for the nearest cover of tall brushwood. Saplings were of no consideration at all, and were prostrated in a flash, leaving a broad trail, as if a mowing machine had passed. But the hampers were well tackled on, and stood the test. Next came a series of ground and lofty tumblings on both sides the creek bank, and in the creek itself, which were equally unsuccessful. Of course we were after him with all our legs; but the freakish course he ran was more than we could follow and keep up the necessary laughter at the same time, and we were much relieved when we saw him suddenly strike out on a bee-line, across the prairies, for Metamoras, the hampers still clinging like wolves to his flanks. Fanny was fully equal to any bee-line that ever was drawn, and though a short-legged mule, when fully under way on a stampede, is "some pumpkins" at going, she made brief work of the intervening distance, and I very soon had the lariat round the pommel of the saddle, and the chop-fallen runaway in tow back to the ford.

These proceedings occupied some time; but the damages we found, on examination, were confined to the breaking of our thermometer and the indiscriminate mixing of some articles that had been better apart. Rain soon began to fall, and we made a short day of it, camping in the lee of a mesquit thicket, some twelve or fourteen miles from San Antonio.

Mr. Brown was securely fastened by the nose to a high branch, and so, for his sins, took supperless a cold standee for the night. When morning came, his ears and spirits were completely wilted, and he always carefully avoided the subject of his private Cibolo stampede—never afterwards offering the least symptom of insurrection.

A WET NORTHER.

Next day the rain continued falling, with occasional dashes of snow, a cutting north wind, making matters very disagreeable. We, of course, kept camp. Without our tent we should have had a sorry time of it; but, with a dry cover, good books, a rousing fire, and a freshly-stocked havre-sack, time passed easily enough. The protection given by the thin clump of trees was astonishing. The tent was hardly shaken, while out of the lee it was difficult to support the furious and continued force of the blast.

February 16.—Rain at intervals. We rode on to the Guadalupe, and camped in the bottom. The country was mesquit prairie, hilly, and much covered with thickets, but fine grazing. We saw many cattle in very fine order, and one large cavallada of about two hundred mares and colts. Our tent stood under a magnificent cypress, overhung with enormous vines. Fuel was abundant, and we did not spare it. The fire-glare lighted up a grand dome of leaves resplendent with the falling rain.

February 17.—A light rain continued. We made a stew for breakfast of such small birds as came within range of the frying-pan. A boy, attracted by our guns or by the savory odor, made his appearance on horseback, attended by a pack of hounds. He seemed somewhat taken aback on observing our comfortable arrangements, and after a tame proposal to " to swop horses," took his departure.

A BLACK LIFE.

Soon afterwards an old negro man and woman came by with a team, going for rails. They stopped near us, and the old man came to our fire for a brand to light their pipes. We asked him if we could get corn at his master's. He didn't reckon we could.

" Why not ?"

" 'Cause he buys all he uses himself."

" Why don't he raise it ?"

" Well, he ha'n't been long in the country."

" How long ?"

"Only one year.   But I've been roun' these parts these four year."

"Where have you lived before?"

"Well, I lived in Arkansaw 'fore I come here."

"Were you born there?"

"Lor' bless you, no.   I was born on the Eastern shore [of Maryland]."

"How came you in Arkansas?"

"My mass'r sold me to go in a drove when I was a little boy, and I was bought out of the drove in South Carolina, and when I was most a man grown my mass'r moved to Tennessee.   Thar I got my old woman, and we raised thirteen chil'en.   Then we was sold to go to Arkansaw."

"Did your children go with you?"

"No, but afterwards my mass'r bought one of my darters. There I stayed some time, and then we was sold to a German, and he sold me to a man that was coming to Texas.   Mass'r couldn' jus' find a place to suit him at first, and I hired my time for three year, and lived in San Antone."

"How did you like San Antonio?"

"I never lived no-where I liked so well as San Antone."

"How did you get on with the Mexicans and the Germans?"

"Oh, very well; they're very civil people and always treated me well.   I never had no complaint to make of anybody, and I b'leeve everybody was sorry when I had to leave."

"Why did you leave?"

"They made a law that no nigger shouldn't hire his time in San Antone, so I had to cl'ar out, and mass'r wanted me, so I come back to him."

"How much did you pay for yourself?"

" Tree hundred dollar a year for both on us. Wasn't that pretty good wages, mass'r, for two old folks?"

" How old are you?"

" Well, sar, so far as I am acquainted, I am sixty-four years old; just about sixty-four, sar."

They remained near us in the rain, cutting at opposite sides of a big tree. We passed, soon after we started, the field to which they were carting the rails. Half-a-dozen women and two or three men were eating their dinner—corn-pone and eggs. A little apart was a woman, nursing her child, sitting on the newly-ploughed wet ground.

SEGUIN.

About a mile from the river we entered Seguin. It is the prettiest town in Texas; at least of those we saw. It stands on elevated ground, in a grove of shaggy live-oaks, which have been left untouched, in their natural number and position, the streets straying through them in convenient directions, not always at right angles. How wonderful, that so cheap and rich an ornamentation should not be more common. The hotel is large and good. We were kindly treated, and furnished with clear information, at the store of Mr. Wuppermann, of whom we purchased some supplies. Irish potatoes were sold by him, we noted, at $6 the bushel, for seed. A number of buildings in Seguin are made of concrete—thick walls of gravel and lime, raised a foot at a time, between boards, which hold the mass in place until it is solidified. As the materials are dug from the cellar, it is a very cheap mode of construction, is neat in appearance, and is said to be as durable, while protected by a good roof, as stone or brick. One man may erect a house in this way, calling in mechanics only to roof and finish.

We camped near the San Geronimo creek, at the edge of a live-oak grove, looking across a charming lawn. The rain continuing, we were obliged to spend the following day in camp. With the help of the mule we got together some huge live-oak logs, and made a quasi-permanent fire-place, which kept a-glow all night.

A negro, who was getting wood near us, informed us that he was born in Tennessee, and wished he was back there again— Texas was a miserable place for the likes o' him. There were several houses in the neighborhood, at which we obtained fowls and eggs. At one house a long consultation on the subject resulted favorably, and three negro girls, two boys, and two dogs were set upon the unfortunate pullets. All the whites with whom we talked were well pleased with the country—they had had uniform good health and satisfactory crops. One family had come from a river county in Missouri, and congratulated themselves much upon the change.

February 19.—The rain ceased, and a light breeze sprung up from the southwest. The road soon entered post-oak woods and sandy land. This alternated with black hog-wallow prairies. The depressions varied from two to six yards across, and had now each a miry centre. The soil is more tenacious than the ordinary prairies, and produces well, only in peculiar seasons, which afford it neither too much nor too little moisture. Here and there were ledges and hills of limestone, and, sometimes, what appeared to be a red sandstone, cropping out. We passed Mount Capote, which is a wooded summit, terminating a long range of hills. Though not high, it is the only object that rises above the general surface, and can be seen for a great distance. We went through some small rich prairies, where the mesquit and sedge grasses were mixed. The cattle upon these looked in good condition, but upon the large hog-wallows were in very bad order.

February is a spring month in Texas, and, in spite of the cold, we had already found one or two feeble flowers near our camps.

To-day, the genial sun warmed the fresh moistened soil, and three or four more species opened into bloom. After this hardly a day passed without some addition, and very soon it was impossible to welcome each new-comer; the whole prairies became radiant and delicious. The beauty of the spring-prairies has never been and never will be expressed. It is inexpressible.

A few days sufficed now, in fact, to change the whole face of nature. A quick flush spread over all; the bosom of old Mother Earth seemed to swell with life.

In another day the elm-buds were green and bursting, and the wild plum in fragrant blossom; the dreary, burnt prairies, from repulsive black, changed at once to a vivid green, like that of young wheat. The cheering effect I leave to be imagined. The herds all left the dry sedge, and flocked to the new pastures. The unburnt districts, covered with the thick mat of last year's growth, were a month behind.

We passed, in the afternoon, a cotton field in the river bottom. The stalks were short, but much cotton remained unpicked. The country is more suited to small farms and grazing than to planting.

Toward night we could find no water for our camp. At a house, where we inquired, they told us they brought water from the river, half a mile. We stopped by a water-hole, fresh filled by the rain. A great many cardinals came about our camp. Their notes were now very clear, varied, and agreeable, their plumage a somewhat dingy scarlet, but flashing bright when on the wing.

GUADALUPE LANDS.

The bottom lands of the Guadalupe here are usually from two to four miles wide. They are said to be less subject to overflow than those of any other large river in Texas. They are covered with timber, which is mainly heavy and very valuable, especially so here where timber of any kind is difficult to be procured. The principal sorts are white-oak, pecan, walnut, hickory, box-alder, mulberry, cotton-wood, and cypress.

Exterior to the timber, on each side, is generally a portion of flat bottom-prairie. It has a rich, black, clay soil, difficult to work, but producing heavy crops. Beyond this bottom-prairie, the surface rises abruptly to uplands, which present a good deal of variety in soil and scenery. The largest part is rolling prairie, with some chapparal and groves of live-oaks near the terrace. Further back are sandy elevated tracks, the soil of which is comparatively poor and covered by a thin growth of post-oaks.

The banks of the river, on both sides, are considered to be well settled. The houses of the residents are, perhaps, a mile apart on the more valuable parts. On the east side are some families who came here before the Revolution. Most of the settlers are extensive herdsmen and small planters. The plantations have a small front on the river, and extend back sometimes several miles over the upland prairie, no part of which is inclosed. Only the best of the bottom land is cultivated, and of that, probably, much less than a hundredth part.

A large proportion, perhaps almost half, of the white residents we saw were Germans. Their tracts are usually small, not more than from twenty to one hundred acres, which they till with their own hands. The American proprietors own, generally, at least, one thousand acres, and work each from five to fifty slaves. There are very few Mexicans. The Americans are exceedingly suspicious of their vicinity, and drive them off at the least provocation. Those who remain are poor, owning small herds.

On the 20th February we reached Gonzales. The prairies through which the road passes were cropped very close, and we passed many carcasses of cattle, that had miserably perished by the road, of cold and starvation.

The late storm coming at the end of winter caused the destruction of a great number of cattle, both working oxen, belonging to teams that were engaged in hauling goods to San Antonio, and the half-starved herds upon the poorer and most exposed prairies. A little care to provide shelter and fodder for these rare occasions would prevent this great suffering and loss; but in not one instance did we see any such forethought.

We passed a number of old places having much the aspect of Virginia plantations, inclosed within very high zigzag fences, with gin-houses, negro women ploughing, and sometimes a small garden, and a half dozen peach-trees.

We were joined by a planter from the opposite side of the river, where there are many Tennesseeans and Mississippians. He was from Tennessee; had moved first to Alabama, afterwards to Mississippi, whence he came to Eastern Texas. He didn't like it there, and pushed on. He liked the country better and better as he came further, and finally reached the lower

Guadalupe, where he hired land, and was able to purchase it with the proceeds of his first crop. But he found it sickly there, and came higher up. Here he was well satisfied. They had no sickness, but a little bilious fever and very light fever and ague. There was a good deal of pneumonia in winter. The land was very fine; he made one bale to the acre always, and always grew twice as much cotton as his hands could pick. Seven bales to the hand was a common crop, and of corn forty to fifty bushels. He had known ten bales to the hand to be made, and had heard of a hundred bushels of corn to the acre, but had never seen it.

Land had "bounced up powerful." A tract that he could have bought, three years ago, for two dollars, had just been sold at ten dollars. The mustang grape, he told us, was very abundant in the bottoms. It was not worth much to eat, but made beautiful wine. The Germans made it right fine, he heard. Last year he thought he'd try it himself. He mashed them in a barrel, and let them stand and work for six or eight days, then drained them, and bottled the juice. "It was splendid; made a splendid drink, sir, splendid; as good as any cider ever you see." He could get a wagon load in a day if he wanted, and next year he would make a good lot, and squeeze them in his cotton-press.

The price of cattle was now very high, six dollars per head for stock-cattle. He had known a sale at seven dollars. A cow and calf sold at from fifteen to twenty dollars. This expression, "stock cattle," is constantly used to express the usual herd of cattle bought as herdsmen's stock. It includes here all the cows of a herd, with their calves, and all young cattle under three years of age.

He spoke very highly of the Germans of the neighborhood. There were some thieves among them, but, in general, they were very steady workers, trustworthy, and needing no watching when hired; they were very friendly-disposed people. The hire of negroes was now very high. First rate hands, $300; ordi-nary hands, $150 to $250.

GONZALES.

Gonzales is a town of perhaps one thousand inhabitants. It is a centre of distribution for hardware and whisky for a rich district, and is probably destined to a steady increase until the soil of the district is exhausted. It has at present nothing to distinguish it from other towns. There is the usual square of dead bare land, surrounded by a collection of stores, shops, drinking and gambling-rooms, a court-house, and a public-house, or two, with the nearly vacant mapped streets behind.

We could procure no flour, meal, corn, or crackers in town. The price of corn, by the load, was seventy-five cents per bushel; of bacon, twenty-five cents per pound. At a German baker's we found wheat-bread. He informed us that there were about fifty Germans in the town—a few were farmers, most were mechanics.

Our camp, at night, was a few miles beyond Gonzales, in thick post-oak woods. We applied at an adjacent house for water, and were directed to a pool half a mile distant. When found, it made a poor beverage, even after boiling, and, by morning light, we discovered it was so extremely dirty that we postponed any personal ablutions till a better opportunity. This was soon offered in the tolerably clear stream of Peach Creek, a few miles on.

BROADER VIEWS.

Beyond Peach Creek bottoms, the scenery becomes more and more open. The bare prairie hills extend to the flowed river bottom. Scattered at distances of about a mile, along the road, are the houses of herdsmen. The soil is black, but sandy. After twenty miles' ride, we camped in a charming spot, by the side of a clear rippling brook, hanging our tent between two superb live-oaks, upon a swell of prairie, on our right a motte of moss-hung trees, through which we saw the sun go down, lurid and swollen, in the smoke of a distant prairie fire. The horses regaled themselves with the fresh grass. For corn, both yesterday and to-day, we paid one dollar the bushel. To-day it proved quite uneatable from mould. Throughout the South, corn is stored in rude cribs, or half-covered piles, always unhusked. The consequence is, it is almost always musty. The bushel is a barrel of ears in the husk, the purchaser stripping it for himself, a task which added not a little to our daily camp labors. Even when carted thirty miles' distance, the corn is left upon the cob and in the husk.

A thick mist came up in the night, which dropped from the oak leaves so rapidly upon the tent as to induce me to get up to rebuild the fire, thinking it rain.

COTTON HAULING—THE ROADS.

February 22.—The country was much more wooded than yesterday, frequent mottes of live-oak, coppices of mesquit, and forests of post-oak, diversifying the prairie. The houses were old, and of a more comfortable sort. We saw near some of them the first peach-blossoms of the season. We passed cotton-fields again, and wagons loaded with cotton. One carrying eight bales, drawn by ten very lean oxen, was from San Marcos, bound to the coast. The teamster, who was on horseback, told us his best day's work was ten miles. Across the wet hog-wallow prairie of the latter part of the day, the road was very heavy. In the creek, near which we made our camp, was a cotton team stalled, and it was late at night before the whipping and swearing came to an end. While we were at breakfast in the morning, the teamster drove by his cattle, which had strayed away in the night for better pasture, and stopped to ask our assistance. He had cut trees for fulcrum and lever, and thought with our help he should be able to get out. We worked for an hour under his guidance, covering ourselves with mire, but effecting nothing. A man appeared on horseback, who added his forces. After perceiving that our combined efforts would not suffice to raise the wheel, he said, "Stranger, I'll give you my advice. I'm sick, and not able to help you much. I'm going now to see a doctor. But your wagon isn't very badly stalled, sir. The mire is not deep here. That wheel is on the gravel now. I'll tell you what's the matter ; your cattle are too weak. Now you take them all out, and give them a feed, and turn them out to graze till another team comes up, and they'll have to help you, because there isn't room to get by. And I'll tell you what I'll do. I'll call at the overseer's (of roads), and tell him you sent for him to help you. He's got plenty of teams and hands, and if he don't come, you return him (to the County Court), because he's no business to leave a place like this in the road." With that he mounted, and rode on. We did the same, the teamster offering us no thanks, but shouting after us, "What'll you take for that mule?"

We saw again along the road to-day many dead cattle. The

herds were miserably poor in flesh.   Most of the carcasses were of working oxen, usually from the carts of Mexicans, who give their teams no corn, depending entirely upon the pasturage. The latter part of the day, the road left the river, and stretched out upon flat, high, sandy prairies, the poorest prairie land we have seen.

SLAVE EMIGRANTS.

Toward night, we entered on the great level prairies of the coast.   Here we met a gang of negroes, three men, two women, and two boys, under guard of a white man and a very large yellow mastiff.   The negroes had each some article to carry, one an axe, another a rifle, another a kettle, a fourth led a horse, to whose saddle were fastened a ham, a coffee-pot, and a buffalo robe.   This last, undoubtedly, would be the white man's covering at night, the negroes having no extra clothing. They were evidently slaves consigned to some planter in the interior, probably by his factor in New Orleans, as part of the proceeds of his crop.

They were much fagged, and sullen with their day's walk. The prospect before them was a boundless flat prairie, with a cold north wind, and rain threatening.   They were evidently intending to camp upon the open prairie, as for eight miles we had passed no house.   Before midnight, a severe rain-storm did, in fact, commence.

VICTORIA.

Shortly before reaching Victoria, we came into a German settlement.   The houses were poor and small, and indicated m uch less thrift than any we had seen.

Victoria is a very ditto of Gonzales, and all the rest. It stands on the great flat coast prairie, near the edge of the river bottom.

It is an old settled town, and has about 1,000 inhabitants. About half its population are Germans, many of whom remained at the first settled spot reached during the great immigration. Several tracts adjacent were divided into plots for them, which they eagerly bought with their savings, or first earnings, and are now unable to sell without the loss of their improvements. Two of them together commonly bought a lot of forty acres. Comparing their position with that of their countrymen in the upper country, it was really pitiful. Many of the lots we saw were undrained flats, now half under water, which sometimes surrounded the houses, covered with a green slime. Yet they told us the town was not unhealthy, and the Americans assured us that it was as healthy as any town in Texas, and much more so than Gonzales, in particular. Yellow fever had visited them the previous year, but was said not to have been epidemic. On the coast we were told that it was an extremely unhealthy town, severe bilious and congestive fevers prevailing every year.

We found the town ill-provided with provisions and goods; and for all small articles we were charged exorbitant prices. Corn was not to be had. Its nominal price was $1 50 per bushel.

NIGHT ON A PLANTATION.

We went on some miles beyond Victoria, and not finding a suitable camping place, stumbled, after dark, into a large plantation upon the river bottom.

The irruption of such a train within the plantation fences caused a furious commotion among the dogs and little negroes, and it was with no little difficulty we could explain to the planter, who appeared with a candle, which was instantly blown out, upon the porch, our peaceable intentions. Finally, after a general

11

striking out of Fanny's heels and the master's boots, aided by the throwing of our loose lariats into the confused crowd, the growling and chattering circle about us was sufficiently enlarged and subdued for us to obtain a hearing, and we were hospitably received.

"Ho Sam! You Tom, here! Call your missus. Suke! if you don't stop that infernal noise I'll have you drowned! Here Bill! Josh! some of you, why don't you help the gentleman? Bring a lantern here! Packed, are you, sir. Hold on, you there, leave the gun alone. Now, clear out with you, you little devils, every one of you! Is there no one in the house? St! after 'em, Tiger! Can't any of you find a lantern? Where's Bill, to take these horses? What are you doing there? I tell you to be off, now, every one of you! Tom! take a rail and keep 'em off there!"

In the midst of the noise we go through the familiar motions, and land our saddles and hampers upon the gallery, then follow what appears to be the headmost negro to the stable, and give him a hint to look well out for the horses.

This is our first reintroduction to negro servants after our German experiences, and the contrast is most striking and disagreeable. Here were thirty or forty slaves, but not an order could be executed without more reiteration, and threats, and oaths, and greater trouble to the master and mistress, than would be needed to get a squadron under way. We heard the master threaten his negroes with flogging, at least six times, before we went to bed. In the night a heavy rain came up, and he rose, on hearing it, to arrange the cistern spout, cursing again his infernal niggers, who had turned it off for some convenience of their own. In the morning, we heard the mistress scolding her girls for having left articles outside which had been spoiled by the wet, after repeated orders to bring them in. On visiting the stables we found the door fastened by a board leaned against it.

All the animals were loose, except the mule, which I had fastened myself. The rope attached to my saddle was stolen, and a shorter one substituted for it, when I mentioned the fact, by which I was deceived, until we were too far off to return. The master, seeing the horses had yet had no fodder, called to a boy to get some for them, then, countermanding his order, told the boy to call some one else, and go himself to drive the cows out of the garden. Then, to another boy, he said, " Go and pull two or three bundles of fodder out of the stack and give these horses." The boy soon came with two small bundles. " You infernal rascal, couldn't you tote more fodder than that? Go back and bring four or five bundles, and be quick about it or I'll lick you." The boy walked slowly back, and returned with four bundles more.

But on entering at night we were struck with the air of comfort that met us. We were seated in rocking-chairs in a well-furnished room, before a blazing fire, offered water to wash, in a little lean-to bed-room, and, though we had two hours to wait for our supper, it was most excellent, and we passed an agreeable evening in intelligent conversation with our host.

After his curiosity about us was satisfied, we learned from him that, though a young man, he was an old settler, and had made a comfortable fortune by his plantation. His wife gave us a picturesque account of their wagon journey here with their people, and described the hardships, dangers, and privations they had at first to endure. Now they were far more comfortable than they could have ever hoped to have been in the state from which they came. They thought their farm the best cotton land in the world. It extended across a mile of timbered bottom land from the river, then over a mile of bottom prairie, and included a large tract of the big prairie " for range." Their field would produce, in a favorable season, three bales to the acre; ordinarily a bale and a half: the "bale" 400 lbs. They had always far more than their hands could pick. It was much more free from weeds than the states, so much so, that three hands would be needed there to cultivate the same area as two here ; that is, with the same hands the crop would be one-third greater.

But so anxious is every one in Texas to give all strangers a favorable impression, that all statements as to the extreme profit and healthfulness of lands must be taken with a grain of allowance. We found it very difficult, without impertinent persistence, to obtain any unfavorable facts. Persons not interested informed us, that from one-third to one-half the cotton crop on some of these rich plantations had been cut off by the worm, on several occasions, and that negroes suffered much with dysentery and pneumonia.

It cost them very little to haul their cotton to the coast or to get supplies. They had not been more sickly than they would have been on the Mississippi. They considered that their steady sea-breeze was almost a sure preventive of such diseases as they had higher up the country.

SUGAR.

There were several sugar-plantations near them, one above Victoria, which had done extremely well, always selling their sugar at the highest price, for the supply of the back country.

As there is, for the present, abundance of fuel in the bottoms, sugar-making will probably be an extensive business on the lower

Guadalupe, for some time to come. The land is very well adapted, and can be bought, improved, for $10 per acre. We were
shown, as high as Seguin, cane, which was of unusual size, and
perfectly developed.

In the garden were peach and fig-trees, and raspberries. Pears
on quince-stocks have produced fine crops in the neighborhood.
The banana is cultivated here and at Indianola, but only as a
curiosity, requiring to be housed or well protected.

They always employed German mechanics, and spoke well of
them. Mexicans were regarded in a somewhat unchristian tone,
not as heretics or heathen to be converted with flannel and tracts,
but rather as vermin, to be exterminated. The lady was particularly strong in her prejudices. White folks and Mexicans
were never made to live together, anyhow, and the Mexicans had
no business here. They were getting so impertinent, and were
so well protected by the laws, that the Americans would just
have to get together and drive them all out of the country.

THE COAST PRAIRIE.

We looked out in the morning upon a real sea of wet grass.
A dead flat extended as far as the eye could reach, reeking with
water. The rain fell in sheets, and the wind blew a gale from
the southward. But we were anxious to reach the coast, and
sheathing ourselves and our hampers in india-rubber, we put off
in the face of the blast.

We had come a long way off the road in finding the plantation,
and on leaving, our host gave us advice how to find it again—advice not at all unnecessary; for we might easily have lost all traces
of our whereabouts on the limitless expanse before us, and have
furnished, perhaps, another example of the accident mentioned

in the " Visit to Texas," and introduced (like all the other available incidents of that little book) into one of Seatsfield's novels,
where the traveler, losing himself upon the great coast prairie,
finally congratulates himself, when, on the second day, he finds
the trail of a horseman. Following it, with the idea that it must
lead *somewhere*, he finds it joined by other tracks, which fill him
with joy, till he eventually discovers that he has for four days
been traveling in his own tracks in a frightful circuit around the
vast prairie.

Our directions were as follows : " The wind is now just about
south, and it will most likely stay so. Well, you keep the wind
right square on your shoulder, and ride straight across the prairie, and when you've gone about a mile, you'll rise the tops of
some timber. Then you go right toward that till you can see
the bottoms of the trees, and when you can see the ground where
they grow, then you can bear off to the right of them till you
see the road."

Following these sailing orders as if we were really at sea, we
at length reached the road. Several times we had to recall the
direction to keep the wind on our right shoulder, finding that in
conversation we had diverged, till quite at right angles with our
course, and each having a different idea, as we looked up, as to
the proper bearing of the point we were aiming at. The road
was a mere collection of straggling wagon-ruts, extending for
more than a quarter of a mile in width, from outside to outside,
it being desirable, in this part of the country, rather to avoid a
road than to follow it. We had heard, the day before, at Victoria, that two parties, who wished to meet, had passed one
another unnoticed, and it now seemed quite credible; one had
taken the right of the road, the other the left. We, ourselves,

usually rode outside all the tracks, using them only as a guide
to our course. We met the mail-coach standing in the opposite
direction, many hundred yards to our left, across the way.

The storm was severe, and during the whole day we saw
no one working to windward but ourselves. The distance to Lavacca was twenty-eight miles. We passed, until near our arrival there, but one house, a miserable, half-drowned ranch, upon
a slight elevation, near a still creek. The rain fell constantly,
and the clay-soil having been saturated before, the whole now
remained upon the surface, so that we waded through water fet-
lock deep. Wherever the turf was not too soft to support the
hoofs of the horses, we went at round trot, splashing sheets of
water over one another. The greater part of the time, our view
was entirely uninterrupted, across a nearly level, treeless space
around three quarters of the horizon. Objects loomed into
vagueness, as at sea. Part of the prairie was hog-wallow, very dis-
tressing to the laboring horses, and now and then came a slightly
elevated long roll. As we approached the coast, the ground became still more perfectly level, and more deeply inundated.
The horses were half-knee deep.

We met seventeen wagons and nine Mexican carts upon the road,
bound up, and ten cotton wagons and seventeen Mexican carts
bound to the coast, laid up in stress of weather, the teamsters huddled in pitiful plight under their slight protection. We passed
near several herds of deer, and saw many wild geese, cranes, and
prairie hens, and innumerable smaller birds and water-fowl.
Two herds of horses came near us; one of about forty we approached closely. They stood tails to windward, scattered and
feeding. When we were within about five hundred yards, all
raised their heads, trotted together, and stood gazing at us in a

troop. When we had approached within three hundred yards, they broke into a frolicsome gallop, stopping after a short run to look at us again.   They were, probably, half-tamed mustangs, though, possibly, a stray troop of wild horses from the desert prairies to the West.

LAVACCA.

Lavacca seemed to recede as we drew near it. We saw the masts of vessels two hours before we reached the town. We found a very indifferent hotel, but, luckily, a capital stable, where we saw our jaded horses rubbed thoroughly dry and well fed.   The town stands on the edge of the bay, the surface of which is some fifteen feet below the prairie.   The streets were now completely flooded. It lacks churches, school-houses, a public square, shade-trees, and Venetian blinds, but, in other respects, reminds one completely of a small New England seaport or fishing village.   There were four New York schooners at the end of long, slightly-built jetties, and three or four smaller bay craft.   There is no rise and fall of tide of consequence, but the depth of water is changed by the prevailing winds.   There are said to be seven feet of water in the channel; the depth, however, varies with the residence of your informant, and is only to be correctly ascertained from the Coast Pilot.

A REFORMED ABOLITIONIST.

We were invited, when we arrived, into the ladies' sitting-room, to dry our wet clothes at the only fire. The room was well filled by a family from Alabama. They were on their way with their negroes to the interior, and had been detained here a week, unable to procure wagons. The mistress was in conversation with an Irish lady upon the subject of negroes.

When she left Ireland she was an abolitionist; she wouldn't own a slave; and, bless you, as to whipping one, why she'd just as soon think of whipping a white person. But she very soon had to change her views on arriving in Texas. She found they couldn't get any servänts they could depend on, except niggers, and now she had just as lief whip a nigger as not. She used to think niggers were hard used, but now she knew they weren't a bit more than they deserved to be. They all deserved to be whipped; if they were whipped more they'd be better; unless they was whipped they was good for nothing. She knew and acknowledged she didn't whip her own servants half enough; they were so saucy, and didn't care a bit for your interests. There was a girl they had owned now four years, and she didn't care a bit more for their interests than she did for anybody else's. The other day, a lady called out to her that the pigs were in the garden, and what do you think she said? Why, she said they weren't any of her pigs, was they? And so she let 'em root up all the potatoes they had planted, and the seed cost them six dollars a bushel, and had to be brought from St. Louis. Did they have white servants in Ireland? one of the young ladies asked. Oh, yes, nothing else. And didn't they whip 'em when they wouldn't mind? Oh, you see, my dear, it's very different; they an't like niggers at all, they're enough sight better; they mind of their own accord. You see, it's their interest to mind, because, if they don't, they'll get sent away; and they're more respectable than niggers, and more humble, too, a great deal, though they are more respectable. But they are spoiled as soon as they come to this country, complete. When I first came here I hired me a seamstress, and it wasn't a day before she wanted higher wages; then she wanted to sit at my
11*

table, she wasn't a nigger, she said; she thought she was our equal. So I discharged her, and she thought she could do better; and, sure enough, there was a lady hired her before night of the same day, and when I took tea with the lady, here was this girl at table as good as anybody, and I thought I should have laughed in her face when she turned to me and asked if she shouldn't help me to something more, just as if she was the mistress herself.

The Alabamians did not seem to appreciate the peculiar fun of this.

The head of the Alabamian family seemed to fear the bill. He was asking the landlord what the charges were, as, now it was storming again, it looked like as if they wouldn't be able to get wagoned up the country for a week more. They were charged one dollar per night, each person and each horse. There was nothing eatable upon the table, save the old corn-bread. Everything else was drenched in bad melted butter. As usual, no milk.

We were shown to bed by a little negro, who led us across an open space, ankle-deep in mud and water. Three beds occupied the room, with scarce space to move between them. The towel was a quarter yard of twilled cotton. We remonstrated. The little negro said, " that ar's a good one, put in here to-day, never been used but once, mass'r." We asked what time breakfast was served. "Jus' as soon as we ken get it ready, mass'r." "What time is that usually?" "Can't till 'ou, mass'r." "Is there any one else to sleep in this room?" "Yes, sar; thar's an old gen'l'm'n sleeps here, but he don' often come in till morning, sar." At midnight two men entered the room, talking loudly, and holding a candle to our faces to see who we were.

They occupied the same bed, half dressed, and continued talking in the most profane manner. They appeared to be professional gamblers, and spoke of a young man of whom they had got, that night, $200. One expressed some compassion for the poor fellow. The other laughed. "Why, damn him, don't he deserve to lose all he's got, if he's fool enough to gamble without knowing more about cards than he does."

We went next day to get some work done at a blacksmith's. He was not at his shop. "Well, mechanics don't work steady here, as they do at the north," said his neighbor, when we asked at what time he could usually be found.

SUBSIDENCE OF MR. BROWN.

At noon, the weather being good, we started for Indianola. We went splashing through the water again, the depth as before. At a short causeway, two or three miles from Lavacca, we paid a heavy toll, crossing the Chockolate, a small, crooked, dirty creek.

Not long after, we noticed we were wading through water deeper than usual, and suddenly the mare sunk through the turf, mired. The doctor jumped off, and, relieved of his weight, after some plunging, she relieved herself. The mule, who had sunk in the same place, only went deeper and deeper for his efforts, and, feeling the ground giving way beneath the pony, I spurred on and joined the doctor, who, up to the knees in water, was leading Fanny, trembling with excitement, cautiously towards the nearest elevation, which was some three hundred yards distant. This we soon reached, and found the ground firm, and tolerably dry. Looking back, to learn the fate of the mule, we beheld one of the most painfully ludicrous sights I have ever seen. Nothing whatever was visible of Mr. Brown, save the horns of the pack-saddle and his own well-known ears, rising piteously above the treacherous waves.   He had exhausted his whole energy in efforts that only served to drag him deeper under, and seeing himself deserted, in the midst of the waters, by all his comrades, he gave up with a loud sigh, and laid upon his side to die, hoisting only his ears as a last signal of distress.   We threw off our saddles, hobbled the horses, and prepared to wade to his help, when we saw him renewing his struggles, and, after getting his fore feet upon some more solid turf, he gradually came forth, and walked eagerly toward us, emerging upon the upland, sleek and dripping like a drowned rat, the water shooting from the wicker hampers as from some patent watering-cart.

We thought, bitterly, for a moment, of our pistols and sugar, our Epsom salts and gunpowder, our gingerbread, our poets and our shirts, then broke into an uncontrollable fit of laughter. But the hampers had become two barrels of water, which, added to our ridicule, the mule, his excitement over, found more than he could bear, and, sitting down, he gave us a beseeching look, as if ready to burst into a torrent of tears.

We at once unlimbered, and selecting the least wet portion of available land, spread our property to dry.   The grateful mule commenced rolling and grunting in his usual manner, and was soon restored to good spirits.   A bright sun and strong northerly wind facilitated our operations, and the damages were less than could have been expected.   The medicine chest was the greatest sufferer, and, if any fishes frequented the neighborhood of the disaster, they must have got a well-sweetened dose of a cold infusion of the pharmacopœia in general, that ought to have prolonged their lives to a most unexpected old age.

INDIANOLA.

After three or four hours' delay, we repacked, and got under way again. Indianola was in plain view, but a good deal of navigable prairie was still to be passed. The sun set in a gray haze, in the flat prairie, giving the horizon a greater apparent distance than even the calm ocean. Half a mile from the town we struck the shore, a narrow, hard, sand beach, between a lagoon and the sea, hardly twenty feet wide. As soon as it expands, the town begins abruptly. At the entrance are some prominent gables, and it was so like the approach to a European seaport that we thought of our passports and the *octroi* officers.

The beach on which the town is built is some three hundred yards in width, and extends about a mile in length, having but two parallel streets, front and back. It has a more busy and prosperous appearance than Lavacca, and is much larger, but is said to have less heavy business, and less capital. The rivalry is extreme and amusing. At Lavacca we heard of Indianola as "a little village down the bay (they call it Indianola), where our vessels sometimes land goods on their way up." Each consider the other to be sickly. Indianola has the advantage of the best water, and of the New Orleans steamers, which land at Powderhorn, a sort of hotel suburb, four miles below, by a hard beachroad, where nine to ten feet of water can be carried. Lavacca has the advantage of twelve miles' distance in land-carriage, which, in the present state of transportation, is an important consideration, though the distance from hard roads across the low level prairie is about the same. Schooners, of ordinary coasting draught, come without difficulty to the wharves of Indianola, and with greater difficulty, and with some liability to detention from grounding, to Lavacca, through a channel kept open by a steam dredge.

Ships from Europe lie several miles below Indianola, outside a bar, as at Mobile, and must employ lighterage to either town. There are two towns, of a speculative character, laid out further down the bay, La Salle and Saluria, the former on the main, the latter upon Matagorda Island, and the proposed terminus of the San Antonio and Gulf Railroad. Of neither of these can we speak from personal observation. The mutual jealousy among the speculators in these several towns is immense. It is only certain, at present, that some one great town must grow up upon Matagorda Bay, which will be forever the great sea-gate of Western Texas. It is said that since our visit a great storm has resulted in the partial removal of the outer bar, and persons interested in Western Texas now claim as much water as Galveston for the entrance to their bay. To any reader who wishes to verify the fact, I can only recommend a series of personal soundings upon the two bars.

We spent a quiet Sunday at Indianola. The beach beyond the town forms a pleasant promenade, and we enjoyed to the full the calm sunny sea, which seemed like a return to an old friend, after our months of inland journeying.

Our hotel was a great improvement on that of the day before. The Germans, who compose half the population, have the enterprise to cultivate vegetable gardens, which furnish, at least, salads at all seasons. Around one of these gardens we noticed a hedge of enormous prickly pear. The native oysters are large and abundant. Game of all kinds is cheap. The landlord complained, as usual, of the difficulty of obtaining meat in a country covered with cattle and sheep. The butcher, in summer, wouldn't kill because it was too warm for keeping meat, and in winter because it was too cold or too rainy, he must go to a "saloon" to keep himself warm.

The yellow fever, last year, was severe, as in all the coast towns. In ordinary years, about half the inhabitants leave during the hot months for the interior; but there are many planters from the Caney and the Colorado who come then to the town as a watering-place. Little business is then done, and the New Orleans steamers make their trips but once instead of twice a week.

There is no wood within many miles of the town. That used for fuel is brought mostly from Texana, on the Navidad, fifty miles distant. The price of wood was nine dollars per cord; it is sometimes more than twenty dollars. Coal, from one dollar upwards; corn, one dollar and fifty cents; potatoes, four dollars. The banana produces an abundant but inferior fruit. In winter it is cut in, to a height of five feet, and covered with hay. Oranges and lemons require protection from northers.

In the evening we heard a din which proved to be a charivari, offered as a tribute of public opinion to a couple who had been married in the morning. The bride was suspected not to be immaculate. After some exhibition of endurance, the bridegroom, we were told, " caved and treated," that is, came to the door, and furnished drinks for the crowd.

RETURN TO THE UPLAND.

We left Indianola on the 27th February. Our intention had been to visit Corpus Christi, and some other parts of the coast; but we found this wading over wet prairies so extremely disagreeable, that we determined to retreat to higher land as fast as possible.

The water still covered the prairies, and we splashed our way through it as before.   Leaving at noon, we stopped for the night upon the Chockolate, twelve miles distant.   The house being somewhat crowded, a noise, which seemed to come from several young babies, attracted great attention.   " The fact is," said the father, proudly, " they're twins, and they've got the measles. Leastways, there was a lady here when they was seven days old, said they looked as if they were going to have the measles, and they've been sick ever since."

" Travlin'?" inquired an old man.

" What, sir ?"

" Was the lady trav'lin'?"

" No, sir.   She come up here to see 'em from the city.   We had a great many come here from all about.   I suppose as many as half of all the ladies in the city come out here.   Such an ex-traordinary interesting event, you see—twins!"

A RUNAWAY.

" Which way did you come ?" asked some one of the old man.

" From ———."

" See anything of a runaway nigger over there, anywhar?"

" No, sir.   What kind of a nigger was it?"

" A small, black, screwed-up-faced nigger."

" How long has he been out?"

" Nigh two weeks."

" Whose is he ?"

" Judge ———'s, up here.   And he cut the judge right bad. Like to have killed the judge.   Cut his young master, too."

" Reckon, if they caught him, 'twould go rather hard with him."

"Reckon 'twould. We caught him once, but he got away from us again. We was just tying his feet together, and he give me a kick in the face, and broke. I had my six-shooter handy, and I tried to shoot him, but every barrel missed fire. Been loaded a week. We shot at him three times with rifles, but he'd got too far off, and we didn't hit, but we must have shaved him close. We chased him, and my dog got close to him once. If he'd grip'd him, we should have got him, but he had a dog himself, and just as my dog got within about a yard of him, his dog turned and fit my dog, and he hurt him so bad we couldn't get him to run him again. We run him close, though, I tell you. Run him out of his coat, and his boots, and a pistol he'd got. But 'twas getting towards dark, and he got into them bayous, and kept swimming from one side to another."

"How long ago was that?"

"Ten days."

"If he's got across the river, he'd get to the Mexicans in two days, and there he'd be safe. The Mexicans'd take care of him.

"What made him run?"

"The judge gave him a week at Christmas, and he made a good deal of money, and when the week was up, I s'pose he didn't want to go to work again. He got unruly, and they was a goin' to whip him."

"Now, how much happier that fellow'd 'a' been, if he'd just stayed and done his duty. He might have just worked and done his duty, and his master'd 'a' taken care of him, and given him another week when Christmas come again, and he'd 'a' had nothing to do but enjoy himself again. These niggers, none of 'em, knows how much happier off they are than if they was free. Now, very likely, he'll starve to death, or get shot."

" Oh, the judge treats his niggers too kind. If he was stricter with them, they'd have more respect for him, and be more contented, too."

" Never do to be too slack with niggers."

We were accompanied, next day, by a California drover, named Rankin. He was in search of cattle to drive across the plains. He had taken a drove before from Illinois, and told us that people in that state, of equal circumstances, lived ten times better than here, in all matters of comfort and refinement. He had suffered more in traveling in Texas,· than ever on the plains or the mountains. Not long before, in driving some mules with his partner, they came to a house, which was the last on the road for fourteen miles. They had nothing in the world in the house but a few ears of corn, they were going to grind in their steel mill for their own breakfast, and wouldn't sell on any terms. "We hadn't eaten anything since breakfast, but we actually could get nothing. The only other thing in the cabin, that could be eaten, was a pile of deer-skins, with the hair on. We had to stake our mules, and make a fire, and coil around it. About twelve o'clock, there came a norther. We heard it coming, and it made us howl. We didn't sleep a wink for cold."

On the banks of the Chockolate we saw a flock of some 500 sheep. They were Mexican, very poor and thin, coarse-wooled, large-framed, long-legged, without wool upon their bellies, legs, or heads. A Mexican shepherd attended them, who could speak no English. A few goats were herded with them, as is the Mexican custom, for the prevention of disease. There could not be a country, we thought, at this season, less adapted for a sheep-walk than this open, flat, wet prairie, without protection of any sort. We learned that these were part of a flock of 7,000, purchased by a Mr. Caldwell, on the Rio Grande, and driven here by Mexican shepherds. They had been taken first to Corpus Christi, afterwards to the upper part of Goliad County, and were now on their way to one of the islands of the coast. During the late northers 1,500 had died from exposure to the cold and wet.

We afterwards examined, in Medina Connty a flock of 300 sheep belonging to a German gentleman named Riecharz, which had been provided during the northers with both shelter and hay. Not one had been lost by exposure. These were mostly Mexican sheep, in process of rapid improvement by admixture of Saxony blood. They were regularly housed at night and the consumption of hay, used only in extreme weather, had been trifling.

The road from Indianola strikes the uplands along the Guadalupe, twelve miles below Victoria, and thence the road was good and dry. We passed one large plantation, where the negroes were planting cotton. The women were sowing from bags, and the men ploughing in. An overseer sat upon the ground looking on.

RAILROAD HOUSE.

We stopped, in Victoria, at the Railroad Hotel. As soon as our baggage was disposed of, the landlord stepped up and said, " Go over and take a drink, gentlemen ?" On our declining, he repeated the invitation to each of us in person. At every other arrival he put the same question, when all, including the inn-loungers, went together, we afterwards discovered, to a bar upon the square, it not being the fashion to have the bar in the house. Before night twenty-four travelers had arrived, all with saddle horses.

The advertisement of the house made a point of the great number of sleeping-rooms. These were made by partitions of white cotton, without doors.   Our own room was furnished with two beds, and was entered by every one, indiscriminately, in search of water, a match, or a candle, at all hours of the night. Of course the whole conversation of the various guests was audible —not always of the most agreeable stamp.

In the public room was a written advertisement, as follows :—

" NOTICE.

" I am a candidate for the vacancy in the Board of Aldermen occasioned by the resignation of the Globe man." (There is a " Globe Hotel" in the city.)   " I am in favor of establishing an Academy, and of the sale of the corporation lands.   Also, for the sale of the square on which the First Presbyterian Church is built.   Also, if elected, I shall go for the removal of —— —— from the office of Clerk of the Corporation.   These are my views ; and, if elected, I shall remain your humble servant,

THE GUADALUPE TO THE SAN ANTONIO.

March 1st.—We crossed the Guadalupe upon a ferry-boat, the bridge having been long ago carried away in a freshet.   The ferryman informed us that a steamboat of light draught used to ply upon the river, reaching Victoria.   In summer there was sometimes not more than eighteen inches water in the channel. Since our visit I understand that both the lower Guadalupe, as far as Victoria, and the San Antonio, as far as Goliad, have been made navigable, by individual enterprise.   The bottom, at the crossing, is heavily timbered.   Very few leaves were yet to be seen.   From the bottom, the ascent is rapid, and our day's ride towards Goliad lay through high prairie, with belts of post-oak. The soil is sandy, and appeared poorer than on the east side the river, but the cattle were in much better order.

Two men overtook us, and made offers of horse-trading.   On learning we were from New York, one of them said, " From New

York! You're a long way from your *native* home, aint you? I expect you seem to think the country here tolerable curious. Folks from up north always think the people here's awful rough. We aint so smart down south as you be up to the north. We don't fix up so much, I reckon, do we? Reckon you see some people that's right curiosities, don't you? Well, folks down south likes to live rough. It takes all sorts to make a world."

We passed a man engaged in firing the prairie. He drew a handful of long, burning grass along the dry grass tops, at a run. Before the high gale it kindled furiously, and in fifteen minutes had progressed a mile to leeward, jumping, with a flash, many feet at a time. In a moderate wind we had once noted the progress of prairie flame, to windward, at about one foot per minute.

Camped on Manahuila creek. The following morning we were writing in the tent, waiting the termination of a gentle shower which was falling, having had before a delicious bath, of agreeable temperature, in the creek, when we heard an indistinct roar advancing toward us. As usual, we did not recognize the sound for an instant, and thought a freshet was, perhaps, coming down the creek. At the door we saw and recognized the black cloud approaching, and jumped to the tent pins, which had been partly drawn before the shower. We were barely in time; the blast struck us before we could fasten down the doors. The tent bellied and swelled and pulled like a balloon, but, securing all tightly, we covered ourselves with blankets, and resumed the portfolios. Heavy rain accompanied the norther, but in an hour the fierceness of the storm was over, and we broke camp and proceeded. As spring comes on, the northers lose much of their force and duration.

We saw large flocks of wild geese, and I crept within two hundred yards of one, and secured—a quill or two. We soon reached Goliad, a settlement of half a dozen houses, two stores, a wheelwright's and a blacksmith's shop.

THE MISSION CHURCH AT GOLIAD.

While the horses were being shod, I rode to the old Mexican town of La Bahia, or old Goliad, on the opposite side of the river, to visit the mission and fort, where the massacre of Fannin took place. There are several of the missions in the neighborhood, of which this seems to have been the principal. The ruins I found quite extensive; there are the remains of a large fort, with bastions, which appears to have been about two hundred feet square. Several stone buildings stand about it, all now in ruins. Behind one of the bastions, in a corner of the inclosure, is the church. It is also of limestone, and in similar style to those of San Antonio. The modern village is composed of about twenty jacals, large, and of a comparatively comfortable character, scattered over two hills. The city was formerly one of some importance, and is said to have contained some thousand inhabitants. It was the head of navigation on the San Antonio, and the port of collection for the Bay of Espiritu Santo, whence its old name.

I rode through the village and the fort, and stopped my horse before the door of the ruined church. I should have probably ridden in, but for a general respect for the worshipful design of a church; for two of those we had lately seen at San Antonio, though less ruinous, are used as stables. As I stopped my horse I saw the figure of a man beyond a dilapidated wall.

" Good evening, sir," said I; " can I look within the church ?"

" Oh, yes, certainly," he replied, " why not?"

Seeing a frame in the court, on which were hanging two old Spanish bells, I rode thither, and fastened my horse. While I was looking at the bells, the man stepped over the broken wall, and looked at me. He might have taken me for a bandit or a Texan Ranger. We had been cautioned against horse-thieves in this region, and I had slept with my Colt and bowie-knife buckled round my waist, and had added, when the norther arose, a blue flannel hunting-shirt, and a low cap, which was drawn over my eyes; the short rifle hung at my saddle-bow.

He was a man of forty years, thin, dark-complexioned, and with features that indicated culture. I raised my cap and saluted him, saying that I had ridden over to look at the ruins, and had not known that they were occupied. I did not wish to intrude upon a family.

" Oh, no," said he, " no family, only myself. And where are you from, sir?"

" From New York."

" Ah, from New York, indeed; you are a long way from home. I am glad to see you here. Ah, it's a poor old ruin; come in and you shall see. It was once a very fine church, but the Americans destroyed it as much as they could. See, there we had a gallery, with the oriel over it; they burned it. All the pictures they burned; the carvings they cut with knives—ah it is all ruins! It is hard, my people here are so very poor; you have no idea. I don't suppose that thirty dollars could be found among them all; as for me, I have just come here, eight days ago, and three days I have been a journey to visit some sick. I had no time to do anything. Ah, it seems as nothing could be done. See, here I have made a beginning."

At the end of the church, he had whitewashed a space of the wall, and covered it with calico; over it, an old and battered image, it was now impossible to guess of what, had been set up, and several glass candlesticks were placed before it. The rain had already beaten in, and stained the walls, and the calico had been half-torn off, and thrown upon the floor.

"The wind," said he, "has done this—the norther this morning. I have not yet had time, since I am back, to replace it."

I asked the history of the church. He knew nothing of it, only that there had been a city and a fort, and the church within the fort; the Americans had taken it, and, so far as they could, had destroyed all. Would I look at the fort? If I would excuse him, he would take me through the room where he lived. He drew aside a curtain from an arched door, and we entered what had been a chapel, with a door at the opposite side leading upon the parade of the fort.

"This," he said, "is my little room; I could get no other. The Mexicans they live like chickens—the men and girls all sleep together in the same room. I could not live with them, so I came here. They are very kind, but so poor; but they tell me when they shall have finished sowing their seed they will give me help. They will clean and repair the church; they will build me a house in the parade ground. Then I shall get some old woman to cook for me. Now, I am sorry I can offer you no refreshment. When I am hungry I must go to one of their houses, and eat what they have prepared for themselves; but I can offer you a very good cigar if you will be so good as to accept it."

The place was cheerless enough. It may be fancied that a dim damp vault-like room after being for years desolate and exposed, with open doors, to the weather, would not be a picture of cheerful comfort. It was lighted only by a round window, high up the wall. The furniture consisted of a table, half a dozen open trunks, a heap of some hundreds of well-bound books, over which the mould was beginning to creep, a few scattered garments, a pallet on the floor, and one chair. This he offered me, and, seating himself upon the table, continued to smoke and talk.

The Mexicans, he said, certainly once owned all the land about here. Now it was all held by Americans, and no Mexican had received any pay for it. He did not know, but his people said it really belonged to them. They told him they were not well treated by the Americans. The Americans thought the Mexicans to be bad people. The Mexicans thought the same of the Americans. The Americans, they said, cheated them in every business. They were not allowed to get wood for their fences where they had always got it. They were too poor and too ignorant to do anything towards insisting upon their rights. The Americans, he heard, talk very hard about the Mexicans, as if they had no business in the neighborhood; but he was sure the treaty declared they should have the rights of citizens, and continue to hold their property. I said I hoped he would be able to help them to secure just treatment. No, his duty was not to mingle in their temporal concerns, but he hoped to do them moral benefit. They were in an unhappy condition. They had no ambition, no desire to improve themselves. If they could have leisure to play cards, and could own a small piece of land for corn, and a cabin, and some oxen for their carts, they did not

12

look for anything better. But they were kind to one another, friendly and cheerful, much more so than the Americans. He had just been sent here by the bishop, to see if he could do anything for them; but it looked very bad; the people had no money; they were very poor, and it was all complete ruin. The bishop hoped they might make here a seminary, by-and-by. He came here the year before, and, after an examination, made a claim to the church, which the corporation allowed. But the parade-ground, the other ruins, he was obliged to purchase. For the country around, so far as he could inform himself, it was unusually healthy, and its beauty and fertility I could see for myself. If I were looking for a residence, he would strongly advise me to settle here. Thanking him for his politeness, I rode away, with his good wishes for my journey. The contrast of the ruin and the good curé with the Texan shop and shop-keeper across the river was strong.

We saw, not far from Goliad, a novel sort of fencing, of squares of turf piled into a handsome wall. The Irishman who was at work upon it, said he had made many such here, and that they had proved strong and firm. Another Irishman rode with us, who was from Refugio, where a colony of Irishmen settled in the early days. The settlement, he said, had not increased very rapidly, but all were comfortable there, and doing well. They owned no negroes, as they were not very safe property there—they could run too easily across the Rio Grande. At Corpus, people who had negroes were obliged to treat them very carefully, almost as if they were the masters, for fear they would run. This man appeared to be a horse-dealer. After trying to buy our mule at one quarter his value, he learned that we were on our way to San Antonio, and that we were willing to exchange the mare, who was now much worn down, for an animal more adapted to rough travel and short fare. He offered us his own horse, recommending him in most captivating terms, and informing us that he had sold a great many finer horses than the mare in San Antonio for $30, and that the market there was particularly well stocked at present. "We were in San Antonio three weeks ago," said I, "and were offered $125 for her." The mention of this fact seemed, as it were, to stun him, and, turning to the weather, after a short conversation, he rode away.

The soil of this neighborhood was sandy. We found it, at two points, two miles apart, to be two and a half feet deep, mainly composed of black vegetable mould, with fine sand closely intermixed. The sub-soil was a whitish clay. At the surface of the sub-soil was a sprinkling of flinty pebbles. The grass was thin, and now in separate shoots, like a crop of young oats.

A STAMPEDE OF THREE.

The following day we camped at night many miles from any house, near a bog, which furnished the only water we could find at sunset. The country was a mesquit prairie, the grass very fine, and the trees in scattered clumps at long intervals. After supper we wrote a while, by the light of a candle, a luxury we took good care to have always with us, then, after seeing that all was quiet without, and the fire in a good state of preservation, we lay down and drew the blankets over us. We had barely fallen into a soft doze, when we heard the sound of hoofs, and in a moment a troop of horses dashed, at frightful speed, past the tent. The thundering sound shook the very ground under us. We sprung to our feet simultaneously, seizing our pistols, which were always put within reach at night, and jumped to the door, saying, " those Mexicans have stampeded our horses!"   A glance was sufficient.   Every horse was gone!   We searched for any signs of life around the tent, but all was still, save the dog, who was growling and uttering an occasional excited yelp.   Far off the sound of galloping hoofs was dying away in the distance.

What was to be done?   Here we were in the centre of a big prairie, with an excellent tent, and three or four hundred pounds of baggage on our hands.   The loss of all our animals would be serious at any time.   Here it was a perfect predicament.   We had been repeatedly cautioned against horse-thieves about here, and, just before night, had met two scowling, ill-dressed Mexicans upon the road.   We had remarked them particularly, as the only really wicked-looking Mexicans we had seen.   We both instantly referred our mishap to them.   Well, nothing was to be gained by waiting, at all events.   We examined the stakes where we had left the horses; they were pulled; the ropes, then, had not been cut.   At the moment, a sudden clattering gave us a new start.   A great flock of geese rose noisily from the bog.   The Mexicans were at once acquitted.   Fanny, who had been nearest, had been undoubtedly frightened by them, as they settled down to feed.   The others had followed her motions, and terrified her anew, until the joint alarm culminated in that terror of travelers on the prairies—a stampede.   After a little reflection, we stationed Jude at the door of the tent, extinguished the light of the fire, and started with the rifle, in the line of the last sound.   It soon struck the road tracks at an acute angle, and these the runaways would undoubtedly follow.   All was now perfectly still.   There was a pale moon, just setting.   We walked briskly for a mile, then, groping by the light of a candle-end, found the trail of the mule, going at full gallop.   After another mile, we examined again, he was still going at the same fiery speed. Shortly after, we lost the trail, and were unable to discover, by the flickering light, where it left the road. Further search was postponed. We anticipated some difficulty in finding the camp again, as the night was now very dark, and the dim outlines of the clumps of mesquit were so similar. But Jude's ringing bark, as we came within hearing of her quick ear, guided us back.

The start we had had, and the image of the two Mexicans lurking about, was not enough to prevent our sleeping as usual, but added a singular fury to our dreams. We were each engaged all night in hand-to-hand conflicts with Mexican marauding bands of ten times our numbers, or fighting our way with the recovered animals, from the city of Mexico to the coast. Once, I was captured by the mad rabble, who were leading me in triumph to the sacrificial block, in the temple, when the mule broke away from the tall Indian who was leading him, and laying out on all sides, opened a stampede-track for himself through the mass, through which, jumping suddenly on the mare, I darted away like the wind, leaping over jacals, and cactus-fences, not without some deep scratches.

When daylight came, we carefully scanned the horizon; but not an animal was in sight.

After getting a substantial breakfast, it was agreed that one of us should remain to guard the tent, while the other went on the almost hopeless search. The wind blew strongly from the north, in which direction the horses had gone. Taking another look about us, we discovered something in motion far to the eastward. With the glass we were fortunate enough to make out three horses, slowly walking before the wind. One of them seemed to bear some resemblance to Fanny. A short walk settled the matter, and in an hour our estrays were in camp again. Their run had luckily been directly to windward, and, following their instincts, after coming to a pause, they turned tail to the wind, and walked slowly to leeward, stopping here and there to crop the grass.   Had the wind been from any other quarter, or had they been a few minutes earlier in passing within our range of vision, we should have infallibly lost them.   They would have fallen into the hands of some happy Mexican, or have joined some wild prairie herd.

THE SAN ANTONIO RIVER COUNTRY—MEXICAN PLANTATIONS.

The remainder of the route to San Antonio lay through a country very similar to that over which we were now passing, with occasional belts of post-oak, and, now and then, a piece of broad river bottom.   It is an undulating surface of very rich but light soil, covered with close, fine, mesquit grass, and checkered, pleasantly, with clumps of mesquit, and other shrubs and trees. Much of it is still uninhabited prairie.   We passed but one American settlement—the little town of Helena, which had been just built.

About five miles above, upon the west bank, a sort of religious colony of Silesian Poles has been established since our return.   One or two hundred arrived on the ground in February, 1855, seven hundred more in the autumn, and some five hundred additional in 1856.   The site was chosen by their ghostly father, who accompanied them, without discrimination, and the spot has proved so unhealthy as to induce a desertion of about one-half the survivors, who have made a settlement in the eastern upper corner of Medina County.

We saw some large herds in the finest condition, and it seemed to us the richest grazing district for cattle or sheep we had yet traversed. As we got nearer San Antonio, we passed a greater number of Mexican ranches than we had before seen. Two of them we had occasion to enter. One was a double cabin, in American style. A man in red sash and drawers lay upon the bed, which was almost the only piece of furniture, tossing and playing with a child. We inquired if we could purchase any meat. He referred us to his wife, who was in the garden behind. Passing through, we found the lady, who took down for us about two yards of meat, from several hundred which were drying on a clothes-line. It was cut in strips an inch thick, and was quite hard and dark-colored. Paying at the rate of a dime a yard, we carried it to camp, but found it so tough and so far tainted as to be quite useless. We handed it over to Jude, who, less fastidious with travel, readily disposed of the whole.

The other house was a respectable stuccoed building, belonging to a man of some education, speaking English, and giving employment to some twenty or thirty Mexican laborers. The ground about the door was neatly swept, and in the yard stood a Jersey wagon. The lady was well dressed, but coolly occupied in a very peculiar search for unconsidered trifles, in the glossy hair of her daughter of twelve, who sat *en chemise* before her ; an occupation which was not at all interrupted by our approach. We succeeded in procuring a chicken and a few eggs. Not far from the house were a number of cabins for laborers. Such groups of cabins we also saw once or twice where the occupants were their own employers, and worked together for sociality. The greater part of the houses were very poor. All were engaged in corn-planting (5th and 10th of March). Some Mexicans here are large landholders and stock-owners. A few of them even own slaves, of which we saw two near the crossing of the Calaveras. They were working indiscriminately with hired Mexicans. Near the house were a gin-house and cotton-press, and twenty or thirty small bales of cotton. The Mexican slaveholders are said to treat their slaves very cruelly, though allowing them at the same time many foolish privileges, which increase their capacities, but render them discontented. The utensils upon these farms were, as usual, very rude: the plough, a sort of long wooden plug, dragged through the soil, having an effect much like that of a subsoil plough. The furrows were not turned over at all, but were regular and straight. The fences were invariably of crooked stakes, of various kinds of wood, planted closely in a line, and bound by withes near the tops. These small landholders are almost certain to disappear before the first American settlers who approach. A quarrel is imme-diate, and the weaker is pushed off the log. But throughout the South the same occurs—the small whites are everywhere crowded upon and elbowed out before the large planters.

CHAP. V.

A TRIP OVER THE FRONTIER.

FINDING no company for any long route in Mexico, we abandoned the idea, and set out on the first of April for a short ride across the frontier, by ourselves. The danger to be apprehended was slight, and confined to the four days we should be compelled to pass on the road through the desert, between the westernmost settlements and the Rio Grande. Here we might lose our scalps, should we chance to be seen by any stray band of Comanches, who came down occasionally in foraying parties, from the upper plains, much as inland farmers come on a pleasure-trip now and then, for a change of diet, to the seaside. But if a mail-rider was satisfied to take the chances once a week for $400 a year, we might well afford to do the same once in a lifetime, for the pleasure of the thing.

The mare being much worn down, we took with us only the mule and little Nack—leaving behind the tent and pack, and trusting to the kind skies for shelter from rain.

TRAINS.

Not far from the edge of the town, on our road, were encamped several trains. One was loading government stores for the frontier posts, the others awaiting herds of cattle which they were to convey to California. This is customary with the de-

12*

parting trains, as with ships which drop down the bay with the tide, and anchor until the final arrangements are made for going to sea.

A California cattle-train, we afterwards saw, consisted of four hundred head of oxen, generally in fine, moderately fat condition. There were twenty-five men to guard and drive them. Only a few of these, old frontier men and drovers, who had before been over the road, and could act as guides, were paid wages. The remainder were young men who wished to emigrate to California, and who were glad to have their expenses paid for their services by the proprietors of the drove. They were all mounted on mules, and supplied with the short government rifle and Colt's repeaters. Two large wagons and a cart, loaded with stores, cooking utensils, and ammunition, followed the herd; and another wagon was in company, belonging to a French family, which was very comfortably fitted up for the six months' residence and conveyance of a woman and several children.

The driving of cattle to California from Texas, as long as the market prices permit, is likely to be of increasing importance, as the hazard of much loss is small, and the profits often large. Four men for a hundred head, where the herd is a large one, is considered a sufficient number. Five or six months are usually spent on the road. If the market is overstocked, and prices unsatisfactory on the arrival of the herd in California, it costs but a trifle, in wages to herdsmen, to keep the cattle at pasture, where they fatten and improve in actual value. When importations have been checked, and the demand increases, the herd can again be brought into market. The cattle were costing here, this year, not more than $14 a head, while those driven out last year brought $100 a head in California. A Texan drover, we were informed, the previous year made $100,000 by purchasing sheep in Mexico at $1 a head, and selling them in California at $20 a head. The exportation of sheep from Mexico is, at present, by law, contraband.

THE WEATHER AND THE ROAD.

The year was now well advanced; summer clothing was already sported in San Antonio, and the markets were abundantly supplied with vegetables from the new-made gardens. The earlier trees were in full leaf, and with the new coloring and the new shadows, the town and environs took on an unfamiliar tone of gay adornment. The coyness of the early season was over; nature had now entered with warm delight upon the honeymoon of the year, and was lavish at once of all her spring charms. A very Linnæus might have been caught in the bewildering beauty, and have forgotten his dry ardor for classifying the quivering petals. If we had enjoyed any day's travel before, we enjoyed these with a tenfold zest. The April weather contributed. There were some frigid changes yet, too sudden to be agreeable, and now and then a hot dampness pervaded the atmosphere, like the sirocco, which caused a great mental and muscular depression. But the ordinary temperature was Italian, and, of itself, delicious.*

We rode before evening to the Medina, twenty-five miles. Imagine, for the country, a rolling sheet of the finest grass, sprinkled thick with bright, many-hued flowers, with here and there a live-oak, and an occasional patch of mesquit trees, which might be

---

* Among the flowering shrubs, we noticed particularly a gay relation of the currant family, and a purplish cluster, with a perfume of grapes, which hung from a dense, glossy, laurel-leaved evergreen, near the San Pedro spring.

pictured as old neglected peach-orchards. The surface undulates, and the road leads over much elevated ground, offering very extended views. Northward, the hills, a part of the long range which stretches from the Colorado to beyond the Nueces, swell gradually higher, until they end in a blue and mountainous line, sharply cutting the cool northern horizon. In the south, they slope gently downwards, into the lap of the Medina. Beyond, they again rise gently, covered at last with a soft, hazy forest, across which the view faints away into the sky, flushed at sundown by the red smoke of an invisible burning prairie.

The country is almost unoccupied. There are one or two little settlements of Mexicans and Germans along the road, owners of the few cattle that luxuriate in this superb pasture. Their houses are *jacals*, of sticks and mud, with a thick projecting thatch. The roof of one of them was stretched over a gallery, surrounding the whole house with a very picturesque and comfortable effect.

The Medina is the very ideal of purity. The road crosses upon white limestone rocks, which give a peculiar brilliancy to its emerald waters. It runs knee deep, and twenty or thirty yards wide, with a rapid descent.

CASTROVILLE.

Upon its bank stands Castroville—a village containing a colony of Alsatians, who are proud here to call themselves Germans, but who speak French, or a mixture of French and German. The cottages are scattered prettily, and there are two churches—the whole aspect being as far from Texan as possible. It might sit for the portrait of one of the poorer villages of the upper Rhone valley. Perhaps the most remarkable thing is the hotel, by M. Tardé, a two-story house, with double galleries, and the best inn we saw in the state. How delighted and astonished many a traveler must have been, on arriving from the plains at this first village, to find not only his dreams of white bread, sweetmeats and potatoes realized, but napkins, silver forks, and radishes, French servants, French neatness, French furniture, delicious French beds, and the *Courrier des Etats Unis;* and more, the lively and entertaining bourgeoise.

Castroville was founded by Mr. Henry Castro, a gentleman of Portuguese origin, still resident in the town, under a colony-contract with the Republic, which passed the legislature the 15th of February, 1842. The enterprise seems to have been under the special patronage of the Roman Church. Every colonist was a Catholic, and the first concern was the founding of the church edifice, the corner-stone of which was laid ten days after their arrival, with imposing ceremonies, by Bishop Odin of Galveston. By the contract with the colonists, each person was to receive a town lot, and a piece of outlying land, as a farm. By the contract with the state, two thousand persons were to be introduced within two years. An extension of two years was granted in January, 1845. Mr. Castro was to receive a quantity of land equal to one-half the whole taken by the colonists, to be located in alternate sections, with the state's reserve.

Seven hundred persons came first in seven ships. Assembling at San Antonio, the advance party started, in a body, for the Medina, on the 1st of September, 1844. One board building was carried in carts, and in it were housed the temporary provisions. The settlers built themselves huts of boughs and leaves, then set to work to make adobes for the construction of more permanent dwellings. Besides their bacon and meal, paid hunters provided abundant supplies of game, and within a fortnight a common garden, a church, and civil officers, chosen by ballot, were in being, and the colony was fully inaugurated.*

After struggling with some difficulties, it is now a decided success. The village itself contains about six hundred inhabitants, and the farms of the neighborhood several hundred more.

FRONTIER COLONIES.

Leaving it, we ascended a high hill, and rode for fifteen miles through a more elevated and broken country, whose beauty is greatly increased by frequent groves of live-oak, elm, and hackberry. I have never seen more charming landscapes than some of the openings here presented. In the elements of turf and foliage, and their disposition, no English park-scenery could surpass them.

Beyond Castroville, there are two small villages, settlements of German colonists, mostly from the west bank of the Rhine; one, Quihi, upon the Quihi creek, a branch of the Seco; the other, Dhanis, upon the Seco itself. A third, Vandenburg, has been lately deserted by most of its inhabitants, after they had built themselves houses and brought a considerable quantity of land into cultivation, because the creek on which they depended for water was found to fail in summer. One of those who remained attempted to dig a well. He reached a depth of one hundred and thirty-five feet, and then finding no water, gave it up. A few days afterwards, water was observed to have collected in the bottom, and the well gradually filled until it now stands

---

* "Le Texas en 1845: Colonie Française." 8vo. pp. 20. Anvers, 1845.

constant within fifteen feet of the surface of the ground, enabling him and a neighbor or two to keep their farms.

We stopped a night at Quihi. It is a scattering village, of ten or twelve habitations, one of them a substantial stone farm-house, the others very picturesque, high-gabled, thatch-roofed, dormer-windowed, whitewashed cottages, usually artistically placed in the shade of large dark live-oaks. The people seem to have been very successful in their venture, to judge by various little improvements they are making and the comforts they have accumulated. We were domiciled in a cottage of a family from Hanover, who came here three years ago. Last year they culti-vated over fifty acres of corn, the produce of which they had sold to the Government at a dollar a bushel; they had fifteen cows, four mares, and fifty hogs. They had also a large kitchen garden, in which was growing a greater quantity and variety of vegetables than I have seen in any planter's garden, with two exceptions, at the South. Their cottage they had built with their own hands entirely; it was small and composed of very simple and inexpensive materials, but was provided with more conveniences of living in comfort than many wealthy slave-holders' habitations. A number of loads of stone had already been carted together, and laid in a square pile near at hand, with the intention of building a better house. "My son and I can build it when we have no other work to do, so it will cost us nothing," said the old peasant. I could not see that the climate was to be accused of having in any degree paralyzed his ambi-tion or his strength. The family had enjoyed excellent health, as had, by their report, all their neighbors.

The road beyond follows a low ridge which skirts the foot of the mountains, at a distance of two or three miles. The live-oaks become more stunted and rare, and the mesquit begins to predominate. Dhanis, which is distant some twenty-five miles from Castroville, presents, certainly, a most singular spectacle, upon the verge of the great American wilderness. It is like one of the smallest and meanest of European peasant hamlets. There are about twenty cottages and hovels, all built in much the same style, the walls being made of poles and logs placed together vertically, and made tight with clay mortar, the floors of beaten earth, the windows without glass, the roofs built so as to overhang the four sides, and deeply shade them, and covered with thatch of fine brown grass, laid in a peculiar manner, the ridge-line and apexes being ornamented with knots, tufts, crosses or weathercocks. There is an odd little church, and the people are rigid Catholics, the priest instructing the children.

We spent the night at one of the cottages, and, though we slept on the floor, we were delighted with the table, which was spread with venison, wheat-bread, eggs, milk, butter, cheese, and crisp salad. The bill was less than half that we had usually paid in Eastern Texas for bacon and mouldy corn-bread.

This was a second colony of Mr. Castro, established in 1846, but he here appears to have done little else than point out the spot and assign the lands to the colonists.

During their first year, they told us, they suffered great hardships, the people being all very poor, and having no means of purchasing food except by the proceeds of their labor. Fortunately, there was then a military station in the vicinity, and the quartermaster gave them some employment in collecting forage. They arrived too late to plant corn to advantage, and not having had time to make sufficient fences, the deer eat the most of what did grow. The second year their crop was destroyed by a nail-storm. They lived on game and weeds, for the most part, during two years. Rattlesnakes were then common about the settlement, and were regularly hunted for as game. In some of the families, where there were many small children whose parents were unable to leave them to labor for wages, they formed a chief article of subsistence. Since their second year they had been remarkably prosperous iu all respects. On their arrival here it was believed that the richest of the colonists was not worth twenty dollars ; now the average wealth of each was estimated at eight hundred dollars. It consists mainly in cattle. They have been every year somewhat annoyed by Indians. The colonists had enjoyed better health than in Germany, doubtless, because, since their first struggles, they have obtained a better supply of wholesome food. Notwithstanding the mean appearance of most of their dwellings, the people evidently lived in greater luxury than most of the slaveholding Texans. Cows were milked, I observed, at every house, night and morning ; and a variety of vegetables was cultivated in their gardens.

The women of the settlement, by the absolute necessity of out-door work, had been rendered, it seemed to us, very coarse and masculine in character. All the ordinary labors of men, such as digging and herding cattle, were performed by them. We saw one of them lasso a wild-looking mustang on the prairie, and, vaulting upon his back, canter away in search of her cows, without saddle or bridle. The condition of the children must be yet, for many years, barbarous and deplorable.

ORGANIZED EMIGRATION.

This is the last of the organized colonies of Texas that we had occasion to examine. We were strongly impressed with the actual results of these enterprises. Not one of them could be pronounced a failure, in spite of the most bungling and cruel mismanagement, and the severest reverses in execution. In the hands of men of sound sense and ability, backed by completely adequate capital, there is every reason, from their present condition, to believe that the general plan would have been found not only remunerative to every party concerned, but would have ranked as, in the highest degree, a beneficent acquisition of experience, inaugurating almost a new era for humanity. I am convinced that some similar plan is destined to be adopted for settling, at the least cost, and in the best manner, the vast territorial regions that still are awaiting the pioneer's fences, and that, by its instrumentality, emigration may be elevated, from a barbarizing scramble, to a civilized and worthy institution. For the trial, Texas yet offers the fairest and most attractive field in the Republic. She is accessible with the greatest ease and the least expense, from the crowded centres of the world, and has every natural quality that can attract population in greater measure than her northern rivals.

The excited experience in emigration of the present year in Kansas, has served, at least, to show what might be realized, in calm times, by the power of organization and capital. From almost every state, emigrants have gone with associated numbers and means; but the operations of the Massachusetts Emigrant Aid Society have been especially well known. Whatever the opinion held of its actuating impulse, there can be no doubt that the plan of a similar but general institution has long been forming in the mind of every humane man, who has felt pity and disgust for the miseries bred by the want of some such system applied to foreign emigration.

Had, in this case, the capital been ample, and no political ob
structions intervened, the economical success would have been
secure and incontrovertible. Even under the present difficult
conditions, it has transferred to the new country many hundreds
of families, at a saving to them and a profit to the society; and
has put directly at their command, conveniences impossible, for
many years, to the isolated settler.

New England villages have appeared upon the wild prairies in
a single fortnight; and, had all parties retained their good-humor
and kept the peace, without foreign interference, Kansas would
now have been covered with farms, plantations, and thriving
towns; and a young state have grown into vigorous being.

Under the existing régime of laisser aller, the Silesian peasant
starts, on vague rumor, from the Polish frontier, for the cheap
and wonderful West. He lugs with him his hereditary loom and
his wooden plough, to be split, in Wisconsin, into fuel for his
kettle. He leaves his senses all along the road, and pays his
passage three times over, in the gauntlet of wolfish sharpers who
beset his path. He hunts rattlesnakes for food, and lets his
children grow to savages, while he subdues his field; and then,
perhaps, discovers that he has spent all for a worthless title.
Were a good mercantile system applied to the transaction, he
might pay for an improved farm with the mere sum saved to his
traveling purse, and be furnished, from the first, from the profits
of the agent, not only with temporary subsistence, but with pastor, doctor, school, newspaper, and saw-mill.

There is no philanthropic enterprise that promises half so
thankful a return as this, or that presses, more peremptorily, for
consideration and action. We are not worthy of the times we
live in, if we cannot devise, and put into smooth-working. prac-

tical operation, some beneficent and thorough system of organized emigration.

BORDER SETTLERS.

For some fifteen miles, the country continued of a similar character to that through which we had before passed. Beyond here the mesquit trees became thicker and more bushy, the live-oaks gradually ceased to appear at all, and we saw that we were approaching the great chaparral desert of the Rio Grande valley. We passed two or three houses near the Rio Frio, lonely settlements of Americans, who cultivate corn for sale at Fort Inge. At one of these houses I stopped to make an inquiry, and found it left in charge of a little black boy of ten years, who could give me no other information than that everybody was away, that he hadn't lived long with these people, and that he didn't know who his father was; he had been sold away a long time ago. As I left the house the child ran after me and called out, " Massa, does you know how long it be to Kis'mas ?"—" Oh, a long time yet. What do you want to know for ?"—" Coss I'se on'y hired to Kis'mas; I'll get away den, go back whar I belong."

The road winds along the spurs of the mountains which bound the great " staked plains." They are very rugged, descending precipitously from the level of the elevated table-land. For many miles there is but one practicable pass, the Cañon Uvalde, from which flows the Sabinal, a small branch of the Frio. It is through this and the Bandera Pass, between the head-waters of the Medina and the Guadalupe, that the roving bands of Indians come on their predatory expeditions from the plains.

VICTOR CONSIDERANT AND HIS COMMUNITY.

At the head of the Sabinal are a number of non-slaveholding

farmers, from northern states, engaged in sheep and cattle-rais-
ing, settled together upon a rich and sheltered tract of pasture.
To the same place, if I am correctly informed, VICTOR CONSIDE-
RANT has brought the remnant of his communist colony. His
first position was a very ill-chosen one, upon Trinity river, in
Dallas county, amid a population of planters, who looked with
extreme coldness and jealousy upon such an incursion as that of
a thousand French "agrarians," all foreigners, and, per force,
free-labor men. The experiment appears to have been a brief
one. The colony, which arrived in the winter of 1854–5, was
already, at the end of one season, shattered and dispersed. A
few remained upon the domain of the association, with some
separate organization; a few were faithful to Considerant, and
have followed him to this new and more hopeful position, while
the great body scattered, to try their own fortunes, over the
state. The more intimate reasons and cicumstances of the failure are not yet public.*

FORT INGE.

At night we reached Fort Inge, the military outpost of the
district. It is situated near the head of the Leona, and adjacent
to a singular conical rocky hill, said to be the only evidence of
volcanic action within a large area around. The force stationed
here was a part of two or three companies of mounted rifles,
under command of Major Simonson. As is usually the case
with our nominal Indian forts, there were no structures for defense, the only thing suggesting them being a stockade of mesquit trunks, surrounding the stables, which were open thatched
sheds. There were, perhaps, a dozen buildings, of various sizes,

* An application for the incorporation of M. Considerant's colony has failed
in the state Senate, at the extra session of 1856.

as officers' quarters, barracks, bakery, hospital, guard-room, and others. These were scattered along the border of a convenient parade-ground, pleasantly shaded by hackberries and elms. Behind runs the Leona—a large brook of clear water. The buildings were all very rough and temporary, some of the officers' lodgings being mere *jacals* of sticks and mud. But all were white-washed, and neatly kept, by taste and discipline.

We camped not far away, but were hardly established when we received a visit from two officers, who, with open hospitality, invited us to the mess-table, and the room of an absent lieutenant. We found our hosts gentlemen of spirit and education, upholding in social bearing the reputation which the officers of our army have always maintained—preserving on the rough and lazy border the cultivation belonging to a more brilliant position. The evening and the table were jovial, but not too free, and many a good story was ready to while the hours smoothly away. Though the force present was very small—a large detachment being absent on a " scout"—all the ceremonies of a large command were, as is usual, rigidly observed; five sentinels were posted and relieved, and the form of guard-mounting was gone through with as much exactness as if a commander-in-chief were looking on. The men and their sergeant in uniform, are inspected by the officer of the day in full dress, and the major in fatigue. At Fort Duncan, a more important post, which we visited a few days later, a fine band played upon a terrace at the close of evening, and a bevy of fashionably-dressed ladies added a strange feature to the remote scene.

THE MAILS.

The United States mail train for El Paso and Santa Fé was

camped near the fort, on the third night of its outward passage. The train consists of two heavy wagons, and an ambulance for passengers, who are carried through to El Paso, seven hundred miles, for one hundred dollars, and found. "Passengers," the contractors advertise, "are allowed forty pounds of baggage, and not required to stand guard." There are four mules to each vehicle, and one spare mule for each team is led.

The train is attended by a mounted guard of six men, armed with Sharp's rifles and Colt's repeaters. Their pay is forty dollars a month. A man is lost on nearly every trip out and back, but usually through his own indiscretion. After passing Fort Inge, there is no change of team for more than five hundred miles. The train usually camps from ten o'clock at night till four in the morning. At eight o'clock, a stop of an hour or more is made, to graze the mules, and for breakfast. Another halt is made between three o'clock and sunset. The average distance accomplished in a day is over fifty miles. No government officer or functionary goes with the mail. The commander was an old Texan ranger captain, and the guard, we understood, was composed of old rangers. They had, however, so much the appearance of drunken ruffians, that we felt no disposition to join the party.

The mail between San Antonio and Eagle Pass "changed horses" at the post also, in the afternoon. The mail-carrier is mounted, and the mail is carried on a pack-mule. The contractor is paid eighty dollars a month, and hires a young man to carry it once a week each way, so that he has but one day's rest a week—for thirty dollars. The labor is severe, and the danger, in the long run, great. A mail-rider, running in a similar manner to another post, had just been murdered. The mail leaves

the Leona usually at four in the afternoon. About midnight,
the rider informed us, he quits the road, and searches for a secluded place, where he shall be hidden by bushes. Having chosen
the spot, he unpacks his mule, and lariating his animals, makes
a pillow of the mail-bags, and sleeps till he wakes from his first
nap—usually after sunrise. Before night he is able to reach
Eagle Pass. The distance between the posts is sixty miles.

AN INDIAN CAMP.

We accompanied, on the following day, an ambulance excursion to visit an Indian camp at the head of the Leona, three
miles north of the fort. It was the first time I had had the opportunity of coming in contact with the native savage unalloyed,
and my curiosity was on the alert. The camp was of a portion
of the tribe of Lipans, with a few Tonkaways, and Mescaleros—
numbering, perhaps, in all, one hundred. They had been recently. brought in from the plains by the Indian agent, according
to a treaty by which they were to receive a certain pension in
clothing and food, for keeping quiet, and for substituting the use
of the plough for that of the scalping-knife.

The approach to the camp was at least satisfactorily picturesque; a group of wigwams, bright blankets, and camp-fires were
scattered through the shady grove round the spring, suggesting
a pleasant sketch of the natural socialism of the uncontaminated
man. But this was the last of the picturesque, or of anything
fanciful or agreeable. I will impart in confidence to the reader,
that the tamed sort of Indians he has seen and carelessly despised at Saratoga and Niagara, Eastport and Montreal, are by
no means as degenerate sons of the forest as I used to think.
They are every bit as real, and ten times as good and decent as

this noble savage of the plains. Here, at least, was nothing but the most miserable squalor, foul obscenity, and disgusting brutishness, if there be excepted the occasional evidence of a sly and impish keenness. We could not find even one man of dignity; the universal expression towards us was either a silly leer or a stupid indifference.

But to write down sensations and reflections in a paragraph of my own would be flat burglary, when I have all the time by me the quenching summary in *Household Words*:

" To come to the point at once, I beg to say that I have not the least belief in the Noble Savage. I consider him a prodigious nuisance and an enormous superstition. His calling rum fire-water and me a pale-face, wholly fail to reconcile me to him. I call him a savage, and I call a savage a something highly desirable to be civilized off the face of the earth. I think a mere gent (which I take to be the lowest form of civilization) better than a howling, whistling, clucking, stamping, jumping, tearing savage. It is all one to me whether he stick a fish-bone through his visage, or bits of trees through the lobes of his ears, or birds' feathers in his hair ; whether he flatten his head between two boards, or spread his nose over the breadth of his face, or drag his lower lip down by great weights, or blacken his teeth, or knock them out, or paint one cheek red and the other blue, or tattoo himself, or oil himself, or rub his body with fat, or crimp it with knives. Yielding to whichsoever of these agreeable eccentricities he is a savage—cruel, false, thievish, murderous ; addicted more or less to grease, entrails, and beastly customs ; a wild animal with the questionable gift of boasting ; a conceited, tiresome, blood-thirsty, monotonous humbug."

Not far from the camp was a solitary house, belonging to Mr. Black, an American who had engaged in cultivating corn here for sale at the fort. It must be an extreme idiosyncrasy or a strong instinct of profit, that would induce a man to settle among such unreliable neighbors. His house was now overrun with a swarm of these vagabonds, who, two weeks later, were loose

13

again upon the settlements, scalping, kidnapping, and throat-cutting.

We spent an hour or two in the camp, visiting almost every hut. These were simply slight tents of poles and skins, of larger or smaller size. In each were a few rude utensils, scattered over a heap of skins and filthy blankets. The faces of both sexes were hideously streaked with paint, the features very coarse, nose arge, and cheek-bones particularly prominent. The faces of the boys and girls were a pleasant relief, containing some possibilities, though after all but a slight mitigation of the parental traits. All were eager for a dime, and went through any amount of de-grading nonsense to secure it. A few half-starved Mexican horses were staked outside the camp. The chief, " Castro," was absent with some of the " braves" on a visit to " Chiquito," the chief of another branch of the tribe now encamped in the Cañon Uvalde.

A RIDE WITH OUR RED BROTHERS.

On our return trip we had the distinguished honor of making a personal acquaintance with this hero, under somewhat dubious circumstances. We were riding over the ridge between Quihi and Castroville, some seven miles from the latter place, when, hearing a noise behind, we looked around, and discovered a squad of armed Indians close upon us, and coming up at a quick trot. There was but a moment for consultation. We well knew that no armed Indians ought to be found where these were, but whe-ther these were a friendly exception we could not tell. If they were on a maraud they could not have fallen on a prettier prize than the mule and horse we rode, the guns and Colts we carried, and the comely scalps we wore. Should we fight, should we run, or should we keep about our business, and trust to circumstances? The odds were against us in any one of these proceedings, and we naturally fell into the last while awaiting decision.

We were so far within the extreme settlements that we had laid aside all precaution, and our Colts had been put in our saddle-bags to relieve us of the weight. We had only time to get them out and buckle them to the waist, and to whisper hurriedly, "Don't let them separate us, at any rate," when they came up—the evident chief upon a mule close on our right, a second on our left, a third insisting upon a place between us. This last we resisted, but a sort of leer from the old chief apparently ordered him to persist. There was nothing for it but to yield the point, as we had, per force, assumed the friendly view of things. The troop had adapted themselves to our pace, and we now presented the odd spectacle of a platoon of three Indians and two white men, filling the road, followed by a similar platoon of Indians. In fact, we were prisoners under escort.

I looked towards the chief who rode by my side, and, assuming as much native dignity as I could command, nodded. He returned the nod with a grunt, which I was unable to translate. For a few minutes more not a word was said. Every one of the squad was devouring, with his eyes, our accoutrements and our animals. Not a screw on the rifle nor a buckle on the bridles seemed to escape a close scrutiny. There were many grunts of satisfaction which yielded us equivocal pleasure. We returned their compliment, by eying, with equal curiosity, their faces, dresses, and arms.

The silence becoming somewhat awkward, I broke it with a venture, that might either do me credit or betray a total inexperience.

" Lipanos ?"

" Si."—Grunt.—Pause.—" Americanos ?"

" Si."—Pause.

" To San Antonio ?"

" Yes."

" Where from ?"

" San Fernando."

" Ho !"—With a look at his companions.—" Indians in San Fernando ?"

" Yes.   Many."

" What kind ?"

" Lipans, Mescaleros, Kickapoos, Comanches, Tonkaways, Seminoles.—All drunk.—All fools."

This seemed to excite a great hilarity in the chief.   He wished me to say it again and again, repeating, " so they were all drunk, were they," and making his friends enjoy it with a sort of sparkling chuckle.

I had evidently succeeded in winning his esteem; for he now entered upon a general conversation on the various merits of whisky, corn, horses, and Germans.

Any apprehensions of sudden violence were now allayed, particularly on our discovering that one of the riders behind was a young female.

I inquired if this girl were the chief's squaw.   " Yes," he said, with a scowl, intended to forbid any further investigation.   I asked if he were the chief of the tribe.   " Yes."   " Castro or Chiquito ?"—I had remembered the names since our excursion to the camp.   " Castro," said he, with a sneer, that indicated no particular respect for his royal brother.   He was going to San Antonio, he told us, to have an audience of the Indian agent, in which he was to submit, on the part of his tribe, the proposition that the Lipans should make a series of journeys into Mexico for the purpose of stealing horses and mules, and bringing them to the Americans. This he seemed to think was a grand, novel and philanthropic idea, which would undoubtedly commend itself to every mind and bring eclat to himself and admiration and respect to his nation.

Castro was dressed in a buckskin shirt, decorated profusely with bead-work. Upon his bare head was a *wreath of fresh oak leaves.* Hanging from the ears were heavy brass rings, and across his face blazed a vermilion streak, including the edge of the eyelids, whose motion had a horrid effect. The eyelashes and eyebrows had, as usual, been pulled. His face was not without some natural dignity and force, but the predominant expression was wily and brutal.

The squaw was a girl of delicate features and slight proportions, showing signs of fatigue and hardship. She rode astride, like the rest, dressed in a tolerably neat and pretty buckskin cape, with fringed leggins. The horses of the party, though probably the best belonging to the tribe, were small, worn, and inferior. The mule on which the chief rode, was alone in tolerable working condition.

At Castroville, which we at length reached, not without some relief, we shook off the infliction of our friends, resisting their invitations to stop with them to fire up at the first grocery. We afterwards came up with the party again, within a few miles of San Antonio—every man on the verge of intoxication, Castro himself begging for the personal loan of four bits, and denouncing us with maudlin ferocity for refusing so slight a favor to so old a friend.

The precise object of this expedition of the chief to San Antonio was left in mystery. It appeared afterward that our ride with them, had not been as little attended with danger as we thought; and that this was probably a sort of final scouting trip before the commencement of hostilities.

INDIAN DEPREDATIONS.

We had hesitated at the Medina, whether to go on to San Antonio or to turn up the valley, and pass the night at a sheep-ranch upon the San Geronimo, belonging to Mr. Callaghan, which we had been invited to visit. The slight inducement of seeing our letters one day earlier, struck the balance. The following morning came news that the ranch had been visited during the night by Indians, who had killed a Mexican shepherd, carried off a second boy, and shot at the third, who brought the news. Later in the day, an express arrived from a settlement ten miles nearer San Antonio, with intelligence of a similar outrage. The savages had appeared at the house of a settler named Forrester, demanding something to eat. As the poor fellow was entering the cabin to comply, he was shot from behind, and fell dead on the threshold. His wife sprang out at the other door, and, looking back, saw two of her children struck down by hatchets, and a third running to the bushes, the Indians in full pursuit. She escaped unobserved to the nearest settlement. This occurrence took place within sixteen miles of the town. An expedition in pursuit was made up, and Castro, who had shown great excitement on hearing the news, offered his services as trailer, affecting the greatest indignation at the deed, which he declared must have been done by the Comanches. But the trail, when found, had evident marks of Lipan origin. When this was whispered, Castro became greatly disturbed, and in the night disappeared with the horse belonging to the leader of the pursuing party. An express was sent back, with orders to detain the remainder of Castro's men, who were encamped at the edge of the town; but they were on the alert, and all escaped save one, who was killed by a musket-ball.

Our own conversational ride had been the last polite intercourse with the tribe, and probably our scalps were only saved to us by the hankering of the brutes for a parting draught of whisky. Open war at once broke out; the Lipans decamped to the plains, and henceforth ranked as outlaws, to be shot down at will. Frontier murders became the order of the day, and for more than two years, hardly a week elapsed without a visit to some exposed settlement from a gang of Indians, who left their arrows sticking in cows and sheep, drove off cattle and horses, shot down whoever appeared least likely to resist, and carried sleepless excitement and terror before them. They must have taken more than a hundred lives by the most horrid means, destroyed many thousands of dollars' worth of property, and, indirectly, by putting an end to the progress of a whole district, have affected landholders and the state to the amount of millions.

INDIAN TRIBES IN TEXAS.

It is extremely difficult to form a trustworthy estimate of the number of Indian tribes. Those beyond civilized bounds are continually upon the move, ignorant even of their own numbers, and prone to make themselves formidable by exaggerated statements. In 1853, there was thought, by the commissioner of Indian affairs, to be within the limits of the state, a total of 20,000. This was probably, even then, a large reckoning, and the diminution has since been rapid. At all points of contact with the white race, they melt gradually away. At least one-half of the Lipans have been exterminated by powder and ball, in the open war of the last years. Many Comanches have perished in the same violent manner. On the other hand, the Apaches have extended themselves in floating parties from the neighboring Mexican states, toward the coast, making now frequent appearance upon the El Paso road. A part of the remaining Comanches have been brought to settle upon eighteen leagues of land given by Texas to the United States for the purpose. This reservation lies within five miles of Fort Belknap, upon the Clear Fork of the Brazos. There are fixed upon it (July, 1856) 1,540 Indians, of various tribes, who have ploughed and cultivated eight hundred acres of corn. They have made crops now for two seasons in succession, and profess to be gratified at the change in their mode of life. In Eastern Texas are some 3,000 of the semi-civilized Creeks, Delawares, and Cherokees. In the north are some of the old Wichita and Waco tribes. If these be estimated at 1,000, the Comanches at 3,000, and the remnant of Lipans, Tonkaways, and Mescaleros at 1,000, and 4,000 be allowed for the wandering, little-known tribes of the great plains, we have a total of about 12,000 living within the bounds of Texas.

Nothing can be more lamentable than the condition of the wandering tribes. They are permanently on the verge of starvation. Having been forced back, step by step, from the hunting-grounds and the fertile soil of Lower Texas to the bare and arid plains, it is no wonder they are driven to violence and angry depredations. As to our policy towards them, we saw too little either of it or of them to justify the expression of an opinion, having any other foundation than common sense. The border-ers' idea, which looks upon them as blood-thirsty vermin, to be exterminated without choice of means, was imperatively upper-most in our minds while in their presence. A look into their treacherous eyes was enough to set the teeth grinding and rouse the self-preservative tigerhood of the animal man, latent since we ran naked like the rest in the jungles. If my wife were in a frontier settlement, I can conceive how I should hunt an Indian and shoot him down with all the eagerness and ten times the malice with which I should follow the panther. Yet the power of even a little education on these chaotic, malicious idiots and lunatics can hardly be over-estimated. How easily has the In-dian element in Mexican nationality been developed into civilized and productive coöperation. After the foundation of Frede-ricksburg by the German settlers, the principal supplies of food were obtained from the Indians, and the people were almost in consternation when the forts were first established near, and the Indians withdrew their supplies and their profitable barter. But while whisky is sold at ten cents a quart, no general melioration of the condition of the grown border savages can be expected; still their young, like those of other animals, can be caught and tamed. This is the excellent suggestion of Secretary McLelland in his last report on our Indian policy. It has even been carried out to a certain extent with gratifying results. The plan of "re-servations" is a good one, but should be considered as only a first step, and, where practicable, the reservation should, for ob-vious reasons, be entirely inclosed by old settlements. The Comanches, for instance, at Fort Belknap, will be almost certain, on some sudden suspicion, or from mere weariness, to make a stampede to their old plains. Had they to run the gauntlet of

13*

a hundred miles of villages, they would be delivered from temptation.* Once confined in small bodies, within rigid limits on all sides, gradual restriction by other laws will be practicable. The Maine law can be attempted, and a compulsory school law be soon enforced. Some other future than extermination will then, at least, be open.

But such governmental philanthropy is only in practice a jolly job, in which, as usual, the least possible is done, and the utmost possible paid. The smaller the reliance on that the better, and, meanwhile, might not a larger portion of the current of religious contributions be turned with advantage into this nearer channel? The Jesuit mission-farms are an example for us. Our neighborly responsibility for these Lipans is certainly more close than for those Feejees, and if the glory of converting them to decency be less, the expense would certainly be in proportion.

FRONTIER DEFENSES.

The deliberate slowness of the national sword is as notorious along the frontier as the good-natured blindness to official larcenies. Justice always comes lumbering one day behind the rogue. With the exception of the "mounted rifles," we have no force that pretends to meet the Indian on his own ground. Keeping a bull-dog to chase musquitoes would be no greater nonsense than the stationing of six-pounders, bayonets, and dragoons for the pursuit of these red wolves. The vicinity of forts is even more dangerous than the unprotected frontier, for the

---

* "On the 12th of June, 1856, a fight took place, on the Sabinal, between five Americans and twenty-five Indians. During the affray, one of the Americans received no less than five arrows in his body. This was undoubtedly a roving band that had escaped from the Reservations."—*San Antonio Paper.*

fine horses and arms of the stolid regulars are an exciting attraction for the savages. Even the mounted rifles furnish them some keen sport; for a few days before we were at Fort Inge, the stable-yard, guarded by four sentinels, had been entered at night, and half a dozen horses run off. The party was fired upon by the guard, but the bold fellows got clear, leaving only one horse and some drops of blood behind them. At Fort Duncan such depredations were frequent. A sergeant, who was bringing in a load of hay, was pounced upon, within a mile of the fort, and, before he could rally the muskets of his escort, three mules were cut from the traces under his nose, and jerked into the chaparral.

The news of the Forrester murder reached San Antonio about nine in the morning. Two Germans hastily borrowed our pistols, telling us what had occurred, and in ten minutes were in the saddle on the plaza. The squad of mounted infantry, ordered to join the volunteers, was ready *six hours after.*

In truth, the inefficiency of regular troops for Indian warfare needs no evidence. Wherever posted, they are the standing butt of the frontiersmen. They should be placed at work, in times of peace, upon the fortifications that will be subject, in war, to regular attacks by disciplined battalions. The system of arming the border-settlers, subjecting them to the call of one of their own number, and paying them in the ratio of their activity and their services, is the only rational one that meets the circumstances. They are on the spot, and being the interested parties, are always sleeplessly alert and versed in every trick of their wily enemies.

TEXAS RANGERS.

A system nearly equivalent was that of ranging-companies

adopted by the Texan Republic. These were so many organized
tribes of civilized white Indians, living in moving camps beyond
the border, always ready for the chase of the red-skin, at or without a moment's notice. Their wild life and exciting combats
were as romantic and attractive to adventurous young men as any
crusade of old, and on their rolls may be read the names of many
men who would never be suspected now of rampant blood and
deviltry. From many road-talks, from Germans who had ranged
in their ranks, and from our companion, B., we collected some
notes of their characteristics.

Any one, having obtained from the government a commission
to form a ranging-company, advertised a rendezvous, where all
wishing to join should be on hand at a specified time, when they
were inspected by the enlisting officer. The men furnished their
own horses (American or large mustangs), saddles, pistols, and
knives—the state providing only rifles. The pay was $25 per
month. The recruiting officer was only provisionally captain,
the corps, when organized for service, choosing its own leaders.
Rations of hard bread and pork, or, sometimes, fresh beef, flour,
rice, sugar, and coffee, were served out once in four days, with a
bushel of corn and hay for the horse. If sent on a separate scout
where rations could not be taken, they were drawn and sold on
their return, the party subsisting upon game.

They carried no tents, and seldom employed baggage-wagons.
Where they were to make a long camp, they usually built log
huts, otherwise, lay, rolled in their blankets, wherever they
pleased, within the lines of their sentinels.

B. told us that he had once been out six months from the settlements, with nothing to eat but game during that time. They
returned, at length, to a post, where a single load of corn and

bacon was found. It was divided and served out, each man's ration consisting of about a pint of mouldy corn and a "right smart chunk of bacon." Every man used it as he pleased. For himself, he took his corn and broke it as fine as he could between two flat stones, and then, with some fat, tried from the bacon, mixed a cake, which he baked, wrapped in green leaves, by a bed of ashes and hot coals in a hole in the ground. He had never eaten anything the memory of which was more delicious.

They dressed as they chose, generally in flannel shirts and felt hats, sometimes in buckskin suits.

One of the gentlemen at Sisterdale described a company he saw coming into San Antonio, after having been out six months. They had only a few rags tied together and drawn round them for decency. After parading the plaza they left their horses with a guard, and all went into the stores. In a few moments were seen negroes coming out of every store with bundles of rags, which they threw into the street, and presently appeared the rangers, in fine cloth, stove-pipe hats, and all the etceteras. Once, while in Mexico, a regiment was in so sorry a plight, that an order was given from head-quarters for supplying it with clothing. A suit of dragoon's uniform was served out for each man; but, disliking the appearance of uniform, they sold or gambled all away, only the officers keeping their new rig. Dissatisfied at the novel plumage of their officers, they managed to steal every suit, and returned it, with the gold lace and ornaments—blackened.

Men and officers were on terms of perfect equality, calling each other by their Christian or nick-names. Their time, when not in actual service, was spent in hunting, riding, and playing cards. The only duty was for four (out of seventy) to stand guard.

Men were often absent, without leave, three or four days, without being reprimanded. They fought, when engaged, quite independently, the only order from the commander usually being—" All ready, boys? Go ahead."

Their principal occupation has always been Indian fighting, but two or three regiments of them were employed, during the Mexican war, with great advantage, mainly as scouts, pioneers, and foragers. At Monterey, they stormed a battery on foot, leaving their horses and rifles, and fighting with only bowie-knife and Colt. After the city was taken they were prepared to enjoy themselves, but when they had caused much annoyance by their riot, a few regiments of volunteers were ordered to *clear the town of the Texas Rangers.*

The commanding-officer of one of the regiments, after their arrival on the Rio Grande, early in the Mexican war, called his men together, and addressed them as follows :

" I've got an order, boys, to parade the regiment to-morrow morning, at ten o'clock, to be reviewed by General Taylor. I don't know what the devil we ought to do about it, but I reckon we'd better all draw up in a line, and when he comes give him three cheers." Accordingly, when the General appeared, the order was given—" Three cheers for General Taylor." The cheers were given, every man waving his hat, after which he tossed it into the air, or sent it scaling over the General's head, and, drawing his revolver, fired five rounds, in a random *feu-de-joie,* whooping, hallooing, yelling, and making whatever independent demonstrations of respect and welcome he saw fit.

During the later years, one-half of some of these companies was composed of Germans, who were not required to understand English, beyond the words of the general orders. We were shown, at Sisterdale, an arrow, which had pierced one of them near by, who was stationed as guard over some horses at pasture. He had solaced himself with a newspaper, and the Comanches, creeping up, had driven the noiseless bolt through its folds and the body of the careless ranger.

A CAPITAL SCOUT.

We were fortunate enough to procure at Fort Inge a good guide for the Rio Grande. He was recommended to us by the officers as an excellent scout, and a very reliable man ; and so we found him. He was also neat, quiet, and orderly; good-natured without being obtrusive, and communicative without being garrulous and tiresome—a combination of good qualities we found in no other frontiersman. He could assume the Mexican manner and tongue so perfectly that the Mexicans would not believe that he had not been born in their country. He could also speak several Indian languages, and could use the signs of various other tribes. His notions of Indian character commended themselves to my judgment in an unusual degree. Though he despised and hated the savages as frontiersmen always do, and loved to find any decent and manly pretext for killing them, he gave them credit for some perceptive character, which made them a little more worthy of respect.

" Why do people who write books," he asked, " always make Indians talk in that hifalutin way they do? Indians don't talk so, and when folks talk that way to them they don't understand it. They don't like it neither. I went up with Lieutenant ——, when he tried to make a treaty with the Northern Apaches. He had been talking up in the clouds, all nonsense, for half an hour, and I was trying to translate it just as foolish as he said it. An old Indian jumped up and stopped me—'What does your chief talk to us in this way for? We an't babies, we are fighting men; if he has got anything to tell us we will hear it, but we didn't come here to be amused, we came to be made drunk, and to get some blankets and tobacco.'"

He was born in London, but came when a child to Ohio, where he was educated. He, at first, said that he remembered nothing at all of England, but afterwards asked—

"Aren't there little flowers that grow along by the fences in England that they call cups?"

"Buttercups—yes."

"And another little flower in the fences that smells very nice—*haws*, is it?—and another in the grass—"

"Primroses," I suggested.

"Ah, yes, that's it—*cups and primroses*. I thought it was in England; there wan't no such in Ohio. I can remember going out with my mother into the country and picking them. That's the only thing I can remember in England."

He came to Mexico with the volunteers, and when his regiment was paid off, joined the Texas Rangers. After having acquired the Mexican dialect he was placed in the spy company. Once, while engaged in a reconnoissance, they were intercepted by a very strong party of the enemy. It was agreed that they should charge pell-mell through their columns, every man to look out for himself. He got through with his life, and escaped pursuit, but received a blow which had left him since nearly powerless in his right arm. After the close of the war he had earned his living as a scout for Government, and as guide and interpreter to people doing business in Mexico. In his wander-derings, in this capacity, he once nearly reached the Gulf of

California. He had been taken prisoner by the Comanches, and moved about with them, as their slave, for a month before he succeeded in making his escape.

A man so trustworthy and competent in his business, and yet so modest, is rarely found. His name is John Woodland, and any one who has occasion for his services may probably obtain them for two dollars a day, by applying to him at Fort Inge.

AN ESCORT.

Fortunately also for us, there arrived at the fort, the night before we left, two officers *en route* to their posts on the Rio Grande. They were provided with an ambulance, or large Jersey wagon, drawn by six mules and an escort of two mounted riflemen. We joined company, and, with their driver and servant, our whole party, for the two days' ride, to Fort Duncan, numbered nine.

BEYOND SETTLEMENTS.

Before noon, although a hearty mess-table breakfast had been eaten too late to permit us yet an appetite for dinner, Woodland advised us to halt, as we arrived at the last point for a long distance at which we could get good water, shade, and grazing. We had, of course, brought no corn, having left our pack behind us. There were rations for the Government horses in the ambulance, and the officers, with their escort, had gone on without stopping. As we lounged on the ground—our horses roped out to graze near us—I asked the scout if he did not smoke.

"No," said he; "I noticed that men who used tobacco, when they had to go far away from the settlements, very often got out of it, and it made them very uncomfortable, so I quit using it altogether; I never use liquor either, except in the way of politeness or for medicine, so I never have to carry any with me, and it's so much weight saved."

After we had eaten our " snack," I took a nap. When I awoke, Woodland remarked—

" A couple of fellows got killed here last year?

" How ?"

" They had been eating their dinner, and afterwards they went to sleep, I reckon, and some Indians crept up and shot them. They were scalped, and everything they had taken away. We buried them just over there, back of you."

"Ah! you did? Well, don't you think we might as well get away from here now? We shall hardly overtake the escort before dark."

" There's a hole, ten miles on from here, where there's water generally at this time of year ; I reckon, if they make a noon-ing at all, we shall find them there—if they don't, we can't catch them before night. But the horses have about filled them-selves ; so, if you are ready, we'll saddle up."

À LA BELLE ÉTOILE.

We did not overtake the soldiers till nine o'clock at night. They were camped on the brow of a little gully, at the bottom of which trickled a weak streamlet of fresh water. Good wood was scarce, and their fires were already smouldering, though a pot of coffee had been kept hot for us. They had finished their own suppers, and the officers sat smoking over one pile of embers, and the riflemen at another. The mules were eating their corn at the tongue of the ambulance ; the soldiers' horses were staked out near their fire ; and the soldiers themselves, wrapped in their great loose overcoats, were frightening out of his wits, with

Indian yarns, the officer's servant—a free Virginia negro. The grass was very scanty, and our first care was to select the best spots within gunshot of our fires to stake our own horses. We had shot a couple of rabbits, and Woodland in a few minutes dressed and cooked them à la Texas Ranger, which we presently agreed with him was the only way in which a rabbit should ever be cooked, when the requisite conveniences could be obtained. The process is thus: the rabbit being dressed, skewer it with a shaft of green mesquit; rub salt over it generously; lay it upon a bed of red embers for from a minute to a minute and a half, according to your appetite; take it up; jerk off any flaky parts, and eat them out of hand; then lay the other side upon the embers, and leave it for from three-quarters of a minute to a minute and a quarter, according to the eagerness of the company; take it up; tear the whole into as many parts as the number of the company requires; serve immediately on sharpened mesquit sticks.

After supper we replenished the fire, and brought our horses closer; then took our saddles and blankets and laid down outside of them, on the edge of the bank—because, as the scout observed, if we should have any visitors in the night, they would be likely to steal up through the gully. The officers had already retired to rest in the ambulance; the driver and servant were snoring under it, and the gleams of the soldiers' pipes appeared like revolving light-houses, one after another, from a little knoll opposite to us, where they had taken their station as our picket-guard. Each one of us had a revolver and a knife at his waist. As we lay down, Woodland instructed us thus: "I've got a habit when I go to sleep to take off my Colt always and stick it under the fork of my saddle; then if it rains—'tisn't no matter how hard—there's no danger of it's getting wet, and I know just where 'tis. I always sleep with my head on my saddle, and if I hear anything in the night I can slide my hand in and get it, without making any rustling, quicker than I could take it out of my belt. I suppose 'twould be just as well if you did so. This here grass is so poor, there wouldn't be any on 'em round here unless they came a purpose to run off travelers' horses, and we are too strong for any *common* stealing gang. Such a lot of mules, though, and them dragoon-horses would be mighty tempting, and if there is a good many of 'em, they'll run some risk, if they've seen us, to get 'em. It's always *just as well*, anyhow, to be ready, tho' I don't reckon there's any particular danger."

The night was truly gorgeous. The Germans have a saying that the sky seems *nearer* in Texas than in Europe. The stars, and especially the nebulæ, do seem to shine more vividly, and to give more light, and the firmament appears more effulgent than in any part of the northern or southern hemisphere in which I have been. The air was nearly calm, but elastic, and of an agreeable temperature. It is difficult to express the delicious freshness of the gentle breeze that flows across your cheek, upon such an open pillow. I slept little, but have seldom enjoyed a more pleasant or refreshing night's rest. Daylight arrived without our having been disturbed by anything more formidable than a mouse, or something like it, which found its way under my blanket, and for a moment startled me by rubbing against my throat.

SNAKES, INSECTS, AND GAME.

Before sunrise we had breakfasted, and were again in the saddle. Just after we had started, we met on the road, and killed, the largest rattlesnake I have ever seen ; it was only five and a half feet long, but very thick, and carried thirteen rattles. When the soldiers overtook us, they said they had just killed a larger one. We saw several others, and their tracks crossing the road were very frequent. Woodland told us that they disliked to go into the wet grass, and it was for that reason we saw them so much on the edge of the dry road, while the dew stood on the leaves in the morning. In grassy land, at this time of day, they were generally *hanging* in bushes; this we also observed. On this account he always chose the heaviest grass to spread his blanket on for the night. He had several times been told that rattlesnakes had crept within the blanket of persons in the same camp with himself—it was supposed to enjoy the warmth of their bodies—but he had never been an eye-witness of it, nor had he ever heard of a man's having been bitten on these occasions.

These were almost the first venomous snakes we had seen. But the torpid season was now over, and from this time forth they were so common as hardly to excite an exclamation, especially here, beyond the settlements, where they were tenfold numerous. Among them, the rattlesnake stands at the head; but as it cannot strike without coiling, and will not coil without rattling, it is, in reality, less dangerous than some others. In the settled parts of Texas it is common, but scarcely more so than in all the southern and western states. Its rattle is a piercing noise, like that of an August grasshopper, and cannot be mistaken. We had testimony in Eastern Texas of the power of charming said to reside in these reptiles, from Mr. Strather, on the Sabine, who had seen, while hunting in Alabama, "a well-marked case." Coming from a little swamp, he heard a bird, upon a tree-trunk before him, in an unusual flutter; and, stopping to examine the cause, saw a huge rattlesnake coiled, with open mouth, at the foot of the tree, towards which the bird, in convulsions of fright, slowly descended. Keeping perfect quiet, he saw it gradually come within reach of the jaws, when it was seized with a jerk, and slowly swallowed.

I share, with many of mankind, a peculiar dread of serpents— and when on our return across this wilderness my horse stepped in the road close upon a huge specimen of this species, who struck, but fortunately did not wound him, I almost fell faint from the saddle. The Texan settlers seemed to care very little anywhere for snakes; and, indeed, they are perfectly right in ignoring them, as fatal accidents are so extremely rare. The physicians in San Antonio corroborated the general declaration on this point. We saw one patient who had been struck by a water-snake, in collecting "tula," for thatch, from the river edge. He was in a fair way, after three weeks' treatment, to lose an arm by erysipelatous sloughing and necrosis of the bones of the fore-arm, but no danger to life was apprehended. From what we could learn, more than one-half the accidents were followed by no consequences whatever, and a very small percentage, only, proved fatal. The immediate remedies were, for the profession, ammonia; for the people, whisky. A medical man from Illinois told us of a patient to whom he was called, "a lady, who was going out barefoot to milk, and was struck in the ankle, while letting down the bars," who instantly returned to the house and drank a pint of whisky. He contented himself with awaiting the result, and found the antidote real.

The principal venomous snakes of Texas, besides the rattle-snake, are the land and water moccasins, cotton-heads, coach-whips, and copper-heads. We saw none of these, however, in a six months' journey, with the exception of the moccasins, so that they must be comparatively rare, and little to be dreaded. With the moccasins we became very familiar, in traversing the coast region of the eastern part of the state, one or two of the black water-moccasins showing themselves in every pool we entered. even twenty times a day. My acquaintance with the land variety originated a week or two before this, in returning from the mountains. I was creeping up to get within shot of a deer (a useless labor, I need not confess), when I suddenly dropped my eyes upon one of these creatures, about five feet before me, and in my direct path. I drew back aghast, for he did look like a devil incarnate, to be sure. He lay coiled, with a short, thick black body, a huge head, a wide-open, flame-colored mouth, long fangs, and a forked tongue, dancing about in ecstasy of malice. It was a moment or two before I recovered my discretion, which, I acquiesced, in such a case, was the better part of valor. The day before, one of the Sisterdale gentlemen had described these creatures to me, while bathing, and had recommended me to be careful in entering the water.

He had seen a calf, on putting his nose to the creek to drink, struck by one of these moccasins. His head immediately swelled to an enormous size, and convulsive movements followed, which terminated in death, in less than ten minutes.*

The variety of harmless snakes is considerable, but the only

---

* Bartlett (*Narrative* ii., 342) mentions the death of a horse, from the bite of a rattlesnake, three days before.

From the *Staats Zeitung*, San Antonio, 7th July, 1856:—" Mr. Gessler was yesterday bitten by a moccasin-snake, while bathing in the Salado. He had shot the snake and cut him in two, when the *forward part* suddenly jumped towards him, and struck his leg, as mentioned above. Gessler at once rode into town and put himself in charge of a physician. The wound was cupped, and hitherto no consequences have followed."

one with which we became familiar was the egg-snake, before mentioned.

As to the peculiar venomous insects of Texas, we saw not one of the family out of scientific collections. The tarantula was described as simply a very rare huge black spider, whose bite is poisonous, in different degrees, to different individuals. The scorpion is a minute flattened, crawling lobster, perhaps half an inch long. Its sting is painful, but not dangerous, occasioning a suffering like that of the hornet. The most formidable insect is the centipede, whose *crawl* is said to be poisonous, when interrupted, leaving upon the body or limb it is traversing an intensely-painful inflamed track. Prostration and great nervous agitation follow. For all these, ammonia, if instantly applied, is considered an antidote. Should it not be at hand or be unsuccessful, the after symptoms are treated according to their nature, without empirical remedies.

Near the Nueces, we saw the first specimen of the "horned frog." This singular creature is apparently a sort of lizard, of the size, and of somewhat the shape, of an ordinary toad, of a yellowish color, having four hard horns sloping backwards upon its head, and a series of imbricated horny scales covering the spine. It has sharp claws, and does not leap, but runs, with great rapidity, along the ground upon its four feet. Its eyes are gentle, its movements active, and its whole expression is not repulsive. It is not rare in this part of the state, as we saw four or five upon this trip, three of which we captured. One of them made his escape; the other two were inclosed in a little paste-board box, and sent by mail from San Antonio to New York. They survived the trip, and came out in good spirits and flesh from their narrow quarters. The box chanced to arrive before the letter of introduction, and when it was found to contain, in lieu of jewels, certain eccentric tropical reptiles, there was some explosive consternation. It was at length opened by the aid of tongs, and after the letter announcing the innocent nature of the visitors, they became household pets. After a month or two of in-doors, they began to lose flesh, when they were lariated by a cotton twine attached to the leg, and left to their own resources in the grass, where they soon recovered their corpulence. One of them escaped, and was recaptured a long time after, in high condition, by the mowers in a field a half mile away, but subsequently broke bonds again, and has not since been heard from. The other was presented to a scientific friend.

Game is abundant in this region. We saw probably fifty deer during the forenoon, and rabbits, hares (mule-rabbits), and quails, almost momentarily. We also saw one small herd of antelope and one wolf. A bird, which we had seen twice before—at San Antonio and near Dhanis—about the size of our robin, with a long forked tail, like a pair of paper shears half opened, was here frequent along the road—(*muscicapa forficata ?*). We had heard it called the tailor-bird; but Woodland said it was known among the rangers as the bird of paradise. If it belong to this particular district, it must have been so denominated in irony; for a more dreary country, of equal extent, I never saw.

THE COUNTRY.—NIGGER HUNTING.

The surface is rolling, like the prairie country, but the soil is generally gravelly, arid, and sterile, and everywhere covered with the same dwarf forest of prickly shrubs.

In riding sixty miles, we encountered but two men; they were on the road, mounted and armed, and met us with the abrupt inquiry :
14

" Seen any niggers ?"

(We, unitedly,) " No."

This was all our conversation. " Nigger-hunting—poor business," some one observed, as we separated, and they were directly lost in the bushes. " Poor business," I repeated, inquiringly. " Yes; it's more trouble to get the money, after you've jugged 'em, than it's worth."

The nearer we approached the great river which now forms the admirable boundary line between the states and Mexico, the more dreary, desolate, dry, and barren became the scene; the more dwarfed and thorny the vegetation—only the cactus more hideously large. Within six miles of the Rio Grande the surface of the ground surges higher, forming rugged hills, easy of ascent on one side, but precipitous on the other.

FORT DUNCAN.

As we ride round the foot of one of these abrupt declivities, there is a sudden flash of light from the tin roofs of a cluster of military store-houses. The American ensign floats over them, and, through the openings of the bright green foliage of a mesquit grove, by which they are surrounded, we soon perceive rows and blocks of white tents, and brown thatched sheds and cabins, and a broad flat surface of green turf, with here and there a blue dot, and a twinkling musket; directly we hear the notes of a bugle. There is a fork in the road, and the ambulance takes the road to the military post. It is Fort Duncan—badly placed, in a military point of view, being commanded from the hills in the rear, but in other respects admirably situated upon a broad and elevated plateau, on the bank of the Rio Grande. On the opposite bank we see the wretched-looking Mexican town of *Piedras Negras*, and beyond it another dreary, hilly desert. Nearer, to the right, over the top of a low hill, are some roofs, towards which we are guided, with somewhat pleasant, though indefinite anticipations, derived from a rose-colored little book, describing a residence here, by a lady, who has since obtained the reputation of a diplomatist: "EAGLE PASS; by Cora Montgomery." She was a bride, and her husband, General Cazneau, was engaged in a promising land-speculation, at the time she made her observations. Perhaps, if we had known this, we should have been a little less disappointed, than I must confess we were, when we reached the place.

EAGLE PASS.

First, as we rode up the hill, there were half a dozen tottering shanties, mere confused piles of poles, brush-wood, and rushes, with hides hung over the apertures for doors; broken cart-wheels, yokes, and other rubbish lay about them; fowls had their nests in the loose thatch, and swine were sleeping in holes they had rooted out on the shady sides. A single woman's garment, long since dry, hung fluttering upon a hide-rope, but no other sign of a human being appeared. Then there were two or three adobe houses, looking like long, two-story sepulchres, but which Woodland said were stores; and then, as we rode over the brow of the hill, and there appeared only a few low huts beyond, and still no living man, I asked our guide where was the town. This was it, he said. And where were the people? He supposed they were all gone to sleep, after dinner. "Hallo!" he shouted, pulling up before the open door of a large mud-walled cabin, within which, standing upon an earth floor, we could see a handsome billiard-table. "Hallo!" A good-natured looking man came yawning to the door. "Why! where are all the people gone to, here?"

" To the berrin'—reckon."

" Buryin'? who's dead?"

" Ole Barrels."

" When did *he* go?"

" Last night."

" What killed him?"

" Whisky."

" Well, I reckoned that was it."

Adjoining the billiard-house is another hut, with a yard inclosed by a stake-fence. The good-natured man—who has a fixed smile on his face—unlocks a gate in the fence, and we ride in, and fasten our horses to a tree, which has chains with padlocks, so they can be locked to it, and then take our saddles into the hut.

" See any niggers?"

" No."

" Two got across last night, and one took. You goin' across?"

" Yes."

" To-night?"

" No."

" These gentlemen want a bed—there's one in t'other room; I don't want it."

" Where do you sleep?"

" Out here on the ground. I don't like the bed, 'count of fleas."

The room into which we have taken our saddles and bags is a bar-room; the other contains a bed, upon a strong New York made bedstead, such as we see at our most fashionable hotels, a stove, a barrel of whisky, a box of candles, some sacks of coffee, a trunk, a pack-saddle, a pair of boots, with spurs on, a revolver, a dirk-knife, and a *Journal of Commerce*. Here we are left while Woodland goes out to see if he cannot get a dinner cooked for us.

"Eagle Pass is not so large a place as I had supposed," I observe to the barkeeper; "I thought there was considerable business done here."

"There is considerable for a place of its size."

"Why, there are no people living here except at the Fort, are there?"

"Yes, there's about twenty-five white folks, I believe. It don't cost much to set a man up in business here: three men will build a doby house in three days, roof and all; then all you need to be set up in business is a few boards to make a counter and some shelves, and some fancy bottles to put on the shelves, and red paint and gilt paper to set it off, a box of tobacco, and a single demijohn of *good* whisky, for them that's a judge of it, *to start with*, and a barrel of rot-gut to keep 'em going when they get tight and for common customers. A barrel of raw whisky goes a long way with these soldiers. A man can make a right good start for a fortune with it."

"Do you own this establishment?"

"Me! No, I'm only 'tendin' bar for the man that owns it. He's gone off for a day or two."

"What do all the people live by, here?"

"Selling liquor and gambling. There's nine groceries and five gamblin' saloons."

"But who is there for them to deal with?"

"Soldiers, of course."

"But are there not several merchants here who do a respectable business?"

"Oh, yes, there's two or three smuggles considerable goods over into Mexico."

"Do the Mexicans come across here to trade?"

"Any of them that ever gets any money comes here to spend it."

We were taken to dine at a small hovel, on the floor of which our dinner was being cooked, the smoke escaping by the doorway through which we entered. We had a good dinner, of roast kid, eggs scrambled with sausage meat, and vegetables, which was very neatly served by a pretty, saddened, lady-like, dark-colored woman, who spoke to us in English perfectly, but addressed her children in Spanish. I asked Woodland, while she had stepped out for a moment, if she were a Mexican.

"Oh, no, she's a mulatto, and was born in Louisiana. Colonel —— is her father; he gave her her freedom. Mr. ——, one of the merchants here, lives with her. These are his children, I suppose, though they are rather dark for quadroons. She keeps a kind of a boarding-house for the clerks here, and she's the best cook on the Rio Grande."

After we had dined, and fed and watered our horses, Woodland said there would be no use in our crossing the river yet, for at this time of day the Mexican commandant would be asleep, and would not be disturbed for us; he would, therefore, go to the funeral, if we did not want him. We occupied the time in writing. When he returned, he said it had been the most respectable funeral he ever saw on the Rio Grande.

"Was there a sermon preached?" I asked, thinking the chaplain of the post probably officiated.

"Oh, no, there ain't no parson here; there weren't no ceremonies, but they had a coffin fixed up for him; first time I ever saw a coffin out in this country."

PIEDRAS NEGRAS.

At five o'clock, we proceeded to cross the river, in order to call on the commandant. The Rio Grande here is a rapid turbid stream, not fordable with safety by a stranger at ordinary stages of the water. On the United States side is a "bottom," or sand-bar, three or four hundred yards wide, which is covered in freshets; on the Mexican side there is an abrupt high bank, shelving and sandy, forty or fifty feet high, with a narrow beach below it. A Mexican ferried us across in a skiff—several of which were waiting for passengers—for a dime apiece. On the beach were nearly twenty women and girls washing clothes. One man, dressed in a red shirt and blue trowsers, reclined in the shade of a broad-brimmed, stiff, black hat, on a blanket, spread upon the ground, smoking a cigarito. His eye turned sleepily towards us as we passed up the bank, but he did not address us. Woodland said he was a Mexican corporal, and was then *standing guard* over the landing.

The town is regularly laid out, with streets crossing at right angles, and is compactly built. I cannot say much for the style of the houses. Those we first passed were made by digging into the bank, as if for a cellar, with one end open upon the road, covering the top first with brush-wood and rushes, and then with sand or clay to the depth of a foot or more, and closing in the front by poles set upright, closely together, the interstices made tight with clay. They had no windows, and a hide hung over the doorway. Most of the houses are made of

poles and mud, with thatched roofs; but in the principal business streets, as well as in the aristocratic quarter, there are
several adobe houses, of one story.   It seemed we had not
waited long enough, for in the open doors we frequently saw
men and women lying asleep on the floor or in beds, and it was
not till we had passed several blocks that we approached any
one in the streets.   Five men wrapped in serapes sat upon the
ground, at a corner, smoking.   They looked at us as we came
up, but did not move out of our way, or in the slightest degree
alter the unpleasantly scrutinizing expression of their faces when
we stopped in their midst, until Woodland asked them in Spanish the way to the capitan's house.   Instantly, like an opera
chorus, they all rose and saluted us gracefully and kindly, before
replying, which they then did, by directing us with an easy, dignified gesture.

In the rear of the town is a considerable square of open
ground—not but that there is limitless open ground in this direction, but this particular part of it is surrounded on three sides by
streets, and on two sides is built upon.   It is, doubtless, destined
to be a grand *plaza*, when the town shall have quadrupled its
present population.   It is now pastured by goats and swine, and
has no imposing effect, except at one end, where are two edifices
of adobes, of noticeable magnitude.   In front of one of them is
a strong wooden frame-work, sustaining three small bells; in
front of the other is a singular piece of artillery.   It consists of
an old old-fashioned sulky, an ammunition-chest placed upon the
springs in place of a seat, and, bolted to the lid of the chest, the
muzzles elevated by the depression of the shafts, a large, iron,
double-barreled blunderbuss.   The first of the two edifices is
the church; the latter the town-hall, and residence of Sr. Don

**** **** **** **** **** **** **** ******, acting alcalde of the loyal town of Piedras Negras, and captain commanding the local forces of the Republic of Mexico.

AN ALCALDE.

After knocking several times at the door, it was unbolted, and a dark-complexioned, thin young man, with an anxious, troubled, and ill-natured expression, as if he suffered under a continual conviction of the entire depravity of the human race, and was always prepared for treachery, opened it sufficiently to examine us and confer with us. The captain was not yet wakened from his siesta, but after a lengthened parley he permitted us to enter, observing all the time a cautiously non-committal formality and politeness. The room into which we were admitted was some thirty feet long, fifteen broad, and as many high, the ceiling being formed by the flat ridge-and-furrow roof itself. The floor was of hard-trodden earth. The adobe walls were whitewashed, and broken only by three doors; one, the entrance from the street, another opposite, opening into a rear court, and a third, at one end, leading to another apartment. Two sides of the room and the end opposite the door were furnished with a plank bench, behind which a piece of printed calico was tacked to the wall; at the end of the room, the bench was covered with red-stuff, and some mats were laid before it. We here seated ourselves, and waited for the capitan.

At length he came—white-haired, wrinkled, keen, but kind-eyed, thin, tall; wearing no coat; a vest, nearly worn out, and very much too small; a dirty shirt, comfortably thrown open at the neck; quiet, self-possessed, gentlemanly and good-natured in his manner, and with a soft and winning voice.

14*

We told him, that being about to make a short trip into Mexico, we had called on him to pay our respects, and at the same time offered him an informal passport, we had obtained of the Mexican consul at New York. He called the young man who had received us at the door, and asked him to read the passport, and then told us he was glad we had taken this precaution, for such was the state of the country, he should otherwise have been under the painful necessity to deny us permission to travel in it. He then inquired by what route we had come from New York; and on our mentioning Nachitoches, in Louisiana, he asked, with interest, how that town now appeared, and what was its present population. Thirty years ago, he informed us, he was a lieutenant in the Spanish garrison there.

After half an hour's conversation, Woodland being our interpreter, he conducted us into the adjoining room. It was less than half the size of the first, and had a projecting window, not glazed, but strongly barred. Six beds, with patch-work coverlids, more or less highly ornamented, were set around the sides of the room, which also contained several packing-boxes, doing duty as wardrobes, and a table with writing materials.

Following his example, we reclined upon the beds, while his clerk made a lengthened examination of us, and recorded our age, birth-place, residence, occupation or profession, state (married or single), religion, our purpose in visiting Mexico, the route we proposed to follow, our proposed destination, the time we expected to spend in the country, a minute description of our persons, etc., to a copy of which we were requested to append our signatures. The original was then given to us, on payment of the very moderate fee of twelve-and-a-half cents; and we were told that one copy of it would be retained in the capitan's official bureau (which appeared to be a small box, distinctly labeled, "COLGATE'S PEARL STARCH—NEW YORK"), and that the other would be sent to the city of Mexico. Woodland told us, that a few weeks before, he had called with a gentleman who had been obliged to pay three dollars apiece for the passport of every man in his company.

RUNAWAY SLAVES IN MEXICO.

Returning through the town, we found the awakened people lounging outside their doors, chatting cheerfully, laughing, and singing a great deal, nearly all smoking, and the softer portion affectionately searching under each other's long, luxuriant, and glossy, but coarse, black hair, for—something which they were constantly finding, and dispatching with their thumb-nails.

Very few persons were moving in the streets, or engaged in any kind of labor—for this searching exercise comes under the head of sport, I suppose. As we turned a corner near the bank, we came suddenly upon two negroes, as they were crossing the street. One of them was startled, and looking ashamed and confounded, turned hesitatingly back and walked away from us; whereat some Mexican children laughed, and the other negro, looking at us, grinned impudently—expressing plainly enough—"I am not afraid of you." He touched his hat, however, when I nodded to him, and then, putting his hands in his pockets, as if he hadn't meant to, stepped up on one of the sand-bank caverns, whistling. Thither, wishing to have some conversation with him, I followed. He very civilly informed me, in answer to inquiries, that he was born in Virginia, and had been brought South by a trader and sold to a gentleman who had brought him to Texas, from whom he had run away four or five years ago. He would like right well to see old Virginia again, that he would—*if he could be free.* He was a mechanic, and could earn a dollar very easily, by his trade, every day. He could speak Spanish fluently, and had traveled extensively in Mexico, sometimes on his own business, and sometimes as a servant or muleteer. Once he had been beyond Durango, or nearly to the Pacific; and, northward, to Chihuahua, and he professed to be competent, as a guide, to any part of Northern Mexico. He had joined the Catholic True Church, he said, and he was very well satisfied with the country.

Runaways were *constantly* arriving here; two had got over, as I had previously been informed, the night before. He could not guess how many came in a year, but he could count forty, that he had known of, in the last three months. At other points, further down the river, a great many more came than here. He supposed a good many got lost and starved to death, or were killed on the way, between the settlements and the river. Most of them brought with them money, which they had earned and hoarded for the purpose, or some small articles which they had stolen from their masters. They had never been used to taking care of themselves, and when they first got here they were so excited with being free, and with being made so much of by these Mexican women, that they spent all they brought very soon; generally they gave it all away to the women, and in a short time they had nothing to live upon, and, not knowing the language of the country, they wouldn't find any work to do, and often they were very poor and miserable. But, after they had learned the language, which did not generally take them long, if they chose to be industrious, they could live very comfortably. Wages were low, but they had all they earned for their own, and a man's living did not cost him much here. Colored men, who were industrious and saving, always did well; they could make money faster than Mexicans themselves could, *because they had more sense.* The Mexican Government was very just to them, they could always have their rights as fully protected as if they were Mexicans born. He mentioned to me several negroes whom he had seen, in different parts of the country, who had acquired wealth, and positions of honor. Some of them had connected themselves, by marriage, with rich old Spanish families, who thought as much of themselves as the best white people in Virginia. In fact, a colored man, if he could behave himself decently, had rather an advantage over a white American, he thought. The people generally liked them better. These Texas folks were too rough to suit them.

I believe these statements to have been pretty nearly true; he had no object, that I could discover, to exaggerate the facts either way, and showed no feeling except a little resentment towards the women, who probably wheedled him out of his earnings. They were confirmed, also, in all essential particulars, by every foreigner I saw, who had lived or traveled in this part of Mexico, as well as by Mexicans themselves, with whom I was able to converse on the subject. It is repeated as a standing joke—I suppose I have heard it fifty times in the Texas taverns, and always to the great amusement of the company—that a nigger in Mexico is just as good as a white man, and if you don't treat him civilly he will have you hauled up and fined by an alcalde. The poor yellow-faced, priest-ridden heathen, actually hold, in earnest, the ideas on this subject put forth in that good old joke of our fathers—the Declaration of American Independence.

The runaways are generally reported to be very poor and miserable, which, it is natural to suppose, they must be. Yet there is something a little strange about this. It is those that remain near the frontier that suffer most; they who have got far into the interior are said to be almost invariably doing passably well. A gang of runaways, who are not generally able to speak Spanish, have settled together within a few days' walk of Eagle Pass, and I have heard them spoken of as being in a more destitute and wretched condition than any others. Let any one of them present himself at Eagle Pass, and he would be greedily snatched up by the first American that he would meet, and restored, at once, to his old comfortable, careless life. The escape from the wretchedness of freedom is certainly much easier to the negro in Mexico than has been his previous flight from slavery, yet I did not hear of a single case of his availing himself of this advantage. If it ever occur, it must be as one to a thousand of those going the other way.

Dr. Stillman (*Letters to the Crayon*, 1856) notices having seen at Fort Inge a powerful and manly-looking mulatto, in the hands of a returning party of last year's filibustering expedition, who had been three times brought from beyond the Rio Grande. Once, when seized, his cries awoke his Mexican neighbors, and the captor had to run for it. Once, after having been captured, and when the claim to him had been sold for fifty dollars, he escaped with a horse and a six-shooter. Once, again, he escaped from the field where his temporary holder had set him at work on the Leona. In revenge for this carelessness, a suit was then pending for these temporary services.

The impulse must be a strong one, the tyranny extremely cruel, the irksomeness of slavery keenly irritating, or the longing for liberty much greater than is usually attributed to the African race, which induces a slave to attempt an escape to Mexico. The masters take care, when negroes are brought into Western Texas, that they are informed (certainly never with any reservation, and sometimes, as I have had personal evidence, with amusing extravagance) of the dangers and difficulties to be encountered by a runaway.

There is a permanent reward offered by the state for their recovery, and a considerable number of men make a business of hunting them. Most of the frontier rangers are ready at any time to make a couple of hundred dollars, by taking them up, if they come in their way. If so taken, they are severely punished, though if they return voluntarily they are commonly pardoned. If they escape immediate capture by dogs or men, there is then the great dry desert country to be crossed, with the danger of falling in with savages, or of being attacked by panthers or wolves, or of being bitten or stung by the numerous reptiles that abound in it; of drowning miserably at the last of the fords; in winter, of freezing in a norther, and, at all seasons, of famishing in the wilderness from the want of means to procure food.

Brave negro! say I. He faces all that is terrible to man for the chance of liberty, from hunger and thirst to every nasty form of four-footed and two-footed devil. I fear I should my-self suffer the last servile indignities before setting foot in such a net of concentrated torture. I pity the man whose sympathies would not warm to a dog under these odds. How can they be held back from the slave who is driven to assert his claim to manhood?

GERMANS AND RUNAWAYS.

The fugitive fears to make a fire lest it should draw attention to his lurking-place. During the day, he ascends a tree or hides silent in a thicket. At night he often follows the roads upon any horse he can lay his hands upon, regardless of ownership. Negro cabins he generally approaches with confidence, and in the hovels of the Mexicans, while he is in the settled country, he often obtains food and shelter. Any man who harbors a negro in Texas is liable to fine and long imprisonment.

Most of the Germans, I presume, would refuse to take in a negro whom they knew to be running away. Once, however, I happened to learn that a poor, ignorant, Roman Catholic emigrant, happening to find a half-starved fugitive, when looking after his cattle, melted in compassion, took pains to prevail upon him to come to his cabin, bound up his wounds, clothed him, gave him food and whisky, and set him rejoicing on his way again.

I could not but take off my cap in involuntary respect for the man when told of this, knowing he would be shamefully punished, legally or illegally, if he were even suspected of such a thing, by his American neighbors.

"That German must be a Judas who would do aught to hinder a man who was fleeing toward liberty!" was the reply of my informant.

But a runaway slave is a lawless and, usually, a very mischievous and desperate man, and with a knowledge of the small chance of his eventual escape, and the dangers of all kinds which beset his flight, I have always heard the Germans, even those who most detested slavery, speak of a negro's running away with pain and regret. The slaveholders, who have the least acquaintance with Germans, knowing their sympathy with the slaves, are very much afraid to have them settle near their plantations; but, as far as I can judge, their apprehensions are without good foundation. A German was brutally treated by a company of ruffians, while we were in Texas, from a suspicion, which afterwards failed to be sustained in a slaveholder's court of justice, that he had incited a negro to escape. I did not hear a single well-defined charge of this kind, though, it was repeatedly vaguely made against the Germans in general. On the other hand, to the credit of the Germans, I must say, I heard of only one of them ever having claimed a reward for returning a runaway.

There are a few Jew-Germans in Texas, and, in Texas, the Jews, as everywhere else, speculate in everything—in popular sympathies, prejudices, and bigotries, in politics, in slavery. Some of them own slaves, others sell them on commission, and others have captured and returned fugitives. Judging by several anecdotes I heard of them, they do not appear to have made as much by it as by most of their operations.

A MAIL BEHIND TIME.

A little fellow was pointed out to me, who, a few years ago, was the mail-carrier between San Antonio and Eagle Pass, and who met with two or three amusing adventures in attempting to arrest and bring in fugitives. Once, in coming from Eagle Pass in the night, he saw upon the road before him two negroes— runaways, of course. He was driving a sulky, and they probably mistook it for a Mexican cart until it was close upon them, and it was too late to dodge into the chaparral. He presented his revolver, when both stopped, rather than take the chance of a shot. Ordering them to come back to the road, and to stand at some distance apart, with their backs towards each other, he took a piece of rope, which he carrried for the purpose, and got down from the sulky, with the intention of pinioning them.

Going behind one of them, he laid the revolver upon the ground, that his hands might be free to lash his captive's elbows behind him. He had no sooner done so, than the negro turned and grappled him, while the other ran up, and, snatching the revolver, put the muzzle to his head. He begged them to spare his life; they threw him upon the ground, bound him with his own rope, jumped into the sulky, and drove off rapidly towards Mexico.

Another Jew is said to have sold himself at a particularly cheap rate. He was returning from Mexico, with the proceeds of a jewelry peddling excursion in Spanish dollars. On the banks of a stream, he observed the foot-prints of a man, and upon further examination saw where he had put on a pair of heavy, much-worn shoes. The trail was fresh, and evidently that of a fugitive by night, as the tracks kept on in a direct course, not turning out for puddles, or picking the smoothest of the road. It was yet early in the day, and the runaway was probably lying not far distant. He proposed to his companion to hunt for him; if they should catch him, they could drive him along before them to San Antonio, and get a hundred dollars apiece, very easily. His companion, however, having no inclination to engage in this sort of sport, plead urgent business as a reason for declining, and continued on his way. The Jew determined to run his own hazard, and secure the whole reward. The trail soon left the road, and he followed it cautiously, to an overgrown gully, where he found his fugitive, overcome with sleep. The poor wretch yielded without a word, only begging for something to eat. But the Jew was too wise not to keep the muscular advantage he had over a negro faint and sick with hunger, and tying his hands behind him, drove him before him to the road. The prostration of the poor fellow was so extreme, however, that the task of driving

him in to settlements would be tedious; and, after a short distance, the Jew mounted his feeble prize behind him, joining his
ankles firmly together by a handkerchief, beneath the mule's belly
For a time, all went well—the Jew vigilant and merry, revolver
in hand. But there came the Nueces to cross; the mule would
drink; the bridle goes loose; the spark of liberty suddenly kin-
dles, and headlong, over the mule's head, goes Jew, revolver, and
all, floundering under the feet of the frightened animal. Up the
bank goes a stampede of mule and crouching runaway, securely
tied together, the bags of dollars and provision not even left to
the dripping speculator. The Jew is the only one of the party
that has ever again been heard from.

PLANS OF SLAVEHOLDERS.

The loss and annoyance from this running of slaves to Mexico
has been so great, in Central and Western Texas, as to lead to
many propositions having in view the means of an effectual stop
to its continuance. Several conventions and public meetings
have been held, to devise and carry out such measures. Among
other plans, it is proposed that a body of one hundred rangers
be organized, to be equipped at the expense of those interested,
and stationed upon the Rio Grande, for the purpose of awing or
catching the runaways.

Another plan put forward in the newspapers is, "that the
slaveholders west of the Colorado organize a mutual insurance
company, each one paying a per cent. upon each negro he may
own, for the purpose of raising a fund, and that the company
offer a standing reward for each slave caught, of a sufficient
amount ($500 has been proposed) to induce men to incur the
fatigue and risk attending the pursuit of fugitives." The editor

of the San Antonio *Ledger* remarks : "If such a plan is adopted, the number of escapes will certainly decrease. The reward that is generally offered, over and above what is allowed by law, is but a poor inducement for men to ride several days and nights in pursuit of fugitives, risking their lives, and ruining their horses. But if there is a certainty of recovering one-half the price of each negro caught, the inducement would be sufficient to insure the arrest of fugitives, if within the limits of possibility. And if negroes are once assured that their chance is almost hopeless, and that they will be pursued to the very limits of the state, *and even beyond, if such a thing can be done,* they will be less apt to attempt escaping. And in case fugitives are killed in attempting resistance, the reward should be the same. This plan, if adopted, will do much toward preventing the escape of fugitive slaves. One thing is certain, unless something be done to arrest the escape of slaves, this class of property will become valueless in Western Texas. As yet, but few of those escaping have been caught."

In the same paper is the following item of local news : "On last Thursday night, two of Major Dashiell's negroes got into a dispute, when one seized a large cedar club, with which he killed the other instantly. He then left. The next night he returned, took one of the Major's best horses, and started for Mexico. At Dunn's rancho, a Mexican attempted to arrest the fugitive, when he drew a knife and made at the Mexican, who shot him. This is the third negro Major Dashiell has lost in a short time—one running away, and two killed."

The plan of mutual insurance is certainly that which would commend itself to adoption, in similar circumstances, in other parts of the world ; but, such is the reluctance of a southern-born man to be taxed, for a mutual benefit, that it will probably never get in operation. He instinctively prefers to gamble with his own risks, and would find a life not worth living which was surrounded with recuperative checks and deprived of exciting possibilities.

The actual pursuit of slaves over the frontier, mentioned above, is, of course, not legally possible, with our present treaty obligations. The scheme of separating the Rio Grande states from the Mexican Republic, and erecting them into the " Republic of the Sierra Madre," by American aid, given under the promise of the immediate passage of a law for the rendition of slaves, has been, therefore, a favorite one with the slave-proprietors of the southwest. A Texas paper lately told its readers, in so many words, that they had " acted like fools" in not having assisted a certain neighboring factionist when he attempted, a few years since, a revolution of this sort. Isolated foraying invasions along the border, with vague intentions in this interest, have been frequent. In 1855 a more deliberate plot was laid, and had any respectable support, within Mexican boundaries, been found, the project might have disclosed itself by a decisive trial. The company of rangers under Callahan, which invaded Mexico at Eagle Pass, ostensibly for the chastisement of Indians, was, in fact, upon a revolutionary reconnaissance. The reception it met gave a quick quietus to the scheme. The Mexicans rallied with the Indians—the party was driven back, and obliged to be content with a contemptible piece of spiteful retaliation, the sacking and burning of this poor little village of Piedras Negras.

Frontier irregularities of all kinds are of continual occurrence, and must be winked at by the law, which has no force, in so sparsely settled and distant a border region. Negroes have been many times kidnapped by armed parties from the American side, and taken back to slavery.   On the other hand, it is said, by the author of "Eagle Pass," that peons are constantly forced back to bondage in Mexico, and the chief object of her spirited descriptions was to call public attention to this latter wrong.   We made particular inquiries, at her point of observation, and were unable to find any recent facts to sustain her charges.   But one case of the return of a peon could we hear of, in which the only force used was that of personal remonstrance.   No doubt injustice may have been done—but not all upon one side—and though I would be the last to defend actual delinquencies like those attributed to Mr. Webster, I can hardly subscribe to the necessity of putting $100,000 at the disposal of the Secretary of War for the purpose of deepening the channel of the Rio Grande, as a defense against the rapacity of the Mexicans.

PEON LAW.

I have often been amused at the horror with which this Mexican Peon Law is viewed at the South.   I have been asked, many times, if I did not think it worse than negro slavery.   But there appears to be nothing in the spirit of the law which is *essentially* unjust.   Its object was, probably, a good one, and it was no more intended for the benefit of the capitalist than the laborer. Its abuses are, no doubt, villainous, and because, as with slavery, its abuses are almost sure to occur so constantly as to more than compensate its advantages, it should be superseded by a more enlightened (not merely a more just) system.   There is one provision of the law, which is very apt to be forgotten by those who use it, as a make-weight in slavery defense, which, if insisted upon by the peon debtor, would prevent the greater part of those evils which are said to arise from it. It is this : that the creditor shall not furnish the peon goods, to a greater amount in value than *one half the wages put to his credit;* beyond which the law allows no indebtedness. A case had lately occurred at San Fernando, in which a peon sued his master before the courts, and, making him produce his books, proved, that his labor in the service of his creditor, at the legally-fixed rate of wages, would more than pay his original debt, and for all the goods which the creditor had the right to supply to him, and the creditor was actually obliged to pay him the balance of wages due, by this rule. True, it is a very rare case that this provision is enforced, but the reason for this is not the same that prevents the enforcement of laws to protect the slave, in our southern system, from gross cruelty—the incompetency of the slave to testify—it is only the same as that which makes slavery possible at all—the want of sufficient intelligence and manliness. Enlighten the slave and slavery will end —enlighten the people and peonage will be almost harmless—in no way more unjust or cruel than our old laws imprisoning for debt.

RULES OF THE ROAD IN MEXICO.

At the conclusion of my conversation with the runaway negro, he asked if I were going to San Fernando ?

Woodland, who had drawn near, immediately answered for me—"No"—and told me that a boat was waiting for us. He afterwards observed to me, " There are some people that think they can't never tell a lie; such people won't do to travel in Mexico. When that black fellow asked you if you was going to San Fernando, if you'd told him you were, just as likely as not he'd 'a gone out with a gang of greasers on the road, and hid in the bushes, and when we came up, popped us off before

we could look round at them.   I never let on to anybody which
way I am traveling in Mexico, and I never pay for anything with
gold.   I never let a Mexican ride behind me on the road, and if
I am in a company where there are Mexicans and Americans
mixed, I always keep one American back of all the rest.   If I
was going far in the country, I should always hire a Mexican
fellow to go with me, so I could dress mean, and make him do
all the business, so I would be thought to be his peon."

Yet Woodland was not, naturally, by any means, a suspicious
man.   All travelers in Mexico soon learn to take such precau-
tions against ambuscades and murderous surprises.   They would
have you believe it impossible to estimate highly enough the
Mexican liability to treachery.

A CALIFORNIA WIDOW.

On the beach, a woman, with uncommonly delicate features
for a Mexican, but a very pitiable expression of pride and deep
sorrow, was walking to and fro with a young child, which was
dressed expensively in the American manner.   As we passed
her, she asked us if we had come from California, and, when she
heard that we had not, walked on without another word or any
perceptible variation in the fixed sad resistance of her face.   As
we rowed away from her, the scout murmured—

"I don't see why a marriage by a Catholic priest shouldn't be
just as binding to a man as any other."

Neither, of course, did I, and I asked who did.

He supposed the fellow that was the father of that girl's child
did not think it was.

" She wouldn't have anything to do with him unless he'd
come over on to this side and marry her according to their

fashion, and he was so much in love with her he did it. But, pretty soon after they were married, he told her he'd got to go to California. She tried very hard to keep him here or to make him take her with him ; but he made her believe he'd be back in a year, and she had to let him go. He's been gone three years, now, and I don't suppose she's ever heard a word from him—the damn'd rascal!"

This energetic epithet, spoken in a guttural aside, was the only "profanity" the scout was guilty of while in our company. He habitually saved his breath by dispensing with such language as characterizes the conversation of most frontiersmen, thereby adding another advantage to those of being able to travel without tobacco or spirits.

BED COMPANIONS.

When we again reached our quarters, we found them occupied by a crowd of drinking and brawling Irish soldiers. A little before nine o'clock, however, they returned to the post—those the least drunk supporting those the most so—and left us to sleep in quietness.

Sharing in our friend, the barkeeper's, aversion to fleas, we declined his offer of a bed in the house, and for the greater security of our horses, made our arrangements to sleep near the tree to which they were locked. The bed, we soon discovered, did not contain all the fleas on the premises. There were other creeping things also, desirous of paying their respects to the strangers in the establishment. Once when I had been awakened suddenly, and had risen with a shudder, on looking quickly where my head had lain, I saw running off, with great agility, a dark spider, nearly as large as a mouse. I struck quickly at him, but he escaped into some rubbish, and saved his life. It

15

looked enough like a tarantula, if it was not one, to gratify my curiosity.

ACROSS THE RIO GRANDE.

I was next aroused by the stirring reveillé of Fort Duncan, and starting up, found that our horses had each eaten low into a measure of corn. Woodland had got up and fed them before daylight, and then slipped between his blankets again to finish his night's rest. We gave them short grooming, took a bath in the river, got our breakfast, and, by sunrise, had started upon our trip into Mexico. There are many quicksands, holes, and eddies in the Rio Grande, which make it dangerous to ford. Woodland declined to undertake it, and we employed a Mexican to get our horses over, crossing ourselves in a skiff. Notwithstanding this danger, I did not hear that any runaways had been known to be drowned, although they must always cross at night, and without any knowledge of the proper fording places.

The same sentinel that we had seen before when we landed, smoking, and wrapped in his serape, lounged on the beach. As we passed him, he turned his eyes upon us, and allowed the smoke for a moment to overflow his face, while he inquired if we were furnished with passports; then, trusting our affirmative answer, he reinserted his cigarito, and slowly closed his eyes, as an intimation that he did not wish to be disturbed by us any further, and we proceeded up the bank.

While waiting for our horses, my colored refugee friend, who had talked so confidently of his own ability to support himself comfortably, the day before, came out of a dram-shop, in which were several bright Mexican girls, and asked me if I would not lend him quarter of a dollar. I inquired how it happened he should be in need, if it was so easy for him to earn his living here. He explained that it was merely a temporary accident; if I would loan it to him he would be able to pay me to-morrow. He was well-dressed, and showed no indication of intemperate habits, and I think that he spoke the truth. Probably he meant to treat the girls in the shop. As I had spoken good-naturedly to him, and he had given me some information, the old slave habit of expecting a gratuity—a "drink-money"—returned to him; but, being somewhat modified by the pride of a freeman, he requested it in the *form* of a loan, rather than beg it servilely, though he, doubtless, had no idea that I should see him again, to ask payment. I happened not to have any silver money with me, and did not give it to him; but he continued in conversation with me, without showing any disappointment. The man was "unfit for freedom," as the saying is, evidently enough (and where is the man who does not sometimes make a bad use of freedom, even under the Maine law, I would like to know?), but I was satisfied, by his manner, that his character had been greatly *improved by liberty*. Even the miserable sort of liberty possessed by a laboring man in Mexico is, probably, more favorable to the development of manliness, than that nominal liberty meanly doled in most of our northern states to the African race.

THE COUNTRY AND THE ROADS.—MILITARY COLONIES.

As soon as we had ridden well out of town, Woodland left the traveled road, and led us across a range of trackless, bleak, rugged and barren hills. After we had toiled over them for several miles, we descended upon a nearly level chaparral plain, and soon afterwards again struck into the road, which had been carried a roundabout way through the hills, so as to be practicable for wheels. Although the road was commonly used only by horsemen and a few Mexican carts; unlike any Texan road, it was laid out three rods wide, cleared of bushes, stumps, and stones, and made moderately smooth, like a speculator's street through a farm. Here was the first striking evidence that we had passed from the dominions of a democratic to those of a centralized government. Two years ago, here was only a cart-track, such as private individuals had made, almost by chance, in carrying goods between San Fernando and Piedras Negras; but then the governor of Coahuila determined to make a tour in this part of the state, and orders were sent forward to the alcaldes of the towns in his intended route to make smooth the roads, and otherwise prepare the way for his coming. Here, therefore, were thirty miles or more of a road across a perfect wilderness, without one single resident upon it, almost entirely constructed for the personal convenience of a provincial magistrate.

The towns in this part of Mexico were all originally established by colonies under the military protection of the government, and being laid out on nearly the same model, have the same general characteristics. The town proper is divided by streets, thirty or forty feet wide, into square blocks. These blocks have been divided into building-lots of a certain size, and distributed to the colonists, to be occupied for residences. To each colonist is also given another tract of land for tillage, in the outer part of the town. The towns are always placed at such a point that water for irrigation can be obtained, and the necessary canals for this purpose are made at public expense, and so carried that the water can be distributed over all the allotments when required. Acequias are also made throughout the town, so that water for domestic purposes, and for irrigating the kitchen-gardens, is brought conveniently near every man's house. Usually these town acequias pass through the centre of each block. Though the right of property in these allotments has since been variously disturbed by trade, the same divisional boundaries and general arrangements continue. With the exception of a few very large private estates—the laborers on which all live together, in a central, fortification-like village—there is no agriculture carried on in the district, except within a circle of a mile or two of these towns. This arises from the fact that the towns have been placed in the centre of the best tracts of land, from the advantages to be obtained by combination for the construction of the necessary works for irrigation, for security against attacks of Indians, and from the very gregarious and social character of the people.

Between these towns, which are from twenty to fifty or more miles apart, and the irrigated land in their immediate vicinity, the whole of the country we saw in a ride of a hundred miles—except the rugged hills which wall in the Rio Grande—is an uninhabited, dreary, desolate plain, sometimes as barren and bare as Sahara, but generally thickly covered with the same thorny chaparral described on the American side of the Rio Grande. The surface of the ground is not quite a dead level, but the slopes are imperceptible, except afar off, and they often rise and fall at the same inappreciable inclination for miles without a curve. The landscape is the most monotonous and uninteresting that I have ever seen. The only variety is occasioned by "openings" among the bushes, seldom exceeding a few rods in breadth, and in the alternate predominance of one sort of thorny shrub over another— now, for half a mile, there will be none higher than your knee, again a taller kind prevails, and you scarcely see over the tops, on horseback. The usual soil is a whitish clay with drifts of gravel and pebbles, and, more rarely, a thin, dark, vegetable mould.

During our day's ride of thirty miles, until we approached San Fernando, we saw no house, no inclosed or cultivated land, and but one herd of cattle or horses. We followed an old acequia for many miles, and saw, near it, the appearance of once-cultivated fields, through which we could trace, by the brighter green of the grass, the course of the minor distributing ditches. Not the slightest remains of houses, or barns, or orchards, or fences could I find, nor was I able to learn, though I afterwards made inquiry of the Mexicans living nearest to the place, when, or by whom they had been constructed, or why, or how long since they had been given up. I was told that a dry aqueduct, or main acequia, passed near here, which a United States officer had followed for sixty miles and found to have been constructed with remarkable engineering skill. It is not, I presume, necessary to carry conjectures, as to the day of these irrigators, back of the Spanish Conquest: probably there have been, at some time, mission-farms here, like those of San Antonio.

These "old fields," as a Carolinian would familiarly call them, gave additional melancholy to the cheerless expanse. During the ride we met but one man. This was a Mexican, who was mounted on a serviceable little horse, and rode with us for several miles. He was extremely polite, but seemed excessively stupid or ignorant, and at length dropped behind, as if he could not keep up. Perhaps he was a little afraid of us. He had a broad deer-skin belt at his waist, lined with cartridges, and supporting a horse-pistol, and, fastened to his sadddle, with the stock at his horse's tail and the muzzle at his head, was a very long musket, in a case of blue cotton stuff. The barrel lay under his knee as he rode. He was dressed in a blue jacket and black leather trowsers, slashed down the leg; with a thick row of brass buttons, and open from the knee, so as to let the white under-clothes flow loosely out. He wore on his head a tall, varnished, broad-brimmed, peaked black hat.

SAN FERNANDO.

A dark mass of lofty trees at length rose refreshingly above the distant horizon, and Woodland, pointing to it, said, "there's San Fernando." A town is always marked here by a grove of fine trees: whether these groves were the original inducements which fixed the site of the towns, I do not know. Several weary miles were passed before we could distinguish houses among the trees, and we were within one mile of them before we met the first evidence of human life. This was a forsaken sugar planta-tion with an adobe house, set close upon our road. A small, rude, wooden cane mill stood behind it. A quarter of a mile further, and the road was lined with well-cultivated fields of maize, sugar-cane, and sweet potatoes, divided into fields of not often more than three acres, by stake fences, and surrounded and crossed by acequias. Men and boys were industriously engaged in hoeing the crops, and in conducting the water between the drills in which they were planted.

There were no more farm-houses outside of the town, and the houses in the outskirts were but little scattered. Except one or two of the low thatch-roofed, stake-walled *jacals*, they were all built of sun-dried bricks, one story in height, with flat, cemented roofs, surrounded by a parapet eighteen inches high. They were of the simplest oblong, rectangular form, in fact, much like a brick-kiln set lengthways upon the street, with a single door in front, sometimes with a window or two, and sometimes with none. There were irrigated gardens and small orchards of peach, and apple, and fig-trees about them, and often they were shaded by lofty forest trees—pecan, walnut, beech, cottonwood, and cypress, remarkably large and beautiful. As soon as we got among these trees we noticed an unusual number of birds : it would seem that they were attracted, by their height and beauty, to leave the wilderness of shrubs (where, doubtless, also, they are exposed to snakes and other sly enemies), and were not much annoyed by the amiable Mexicans; they were, indeed, as I afterwards ascertained, more tame and confident than field-birds' usually are in our country.

As we came among the houses, considerable curiosity was shown by the people to see us—children, who had been lounging or playing outside the doors, often calling to the people in the houses to come and look at " *los Americanos*" (though Mexican writers say we arrogate that title to ourselves). The women were dressed loosely, and rather scantily, but not untidily ; numbers of them were sitting at their doors, sewing, or engaged in that other friendly occupation to which I have before alluded. They looked at us modestly and good-naturedly as we passed, often giving us a gracious smile if we turned our faces toward them. At one house the inmates were kneeling near the door, and seemed to be engaged in prayer. Very few men were to be seen, but many girls and boys, the latter, when not more than two years old, generally stark naked. When we reached the principal street, we found upon the corner a company of Indians, on horseback and on foot, around the door of a shop where Woodland had hoped to obtain lodgings for us, for there was no public-house in the town.

"Mescalero—Lipan—Tonkaway!" he muttered, scowling anxiously as we approached them; "I know that fellow; I've seen him on the Leona. What are they here for?"

We halted while he rode among the group, and conversed with a Mexican a moment. When he came out, he said—

"They won't take us in here. I don't know what we shall do. Do you see that old fellow with the squaw—that's a Comanche. I wonder what he's here for? Some of Wildcat's deviltry, I expect."

As we rode on past the Indians, they turned to look at us, speaking loudly to one another, and laughing, and some of the younger ones beckoning to us to stop, and shouting, "Hi! hi!"

"Don't mind them; ride on, ride on!" whispered Woodland, "they are looking at your rifle."

The houses in this main street were, generally, of a superior character, many of them being built of stone, and most of them plastered over and whitewashed. Some were ornamented with bright colored stripes about the doors and windows, and with stenciled leaves and rosettes. The doors, window-cages, and roof-spouts were much carved, often with representations in relief, facetiously rude, of course, of men and angels, and birds and beasts. There was only a single house in the town more than one story in height, but the parapet of many of those on this street was fifteen to twenty feet above the ground, their apartments having correspondingly lofty ceilings.

Stopping next at the store of a French merchant, we were directed to a house where we might probably obtain lodgings. While I remained a moment behind the rest of the party, in conversation with the Frenchman, who was anxious to learn what was last

15*

doing at the opera in New Orleans, and what progress the Cuban filibusters had made, an Indian came up, and tried to take my Sharp's rifle. I drew it away from him, and he, addressing me angrily, took hold of my arm, and tried to pull it towards him.

"Keep it away from him, keep it away!" cried the Frenchman.

I spurred my horse, and, with my free hand, disengaged myself from him, laughing, and cantering off. He followed me for a few rods, yelling and gesticulating violently. The Indians all seemed to know the "Sharp" by sight, and to have a great desire to handle it. One of them told Woodland that he knew it had miraculous power to kill Indians.

My companions had arrived at the house pointed out, and the proprietor, a quizzical, bald-headed, pug-nosed, fat, waddling, little man, had summoned his family to the door to look at us, and say whether they would receive us. They immediately concluded to do so, with evident pleasure. We dismounted, and stood holding our horses.

"Well, come in," said our host.

"Thank you," thought I, "but what is to become of our horses?"

He understood me, and took my horse by the head, bowing to the door again. So, leaving Woodland to look to the horses, I walked in. Outside, the house appeared a mere plain, dead wall of adobes, having, except the single door of entrance, no other openings than the spout-holes of the roof. Within, was a single room, about forty feet long and fifteen broad, the floor of hard-trodden earth, and the ceiling some sixteen feet above it, of bamboo, laid with cement, on small, crooked, unhewn rafters. As there were no windows, and but two small, low doors, there was a great depth of gloom overhead. At one end, upon the whitewashed wall, hung a large old painting, the subject imperceptible except to the eye of faith; a crucifix over it; a small painting of a mermaid-like martyr, with long, draggling, unsinged hair, rising, head and shoulders, out from a sea of fire; and several coarse woodcuts of saints and friars. Near this, on a narrow shelf, was a blunderbuss, a horse-pistol, and a thin prayer-book, the only literature in the house. At this end of the room were three broad beds, with elaborately worked coverlids, used in the day as lounges. Two large chests, containing finery and valuables, stood next the beds, then a sort of settle, or high-backed bench, against the wall, wide enough to be used for a bed; then a broad, low table, used for a dining table when any one dined in the house, also as a bedstead for two at night. A little box or crib, in which a baby lay sucking its fists, swung near the floor by a hide rope from the ceiling. A tall, comely, Madonna-like woman was kneeling on one of the beds, in the act of putting on a dress which lay before her. Pausing at my entrance, she meets my eye, when it turns curious in that direction, unabashed, and with an indolent welcome. Three other women, the eldest—the señora—a dumpy little person, with soft, half-closed eyes, and a large mouth continually smiling. Troops of children, quite too numerous to mention, among whom it is hardly gentlemanly to include a dignified girl, doubtfully young, very dark-colored, but with beautiful liquid eyes, sweetly shaded by long, curving, black lashes.

I might have seen all I have described at one end of the house, before, somewhat to my consternation, I found that the señor was leading my horse in at the door. The horse followed him readily enough, no doubt thinking it a stable, and feeling fully as much at home as I did.   However, he was not to be quartered in the dwelling exactly.   Near the end opposite to that I have described, was a back door; out of this, presently, they went, our host and the pony, the others following.   This end of the house had no other furniture than a cupboard and a few forms, on which were calabashes and earthen pots.   A saddle or two, also, hung here, and some fowls were picking about.   The door opened upon a house-court and garden, which was inclosed by high and strong palisades.   Woodland examined it, and was apparently somewhat relieved as he did so.   "This will do," he said, "better than I expected; some of them Indians wouldn't be at all backward about taking these horses if we gave 'em a chance—that old Comanche devil squeezed his eye at this mule—he don't see such in Mexico very often."

Saddles and bridles were taken off and carried into the house, and we divested ourselves of our Colts and belt-knives, which were immediately deposited in one of the big chests in the house. A fanega of maize was then sent for to feed the horses, who, meantime, were rolling on the smooth ground of the court-yard, and drinking from the acequia which divided it from the garden. In this court-yard were several walnut and fig-trees, under which our horses were fastened; also, a high, dome-formed oven, made of adobes, one of which is to be seen behind every Mexican house, though I nowhere saw one in use, except for a chicken-coop or dog-kennel.   Various vegetables were growing in the garden, but more maize than all else.

Hearing a continual slap, slap, slap, in the next yard, I looked between the stakes to see what made the sound.   A woman, with her back toward me, was kneeling upon the ground, under a fig-tree close to the fence, rubbing the *matate*, and a pretty girl of fifteen was kneeling before her, clapping her hands, or rather slapping a tortilla between them. She stopped a moment to look at me, and, dropping her arms, her chemise—the only garment she wore—fell loosely off her shoulders, disclosing a beautiful little bust; she tossed back the thick, dark locks from her face, then, smiling frankly and cordially, in return to my smile, began to clap her hands again, bending so as still to look at me and let me see her face under the arch of her uplifted elbow. Woodland interrupted the pretty study by asking for our landlady what we would have for dinner. "Some meat, cooked Mexican fashion, tortillas and frijoles, and anything else she likes, so it be Mexican —whatever she would get for her husband if he was uncommonly hungry, and she wanted him to be uncommonly good-natured after it."

A fire was made upon the ground in a corner of the yard near the door of the house, one woman went to hashing a haunch of kid, another sliced some onions, leeks, and red peppers, getting a caution from Woodland about these things, to which she replied, with a laugh—"the Americans are not Mexicans;" the matron brought a calabash of soaked maize, rubbed it, with great labor, on the matate to a paste, which the handsome lady, who had returned from church, and was now dressed like the rest, in a loose, low-necked, sleeveless garment of white, fell to slapping into thin round cakes, displaying much grace and dexterity. A dish of the small brown beans, which constitute, next to maize, and with red pepper (chile colorado), the principal food of the people of Mexico, was also brought to be warmed up for us. When boiled for twelve hours or more, then dried in a saucepan with their sauce of butter and pepper, these Mexican beans, as we had found in Texas, are excellent to the taste and a very wholesome and nourishing, and extremely cheap food.

The tortillas having been cooked upon a flat piece of iron held over the fire, we sat down to dinner, at a low table, the family standing good-humoredly around to watch our American proceedings. Our first difficulty was the absence of fork or spoon, but we soon learned from Woodland the secret of twisting a tortilla into a substitute, and disposed of a hearty meal. The whole we found excellent after our Texan experiences. The tortillas are decidedly superior to the southern corn "pone." The removal of the hull from the meal by lye, changes the character of the dish, and though really less cooked than the baked bread, it has the taste and the digestion of something more ready for the stomach. The constant and severe labor of the women of the family during all our stay was the manufacture of this bread.

Dinner over, we sauntered· through the town. The houses were of a better class than most of those in San Antonio. Low-roofed and without windows, they give a silent, Sunday air to the town. The place had a comfortable look, and the people had the characteristics of a slow, kind, light-hearted and contented peasantry. As strangers, we were much observed, but with a polite, hospitable sort of curiosity. The implements and carts were of the real unimproved Mexican stamp.

The principal movement was given to the streets by the Indians, who were, in numbers, riding helter-skelter about, knocking down black-birds with arrows, having trials of skill at cart-hubs, lying about in all postures of real or affected drunkenness, lounging in and out of every house, and carrying themselves everywhere with such an air as indicated they were masters of the town. In fact, their tone was unendurable on any other supposition. They entered every door, fell on every neck, patted the women on the cheek, helped themselves to whatever suited their fancy, and distributed their scowls or grunts of pleasure according to their sensations. The inhabitants seemed to be quite used to this state of things, which to us was astonishing to the last degree.

While we were standing in the door of our French acquaintance, one of the rascals rode up, and, slapping him upon the back, demanded whisky.

"None."

"Tobacco?"

"None.

"Colors, for daubing the face?"

"None."

"Friend?"

"Yes."

He then repeated the same list, with the same replies. Then fixing his eye upon the Frenchman, he gazed steadily in his face a few moments. The Frenchman not flinching, he slowly, and without changing his look, drew an iron-barbed arrow from his quiver, fixed it upon the bowstring, aimed the point at the merchant's breast, and pulled the bow up to the arrow-head. I expected to see it go through the body—a slip of the finger would have sent it. The Frenchman stood quiet for a moment, but suddenly, with a jerk of the arm, turned the arrow aside, then reaching inside his door, brought out a double-barreled gun, cocked it, and put the muzzle to the Indian's head. The Indian made no effort to remove it, but grunted, and seemed particularly relieved when the gun was taken down. Taking the Indian's bow, the Frenchman, with a slight snap of the string, sent an arrow across the street. It stuck in a wooden door so fast as to require the use of a hammer to extract it. The Indian asked, with a nudge toward us, of what nation we were.

" Germans," said the Frenchman; then to us, " he would be capable of doing you some harm if he knew you to be Americans."

The Indian gave a great shrug, and rode away.

A tall American, wrapped in a shabby cloak, was pointed out to us as a deserter from the other side the Rio Grande. He had arrived in exceedingly destitute circumstances, and had at once commenced *the practice of medicine*. Woodland, apropos, had several good stories of old friends of his in the same business, he had come across in his various journeys in Mexico. One of them, who had served in the ranks with himself, he found in Saltillo lately.

" But, Jim," said he, " what do you do in real serious cases, now—child-bed, for instance ?"

" Oh, I pile in the calomel, and let 'em slide," was the reply of the Señor Medico. The poorer Mexicans seem to consider us as a nation of seventh sons.

Returning to our house in the evening, we found our beds made upon the ground in the court-yard, exposed to the bright moon. This was a precaution of Woodland's against Indian horse-stealers. Our arms were brought out with great formality and placed by our sides—a Colt and knife under each pillow. These preparations for a pleasant night's rest were made for us with perfect seriousness by our host, and, on our laughing at the warlike appearance of our beds, he smilingly said, " It is but a proper precaution." The air was delicious, and we slept well.

For breakfast, we demanded chocolate, expecting the pure

native production. It came frothing in French fashion, and we discovered had actually come from Paris, an importation of the Frenchman's from New Orleans. The town was even more crowded with Indians than the day before, and we found it difficult to avoid collision with them, so disgusting and extreme was their familiarity. They seemed to regard us with a skulking malice, and we resolved to withdraw from their neighborhood as soon as possible. During the day, we made some efforts to talk with intelligent people, but could find no one who was communicable. Even those living in easy circumstances were surprisingly uninstructed. They seemed to dislike to approach the topic of annexation; but gave us to understand that they did not so much fear a change of allegiance as the loss of their property, by the private rapacity of bullying Americans, referring us to what had taken place in Texas.

The alcalde, with all the affable dignity of him at Piedras Negras, gave us visas for our passports, and a welcome to the country. His dwelling, the most imposing of the town, was upon the grand plaza, opposite the church, which had once been a considerable structure, but was now in extreme dilapidation, partly occupied, as were all the tall trees of the town, by flocks of daws, or large long-tailed blackbirds, who filled the air with an inconceivably strepitant chatter.

OUT OF MEXICO.

The following day, we rode southward, through the little towns of Morelos and San Juan to Nava. The country was flat, and, everywhere, away from the villages, covered with dense chaparral. The towns, though varying in size, were upon the same model as San Fernando, and the people of a precisely similar character. We dined, again, upon stewed kid, with a fat old gentleman, who entertained us for half an hour with an account of his running the American lines, with dispatches, during the last war. He affected deafness, and the sentries, considering it too absurd to believe that such a slow, waddling old customer could be bent on any mischief, allowed him to pass.

We saw no Indians beyond San Fernando. At Nava we were hospitably received in the best house of the town, a stuccoed mansion of much pretension. Behind were two courts, reached through a *porte cochère*, the first small and surrounded by out-houses, the second large and walled, having the stables, and a supply of running water for animals. The ladies were beaming but vague. The host, Señor Don Tomas Cantu, appeared to be a land proprietor, and had interest in our descriptions of American agriculture. He told us that much of the land of the neighborhood had been gradually worn out by constant cropping, and that new ditches were now in construction, through land still to be cleared of bushes. Corn was planted, at one foot apart, in drills three feet apart, and the usual production was three hundred fold. As on the upper Rio Grande, nothing is raised without irrigation.

We saw several large flocks of sheep, brought in to be folded. They were of very inferior quality, and were held at fifty cents a head. Before the late edict, prohibiting exportation, they were worth seventy-five cents. They had here no horses for sale, but farther back from the river were large stocks, whence herds were constantly driven into Texas. They were sold at six dollars the head, a mare with her colt counting as one, and one stallion being added without charge to every twenty head purchased. They are broken upon the road, the Mexican drivers receiving one dollar per day for this work.

As at San Fernando, the streets of Nava were shaded by magnificent trees, some of the Pecans, now barely in open leaf, reaching ninety feet in height. The cypresses were in full foliage, the apples and quinces had dropped their blossoms, and showed young fruit upon their branches (April 8).

The following day we rode through thirty miles of chaparral, down a gentle slope, to Piedras Negras. After one lonely, dewy, snaky, starlit camp in the desert, interrupted, after midnight, by a suspicious black or red nocturnal traveler, who passed close by our lurking-place without discovering us, we reached the Texan settlements, and, parting with our guide as from a friend, returned by easy stages, without other incident than our ride with Castro, to San Antonio.

The Mexican towns we had visited, were in no matter of life different, upon this frontier, from those of Central Mexico. The impression had been of a fixed stagnancy, amounting to a slow national decay; the cause, a religious enslavement of the mind, preventing education, communication, and growth, giving rise to bigotry, hypocrisy, political and social tyranny, bad faith, priestly spoliation, and, worst of all, utter degradation of labor.

CHAP VI.

ALONG THE EASTERN COAST.

FOR the return route, we adopted a line that should lead us as nearly as possible along the eastern shore toward New Orleans, hoping to see something of the old-established herdsmen of the coast-prairies, and of the Creole life of Western Louisiana.

On the morning of the twenty-fourth of April, we looked back for the last time, from the San Pedro spring, on the familiar roofs of San Antonio. Having divested ourselves of our pack and of all useless weight, we were prepared for more rapid travel, carrying each a single blanket, to preserve the delightful nocturnal freedom of the prairie. We had learned, like all who make the experience, to love the sweet breath of night and the company of the stars. We took for variety the old and longer road to Neu-Braunfels, which follows the Comal creek, and found it, though almost disused, much more shaded and various than the direct road across the open hills. As we approached within ten or fifteen miles of the town, small German farms appeared, and for the remaining distance they lined the road upon both sides.

About four miles from San Antonio we passed the stock farm of Mr. Ujhazy, late governor of Comorn. We stopped a few moments to pay him our respects, and were very cordially received. He had but recently entered his new log-house, and was hardly yet established. His first settlement was made in Iowa, whence, finding the climate too severe, he had moved by the long inland route to Texas, driving his herd of valuable mares through the friendly Indian country, and camping nightly with all his family, while on the journey. He had spent some time in looking about the State, and finally purchased a large tract of land here, on which he was now making a new home. His wife having died during his residence in Iowa, he lives secluded with his faithful daughter, the very picture of a staunch, hale old gentleman, who supports with quiet dignity what fortunes the gods have decreed. He finds the climate here not to differ greatly from that to which he was accustomed in Hungary, and thinks it more salubrious than that of Iowa. He told us that Kossuth still held near Corpus Christi a thousand acres of prairie, presented him during his visit to this country.

FROM THE GUADALUPE TO THE BRAZOS.

From Braunfels to the Colorado our road lay over long gentle swells, with an occasional creek of pure water and patch of shade. The prairies were laughing with flowers in ravishing luxuriance, whole acres of green being often entirely lost under their decoration of blue and purple. Near Bastrop we entered a tedious sandy tract of post-oak, a camp which, under our single blankets, I remember as one of the chilliest. To Lagrange, a pleasant and busy village, the road keeps the pine-bearing sand, rarely descending into the Colorado bottoms, which are very fertile, and well stocked with old plantations. This large island of lumber is very valuable and important to the western part of the State. It is sprinkled with saw-mills, driven by the numerous streamlets that drain it. Several leagues near Bastrop are the property of the town, and yield a considerable revenue.

In crossing to the Brazos at San Felipe, we rode through a district occupied by German farmers of some means, and apparently in thriving condition, for many of them were engaged in enlarging and decorating their houses. All cultivated cotton, and some had very extensive fields of excellent promise. We saw no negroes among them. The night before (April 28th) we had noticed a slight hoar frost in the bottom, where we camped; but, though some delicate weeds were wilted, the cotton-leaves showed no signs of injury. The cotton plant had now a general resemblance to the young growth of the ruta-baga, before the rough leaves are fully developed. Corn was from two to four feet high wherever early planted. Blackberries and mulberries were ripe, and string-beans, peas, and new potatoes were upon the table before we left San Antonio.

NORTHERN SETTLERS.

The soil throughout the district we were crossing, was admirably adapted for cotton—a rich, dark, sandy loam, with a rolling surface, beautifully broken by clusters and irregular groves of trees.

On the ridge between the Colorado and the Brazos, we traversed for ten miles another poor sandy tract, covered with post-oak. Approaching the Brazos, we came upon twelve miles of high, open prairies, which gradually descended toward the river bottom.

Here we spent a night in the house of a settler from Maine, in whose family we found unusual comforts. He had moved here because he was threatened with consumption; but since his settlement had had none of nis old symptoms, unless after some unusual exertion. He had found the summers very long, but on the whole he thought less oppressive, because the heat was less concentrated and intense, than those of Maine. He was dissatisfied with his position here, and intended to move westward.

The only salable production of his farm was corn, which in a good year produced forty to sixty bushels per acre; but the last year, owing to a two months' drought, he had made but ten bushels.

Sheep were not kept here. He had known one flock of fifty, which perished of neglect in winter. Cattle were very profitable. Beef cattle were now worth $15, and working oxen from $50 to $75 the yoke.

He sneered at his planting neighbors for living without comfort, saying that all the money they got went to buy "more nigger help." He employed himself four free laborers—two English and two Germans. There were many Germans in his neighborhood, all small farmers or farm-laborers; he thought two hundred might be mustered at two hours' notice, at his house. When first arriving they were very poor, and hired themselves to labor at such wages as they could get. As soon as they could, they acquired farms of their own, living very poorly until they had a good herd of cattle; then better, as to their table, than any American. He knew but two Mexicans in the country—one of whom had lately taken a German wife, having established himself upon a farm of his own.

At the house of another Northern man, who had lived in this part of Texas many years, we found two negroes—a male and a female—and seven white hired hands. He was well convinced, from his experience, that white men trained to labor could do more work, the summer through, than negroes. From June to August he allowed his hands, both white and black, to knock off work for three hours in the heat of the day. He believed he had done more hard work during his first five years in the State than any negro in Texas, and had never felt the worse for it.

At his house we were furnished with corn for our horses which had come in bags from Ohio, by Galveston. He had paid $1 50 per bushel for it, and thought it would be the last time he should not raise corn enough for his own purposes. Many a planter near him, he said, had allowed his corn to go to waste in order to apply the time of his hands to picking cotton. One of his neighbors had lost at least 1,000 bushels—now worth $1,500—from mould, mice, hogs, and neglect.

The town of San Felipe, famous as the first American village in Texas, we found composed of two stores and six dwellings—making progress only toward dilapidation.

The Brazos bottoms near by, are four or five miles wide. They are of very great fertility, and the land commands high prices. . A gentleman from Alabama had recently purchased a league (4,400 acres) for $40,000, and during the winter, with three hundred negroes, had cleared and planted seven hundred acres. The bottom is seldom reached by freshets, but was covered in those of the years 1833, 1843, and 1852. We were landed from the ferry near night, and, barely accomplishing the dark and heavy miles of bottom by twilight, camped under a group of huge oaks, at the edge of the great coast-prairie.

To Houston the road lay across a flat surface, having a wet, sandy or "craw-fish" soil, bearing a coarse, rushy grass, diversified by occasional belts of pine and black-jack. We had reached the level prairie region of the coast, and in fact saw henceforth not one appreciable elevation until we crossed the Mississippi. Five miles from Houston we entered a pine forest, which extends to the town.

HOUSTON.

Houston, at the head of the navigation of Buffalo Bayou, has had for many years the advantage of being the point of transhipment of a great part of the merchandise that enters or leaves the State. It shows many agreeable signs of the wealth accumulated, in homelike, retired residences, its large and good hotel, its well-supplied shops, and its shaded streets. The principal thoroughfare, opening from the steamboat landing, is the busiest we saw in Texas. Near the bayou are extensive cotton-sheds, and huge exposed piles of bales.* The bayou itself is hardly larger than an ordinary canal, and steamboats would be unable to turn, were it not for a deep creek opposite the levee, up which they can push their stems. There are several neat churches, a theatre (within the walls of a steam saw-mill), and a most remarkable number of showy bar-rooms and gambling saloons. A poster announced that the " cock-pit is open every night, and on Saturday night five fights will come off for a stake of $100."

A curious feature of the town is the appearance of small cisterns of tar, in which long-handled dippers are floating, at the edge of the sidewalk, at the front of each store. This is for the use of the swarming wagoners.

Houston (pronounced Hewston) has the reputation of being an unhealthy residence. The country around it is low and flat,

---

* The receipts of cotton for the year ending Sept. 1, 1856, were 45,557 bales, or about one-half the receipts of Galveston.

16

and generally covered by pines. It is settled by small farmers, many of whom are Germans, owning a few cattle, and drawing a meagre subsistence from the thin soil. A large number of unfortunate emigrants, who arrive with exhausted purses, remain in the town at labor, or purchase a little patch or cabin in the vicinity. The greater part of the small tradesmen and mechanics of the town are German.

In the bayou bottoms near by, we noticed many magnolias, now in full glory of bloom, perfuming delicately the whole atmosphere. We sketched one which stood one hundred and ten feet high, in perfect symmetry of development, superbly dark and lustrous in foliage, and studded from top to lowest branch with hundreds of great delicious white flowers.

A CAPTURED RUNAWAY.

Sitting, one morning of our stay, upon the gallery of the hotel, we witnessed a revolting scene. A tall, jet black negro came up, leading by a rope a downcast mulatto, whose hands were lashed by a cord to his waist, and whose face was horribly cut, and dripping with blood. The wounded man crouched and leaned for support against one of the columns of the gallery.

" What's the matter with that boy?" asked a smoking lounger.

" I run a fork into his face," answered the negro.

" What are his hands tied for?"

" He's a runaway, sir."

" Did you catch him?"

" Yes, sir. He was hiding in the hay-loft, and when I went up to throw some hay to the horses, I pushed the fork down into the mow and it struck something hard. I didn't know what it was, and I pushed hard, and gave it a turn, and then he hollered, and I took it out.

"What do you bring him here, for?"

"Come for the key of the jail, sir, to lock him up."

"What!" said another, "one darkey catch another darkey? Don't believe that story."

"Oh yes, Mass'r, I tell for true. He was down in our hay-loft, and so you see when I stab him, I *have to* catch him."

"Why, he's hurt bad, isn't he?"

"Yes, he says I pushed through the bones."

"Whose nigger is he?"

"He says he belong to Mass'r Frost, sir, on the Brazos."

The key was soon brought, and the negro led the mulatto away to jail. He seemed sick and faint, and walked away limping and crouching, as if he had received other injuries than those on his face. The bystanders remarked that the negro had not probably told the whole story.

We afterwards happened to see a gentleman on horseback, and smoking, leading by a long rope through the deep mud, out into the country, the poor mulatto, still limping and crouching, his hands manacled, and his arms pinioned.

There is a prominent slave-mart in town, which held a large lot of likely-looking negroes, waiting purchasers. In the windows of shops, and on the doors and columns of the hotel, were many written advertisements headed, "A likely negro girl for sale." "Two negroes for sale." "Twenty negro boys for sale," etc.

THE LOW PRAIRIES.

We were unable to procure at Houston, any definite information with regard to our proposed route. The known roads thence, are those that branch northward and westward from their levee, and so thoroughly within lines of business does local knowledge lie, that the eastern shore is completely terra incognita.   The roads east were said to be bad after heavy rains, but the season had been dry and we determined to follow the direct and distinct road, laid down upon our map.

Now that I am in a position to give preliminary information, however, there is no reason why the reader should enter this region as ignorant as we did.

Our route took us by Harrisburg and San Jacinto to Liberty, upon the Trinity; thence by Beaumont to the Sabine at Turner's ferry; thence by the Big Woods and Lake Charles to Opelousas, the old capital of St. Landry Parish, at the western head of the intricate navigation from New Orleans.

This large district, extending from the Trinity river to the bayous of the Mississippi, has, throughout, the same general characteristics, the principal of which are, lowness, flatness, and wetness.   The soil is variable, but is in greater part a loose, sandy loam, covered with coarse grasses, forming level prairies, which are everywhere broken by belts of pine forests, usually bordering creeks and bayous, but often standing in islands.   The surface is but very slightly elevated above the sea; I suppose, upon an average, less than ten feet.   It is, consequently, imperfectly drained, and in a wet season a large proportion is literally covered with water, as in crossing it, even in a dry time, we were obliged to wade through many miles of marshy pools.   The river-bottoms, still lower than the general level, are subject to constant overflow by tide-water, and what with the fallen timber, the dense undergrowth, the mire-quags, the abrupt gullies, the patches of rotten or floating corduroy, and three or four feet of dirty salt-water, the roads through them are not such as one would choose for a morning ride. The country is sparsely settled, containing less than one inhabitant to the square mile, one in four being a slave.

The people are herdsmen, cultivating no other crop than corn, and of that, not enough to supply their own bread demand. The greater part are of Louisiana origin. They live in isolated cabins, hold little intercourse with one another, and almost none with the outside world. Steamboats land their coffee and salt on the Sabine and Trinity, at irregular intervals, but no wheeled vehicles traverse the region. In two weeks' ride we met with but one specimen, the "mud-cart" of a grocery-peddler, whose wheels were broad blocks sawn from a log. No other road is known than the one by which cattle are driven to the New Orleans market, and this one so imperfectly, that we added probably fifty stray miles to our distance, by following indistinct paths and erroneous information. As hogs do not flourish upon the grass or beneath the pines, the table is relieved by the substitute of ,erked, and, sometimes, fresh beef, and in the best houses we found biscuit, of wheat-flour and lard, a common comfort. In fact, the cuisine is modified even in Texas, by a soupçon of Frenchiness, and in Louisiana, as we approached the confines of civilization, we obtained, now and then, a supper that made our mouths water with Creole sauces. A traveler, other than a beef-speculator, was a thing unknown, and our object was usually an incomprehensible mystery. Hardly once did we see a newspaper or a book, other than an almanac or a franked patent-office report.

The many pools, through which the usual track took us, were swarming with venomous water-snakes, four or five black moccasins often lifting at once their devilish heads above the dirty surface, and wriggling about our horses' heels. Beyond the Sabine, alligator holes are an additional excitement, the unsuspicious traveler suddenly sinking through the treacherous surface, and sometimes falling a victim, horse and all, to the hideous jaws of the reptile, while overwhelmed by the engulfing mire in which he lurks.

Upon the whole, this is not the spot in which I should prefer to come to light, burn, and expire; in fact, if the nether regions, as was suggested by the dream-gentleman of Natchitoches, be " a boggy country," the avernal entrance might, I should think, with good probabilities, be looked for in this region. With these general notions, the reader may, if he please, save himself the following particulars.

TO THE TRINITY.

Leaving Houston, we followed a well-marked road, as far as a bayou, beyond which we entered a settlement of half-a-dozen houses, that, to our surprise, proved to be the town of Harrisburg, a rival (at some distance) of Houston. It is the starling-point of the only railroad yet completed in Texas, extending to Richmond on the Brazos, and has a depth of water in the bayou sufficient for a larger class of boats from Galveston. Houston, however, having ten or fifteen years, and odd millions of dollars, the start, will not be easily overridden. Taking a road here, by direction, which, after two miles, only ran " up a tree," we were obliged to return for more precise information.

At noon, we were ferried over a small bayou by a shining black bundle of rags, and instructed by her as follows:

" Yer see dem two tall pine in de timber ober dar cross de parara, yandar. Yer go right straight da, and da yer'll see de trail

somewar. Dat ar go to Lynchburg. Lor! I'se nebber been da—
don'no wedder's ary house or no—don'no wedder's ary deep
byoo or no—reckon yer can go, been so dry."

Two miles across the grass we found the pines and a trail,
which continually broke into cattle-paths, but, by following the
general course, we duly reached San Jacinto, a city somewhat
smaller than Harrisburg, laid out upon the edge of the old bat-
tle-field.

Upon the opposite shore of the river lies the "town of Lynchburg," which has been recommended, by a commission, for a
national naval dépôt. It consists, at present, of one house and
out-buildings. Within this house is the city post-office, where,
when we mailed a letter, we received, for the first time in six
months, a *cent* in change. A Texan, who was standing by, demanded to see it, saying that he had never known before that
there existed such a coin ; he had supposed it as imaginary as
the mill. The South has no copper currency, the fraction of a
dime being considered too minute for attention. There is a certain vague and agreeable largeness in this, but the contrast of
her working and lounging class with the penny-papered and
penny-lettered corresponding class in the copper-circulating
States is not so pleasing.

A FIRST-CLASS TEXAS GRAZIER.

A ride of thirty-five miles took us to the Trinity. On the
way we spent a night at one of the largest stock-farms of the
district. Its management will afford a better idea of the local
system of stock-raising than any subsequently examined.

The residence was large but rude, and no more descriptive
adjectives could be applied to our style of welcome on arrival

We rode up at evening, at the same moment with a cavalcade of young men, partly of the family, partly invited neighbors. We were permitted without much auxiliary explanation, and with some indirect jeers, to follow the example of the rest and turn our horses, after stripping them, into a fenced pasture, almost the only one we saw in Texas, where five or six fathoms of rope are the usual substitute for stable and paddock. The young men then proceeded to lasso and slaughter a bullock for supper, while we were suffered to wander about like strange cats and familiarize ourselves with the premises. The ground adjacent to the house was nearly all fenced and divided into large and small pens, pleasantly shaded by groves of oak. Among the inclosures were a good garden and a large field planted in corn and sweet-potatoes.

The process of obtaining milk for the table was somewhat singular. In a small pen are kept a number of calves, whose mothers come in morning and evening to give them suck. The lady of the house lets down the bars, holding a little piggin, a bucket, and a short rope, and accompanied by a small boy. The cows enter eagerly, and the calves at once commence drawing their respective rations. The lady then throws a lasso over the horns of one of the cows, the boy attaching the other end of the rope to the neck of the calf, whose lips are drawn beyond reach of the udder. The lady then takes its place and milks into the piggin, held closely by one hand. After about a pint is drawn, the tantalized calf is allowed to squirm back to his natural place, and when the milk is emptied into the bucket outside the fence, the bosom of another happy family is invaded. Thus, in about half an hour, a dozen cows were milked and the pail filled.

The supper was of fresh beef, corn bread, and coffee. On a

side-table stood a decanter of whisky, out of which all, men and boys, had a pull on entering. Our host, we found, was originally a Kentuckian, now many years settled here. He was a man of intelligence, and after supper had leisure for some civil conversation with us upon the gallery. His sons and their friends were silly, rude, illiterate, and stupid, as, perhaps, might be expected from their isolation.

The year's increase of their herd was now five hundred head. This was the season for the annual gathering and branding of the calves. They had been returning from " a drive," when we came up, but one so small as to be of no account. When a regular drive is made, a dozen neighbors, from twenty miles or more about, assemble at a place agreed upon, each man bringing two or three extra horses. These are driven before the company, and form the nucleus of the cattle-herd collected. They first drive the outer part of the circuit, within which their cattle are supposed to range, the *radius* of which is here about forty miles. All cattle having their marks, and all calves following their cows, are herded and driven to pens which have been prepared, in this case to the number of ten, at different points upon the circuit. They are absent from two to three weeks upon this first drive, usually contriving to arrive by night at a pen in which the stock are inclosed, otherwise guarding them in the open prairie. When the vicinity of a house is reached, the cattle are divided, each man's driven into a separate pen, the calves are branded and all turned loose again.

The law allows no property in a weaned calf unbranded, and any one finding such, places his own brand upon them, or slaughters them for his personal use. Dishonest people often take advantage of this, by splitting the tongues of calves to prevent

16*

their sucking, and branding them as if found weaned. This charge we heard especially made at Houston, against the poor Germans of the neighborhood. Here the complaint was, that calves were sometimes stolen and killed, when straying into the swamps, by vagabonds, who did not dare kill them upon open prairie. When cattle are sold, the new brand is placed above the old one, and such double brand is prima-facie evidence of a transfer. A drive usually consisted of 600 cattle, as large a number as it is convenient to manage. It may be conceived that the labor of gathering and confining in pens so many wild cattle, many of which see no human face in a twelvemonth, is not slight. In fact, a drive calls out all a man's energy, adroitness, perseverance, and horsemanship.

Except during the driving season, there was very little to do. Once every month or two they rode through the range, driving in the cattle that were ranging wide. In spite of rogues and accidents of all sorts, the increase was very rapid. Cows are never sold, except as part of a "stock," so that the herd enlarges in compound ratio.

Among the drawbacks are insects and bogs. In a dry and cold winter, when the feed is exceedingly poor, the cattle seek the low grounds near the mouths of bayous or on the sea-shore, where the old grass is more rank and less eaten, and sometimes perish in considerable numbers in the mire. At the end of summer, flies become a very severe annoyance, driving the cattle almost mad with pain and loss of blood. "Ticks," too, sometimes make very bad wounds, clustering together, and filling themselves with blood, until they drop, like bunches of grapes, from the neck, leaving flayed ulcers, in which blow-flies lay their eggs. This takes place frequently in the ears of horses, producing a cicatrix, which gives a singular twist to the ear, horses having which are termed "goched." "Out" cattle are less liable to be troubled by these insects than the "gentled," probably because they frequent timber less, remaining in the open prairies. Calves occasionally suffer so much as to die. We were told, upon the Sabine, that horses sometimes succumbed to attacks of insects, in hauling cotton through the bad roads of the bottom. For cattle, nothing is done, but horses are sometimes driven in, and smeared with sulphur ointment, which gives a temporary relief.

The herdsman's sales are of steers, which are sent to market at four years old. The beef is considered better at five years, but the profit to the herdsman less. In early summer, after the cattle are in good condition with the spring pasture, drovers make their appearance for the purchase. A contract is made, by which, at a price agreed upon, the herdsman shall deliver a certain number of beeves, in marketable order, at a point where it will be convenient to add them to the drove for New Orleans. The range is then scoured, and the requisite number obtained, including all steers found that have escaped the previous years. The price of steers was now $15 to $18 ; that of " stock-cattle," $6 ; that of working oxen, $50 to $75 per yoke.

No pains were here taken to improve the breed. Some cows had been brought to this region from the States, but did not do well. Their calves, however, became acclimated, and were much superior to the common prairie stock.

Attempts to introduce sheep had always failed. Our host had purchased a flock of fifty, which was now reduced, by attacks of wolves and other accidents—all resulting, as he confessed, from lazy neglect—to eighteen. He owned a considerable herd of horses, American and Spanish mares, from which he supplied himself with the large number required in stock driving. The colts were usually caught for the first time, and broken at four years old. The process is a summary one.

Two colts which had been brought in, for the first time, during the day's drive, were taken from the pen after supper, and introduced to the saddle and bridle as follows. A lasso was first thrown over the neck, the colt hauled to a tree—excited and resisting with all his power—and closely blindfolded. A bridle, without bit, was buckled on, a blanket and saddle strapped to his back. The blind was then removed, and the rope slackened. The colt is frantic at the indignity, rears, bounds, kicks, and rolls, until every muscle trembles. If he lies down, he is whipped up until thoroughly fatigued. He is then hauled in again, blinded, led out upon the open prairie, and mounted by the best young man that volunteers. The saddle is Spanish, and has attached to the pommel a strong wooden bar, rolled in sheepskin, extending across the thighs of the rider, almost bolting him to the animal. The blind is now removed, and then comes a scene.

What muscle and wit the colt has in him are put to the test against the tenacity of the rider. Every antic conceivable is played, and when these are exhausted without avail, the pair fly off at a mad gallop, urged on from behind by a horseman with a whip, and led, if possible, by a second towards the safe open country. The pluck and wind of the colt are soon known; and after an hour, more or less, of absence, he comes walking back, peaceable and dejected.

The only accident feared, is a sudden halt and somerset, on the part of the colt, which very rarely happens. The proprietor had once been crushed and stunned in this way. He was found upon the prairie sitting upon the neck of the colt, looking stupidly about. When asked what he was doing, he replied, "holding the horse down." He was able to remount and ride home, but could never remember what had occurred after leaving the others at a gallop. His eldest son had been seriously injured the year before in the same manner.

The horses, like the cattle, were of a mixed and inferior stock. They are mostly undersized, shaggy, vicious, narrow in chest, and low in haunch, like the Mexican and mustang, but, by hereditary education, tough and hardy. They are sold here at from $25 to $40.

We were shown to a crowded loft to sleep, with an apology for the absence of side-boarding under the roof, "it was so difficult to procure lumber." It had been previously mentioned that there were three steam saw-mills within twelve miles. It was not the ventilation, however, but the insatiate bugs, of which we found reason to complain. We rose exhausted at daylight, and were led, as usual, to the common wash-basin upon the gallery. After our ablutions therein, and a sparing use of the one common napkin, we were incidentally informed that the family were recovering from an epidemic of purulent ophthalmia. After breakfast, a child, suffering with the disease, was led out and administered, by force, a dose, of which spirits of turpentine was a principal ingredient, with the promise of whisky and candy, both which it immediately afterwards received.

Our course was pointed out to us across eight or ten miles of grass, to the next timber, the trail being so obscured by the intricate branches of cattle-paths, as to be of no guiding value.

LIBERTY COUNTY.

The Trinity bottoms, opposite Liberty, are about four miles in width, filled with the most luxuriant and varied growth of wood we had seen, amongst it the palmetto, the magnolia, in bloom, and, in greatest number, immense cotton-woods.

Liberty is a stunted hamlet, a short mile east of the river, which is said to be permanently navigable to this point; but we learned that, except two, which lay aground a few miles below, no boats had made their appearance this year. In conversation, we were informed that the country was retrograding rather than improving—an old class of planters gradually disappearing, leaving their places to be occupied by graziers. But the Trinity bottoms, higher up, were being constantly settled—more negroes having been taken there this season than ever before.

Upon the borders of the prairies about here are many Creole French, who came in from Louisiana during the early days of the Republic. They were then in good circumstances, but have now fallen into poverty, owing chiefly, it is said, to injudicious speculations in land. A gentleman told us he had often seen Galveston merchants leave the town with a gang of ten or fifteen negroes, taken in satisfaction of debt from these French planters. Prairie land has very little value; when a sale is made, it is at about fifty cents an acre. The cheapness of land and the facility of access from Galveston attract many Germans here; but, it was said, that bilious diseases made havoc among them—"they don't have no showing to live at all here." Even the Americans acknowledged a great deal of "chills and fever," but seemed to think the Germans were served about right for living without bacon, and eating trash, such as "fresh fish and *ripe cucumbers !*"

From the Trinity to the Neches the face of the country was the same. It is as beautiful, perhaps, as an uncultivated flat can be, the prairies being pleasantly broken by islands and large masses of wood; pine and oak predominating, but cypresses, gums, and magnolias appearing in the bayou bottoms, as the banks of the sluggish brooks are here called. It is occupied by graziers, who rarely raise corn enough to "bread them." They cannot well be nearer one another without the adoption of some different system of living, and are generally squatters—partly because of the vagueness of land-titles in the region, land, where it has any improved value, being often claimed under old Spanish grants. A claim of *forty leagues* (nearly 275 square miles) had lately been confirmed by the courts, and the occupied lands taken by a stranger. The predominant soil is sandy, usually overcharged with water, bearing a rank but very coarse grass, mixed with useless weeds. Though the heat was now sweltering at midday, we were not much troubled with flies, and the traveling might be called agreeable, but somewhat tame, no incident serving to mark the level hours, more remarkable than that of "making" a distant belt of timber, passing it, and leaving it behind. Our horses grew tired of the monotony, and strained eye and ear continually towards the distance, hoping at last to arrive somewhere, and having, perhaps, an instinct that their incessant march was soon to terminate.

SOUR LAKE.

Near the western limit of Jefferson county is the odd natural phenomenon of a "fountain of lemonade." The supply is abundant, and a barrack has been built for summer visitors, who frequent the spring for the relief of every variety of disease—a cure, provided the use of the waters be sufficiently persevered in, being guaranteed by the proprietor. There are, certainly, attractions in the cool shade, the gulf-breeze, the agreeable beverage, and the limpid bath, that should draw a throng, were the spot made accessible. There are two springs, of cold, clear, acid, slightly astringent water, boiling with the outburst of an inflammable gas, having a slight odor of sulphuretted hydrogen. The overflow forms a pond of an acre in extent, which gives to the locality its name of "Sour Lake." Upon the banks and bottom is a deposit of sulphur. The approach to the rude bathing-houses is over a boggy margin, sending up a strong bituminous odor, upon pools in which rises a dense brown, transparent liquid, described as having the properties of the Persian and Italian naphthas.

A BOTTOM BOGGLE.

At Beaumont we were told that the tide was up in the Neches bottoms, and that we should find the road "pretty wet." It was not, however, intimated that we should meet with any great difficulty. The aspect of things from the ferry-boat, therefore, a little surprised us, the bank on which we were landed—some ten feet in width—being the only earth visible above the turbid water. Our directions were, to follow up the course of the stream for about a mile, as far as a certain "big tree," then to bear to the right, and three miles would take us clear of the bottom. At certain spots, where the logs of the corduroy had floated away, we were cautioned to avoid the road, and pick a way for ourselves, wherever we found best footing.

The forest was dense, and filled with all manner of vines and rank undergrowth; the road was a vague opening, where obstructing trees had been felled, the stumps and rotten trunks remaining. Across actual quags a track of logs and saplings had been laid, but long ago, now rotten and in broken patches. As far as the eye could reach, muddy water, sent back by a south wind from the gulf, extended over the vast flat before us, to a depth of from two to six feet, as per immediate personal measurement. We spurred in.

One foot:

Two feet, with hard bottom:

Belly-deep, hard bottom:

Shoulder-deep, soft bottom:

Shoulder-deep, with a sucking mire:

The same, with a network of roots, in which a part of the legs are entangled, while the rest are plunging.

The same, with a middle ground of loose poles; a rotten log, on which we rise dripping, to slip forward next moment, head under, haunches in air. It is evident we have reached one of the spots it would have been better to avoid.

The horses, reluctant and excited from the first, become furious and wild. At the next shoal—personal nastiness being past consideration—we dismount, at knee-deep, to give them a moment's rest, shifting the mule's saddle to the trembling long-legged mare, and turning Mr. Brown loose, to follow as he could.

After a breathing-spell we resume our splashed seats and the line of wade. Experience has taught us something, and we are more shrewd in choice of footing, the slopes around large trees being attractively high ground, until, by a stumble on a covered root, a knee is nearly crushed against a cypress trunk. Gullies now commence, cut by the rapid course of waters flowing off before north winds, in which it is good luck to escape instant drowning. Then quag again; the pony bogs; the mare, quiver-

ing and unmanageable, jumps sidelong among loose corduroy;
and here are two riders standing waist-deep in mud and water
between two frantic, plunging horses, fortunately not beneath
them.

Nack soon extricates himself, and joins the mule, looking on
terrified from behind.

Fanny, delirious, believes all her legs broken and strewn about
her, and falls, with a whining snort, upon her side.   With incessant struggles she makes herself a mud bath, in which, with
blood-shot eyes, she furiously rotates, striking, now and then,
some stump, against which she rises only to fall upon the other
side, or upon her back, until her powers are exhausted, and her
head sinks beneath the surface.   Mingled with our uppermost
sympathy are thoughts of the soaked note-books, and other contents of the saddle-bags, and of the hundred dollars that drown
with her.   What of dense soil there was beneath her is now
stirred to porridge, and it is a dangerous exploit to approach.
But, with joined hands, we at length succeed in grappling her
bridle, and then in hauling her nostrils above water.   She revives
only for a new tumult of dizzy pawing, before which we hastily
retreat.   At a second pause her lariat is secured, and the saddle
cut adrift.   For a half-hour the alternate resuscitation continues,
until we are able to drag the head of the poor beast, half stran-
gled by the rope, as well as the mud and water, toward firmer
ground, where she recovers slowly her senses and her footing.

Any further attempts at crossing the somewhat " wet" Neches
bottoms are, of course, abandoned, and even the return to the
ferry is a serious sort of joke.   However, we congratulate ourselves that we are leaving, not entering the State, by this lower
road, as such a prolonged immersion, during a December sleet-

storm, might have had more serious consequences than the same bedraggled soaking in May. The ferry-man receives us and our second payment of six dimes with a dry nod, that indicates that he considers his advice to us, to try the bottoms, as a good investment, for a man born no nearer Connecticut than the banks of Tennessee river. After a day of scraping, rinsing, wringing out, and drying, at the very tolerable little village hotel, we make a new start, toward a ferry six miles higher up the stream, where the passage is effected without especial trouble.

Our horses being much jaded, we made, before leaving Beaumont, an exchange, by which Mr. Brown was left to the pleasant business of guiding future travelers through the bottoms, and Fanny to the quiet and restorative condition of a prairie brood mare, while we acquired a fresh, lusty, good-natured American stallion, who went satisfactorily through his task of a thousand hot and dusty summer miles, among the hills and valleys that lie between the Mississippi and the Atlantic slopes.

Alas, poor Nack! The dear little brute was sold, a few days later, for twenty-six dollars, and I hardly know what to regret most, the necessary parting, the pitiful price, or the ruthless stable-man's hands, into which he fell. A solemn promise that he should have a month's vacation, and free range of a beautiful unfenced prairie, gave formal salvo to our conscience, but affection still upbraids us for the mercenary separation from our faithful companion. Flesh and blood were never made for cash investments.

As for Judy, the terrier, the wet country had proved for her a great relief. Her ulcerated paws had been carefully covered with moccasins, and, from the beginning of the marshy country, daily improved, until she was able to accomplish the rare canine feat of over two thousand miles of steady travel. A day's pause was now to the tired creature a priceless boon, spent in a rest that was no less than *intense*. Selecting the quietest nook, she would coil herself with great deliberation, and for hour after hour not so much as move a muscle ; immersed in a terrier's sleep, the tip of an eyelid never unlifted. I shall not soon forget her appearance in the Neches bottom. She was very averse—being anything but a water-dog—to enter at all ; but seeing herself abandoned, as we waded away, jumped, with a yelp, into the water, and swam for the nearest stump ; and so followed, alternately submerged in silence and mounted, with a series of dripping howls, upon these rotten pedestals.

For ourselves, we had derived less physical advantage, from our two thousand miles of active exposure, than we had buoyantly anticipated. The abominable diet, and the fatigue, sometimes relatively too severe, had served to null the fresh benefits of pure air and stimulating travel. Lungs, oppressed at home, played, perhaps, a little more freely ; but the frame had not absorbed the sanguine sturdiness that should enable it to resist subtle tendencies, and get itself rudely superior to circumstances.

In this low district, the hot, soggy breath of the approaching summer was extremely depressing ; so much so, as to cause me once a fall from the saddle in faint exhaustion. I retained consciousness enough to loose the lariat and wind it upon my arm ; but, as such loitering was not unfrequent, this was not observed, and I lay half an hour alone, face to the ground, hardly breathing, and unable to speak.

But, to a pulmonary invalid, who can throw off cares, and who has any recuperative elasticity in him, I can recommend nothing more heartily than a winter's ride or sporting trip upon the Texan prairies. For many a case of incipient phthisis, such a course would be the nearest to specific. With money and sufficient pains-taking, it is possible to command a wholesome diet; with clothing and patience, the northers are easily endured. I believe our experience of them to have been unusually severe; but it is remarkable that, owing, perhaps, to some peculiar property of the air from the dry plains, we did not once take cold in them, nor ever suffer anything worse than inconvenience. Six months of leisurely prairie-life, along the pure mountain streams of the West, would, for many a man, now hacking away at his young tubercles in hot rooms, and a weary routine of business, double not only the length but the enjoyable value of life, and at no greater outlay than the sum of his medical bills.

OUT OF TEXAS.

Our road, as far as the Sabine, lay through a district of poorer and more sandy soil, thickly wooded with pine, having small and unfrequent wet prairies. Although rain was much needed for crops, we estimated that one-eighth of the surface was covered by water in stagnant pools. We passed, on both sides the Sabine, many abandoned farms, and the country is but thinly settled. We found it impossible to obtain information about roads, and frequently went astray upon cattle-paths, once losing twenty miles in a day's journey. The people were still herdsmen, cultivating a little cotton upon river-banks, but ordinarily only corn, with a patch of cane to furnish household sugar. We tried in vain to purchase corn for our horses, and were told that "folks didn't make corn enough to bread them, and if anybody had corn to give his horse, he carried it in his hat and went out behind somewhere." The herds were in poor condition, and must in winter be reduced to the verge of starvation. We saw a few hogs, converted by hardship to figures so unnatural, that we at first took them for goats. Most of the people we met, were old emigrants, from Southern Louisiana and Mississippi, and more disposed to gayety and cheer than the Texan planters. The houses showed a tendency to Louisiana forms, and the table to a French style of serving the jerked beef, which is the general dish of the country. The meat is dried in strips, over smoky fires, and, if untainted and well prepared, is a tolerably savory food. I hardly know whether to chronicle it as a border barbarism, or a Creolism, that we were several times, in this neighborhood, shown to a bed standing next to that occupied by the host and his wife, sometimes with the screen of a shawl, sometimes without.

We met with one specimen of the Virginia habit of "dipping," or snuff-chewing, in the person of a woman who was otherwise neat and agreeable, and observed that a young lady, well-dressed, and apparently engaged, while we were present, in reading, went afterward to light her pipe at the kitchen fire, and had a smoke behind the house.

The condition of the young men appeared to incline decidedly to barbarism. We stopped a night at a house in which a drover, bringing mules from Mexico, was staying; and, with the neighbors who had come to look at the drove, we were thirteen men at table. When speaking with us, all were polite and respectful, the women especially so; but among one another, their coarseness was incredible. The master of the house, a well-known gentleman of the county, came after supper upon the gallery and commenced cursing furiously, because some one had taken his pipe. Seeing us, he stopped, and after lighting the pipe said, "Where are you from, gentlemen?"

"From Beaumont, sir, last."

"Been out West?"

"Yes, sir."

"Traveling?"

"Yes, sir."

After pausing a moment to make up his mind—

"Where do you live when you are at home, gentlemen, and what's your business in this country?"

"We live in New York, and are traveling to see the country."

"How do you like it?"

"Just here we find it flat and wet."

"What's your name?"

"Olmsted."

"And what's this gentleman's name?"

"Olmsted."

"Is it a Spanish name?"

"No, sir."

He then abruptly left us, and the young men entertained one another with stories of fights and horse-trades, and with vulgar obscenities.

Shortly he returned, saying—

"Show you to bed now, gentlemen, if you wish?"

"We are ready, sir, if you will be good enough to get a light."

"A light?"

"Yes, sir."

"*A light?*"

"Yes, sir."

"Get a light?"

"Yes, sir."

"Well, I'll get one."

On reaching the bed-room, which was in a building adjoining, he stood awaiting our pleasure. Thanking him, I turned to take the light, but found his fingers were the candlestick. He continued to hold it, and six young men, who had followed us, stood grouped around while we undressed, placing our clothes upon the floor. Judy advanced to lie down by them. One of the young men started forward, and said—

"I've got a right good knife."

"What?"

"I've got a right good knife, if you want it."

"What do you mean?"

"Nothing, only I've got a right good knife, and if you'd like to kill that dog, I'll lend it to you."

"Please to tell me what you mean?"

"Oh, nothing."

"Keep your dog quiet, or I'll kill her," I suppose was the interpretation. When we had covered ourselves in bed, the host said—

"I suppose you don't want the light no more?"

"No, sir;" and all bade us good-night, but, leaving the door open, commenced feats of prolonged dancing, or stamping upon the gallery, which were uproariously applauded. Then came more obscenities and profanities, apropos to fandango frolics described by the drovers. As we had barely got to sleep, several came to occupy other beds in our room. They had been drinking freely, and continued smoking in bed.

Upon the floor lay two boys of fourteen, who continued shouting and laughing after the others had at length become quiet. Some one soon said to one of them—

" You had better stop your noise ; Frank says he'll be damn'd if he don't come in and give you a hiding."

Frank was trying to sleep upon the gallery.

" By God," the boy cried, raising himself, and drawing a coat from under the pillow, " if he comes in here, I'll be damn'd if I don't kill him. He dare not come in here. I would like to see him come in here," drawing from his coat pocket a revolver, and cocking it. " By God, you may come in here now. Come in here, come in here ! Do you hear that ?" revolving the pistol rapidly. " God damn me, if I don't kill you, if you come near the door."

This continued without remonstrance for some time, when he lay down, asking his companion for a light for his pipe, and continuing the noisy conversation until we fell asleep. The previous talk had been much of knife and pistol fights which had taken place in the county. The same boy was obliging and amiable next morning, assisting us to bring in and saddle the horses at our departure.

One of the men here was a Yankee, who had lived so long in the Slave States that he had added to his original ruralisms a very complete collection of Southernisms, some of which were of the richest we met with. He had been in the Texas Rangers, and, speaking of the West, said he had been up round the head of the Guadalupe " heaps and cords of times," at the same time giving us a very picturesque account of the county. Speaking of wolves, he informed us that on the San Jacinto there were " *any dimensions* of them." Obstinacy, in his vocabulary, was represented by " damnation *cussedness*." He was unable to conceive of us in any other light than as two peddlers who had mistaken their ground in coming here.

17

At another house where we stopped (in which, by the way, we eat our supper by the light of pine knots blazing in the chimney, with an apology for the absence of candles), we heard some conversation upon a negro of the neighborhood, who had been sold to a free negro, and who refused to live with him, saying he wouldn't be a servant to a nigger. All agreed that he was right, although the man was well known to be kind to his negroes, and would always sell any of them who wished it. The slave had been sold because he wouldn't mind. "If I had a negro that wouldn't mind," said the woman of the house, "I'd break his head, or I'd sell him. I wouldn't have one about me." Her own servant was standing behind her. "I do think it would be better if there wasn't any niggers in the world, they do behave so bad, some of 'em. They steal just like hogs."

We inquired about the free negroes of whom they were speaking, and were told that there were a number in the county, all mulattoes, who had come from Louisiana. Some of them owned many negroes, and large stocks. There were some white people, good-for-nothing people, that married in with them, but they couldn't live in Texas after it; all went over into Louisiana. They knew of no law excluding free negroes from the State; if there were any such law, no one here cared for it.

This county has been lately the scene of events, which prove that it must have contained a much larger number of free negroes and persons of mixed blood than we were informed on the spot, in spite of the very severe statute forbidding their introduction, which has been backed by additional legislative penalties in 1856. Banded together, they have been able to resist the power, not only of the legal authorities, but of a local "Vigilance Committee," which gave them a certain number of hours to leave the State, and a guerrilla of skirmishes and murders has been carried on for many months, upon the banks of the Sabine, with the revival of the old names of "Moderators and Regulators," of the early Texans.

The feud appears to have commenced with the condemnation, by a justice of the peace, of a free mulatto, named Samuel Ashworth, to receive twenty-five lashes, on a charge of malicious killing of his neighbor's hogs, and of impertinent talking. The Ashworths were a rich mulatto family, settled in Texas in the earliest days of the Republic, and exempted by special mention from the operation of the law forbidding residence to free negroes. They are now three and four generations removed from black blood, and have had a reputation for great hospitality, keeping open house for all who call. The member of the family who was condemned to the indignity of being publicly whipped, rose upon his guard while in the hands of the sheriff, and escaped. In a few days after, he returned with a mulatto companion, and shot the man on whose testimony he was condemned. Upon this the Vigilance Committee was organized, and the sheriff, who was suspected of connivance at the escape of Ashworth, and all the Ashworth family with their relatives and supporters, summoned to leave the county on pain of death. On the other hand, all free men of color on the border, to the number of one hundred and fifty, or more, joined with a few whites and Spaniards, formed an organized band, and defied the Committee, and then ensued a series of assassinations, burnings of houses and saw-mills, and open fights. The Moderators, or Committee-men, became strong enough to range the county, and demand that every man, capable of bearing arms, should join them, or quit the county on pain of death. This increased the resistance and the bloody retaliation, and, at the last accounts they were laying regular siege to the house of a family who had refused to join them. Thirty families had been compelled to leave the county, and murders were still occurring every week. Among those killed were two strangers, traveling through the county; also the deputy sheriff, and the sheriff himself, who was found concealed under the floor of a lonely house, with a quantity of machinery for the issue of false money, and instantly shot: the proprietor of the house, defending himself, revolver in hand, fell pierced with many balls. The aid of the military power of the State had been invoked by the legal authorities; but the issue I have not seen in the newspapers.

CATTLE CROSSING AT THE SABINE.

We arrived, without serious difficulty from swamps, at the west bank of the Sabine, but with soft splashing and floundering enough to recall our wetting at the Neches, and render us extremely reluctant to enter the road across three miles of low bottom on the other side. For my own part, so disagreeable a sensation, in memory, was that of the sinking of a horse under one, in soft mud under water, until his control over himself is lost, that I would have been ready to embark in the first chicken boat for New Orleans, rather than undertake a second wade like that one. But there was no alternative.

There came to the ferry, at the same moment, a drove of mules, and we were curious to see the operation of crossing them. They were first herded in a high-fenced pen upon the shore. After we had crossed, the ferry-man returned in a small skiff, and led into the water a horse accustomed to the work, who was held by the bridle to swim behind the boat, as she receded from the shore. The mules were then driven on with loud shouts and charges from behind, and the foremost being pushed over the bank, on taking to the water, naturally, after a moment's hesitation, followed the horse before them. Men are stationed above and below, to frighten off any who attempt to turn back, and others have the same duty on the opposite side. It is a moment of anxiety; for, should the drove go up or down the stream, or simply insist, through fright or obstinacy, in landing above or below the wings of the pen in which they are received, the greater part would be lost in the swamp forever.

We learned upon the other side, that it was practicable "to take long ferriage," and avoid the bottom almost entirely, by pulling the ferry-boat an hour or two up the stream, to a bluff which the road touched. But, although we were willing to pay the regular charge of four dollars, the ferryman, having an idle turn, refused to gratify us, and we were forced to engage a pilot to take us out by the saddle channel. Following him closely, we were soon upon dry ground, without so much as bedraggled skirts. The pilot was also paid by the drover, whose mules came behind without accident.

The drover considered the Neches bottoms to be in better condition than usual, at present. He had crossed them twice within a year, when he was obliged to swim the horse he rode no inconsiderable part of the way. Once he had horses which he got over without loss.

The second time, he had cattle, and had engaged twelve extra hands to assist him, at three dollars each. Nineteen of the cattle bogged, and he lost them; for, if these wild prairie cattle are left behind or become separated from the drove, they can never be driven. There is danger that they will drive the drivers.

THE DROVER'S STORY.

"I had a splendid pony that trip—a large, powerful pony I called Crockett. When those nineteen beeves bogged, Crockett bogged in behind them. There were two other men near me, one of them on horseback and the other on foot, trying to drive up the bogged cattle. Crockett was in clear up to his withers. Of course, I got off. The mud was about knee-deep, and the water was up to my breast. Among the beeves that were bogged, there was one big old ox that got fiery mad, and he struggled out and turned round and made at the man on the horse, and that was right towards me. 'For God's sake,' says I, 'turn off and get your horse tother side of the tree; if he comes this way he'll kill me, or, if he don't, he'll kill Crockett, sure,' for Crockett and I were both bogged, and couldn't get out of his way. The man turned his horse and got him to one side; but then he saw the man who was on foot. He was a Dutch fellow named Christian—a great big man, six foot, and very fat and heavy. He was very strong and active, though—a great deal more than you'd think, to look at him—and a first-rate fellow.

"Well, when the ox took sight of Christian, he put after him, and you ought to've seen them two! I couldn't help laughing then, though I had nineteen beeves bogged down and my best horse, and I was bogged in myself, and didn't know how soon he'd turn at me. I couldn't help laughing, for all, to see them two dig. Christian, he was working for his life, and the ox was fiery mad and putting in with all his might; but they were both belly-deep in mud, and though they both laid down all they had in 'em, they'd ha' made about as good time if they'd had all their legs sawed off. Finally, he got to a tree, and hauled himself up before the ox got to him, and then it struck off into the swamp."

" And what became of the rest ?"

" Oh, we had to push on and leave 'em there."

" You got Crockett out, then ?"

" Yes; let him rest awhile, and then he worked himself out— a good horse almost always will."

" And what became of the cattle you left ?"

" God knows.   They got off into the swamp, I suppose, after awhile.   There's lots of beef cattle that stray off so from a drove, and are never recovered."

" As nobody owns these cattle but the drover, and they are all branded so nobody else will claim them, and he never comes after them, I suppose they live out the natural life of beef-cattle."

" I suppose so."

WESTERN LOUISIANA.

Soon after crossing the Sabine, we entered a " hummock," or tract of more fertile, oak-bearing land, known as the Big Woods. The soil is not rich, but produces cotton, in good seasons nearly a bale to the acre, and the limited area is fully occupied.   Upon one plantation we found an intelligent emigrant from Mississippi, who had just bought the place, having stopped on his way into Texas, because the time drew near for the confinement of his wife.   Many farms are bought by emigrants, he said, from such temporary considerations: a child is sick, or a horse exhausted; they stop for a few weeks; but summer comes, and they conclude to put in a crop, and often never move again.

It was before reaching the Big Woods, that alligator-holes were first pointed out to us, with a caution to avoid them. They extend from an aperture, obliquely, under ground to a large cavern, the walls of which are puddled by the motions of the animal; and, being partly filled with water, form a comfortable amphibious residence. A horseman is liable, not only to breaking through near the orifice, but to being precipitated into the den itself, where he will find awaiting him, a disagreeable mixture of mire and angry jaws. In the deep water of the bottoms, we met with no snakes; but the pools were everywhere alive with them. We saw a great variety of long-legged birds, apparently on friendly terms with all the reptiles.

A day's journey took us through the Big Woods, and across the Calcasieu to Lake Charles. We were not prepared to find the Calcasieu a superb and solemn river, two hundred and thirty yards across and forty-five feet deep. It is navigable for forty miles, but at its mouth has a bar, on which is sometimes only eighteen inches water, ordinarily thirty inches. Schooners of light draft ascend it, bringing supplies, and taking out the cotton raised within its reach. Lake Charles is an insignificant village, upon the bank of a pleasant, clear lakelet, several miles in extent.

From the Big Woods to Opelousas, there was no change in the monotonous scenery. Everywhere extended the immense moist plain, bearing alternate tracts of grass and pine. Nearer Opelousas, oak appears in groups with the pine, and the soil is darker and more fertile. Here the land was mostly taken up, partly by speculators, in view of the Opelousas Railway, then commenced. But, in all the western portion of the district, the land is still government property, and many of the people squatters. Sales are seldom made, but the estimated price of the land is fifty cents an acre. It is of no value, except as range for herds, and is as thickly settled as it can profitably be, for this purpose.

The herds here are principally of horses, which are of the kind known as "Creole ponies," descended from Norman and Arabian blood, and more valuable than the Spanish stock of Texas, being more intelligent, less vicious, and better formed; but so small as to be suitable only for the saddle. They are valued at from twenty to sixty dollars, the wilder and more neglected herds being of inferior development.

Some of the timbered land, for a few years after clearing, yields good crops of corn and sweet potatoes. Cotton is seldom attempted, and sugar only for family use. Oats are sometimes grown, but the yield is small, and seldom thrashed from the straw. We noted one field of poor rye. So wet a region and so warm a climate suggest rice, and, were the land sufficiently fertile, it would, doubtless, become a staple production. It is now only cultivated for home use, the bayou bottoms being rudely arranged for flowing the crop. But, without manure, no profitable return can be obtained from breaking the prairie, and the only system of manuring in use is that of plowing up occasionally the cow-pens of the herdsmen.

The management of cattle is the same here as in Texas, the laws slightly varying in respect to unbranded yearlings, which are subjected to what is termed the "Congress brand," or mark of the parish, and are sold at auction for the public benefit. But in practice they are usually branded by the first comer, though the penalty is severe. The price of beef cattle was twenty dollars; of cows about the same; that of "stock-cattle," ten dollars. The numbers of the last are roughly calculated, by multiplying by three the total of calves branded in the year.

The road was now distinctly marked enough, but had frequent and embarrassing forks, which occasioned us almost as much an-

17*

noyance as the clouds of musquitoes which, east of the Sabine, hovered continually about our horses and our heads. Notions of distance we found incredibly vague. At Lake Charles we were informed that the exact distance to Opelousas was ninety-six miles. After riding eight hours, we were told by a respectable gentleman that the distance from his house was one hundred and twenty miles. The next evening the distance was forty miles, and the following evening a gentleman who met us stated first that it was " a good long way," next that it was "thirty or forty miles, and damn'd long ones, too." About four miles beyond him, we reached the twentieth *mile-post*.

Across the bayous of any size, bridges had been constructed, but so rudely built of logs that the traveler, where possible, left them for a ford.

The people, after passing the frontier, changed in every prominent characteristic. French became the prevailing language, and French the prevailing manners. The gruff Texan bidding, " Sit up, stranger, take some fry!" became a matter of recollection, of which " Monsieur, la soupe est servie," was the smooth substitute. The good-nature of the people was an incessant astonishment. If we inquired the way, a contented old gentleman waddled out and showed us also his wife's house-pet, an immense white crane, his big crop of peaches, his old fig-tree, thirty feet in diameter of shade, and to his wish of "bon voyage" added for each a bouquet of the jessamines we were admiring. The homes were homes, not settlements on speculation ; the house, sometimes of logs, it is true, but hereditary logs, and more often of smooth lumber, with deep and spreading galleries on all sides for the coolest comfort. For form, all ran or tended to run to a peaked and many-chimneyed centre, with, here and there, a suggestion of a dormar window. Not all were provided with figs and jessamines, but each had some inclosure betraying good intentions.

AMONG THE CREOLES.

The monotonous landscape did not invite to loitering, and we passed but three nights in houses by the road. The first was that of an old Italian-French emigrant, known as " Old Man Corse." He had a name of his own, which he recalled for us, but in forty years it had been lost and superseded by this designation, derived from his birth-place, the island of Corsica. This mixture of nationalities in language must be breeding for future antiquaries a good deal of amusing labor. Next day we were recommended to stop at Jack Bacon's, and, although we would have preferred to avoid an American's, did so rather than go further, and found our Jack Bacon a Creole, named Jacques Béguin. This is equal to Tuckapaw and Nakitosh, the general pronunciation of Attakapas' and Natchitoches.

The house of Old Man Corse stood in the shade of oaks, figs, and cypresses, upon the bank of a little bayou, looking out upon the broad prairie. It was large and comfortable, with wide galleries and dormar windows, supported by a negro-hut and a stable. Ornamental axe-work and rude decorative joinery were abundant. The roof was of large split shingles, much warped in the sun. As we entered and took' seats by the fire, the room reminded us, with its big fire-place, and old smoke-stained and time-toned cypress beams and ceiling, and its rude but comfortable aspect, of the Acadian fireside:

"In doors, warm by the wide-mouthed fire-place, idly the farmer
Sat in his elbow-chair, and watched how the flames and the smoke wreaths
Struggled together, like foes in a burning city. Behind him
Nodding and mocking along the wall, with gestures fantastic,

Darted his own huge shadow, and vanished away into darkness,
Faces, clumsily carved in oak, on the back of his arm-chair,
Laughed in the flickering light, and the pewter plates on the dresser
Caught and reflected the flame, as shields of armies the sunshine."

The tall, elderly, busy housewife bustled about with preparations for supper, while we learned that they had been settled here forty years, and had never had reason to regret their emigration. The old man had learned French, but no English. The woman could speak some "American," as she properly termed it. Asking her about musquitoes, we received a reply in French, that they were more abundant some years than others; then, as no quantitative adjective of sufficient force occurred to her, she added, "Three years ago, oh! heaps of musquitoes, sir, *heaps!*—worse as now."

She laid the table to the last item, and prepared everything nicely, but called a negro girl to wait upon us. The girl stood quiet behind us, the mistress helping us, and practically anticipating all our wants.

The supper was of venison, in ragout, with a sauce that savored of the south of France; there was a side-dish of hominy, a jug of sweet milk, and wheat-bread in loaf—the first since Houston.

In an evening smoke, upon the settle, we learned that there were many Creoles about here, most of whom learned English, and had their children taught English at the schools. The Americans would not take the trouble to learn French. They often intermarried. A daughter of their own was the wife of an American neighbor. We asked if they knew of a distinct people here called Acadians. Oh yes, they knew many settled in the vicinity, descended from some nation that came here in the last century. They had now no peculiarities. There were but few free negroes just here, but at Opelousas and Niggerville there were many, some of whom were rich and owned slaves, though a part were unmixed black in color. They kept pretty much by themselves, not attempting to enter white society.

OLD VIRGINIA.

As we went to look at our horses, two negroes followed us to the stable.

"Dat horse a Tennessee horse, Mass'r," said one.

"Yes, he was born in Tennessee."

"Born in Tennessee and raised by a Dutchman," said the other, sotto voce, I suppose, quoting a song.

"Why, were you born in Tennessee?" I asked.

"No, sar, I was born in dis State.

"How comes it you speak English so much better than your master?"

"O Lord! my old mass'r, he don' speak it at all; my missus she speak it better'n my mass'r do, but you see I war raised on de parara, to der eastward, whar thar's heaps of 'Mericans; so I larned it good."

He spoke it with a slight accent, while the other, whom he called Uncle Tom, I observed did not. I asked Uncle Tom if he was born in the State.

"*No, sar*, I was born in *Varginny*, in ole Varginny, mass'r. I was raised in —— county [in the west]. I was twenty-two year ole when I came away from thar, and I've been in this country forty year come next Christmas."

"Then you are sixty years old."

"Yes, sar, amos' sixty. But I'd like to go back to Varginny. Ho, ho! I 'ould like to go back and live in ole Varginny, again."

"Why so? I thought niggers generally liked this country best—I've been told so—because it is so warm here."

"Ho, ho! it's mos' too warm here, sometime, and I can't work at my trade here. Sometimes for three months I don' go in my shop, on'y Sundays to work for mysef."

"What is your trade?"

"I'm a blacksmith, mass'r. I used to work at blacksmithing all the time in ole Virginny, ironin' wagons and shoein' horses for the folks that work in the mines. But here, can't get no-thun to do. In this here sile, if you sharpen up a plough in the spring o' the year, it'll last all summer, and horses don' want shoeing once a year here on the parara. I've got a good mass'r here, tho'; the ole man ain't hard on his niggers."

"Was your master hard in Virginia?"

"Well, I wos hired to different mass'rs, sar, thar, afore I wos sole off. I was sole off to a sheriff's sale, mass'r; I wos sole for fifteen hunerd an' fifty dollars; I fetched that on the block, cash, I did, and the man as bought me he brung me down here, and sole me for two thousand two hunerd dollars."

"That was a good price; a very high price in those days."

"Yes, sar, it was that—ho, ho, ho! It was a man by the name of ———, from Tennessee, what bought me. He made a business of goin' roun' and buyin' up people, and bringin' 'em down here, speculatin' on 'em. Ho, ho! he did well that time. But I'd 'a' liked it better, for all that, to have stayed in ole Varginny. 'Tain't the heat, tho' it's too hot here sometimes, but you know, sar, I wos born and raised in Varginny, and seems like 'twould be pleasanter to live thar. It's kinder natural to people to hanker arter the place they wos raised in. Ho, ho! I'd like it a heap better, tho' this ole man's a good mass'r; never had no better mass'r."

"I suppose you became a Catholic after you got here?"

"Yes, sar" (hesitatingly).

"I suppose all the people are Catholics here?"

"Here? Oh, no, sar; that was whar I wos first in this here country; they wos all Catholics there."

"Well, they are all Catholics here, too—ain't they?"

"Here, sar? Here, sar? Oh, no, sar!"

"Why, your master is not a Protestant, is he?"

After two deep groans, he replied in a whisper:

"Oh, sar, they don' have no meetin' o' no kind roun' here!"

"There are a good many free negroes in this country, ain't there?"

"What! here, sar? Oh, no, sar; no such good luck as that in this country."

"At Opelousas, I understood, there were a good many."

"Oh, but them wos born free, sar, under old Spain, sar."

"Yes, those I mean."

"Oh, yes, there's lots o' *them;* some of 'em rich, and some of 'em—a good many of 'em—goes to the penitentiary—you know what that is. White folks goes to the penitenti'ry, too—ho! ho! —sometimes."

"I have understood many of them were quite rich."

"Oh, yes, o' course they is; they started free, and hain't got nobody to work for but theirselves; of course they gets rich. Some of 'em owns slaves—heaps of 'em. *That ar ain't right.*"

"Not right! why not?"

"Why, you don' think it's right for one nigger to own another nigger! One nigger's no business to sarve another. It's bad enough to have to sarve a white man without being paid for it, without having to sarve a black man."

" Don't they treat their slaves well ?"

" No, sar, they don't.   There ain't no nations so bad masters to niggers as them free niggers, though there's some, I've heard, wos very kind; but—I wouldn't sarve 'em if they wos—no !— Does you live in Tennessee, mass'r ?"

" No—in New York."

" There's heaps of Quakers in New York, ain't there, mass'r ?"

" No—not many."

" I've always heard there was."

" In Philadelphia there are a good many."

" Oh, yes ! in Philadelphia, and in Winchester, and in New Jarsey.   I know—ho! ho !   I've been in those countries, and I've seen 'em.   I wos raised nigh by Winchester, and I've been all about there.   Used to iron wagons and shoe horses in that country.   Dar's a road from Winchester to Philadelphia—right straight.   Quakers all along.   Right good people, dem Quakers —ho! ho !—I know."

We slept in well-barred beds, and awoke long after sunrise. As soon as we were stirring, black coffee was sent into us, and at breakfast we had *café au lait* in immense bowls, in the style of the *crêmeries* of Paris.   The woman remarked that our dog had slept in their bed-room.   They had taken our saddle-bags and blankets with them for security, and Judy had insisted on following them.   " Dishonest black people might come here and get into the room," explained the old man.   " Yes ; and some of our own people in the house might come to them.   Such things have happened here, and you never can trust any of them," said the woman, her own black girl behind her chair.

At Mr. Béguin's (Bacon's) we stopped on a Saturday night; and I was obliged to feed my own horse in the morning, the negroes having all gone off before daylight. The proprietor was a Creole farmer, owning a number of laborers, and living in comfort. The house was of the ordinary Southern double-cabined style, the people speaking English, intelligent, lively and polite, giving us good entertainment at the usual price. At a rude corn-mill belonging to Mr. Béguin, we had noticed among the negroes an Indian boy, in negro clothing, and about the house were two other Indians—an old man and a young man ; the first poorly clad, the other gaily dressed in a showy printed calico frock, and worked buckskin leggins, with beads and tinsel ornaments, a great turban of Scotch shawl-stuff on his head. It appeared they were Choctaws, of whom a good many lived in the neighborhood. The two were hired for farm labor at three bits (37½ cents) a day. The old man had a field of his own, in which stood handsome corn. Some of them were industrious, but none were steady at work—often refusing to go on, or absenting themselves, from freaks. I asked about the boy at the mill. He lived there and did work, getting no wages, but "living there with the niggers." They seldom consort; our host knew but one case in which a negro had an Indian wife.

At Lake Charles we had seen a troop of Alabamas, riding through the town with baskets and dressed deer-skins for sale. They were decked with feathers, and dressed more showily than the Choctaws, but in calico : and over their heads, on horseback, —curious progress of manners—all carried open black cotton *umbrellas.*

A "NATIVE DUTCH FRENCHMAN'S" FARM.

Our last night beyond hotels was spent in a house which we reached at sundown of a Sunday afternoon. It proved to be a mere cottage, in a style which has grown to be common along our road. The walls are low, of timber and mud; the roof, high, and sloping from a short ridge in all directions; and the chimney of sticks and mud. The space is divided into one long living-room, having a kitchen at one end and a bed-room at the other. As we rode up, we found only a little boy, who answered us in French. His mother was milking, and his father out in the field.

We rode on to the fence of the field, which enclosed twenty acres, planted in cotton, corn, and sweet potatoes, and waited until the proprietor reached us and the end of his furrow. He stopped before replying, to unhitch his horse, then gave consent to our staying in his house, and we followed his lead to the yard, where we unsaddled our horses. He was a tall, stalwart man in figure, with a large, intellectual head, but as uninformed, we afterwards discovered, as any European peasant; though he wore, as it were, an ill-fitting dress of rude independence in manner, such as characterizes the Western man.

The field was well cultivated, and showed the best corn we had seen east of the Brazos. Three negro men and two women were at work, and continued hoeing until sunset. They were hired, it appeared, by the proprietor, at four bits (fifty cents) a day. He was in the habit of making use of the Sundays of the slaves of the neighborhood in this way, paying them sometimes seventy-five cents a day.

On entering the house, we were met by two young boys, gentle and winning in manner, coming up of their own accord to offer us their hands. They were immediately set to work by their father at grinding corn, in the steel-mill, for supper. The task seemed their usual one, yet very much too severe for their strength, as they were slightly built, and not over ten years old. Taking hold at opposite sides of the winch, they ground away, outside the door, for more than an hour, constantly stopping to take breath, and spurred on by the voice of the papa, if the delay were long.

They spoke only French, though understanding questions in English. The man and his wife—an energetic but worn woman— spoke French or English indifferently, even to one another, changing, often, in a single sentence. He could not tell us which was his mother tongue; he had always been as much accustomed to the one as to the other. He said he was not a Frenchman, but a native, American-born; but afterwards called himself a "Dutch-American," a phrase he was unable to explain. He informed us that there were many "Dutch-French" here, that is, people who were Dutch, but who spoke French.

The room into which we were ushered, was actually without an article of furniture. The floor was of boards, while those of the other two rooms were of trodden clay. The mud-walls had no other relief than the mantel, on which stood a Connecticut clock, two small mirrors, three or four cheap cups and saucers, and a paste brooch in the form of a cross, pinned upon paper, as in a jeweler's shop. Chairs were brought in from the kitchen, having deer-hide seats, from which sprang forth an atrocious number of fresh fleas.

We had two or three hours to wait for our late supper, and thus more than ample time to converse with our host, who proceeded to twist and light a shuck cigar. He made, he said, a little cotton, which he hauled ten miles to be ginned and baled. For this service he paid seventy-five cents a hundred weight, in which the cost of bagging was not included. The planter who baled it, also sold it for him, sending it, with his own, to a factor in New Orleans, by steamboat from Niggerville, just beyond Opelousas. Beside cotton, he sold every year some beef cattle. He had a good many cows, but didn't exactly know how many. Corn, too, he sometimes sold, but only to neighbors, who had not raised enough for themselves. It would not pay to haul it to any market. The same applied to sweet-potatoes, which were considered worth seventy-five cents a barrel.

The "range" was much poorer than formerly. It was crowded, and people would have to take their stock somewhere else in four or five years more, or they would starve. He didn't know what was going to become of poor folks, rich people were taking up the public land so fast, induced by the proposed railroad to New Orleans.

More or less stock was always starved in winter. The worst time for them was when a black gnat, called the "eye-breaker," comes out. This insect breeds in the low woodlands, and when a freshet occurs in winter is driven out in swarms upon the prairies, attacking cattle terribly. They were worse than all manner of musquitoes, flies, or other insects. Cattle would herd together then, and wander wildly about, not looking for the best feed, and many would get killed. But this did not often happen.

Horses and cattle had degenerated much within his recollection. No pains were taken to improve breeds. People, now-a-days, had got proud, and when they had a fine colt would break him for a carriage or riding-horse, leaving only the common, scurvy sort to run with the mares. This was confirmed by our observation, the horses about here being wretched in appearance, and the grass short and coarse.

When we asked to wash before supper, a shallow cake-pan was brought and set upon the window-seat, and a mere rag offered us for towel. Upon the supper-table, we found two wash-bowls, one filled with milk, the other with molasses. We asked for water, which was given us in one battered tin cup. The dishes, besides the bacon and bread, were fried eggs and sweet potatoes. The bowl of molasses stood in the centre of the table, and we were pressed to partake of it, as the family did, by dipping in it bits of bread. But how it was expected to be used at breakfast, when we had bacon and potatoes, with spoons, but no bread, I cannot imagine.

The night was warm, and musquitoes swarmed, but we had with us a portable tent-shaped bar, which we hung over the feather bed, upon the floor, and rested soundly amid their mad singing.

The distance to Opelousas, our Frenchman told us, was fifteen miles by the road, though only ten miles in a direct line. We found it lined with farms, whose division-fences the road always followed, frequently changing its course in so doing at a right angle. The country was very wet and unattractive. About five miles from the town, begin plantations on an extensive scale, upon better soil, and here were large gangs of negroes at work upon cotton, with their hoes.

At the outskirts of the town, we waded the last pool, and entered, with a good deal of satisfaction, the peaceful shaded streets. Reaching the hotel, we were not so instantly struck as perhaps we should have been, with the overwhelming advantages of civilization, which sat in the form of a landlord, slapping with an agate-headed, pliable cane, her patent-leather boots, poised, at easy height, upon one of the columns of the gallery.

We were suffered to take off our saddle-bags, and to wait until waiting was no longer a pleasure, before civilization, wringing his cane against the floor, but not removing his cigar, brought his patent leathers to our vicinity.

After some conversation, intended as animated upon one side and ineffably indifferent on the other, our horses obtained notice from that exquisitely vague eye, but a further introduction was required before our persons became less than transparent, for the boots walked away, and became again a subject of contemplation upon the column, leaving us, with our saddle-bags, upon the steps. After inquiring of a bystander if this glossy individual were the actual landlord, we attacked him in a tone likely to produce either a revolver-shot or a room, but whose effect was to obtain a removal of the cigar and a gentle survey, ending in a call for a boy to show the gentlemen to number thirteen.

After an hour's delay, we procured water, and were about to enjoy very necessary ablutions, when we observed that the door of our room was partly of uncurtained glass. A shirt was pinned to this, and ceremonies were about beginning, when a step came down the passage, and a gentleman put his hand through a broken pane, and lifted the obstruction, wishing, no doubt, "to see what was going on so damn'd secret in number thirteen." He drew back hastily, and entered the next room, when I walked toward him hurriedly, *in puris naturalibus.*

But civilization vindicated itself a few days later, in the rapid wheels and clean state-rooms of the "Alice W. Glaize."

Twenty-four hours took us through the alligator-bayous to the Mississippi. Here we separated, one of us resuming the saddle-bags for a two or three months' trip across the mountains, the other steaming on to New Orleans, where, twenty-four hours later, a six months' flavor of bacon and corn was washed out in the cheer of the St. Charles.

CHAP. VII.

GENERAL CHARACTERISTICS.

HISTORICAL AND ACTUAL POSITION.

WHEN, in 1821, the government at Mexico lent an ear to the plans of Moses Austin, they had not the shrewdness to detect in his proposition to introduce upon their idle lands of Texas, three hundred Catholic families from Louisiana,* the concealed point of a wedge that was one day to sunder the Mexican Republic. And when, the same year, the son of the Connecticut empresario staked upon the Brazos prairie the outlines of the first American settlement in Texas, neither he nor the most sanguine of the handful of pioneers, who joined in his venture, could have foreseen the wonderful progress to follow on their little beginning.

These original colonists were not slow at calculating the value of the rich acres their lucky eyes fell upon, nor in sending for their relatives to come on and help take possession. The first advance was quiet, and after all due Spanish formality; and it was not until a firm foothold had been secured, that Americans began to assert their natural rights as the smartest, to the biggest and fairest inheritance. It seems to have been understood that the introduction of slaves was prohibited. They brought

* Yoakum, i , p. 211.

them—none the less—under an attested signature to a ninety-nine years' indenture.* As to Catholicism, not to jeopard their titles or the legitimacy of their children, they were put, grinning, in squads, through the farce of a Roman baptism and re-marriage, by a rollicking vagabond father from Ireland.

Excusing or ignoring a few little moral irregularities like these, as stratagems likely to occur in the progress of any nation before its destiny has become sufficiently manifest to warrant the blunt use of force, we have no reason to be ashamed of the sagacity and determination of our fellow-citizens who chose Texas to build their homes in, nor of the manner in which they bore themselves when, after they were in fair majority, they preferred English taxes and courts to Spanish. They sturdily subdued the lands, the savages, and when necessity was, the impertinent Spaniards.

Every successive attempt at management of their political landlords was bad; and at the last, had these been content to live in democratic peace with their new tenants and neighbors, their flag might at least have floated years longer over their province.

We saw the land lying idle; we took it. This to other nations is all that we can say. Which one of them can cast the first stone?

When the history is candidly re-read, the story that the whole movement was the development of a deliberate and treacherous plot for the conquest of Texas, appears a needless exaggeration of influences that really played a secondary part. Plotting there was, no doubt, and schemes little and big hung on the

---

* "Visit to Texas in 1831."

18

progress of circumstances. Mr. Featherstonaugh attests it, who came upon Houston and other bold spirits, sitting up all night, on the Arkansas border. But Texas had long been coveted, and various idle attempts at seizure had before been made. The event, when by a false step Americans were once invited to enter, was easily foreseen, and heroes of various sorts swarmed around, to glut their ambition as civil and military chieftains, and to get their names emblazoned upon the new map. The class, whose property is invested in slaves, too, saw, clearly enough, its interest in the issue, and resolutely helped it on; and the South, as a section, was not blind to the prospect of so vast a possible increase to its weight in the confederacy. But open movement, under motives so palpable to all the world, cannot be characterized as the workings of a plot, but rather as the first strategetical movements for a free fight.

Austin was, I believe, no mischievous conspirator against Spain, Mexico, or the interests of free labor, though, doubtless, not unwilling to initiate events whose course would pass beyond his responsibility and control. The colonists themselves went as individuals—not as troops or emissaries—and with the single motive, in most cases, of making more money and having a better time in Texas than they could have in the States. The movement was, first of all, agricultural; other influences, as the fillibuster and slavery-extension spirit, were subordinate, and only afterwards got the helm. The land was fertile; that was the kernel of the matter.

For a traveler who has lately ridden over the field, it is not easy to express regret for the simple fact that the fates have ordered such an addition to our national estate, though he may believe it dearly purchased, if it serve to delay for a single year our ultimate riddance of the curse of slavery. Since an English plough first broke the virgin sward of the sea-slope of Virginia, Saxons have not entered on so magnificent a domain. Many times, while making these notes, I have stopped to seek a superlative equal to some individual feature of the scenery to be described, and one is more than ever wanting to apply to the country as a whole. With a front on the highway of the world, the high central deserts of the continent behind, a gentle slope stretching between, of soil unmatched in any known equal area, and a climate tempered for either work or balmy enjoyment, Texas has an Arcadian preëminence of position among our States, and an opulent future before her, that only wanton mismanagement can forfeit.

SURFACE AND STRUCTURE.

A summary review of her present condition will be best given in regional divisions; but a few common characteristics must first be considered.

An outline of the surface is easily conceived. For fifty miles from the sea, extends throughout, a plain, with an imperceptible slope upward from the sea-level. Above comes an undulating interval, rising into broken hills which terminate at the base of the abrupt face of the great desert table-land. The level and undulating regions are an alluvial deposit, from which the waters, it is thought, have not long ago receded. Here and there, as near Seguin, a drift of gravel, superficially deposited, may be found; and, north of the high hills of the upper Guadalupe, primitive rocks and boulders. The hilly region is a vast line of cretaceous formation, extending from the Rio Grande, northeast, (through San Antonio and Austin), to the Red River, corresponding, in many respects, with the similar formation lying parallel with the Atlantic sea-board. It yields everywhere an excellent limestone for building purposes. Near the limit of the table-lands, and following its general exterior line, is a belt of gypsum of rare extent, lying between the Canadian and the Rio Grande, and from fifty to one hundred miles in width. From it a specimen of pure selenite was taken by Capt. Marcy, three feet by four, and two inches in thickness, and perfectly transparent. This bed of plaster may one day be of great agricultural value. On Upper Red River, primitive rocks again appear, and a wide deposit of red clay, giving its coloring mattter to this river. The great plains, according to recent investigations, are themselves deposits of clays in strata, and cretaceous marls.

Coal-beds are found at various points, especially well recognized upon the Rio Grande and at the Clear Fork of the Brazos. Copper ores are abundant; and both copper and iron, it is believed, will be found within the limits of profitable working, when their districts become more settled. Salt has been lately brought to market from the Upper Colorado.

CLIMATE.

In point of climate, Texas claims, with, at least, as much justice as any other State, to be called the Italy of America. The general average of temperature corresponds, and the skies are equally clear and glowing. The peculiarities, over other climates, of the latitude, are found in its unwavering summer sea-breeze and its winter northers. The first is a delightful alleviation of its summer heats, flowing in each day from the gulf, as the sun's rays become oppressive, and extending remotely inland to the furthest settlements, with the same trustworthy steadiness. It continues through the evening, and is described as having so great effect that, however oppressive the day may have been, the nights are always cool enough to demand a blanket and yield invigorating rest. The range of thermometer in summer is uniformly high, though seldom reaching the extremes that occur at the North. A new-comer feels principally in irritating eruptions, that he has entered a semi-tropical atmosphere.

The northers prevail, during the winter months, in the western parts of the State, where the sweep of the air down from the great plains is unimpeded by forests. They alternate, at intervals of a few days, with mild weather, and cause a great and sudden change in the temperature, piercing to the bone, by their force and penetrating chill, any one inadequately prepared to meet them. There is some exhilarating quality, however, about them, that tempers their malice, and with shelter, they are easily endurable.

No part of the State is, probably, entirely free from malaria, the common bane of all our new countries. An unacclimated person must expect to have his attack of " chills," or, if he be imprudent in the situation of his residence, or in exposure, his course of bilious fever. With unusual pains, such as the selection of a dry, breezy hill for the house, and a distant spot for the breaking up of the soil, possibly both may be escaped. The coast towns are visited, sometimes ravaged, by yellow fever (always imported), and, during its season, must be avoided by the traveler. Diseases of the lungs are generally reputed more rare in Texas than in more northern States; but definite statistics are yet wanting. Liability to consumption is not to be escaped by a mere residence, though its course, when established, has, in many cases, been found to be alleviated and retarded.

The soil is always open to the plow, and, if pressed, will not refuse to yield its two crops within the twelvemonth. The long interval between the ripening and the necessary replanting of crops, gives the farmer or planter double advantage from his cultivating force. The plowing may be distributed over many months, and one hand thus do the work of several, where all is condensed into spring.

The season advances somewhat more rapidly than on the Atlantic. Corn and cotton are planted in February, and ripen at the end of July. Wheat is cut in May. In San Antonio market, peas and potatoes, blackberries and mulberries appear early in April, apricots at the end of May, peaches at the end of June, and grapes at the beginning of July. The first bale of cotton at New Orleans, of the crop of 1855, was from Texas, and appeared on the 15th of July.

The temperature of the earth, immediately below the influence of the seasons, is given at about 72° F., as indicated by all springs of considerable volume, at their outburst.

The highest range of the atmosphere which I have seen noted, is 110° F., by Mr. Parker, in Northern Texas: the lowest range at Galveston is reported, by Hon. Ashbel Smith, to have occurred in the winter of 1837–8, when the mercury stood for a few hours at 12° F.

SOURCES OF WEALTH.

The principal wealth of Texas, both of the State and of individual Texans, lies yet in land, the acres held for sale being still in enormous proportion to those brought into use. The land-holders are the chief power in the State, and, did they form a compact and sensitive body, their influence would entirely outweigh that of property in slaves. The cultivable area of the State is estimated at over a hundred millions of acres, about twenty millions of which is called good cotton land, capable of producing, if all put in requisition, in a single year, more than three times our whole actual cotton crop, or upwards of nine millions of bales.

The pastures of the State are a still greater source of future wealth, the production of beef and wool, if stimulated by the means of communication with a steady market, being almost incalculable. At present, it is simply one of the great interests in the commonwealth; and the demand from New Orleans being limited, and the connection with the great northern and European centres of consumption being hardly established,* the chief source of profit is found in the very progress of the interest within itself, the annual growth not keeping pace with the wants of immigrant herdsmen, who desire to purchase their outfit of stocks.

Agriculture in Texas, with some exception among the Germans, is yet almost as rude and wasteful as it is possible to be. No rotation is ordinarily attempted: upon the same field the same crop is repeated, until all the elements of yield are exhausted, when a new area is taken for the same process. In fact, with cotton as the only export, and slaves as the only labor, no better system will ever be adopted. The growth of wealth is in almost nothing else than slaves, and each crop must go to be capitalized in more laborers. The demand upon the soil being thus incessant, immediate return in quantity, without reference to duration, becomes the measure of success, and must remain so as long as virgin soils are at hand.

---

* Within a year or two, Texas droves have not unfrequently been quoted in the New York market reports. They are driven to Illinois, where they are fatted, and forwarded by rail.

The capabilities of the soil for a variety of crops, are, not-withstanding, very great. In the course of years, wine and tobacco will probably appear in the list of exports, with wheat, which is now produced in certain districts in sufficient quantities for a local supply. Maize, with an inconceivable shiftlessness, is still an import of the State.

RAILROADS.

That Texas, with all these capabilities of production, lacks only the means of cheap and steady transportation, to become the richest and most attractive slave State in the Union, is the very first and last reflection that forces itself upon a traveler. For want of such facilities as have shot, like diverging rays of light, from our Northern cities over our northwestern prairies, its vast land-capital must remain locked up and comparatively useless, in spite of its unrivaled capacities. It is, of course, the simplest idea in the world, to mortgage a small part of the idle land for the tenfold benefit of the remainder; and on this principle have been founded various schemes, which, had they to encounter no Northern rivals in the world's market, would surely have been successful long ago. But such an air of delinquency and pound-foolish repudiation, hangs over the young financial character of Texas, that capital is extremely shy, and flows into Northern enterprises at half the price and half the security.

The railway system for the State, is simple and natural: a net-work of parallel roads, at remunerating distances from one another, running from the coast inland, and from the west towards the Mississippi. None of them have failed to be projected; but not one of them is yet completed.

During our winter in Texas, the most profusely liberal offers, under the most riveted State obligations, were made, to further one main line of railway across the State, designed to be the stem of the great Pacific road. But the new obligations had the old Texan odor of evaded contracts about them, and, though adventurers buzzed about, not a capitalist appeared.

Charters, with handsome douceurs in land attached, have a long time existed, for a number of railways. And, during the last session of the legislature, a union of all conflicting plans was effected, in passing a law loaning, in cash, $6,000 per mile to all railways in actual construction. The effect of this remains to be seen; but a new impulse has at last been given to railway enterprises, and the promise is good. But one road is yet in operation, so far as I can learn, in Texas, at the end of 1856— that from Harrisburg and Houston to Richmond, on the Brazos, a distance of twenty-five miles.*

---

* This road is intended to reach Austin. Two competing lines from the Gulf at Galveston, northward, are in course of construction—the "Galveston, Houston, and Henderson," and the "Galveston and Red River." The former has some miles ready for traffic.

18*

CHAP. VIII.

REGIONAL CHARACTERISTICS.

NEW STATES.

THE actual limits of the State of Texas include an area of 274,362 square miles—or a territory greater than the aggregate areas of Kentucky, Virginia, Maryland, Pennsylvania, New Jersey, New York, and all New England.* This immense region, as is well known, is to be divided ere long into five States, according to the terms of the Joint Resolution of Annexation.†

The boundaries of these new States are, of course, not yet mapped, but in local acceptance they are clearly enough indi-cated. The vaguest tavern conversation assumes a natural

---

* Area of Texas, 274,362 miles; of France, 200,000 square miles; of England and Wales, 57,955; of Virginia, 61,000; of New York, 46,000.

† "New States of convenient size, not exceeding four in number, in addition to the said State of Texas, and having sufficient population, may hereafter, by the consent of said State, be formed out of the territory thereof, which shall be entitled to admission under the provisions of the Federal Constitution; and such States as may be formed out of that portion of said territory lying south of thirty-six degrees thirty minutes north latitude, commonly known as the Missouri Compromise line, shall be admitted into the Union with or without slavery, as the people of each State asking admission may desire. And in such State or States as shall be formed out of said territory north of said Missouri Compromise line, slavery, or involuntary servitude (except for crime), shall be prohibited." The limits of the State have been since so defined, that no part now lies north of the Compromise line.

antagonism and future division between Eastern and Western Texas. The limiting line is not drawn—the people of the East assuming the Trinity as their western boundary, while those of the West call all beyond the Colorado, Eastern Texas. This leaves between the Trinity and the Colorado, Central Texas, a convenient and probable disposition.

Northeastern Texas, or the region above the navigable heads of the gulf rivers, and having its principal commercial relations with Red River, is a fourth district, also distinct from the body of the State. The line of the proposed Pacific railroad along the thirty-second parallel, extending upon the map from the Brazos to Shrieveport in Louisiana, may indicate its southern limit.

Northwestern Texas remains. It will still be the largest State of the Union, as its great plains are only adapted, so far as known, for a sparse population of herdsmen and shepherds. It would extend as far east, perhaps, as a line drawn north from the Brazos at 32°, and as far south as a line drawn from the same point to the mouth of the Pecos.

But political necessities, and local jealousies and rivalries will control the limits as well as the time of erection of these five States, and the outlines sketched can only indicate the crystallizing tendencies, and serve for purposes of description.*

NORTHEASTERN TEXAS.

This portion of the State is that which, for the last three or four years, has been most attractive to emigration. We learned,

---

* We have been fortunate in the names of our new States. Do not let us admit these as exceptions, with such names as Houston, Smith, Rusk—but demand the euphonious appellations found within their respective limits. Thus, Caddonia, Sabina, Waco, Comanche; Angelina, Lanana, Panola; Matagorda, Navasota; Bexar, Atascosa, Uvalde, Bandera; Estacada.

very soon after entering Texas, to have a respect for it as receiving general conversational encomiums, and much regretted that it was not in our power to examine it at our leisure. We took pains, however, to preserve such data respecting it as we considered trustworthy, and find them confirmed by an excellent and definite report of Mr. Edward Smith, the commissioner of a proposed English emigration, in 1849.

The region is characterized by its direct business relations, through Red River, with the Mississippi; by its capabilities for the agricultural productions of more northern States; and by the active class of emigrants by which it has been settled. The nearer districts have been peopled from Tennessee and Kentucky, and from the northernmost portions of the gulf States, by farmers and small planters, who hold few field hands, and frequently only household servants, not disdaining to give their personal labor to their lands. Large plantations, with their beggarly accompaniments of poor whites, are comparatively rare, and the country feels the progressive life of its energetic citizens.

The eastern counties are covered with forest; in the central, prairies alternate with wood; while in the western they predominate, although timber enough for agricultural purposes is everywhere within reach. The soil of the east is the red " Red-River soil," sometimes gravelly, usually rich and productive. It is upon this last that the best cotton is produced—that of Cass, Harrison, and Bowie counties bearing a higher price in market than that sent from other districts.

In the north, a rich, black soil is found, commencing in Red-River county, and extending west and south into Dallas county. In the intermediate country lies a gray, sandy soil, alternating in the southeast with the red soil from Red-River.

The prairies are stocked with a "wire-grass," described as very nutritious, which, on the black soils, is found mingled with the "calamus," a sort preferred by horses. Neither is considered equal to the mesquit.

The whole region, but particularly the black calcareous soil of the northwest, is found to be adapted to wheat, and on many farms it is the principal crop. Samples have been shown weighing upwards of seventy-two pounds to the bushel, and sixty-two pounds is considered the miller's average. It is said that the demand of the whole State, were means of transportation provided, could be supplied from the country lying between Fort Towson and the west fork of the Trinity. The crop is ready for the reaper early in May, and new wheat may be placed in market by the middle of the month.

The steady breeze, which prevails nearer the coast, is not wanting, according to the best authorities, in this section, to mitigate the unvarying heats of summer; and Mr. Smith reports abundant testimony of the capabilities of whites for agricultural labor. Thus, Mr. Peacock, near Dangerfield, the owner of several slaves left by his father, states that he works himself in the field, and that cotton is cultivated by white labor with perfect success. A brother-in-law of Mr. Peacock, who would not employ slaves, produced more bales to the hand than any planter around him. Mr. Houndsdell, of Lamar County (whose wheat, yielding twenty bushels to the acre, weighs sixty-seven pounds), knows from experience that a white man can labor as well in cotton-growing, and do as much work in general, as the black man. Dr. Garey, on Sulphur Prairie, says that slavery is almost unknown there, and the settlers are far more industrious than in the South, etc.

The principal planting counties are the easternmost—Harrison, the oldest, having more than one quarter of the slaves found in the twenty-eight counties of this part of the State.

The whole population of Northeastern Texas, in 1850, was about 60,000—one quarter slaves.* At the beginning of 1857, it may be estimated at 135,000—twenty-two per cent. slaves. Harrison, Cass, and Bowie counties, have together nearly one-half. These, with the three adjacent counties, and Lamar, Fannin, and part of Smith, have eight-tenths. But two of the remaining twenty-one counties have as many as five hundred each.*

The increase of slaves, from 1850 to 1855, has been, in round numbers, from 15,000 to 25,000, the principal part of which has taken place in Smith, Cass, Upshur, Harrison, and Titus counties.

The unsettled parts of Northeastern Texas and the adjoining regions, comprising the heads of all the Texan streams as far as the Llano Estacado, have been explored by Capt. Marcy in his various expeditions. They are described in his reports, and in a pleasant volume of "Notes" by Mr. Parker, his companion upon his last trip around the head of the Brazos. No large tracts of land suitable for agricultural purposes, appear to lie beyond the natural boundary of the Cross Timbers, though a part of the surface affords good sheep and cattle range, and here and there a single farm may be placed in a fertile creek-bottom. The Cross Timbers themselves are a curious phenomenon, being two belts of timber (mostly post-oak and black-jack), extending in nearly parallel lines the whole distance from the Brazos to the Canadian, having each a width of five to twenty-five miles. The

---

* The figures are derived from the Census of 1850, and the Report of the State Comptroller for 1855.

water of the streams above them is frequently brackish, bitter, and unsuitable for use, and the country, as the verge of the great plains is approached, becomes desolate, and broken into almost impassable ridges, offering no temptation for any second visit, even of exploration, save by geologists. As to climate, the summer heats and accompanying droughts are extreme, the thermometer for two months ranging from 100° to 110°.

The Brazos has good lands in limited quantities, as high as its Clear Fork, and upon the latter, not only excellent soil, but valuable beds of coal. The Little Wichita and Upper Red River have some fertile bottoms; but the only other region of agricultural value is found at the base of the Wichita mountains, of which Capt. Marcy speaks with enthusiasm. This, however, will not only be long remote from markets, but lies within the limits of the Indian Territory. That large projection of Texan area, from Red River northward to 36° 30, appears to be nearly worthless.

EASTERN TEXAS.

Particular observations in this part of Texas have been given in describing our route, which lay twice across it. The grassed flats of the coast extend some fifty miles from the gulf. Above this is a wooded region, having a western edging of small prairies along the Trinity, and an eastern of pine-bearing sand along the Sabine. It is considered to be less fertile, except in limited spots, than the other sections of the State; and in certain portions the lands of considerable districts have already been exhausted. Judged by the increase of slaves, the northern and northwestern counties are in a progressive condition, while the eastern central are retrograding — the comptroller's report showing an actual decrease of numbers.

Its population, in 1850 about 45,000, may be estimated, in 1857, at 70,000, of which thirty-six per cent. are slaves.

CENTRAL TEXAS.

Central Texas comprises the oldest American settlements, the principal sugar-district, and some of the richest bottom-lands of the State, as well as the two chief towns of Houston and Galveston.* The coast-prairies extend sixty or eighty miles inland, but are far more fertile and valuable than those either of the East or the West; being traversed by small streams, in whose bottoms lie the productive fields of great plantations. The undulating region above, has the characteristics of both the wooded and the prairie districts; high pastures covering the ridges between the streams, dense forests following their courses. The prairie soil is lighter than the black soils of the west, and easily exhausted; but the low lands are unsurpassed. The country is probably destined to the occupation of a mixed population of herdsmen and planters. In the extreme north, the undulations rise into broken, rocky hills, with narrow intervals of level land along the wooded valleys. Here a good bituminous coal is found.

---

* Galveston, the principal port of the State, stands near the eastern extremity of one of the flat sand-islands of the gulf, some twelve miles from the main. Its streets are regular, lined by buildings of wood; its business active, giving it a rapid growth, its population being now about 10,000. Its remarkable points are, its cotton warehouses, its direct foreign trade, its bare elevation above the gulf, the depth of water on its bar—called ordinarily fourteen feet, but varying with the wind—its good hotels, its beach-sand drive, its periodical devastation by yellow fever, its bleak and piercing northers, and the bigoted devotion of its inhabitants to African slavery as the social ideal. In the latter respect, it affects to rival Charleston, its citizens having recently refused even to receive the explanations of their own representative, Mr. Sherwood, for one of his votes in the State legislature, burning him instantly at the moral stake.

SUGAR.

The sugar lands of Texas are estimated roughly to embrace an area of more than seven millions of acres; sufficient, should their capacities ever be developed, to supply three times the whole amount now consumed in the United States. It is not probable that one-tenth part will be put to use; but, should the present import duty be maintained, and Cuba, with her irresistible tropical advantages, remain under foreign dominion, a steady development of production will probably go on. The best lands are quite equal to those of Louisiana, while the capital required for new establishments is far less than there—lands bearing one-eighth the price, no levees, drains, or canals being required, and fuel, for the present, being at hand.

The principal sugar-growing counties are Brazoria and Matagorda, upon the coast, which, as long ago as 1850, indicated their capacities, by sending to market over 5,000 hogsheads. Within their limits are some of the richest soils in the world. One cane-brake (the best indication) extends over a strip seventy-five miles in length, along the Caney, a little coast stream.

Central Texas is also the region whence comes the bulk of the cotton exported by the State—the counties of Colorado and Washington contributing nearly one-fifth to the total.

The population of the region in 1850—61,000—thirty-six per cent. slaves—may be assumed to have doubled in six years, and to be now about 122,000—thirty per cent. slaves.

WESTERN TEXAS.

Western Texas must be considered in two parts—the settled district lying between the Colorado and the Nueces, and the barren wastes bordering the Rio Grande.

Of the genial portion I have already spoken with unfeigned enthusiasm. For sunny beauty of scenery and luxuriance of soil, it stands quite unsurpassed in my experience, and I believe no region of equal extent in the world can show equal attractions. It has certainly left such pictures in memory, as bring it first to mind as a field for emigration, when any motive suggests a change of my own residence.

Its surface has a general similarity to that of Central Texas. Beyond the flat coast prairies, which extend some forty miles inland, commence gentle swells, continuing to the base of the Guadalupe range of hills, 150 miles from the gulf.

Its superb pastures are the characteristic of the country. The whole extent, except an occasional cedar-brake or patch of post-oak, and away from the immediate banks of the streams, is covered with the finest and most nutritious grasses, supplying, even in winter, sufficient sustenance for cattle, and in summer, a luxurious superabundance. Herds and flocks form, consequently, its natural riches; and of these, where so little care is required, it is almost impossible to over-estimate the productive capacity.

The streams which, in other parts of the State, are thick and discolored with mud, flow here clear as crystal; and the soil, which, as you advance from east to west, across the State, steadily improves in fertility, here culminates in a black calcareous loam, which is universally distributed.

Its disadvantages are, the comparative scarcity of timber for building and fencing, the reported greater liability to loss from dry seasons, the distance from market, and, temporarily, the exposure to Indian marauds upon its frontier. The north winds, too, which come in winter with fury, from the plains above, are to be dreaded, though they are partly counterbalanced by the luxurious steadiness of the summer sea-breeze.

In respect of population, Western Texas is characterized by the presence of a large foreign element.

The Mexicans alone, obtained by annexation, number here nearly twenty thousand. Such particulars as we could gather respecting their condition, have been already offered. Of those who had property and intelligence, the greater number at once withdrew from Texas; of the remainder, the stagnant life has been little changed by the new laws and the new circumstances; and, being regarded by the Americans as, socially, only a step above the negroes, they have little or no influence within the community, in which they possess, notwithstanding, an equal voice in all questions open to suffrage. In these matters they are, to a great degree, under the control of their church, though much less absolutely so than in Mexico. They have been of value as furnishing a temporary though ill-regulated supply of cheap labor, already familiar with the details of local agriculture, and especially adapted to its most profitable branch of stock-raising. But as they have the reputation of naturally consorting with negroes, and falling into an intercourse with them immediately demoralizing and dangerous, they have done much to prevent the approach toward the frontier, of agricultural capital. They make, however, themselves docile and patient laborers, and, by dint of education and suitable management, are not incapable of being elevated into a class that shall occupy a valuable position in the development of the resources of the region.

A singular offshoot of the great European current has poured, almost coincidently with American occupation, a considerable stream of German immigration into the same territory. An account of its origin and course, and our observations among the settlers thus introduced, have been given. Some details of their actual numbers, character, and political position remain to be added.

NUMBER AND POSITION OF THE GERMANS.

There are estimated to be, at the commencement of 1857, 35,000 Germans in Texas, of whom about 25,000 are settled in the German and half-German counties of Western Texas.*

The early emigration was of a somewhat humble and promiscuous description. While the great part was composed of peasants and mechanics, who had no other reproach than that of honest poverty, and a desire for improving their condition, there were a certain number, as among the early settlers of Virginia, who were suffered to escape justice at home on condition of becoming colonists; who were, in short, *sentenced* to Texas. But whatever of reckless energy was thus disposed of, seems to

---

* In Comal, Gillespie, and Medina counties, nearly all the inhabitants are Germans. In Victoria and Colorado counties they constitute about three-fourths the population; in Calhoun, Bastrop, and Bexar (excluding San Antonio), about one-half; in Fayette, Caldwell, Travis, and San Antonio city, about one-third, and in Hays about one-fourth. I have, from an intelligent source, the following estimate by counties, with a larger footing. The census of 1850 is thought to be of little value in respect of reports upon the nativities of Texans :

EASTERN TEXAS.—Galveston, 3,500 ; Houston, 3,000 ; Harris Co., 1,000 ; scattered, 1,000. Total, 8,500.

CENTRAL TEXAS.—Austin, 3,000 ; Washington, 1,000 ; Travis, 2,000 ; Colorado, 1,200 ; Bastrop, 1,100 ; Fayette, 1,000 ; Milam, 500 ; other counties, 400. Total, 10,200 (part west of Colorado).

WESTERN TEXAS.—Comal, 3,500 ; Gillespie, 2,000 ; Bexar, 5,000 ; Medina, 1,500 ; Guadalupe, 1,500 ; Victoria, 1,500 ; Dewitt, 1,500 ; Calhoun, 1,200 ; Karnes, 800 ; Caldwell, 400 ; Nueces, 400 ; Llano, 400 ; Hayes, 300 ; Kerr, 300 ; Gonzales, 300 ; Rio Grande Cos., 1,100. Total, 21,700. Total in State 40,400.

have found for itself a natural and harmless vent among the rough demands of frontier life. The result, at least, favors an offer to every rogue of the chance to show himself the victim of circumstances; for it is certainly remarkable with what success the unpractical nation has joined issue with nature and the savages; and how here, where the comparison may every day be made, even Americans acknowledge the Germans their equals as pioneers.*

After the events of 1848, the emigration became of a more valuable character, and included a large proportion of farmers and persons in moderate circumstances, who sought a hopeful future in the New World. With them came numbers of cultivated and high-minded men, some distinctly refugees, others simply compromised, in various degrees, by their democratic tendencies, who found themselves exposed to disagreeable surveillance, or to obstructions, through police management, in whatever honorable career they wished to enter, while others merely followed, from affection or curiosity, this current of their friends.

Few of this class have been able to bring with them any large amount of property; and, with the German tendency to invest in lands, they have chiefly lost the advantages belonging to even a limited capital-in-hand in a new country.

I have described how wonderfully some of them are still able to sustain their intellectual life and retain their refined taste, and, more than all, with their antecedents, to be seemingly contented

---

* Our information upon this point may be incorrect. At all events, the number of vagabonds was very small, as only cash subscribers were received by the association. Single men were required to be in possession of $120, married men of $240. This regulation excluded from Texas a pauper class, which has since furnished thousands of vigorous and valuable laborers to the northwestern States. *Gesammelte Aktenstuecke des Vereins*, p. 27.

and happy, while under the necessity of supporting life in the most frugal manner by hard manual labor.

There is, as I have before intimated, something extremely striking in the temporary incongruities and bizarre contrasts of the backwoods life of these settlers. You are welcomed by a figure in blue flannel shirt and pendant beard, quoting Tacitus, having in one hand a long pipe, in the other a butcher's knife; Madonnas upon log-walls; coffee in tin cups upon Dresden saucers; barrels for seats, to hear a Beethoven's symphony on the grand piano; "My wife made these pantaloons, and my stockings grew in the field yonder;" a fowling-piece that cost $300, and a saddle that cost $5; a book-case half filled with classics, half with sweet potatoes.

But, as lands are subdued, and capital is amassed, these inconveniences will disappear, and pass into amusing traditions, while the sterling education and high-toned character of the fathers will be unconsciously transmitted to the social benefit of the coming generation. The virtues I have ascribed to them as a class are not, however, without the relief of faults, the most prominent among which are a free-thinking and a devotion to reason, carried, in their turn, to the verge of bigotry, and expanded to a certain rude license of manners and habits, consonant with their wild prairies, but hardly with the fitness of things, and, what in practical matters is even a worse error, an insane mutual jealousy, and petty personal bickering, that prevents all prolonged and effective coöperation—an old German ail, which the Atlantic has not sufficed to cleanse.

The poorer emigrants, who were able to purchase farms, have made the happiest progress, meeting a steady market for their productions, and a continuous appreciation in the value of their improved lands. The mechanics and laborers, after the first distress, found more work awaiting them than their hands could perform, and have constantly advanced to become themselves employers, offering their old wages to the new-comers of each successive emigration.

This is the source whence has been supplied the patient and well-directed muscle, which is the first demand of a new country, and which, had American, or even African arms been awaited, Western Texas must have long wanted.

In social and political relations, the Germans do not occupy the position to which their force and character should entitle them. They mingle little with the Americans, except for the necessary buying and selling. The manners and ideals of the Texans and of the Germans are hopelessly divergent, and the two races have made little acquaintance, observing one another apart with unfeigned curiosity, often tempered with mutual contempt. The Americans have the prestige of preoccupation, of accustomed dominance over Mexicans and slaves, of language, capital, political power, and vociferous assumption. The Germans, quiet, and engrossed in their own business, by nature law-abiding and patient, submit to be governed with little murmuring.

A large proportion of the emigrants have remained apart, in German communities, and have contented themselves with the novel opportunity of managing, after republican forms, their own little public affairs. Others, by their scattered residence in isolated positions, are excluded from any other than individual life. Such as have settled in American neighborhoods or towns, feeling the awkwardness of new-comers, and ignorant of the language, have hitherto almost refrained from taking part in politics.

The intelligent portion as early as possible make themselves citizens, and become voters; but until the recent agitation of the idea of restricting the privileges of persons of foreign birth, there has been, in fact, no topic of sufficient general interest to give rise to parties among them, or to force them, as is the result of this, into united action.

As to slavery, the mass living by themselves, where no slaves are seen, and having no instinctive prejudice of color, feel simply the natural repugnance for a system of forced labor, universal in free society. Few of them concern themselves with the theoretical right or wrong of the institution, and while it does not interfere with their own liberty or progress, are careless of its existence.

But this mass is easily swayed by political management, and if brought to any direct vote, examining every question only in the light of personal interest, would move together against slave-owners as their natural enemies.

Among the Germans of the west we met not one slave-owner, and there are not probably thirty among them all who have purchased slaves.* The whole capital of most of them lies in their hands, and with these every black hand comes into tangible and irritating competition. With the approach of the slave, too, comes an implied degradation, attaching itself to all labor of the hands.

The planter is by no means satisfied to find himself in the

---

* A gentleman of San Antonio, from his business relations with Germans particularly well-informed in the matter, told me he knew, in all, of twelve German slave-proprietors in Texas. Ten of these have unwillingly bought house-maids, to relieve their wives, who were unable to find German servants; one gentleman owns four field-hands in Gillespie county; another about the same number in Washington county—both old Texans of '36.

neighborhood of the German. He is not only by education un-congenial, as well as suspicious of danger to his property, already somewhat precariously near the frontier, but finds, in his turn, a direct competition of interests, which can be readily compre-hended in figures.

The ordinary Texan wages for an able field-hand are $200. The German laborer hires at $150, and clothes and insures him-self. The planter for one hand must have paid $1,000. The German with this sum can hire six hands. It is here the con-tact galls.

But actual collision is comparatively rare. The German shop-keepers and mechanics, in American towns, occupy, of ne-cessity, an almost suspected position, and whatever their senti-ments, they carefully avoid all open expression.* In the German settlements there is no direct occasion for thought on the subject. It is only where the population mixes in equal proportion—as in San Antonio—that ideas and interests clash, and bitter feelings are stirred.

The great body of Germans being devoted exclusively to their own material progress, there are, as might be expected, two rival influences at work among them. It is not to be believed that European democrats, who have suffered exile for their social theories, would at once abandon them, and, by fraternizing with an aristocracy of slave proprietors, belie here every principle for which they had struggled at home. On the other hand, in every community a certain number of hangers-on are sure, from mo-

---

* Not, however, from any motives of direct interest, as might be surmised, in business with planters. The empty cotton-wagons bring these their supplies from the coast direct, and they own their own slave-mechanics, avoiding Ger-mans when possible.

19

tives of petty selfishness, to attach themselves to any dominant party. The Americans have thus their allies among the Germans, who, with those who fear the agitation of any subject, but especially this, as detrimental or inopportune, form the party of eager subservience. In a slave state the opportunity does not often arise for any public expression of an opinion upon slavery, and for want of a practical question for discussion, neither of these divisions has been able to show any great activity, except of jealousy and acrimonious feeling.

Their existence and relative power are best illustrated by the history of an attempt at the free discussion of slavery in the columns of their German newspaper. Feeling themselves strong enough in San Antonio to support a local journal, which should be a means of intercommunication, of literary sustenance, and of expression of their opinions, the leading Germans raised, about four years since, by small joint subscriptions, a capital for the purchase of a press and materials. A prominent exile, of literary experience, was elected editor by general acclamation, and the issue of a weekly commenced. In his prospectus, the editor announced himself a radical democrat, and his determination to regard every political question from the point of view of social progress.

Slavery could not of course be ignored, and, although the position was delicate, the subject was discussed like others, as often as its importance, under the circumstances, demanded. Its economical variance with the interests of the German free laborers, and with the natural future of the Western prairies, was now and then dwelt upon; and on the main question of the essential temporariness or permanence of slavery in America, involving, in national politics, extension and furtherance, or restriction and localization, the ground natural to a democrat by principle, was taken. But the tone of the paper was rather literary and educational, and slavery had apparently no special prominence. What was said on the subject, circulated only among Germans, and, though distasteful to the Americans, was, for a long time, hardly noticed by them.

The journal was a decided success, and, at the annual election, the same editor was, with great unanimity, chosen by the stockholders to continue its conductor. Meanwhile, the Germans feeling their social influence too small upon the public opinion of a community of which they constituted by intelligence and numbers, at least the equal half, undertook to assert themselves by some combined action. In May, 1854, advantage was taken of the concourse at their annual musical festival in San Antonio, to hold a simultaneous political convention. An extended " platform" was adopted and published, containing the condensed expression of their radical opinions. It had the disadvantage of proposing no particular action, but of being put forth as a simple manifesto of principles.

One of the resolutions discussed slavery, and declared it to be an evil which should be eventually removed.*

---

* " Slavery is an evil whose ultimate removal is, according to Democratic principles, indispensable; but as it affects only individual States, we demand : That the Federal Government refrain from all interference in affairs of Slavery; but that, when any single State shall resolve on the removal of this evil, the aid of the government may be claimed.' (Die Sklaverei ist ein Uebel, dessen endliche Beseitigung, den Grundsätzen der Demokratie gemäss, nothwendig-ist; da sie aber nur einzelne Staaten betrifft, so fordern wir : Dass die Bundesregierung sich aller Einmischung in Sachen der Sklaverei enthalte ; dass aber, wenn ein einzelner Staat die Beseitigung dieses Uebels beschliesst, alsdann zur Ausführung dieses Beschlusses die Bundeshülfe in Anspruch genommen werden kann.)

The following amendments were rejected :

" Slavery is according to our views a social evil, and possibly liable to conflict

The novel attitude of the Germans was disagreeable to the Americans, and this resolution, meddling with the question of slave-property, particularly offensive. An excitement sprung up, which for a month or more was kept within the limits of conversation, but broke out into newspaper clamor and open threats of violence, when, by a series of articles from a German source, it was discovered that the Germans were not unanimous in their opinions.

In fact, the time was unpropitious for such a political demonstration. "Americanism" was just beginning to show its strength in the East, and to extend its lodges and its barbarizing prejudices into Texas. This independent movement on the part of foreigners, was a god-send to the new party. It gave it a tangible point of attack, and what with the cry of "foreign interference in politics," and "abolitionism in Texas," a universal howl from the American papers went up against the Germans.

The German newspaper had the brunt to bear. It had published and defended the resolutions, and could not, like the convention, dissolve into silence. The editor, reading in the State Constitution the guarantee of his right to free speech, continued on his way, taking little notice of the outcry, answering only in earnest, such arguments as were worth the pains. He soon, however, found that some of his subscribers were disposed to flinch. Two parties were evidently forming among them.

with white labor. But this institution comes too little home to Germans, and is too much connected with the interests of our American fellow-citizens, for us to feel ourselves urged to take, in this question, initiatory-steps, or to act upon it politically."

"Negro-Slavery is an evil, perilous to the duration of the Union. Its abolition must be left to the individual States in which it exists. We German-speaking Texans, are not naturally in a position to initiate measures, but we wish the Federal Government's patronage of the same dispensed with."

At his suggestion, a general meeting of the stockholders was called, at which the course of the paper was sustained, but as a measure of justice to the dissentients it was resolved to sell the press, and allow the paper to stand upon its merits. The editor now became proprietor, and for a time was well supported. An English department was added to his sheet, that Americans might read his principles for themselves, not in garbled extracts and translations with a purpose. This aroused again the fury of the American papers, which, as time passed, had somewhat subsided. A determined effort was made for the suppression of the sheet. Under threat of being denounced as secret abolitionists, the American merchants were induced to withdraw their advertisements. The publication was then carried on at a loss. Friends began to waver, and to condemn the editor's course as "ultra," terminating one by one their subscriptions. The editor saw himself becoming a victim to his allegiance to principles, but, for more than a year, sustained with dignity his supposed right to free expression in Texas. His resources at length exhausted, he surrendered to starvation, and became a second time an exile, the press falling into the hands of the opposite party, who have established a journal whose first principle is not to give offense to slaveholders.

During this singular struggle, threats of the application of Lynch law were incessant on the part of the Americans. The American journals even advocated it, the "*State Times*" of Austin going so far as to indicate the mode of punishment, by drowning. The locality was favorable, to the last degree, for this mode of disposing of opposition. The respect for law is of the weakest, and the tribe of border-idlers, always ready for an excitement, has its very headquarters in San Antonio. In fact, the danger was imminent, and only averted by the personal pluck of the editor, and the determination on the part of the Germans, without regard to party, to resist force by force, and to stand by their countryman, bullet for bullet, in a collision of races where the laws were on their side.

The editor has since become a resident of Boston. He has some amusing details of the various means brought to bear upon his obstinacy. While at work at his press one morning, he was interrupted by a knock, which introduced a six-foot citizen of the region, holding in his hand a heavy stick, and accompanied by a friend.

"Are you the editor of this German newspaper?" he asked.

" Yes, sir."

" You're an abolitionist, are you?"

" Yes, sir."

Then came a pause, after which the inquiry—

" What do you mean by an abolitionist?"

The editor very briefly explained.

Another pause followed, after which the citizen announced that he would consult with his friend a moment outside. He shortly reëntered, saying:

" Well, sir, we've concluded that you are a God damn'd abolitionist, and that such a scoundrel as you are ought to be thrashed out of the town."

" Very well, sir. Try it."

A third pause ensued, to terminate which, the editor opened the door, whereupon the individuals walked out.

The same persons hovered about for some days, not coming, however, nearer than the door-yard, and at length became such a nuisance that he was forced to obtain the services of a friend, to explain in a quiet way his precise opinions; upon which they made a bluff apology, and acknowledged him to be not so bad a fellow, after all. Once, an offered blow produced a blow in return, which was followed by a profuse discharge of apologies from the floor, further explanations not being required. In fact, a little muscle is not a bad adjunct to a martyr who is willing to prolong his misery.

The obnoxious premises were several times reconnoitered by armed gangs, once by a company sent, in order to help to end the matter, from the east; but a larger force was always at once found quietly awaiting the reconnoiterers, who thereupon retired. The reputation of the city being at stake, and having nothing to lose, the Americans were by no means unanimous in approving extreme measures.

The "abolitionism" of the editor was, it is fair to say, of a very mild type, confined to the belief—until lately universal at the South—that slavery was an evil; he being by no means ready to propose any practical measures for its removal. Nor did any German with whom we conversed during our journey, so far as I recollect, go beyond this not very treasonable idea in actual politics. Any process of terminating slavery without regard to the established tenures of slave proprietors, would have an *ex post facto* nature, vitiating its benefits and making it inadmissible. But that, for Western Texas, laws should discourage the further introduction of negroes, and offer inducements for the application of capital to varied employments, requiring educated laborers, they were not less decided. And in social relations, they are sensitive to the overbearing propensities of a proprietary who are accustomed to regard all neighbors out of their own class as White Trash.

I have been thus particular in describing the condition and attitude of the Germans, as the position in which fortune has placed them, in the very line of advance of slavery, is peculiar, and so far as it bears upon the questions of the continued extension of cotton limits, the capacity of whites for independent agriculture at the South, and the relative profit and vigor of free and slave labor, is of national interest.

The presence of this incongruous foreign element of Mexicans and Germans tends, as may be conceived, to hinder any rapid and extensive settlement of Western Texas by planters. There are other circumstances contributing to the same effect. The proximity of the frontier, suggesting and making easy the escape of·slaves, is a chief difficulty. Then there are the border disquiets from Indians, who regard slaves as fair booty when placed in their way. Besides which, the profit of cotton-planting far from market, is small, the distance, for large emigrant trains, fatiguing, and the long travel expensive.

So great, too, is the force of custom, that thousands of emigrants from the lower slave states, deliberately prefer an inferior soil covered with forest, to any field prepared by nature for the plow. They have never seen a good field free from the familiar stumps and half-burnt trunks; and, shaking their heads, stop with their hands and their axes to conquer their own space, where the cabin shall be sheltered and secluded, as "at home."

Planters have hitherto consequently settled in masses, almost exclusively upon the Colorado and Lower Guadalupe bottoms, leaving the great remaining western pasture regions to their more natural occupation of herdsmen and small farmers.

The herdsmen have no use for slaves, which are only

adapted for working in gangs under constant supervision, and cannot be trusted in an employment requiring isolation and discretion. And both herdsmen and farmers find in the proximity and society of planters, a mutual incompatibility.

The result has been the formation of a social condition, differing from that of the rest of the State, which, if its development be not interfered with, will, probably, assimilate in general aspect to that of the western portions of the Atlantic slave states, with such advantages as will accrue from a more fertile soil and greater wealth.

It will only be by a forced and uneconomical change, that this prairie soil can ever be devoted to large plantations and cotton as their staple production. Beef and wool must, for a long time, yield a far more profitable return. Water, however, is abundant, and an intelligent population is already on the spot, perfectly adapted to become manufacturing, if capital be furnished it. These considerations render it probable that Western Texas will have ultimately a position similar to that of Western Virginia and Georgia, when the planting interest will remain subordinate to that of farmers and manufacturers.

The population of Western Texas, in 1850, was about 41,000, of which 7,000 were slaves. It is now estimated at 93,000, divided roughly—as, Americans, 30,000; Germans, 25,000; negroes, 23,000;* Mexicans (excluding El Paso co.), 16,000.

THE MEXICAN BORDER.

That part of Western Texas lying near the Rio Grande, has a character of its own. It is a region so sterile and valueless, as

* The principal increase in negroes has taken place in Gonzales, Guadalupe, Caldwell, and Fayette cos. The number of actual slaveholders is about 700.

19*

to be commonly reputed a desert, and, being incapable of settlement, serves as a barrier—separating the nationalities, and protecting from encroachment, at least temporarily, the retreating race.

The extreme Texan settlements have reached the verge of this waste region. A line drawn from the head of the San Saba southward, to the upper waters of the Guadalupe, thence westward, along the mountain-range bordering the sterile plains, to the head of the Leona at Fort Inge, thence along the course of the Leona, the Frio, and the Nueces to the coast, will mark the limits of valuable land, of probable agricultural occupation.

Along the coast lies a sandy tract, with salt lagoons and small, brackish streams. This is the desert country, which became familiar to our army on its way from Corpus to Point Isabel, at the outbreak of the Mexican war in 1846. It merges into the level coast prairies which, forty to sixty miles inland, become undulating and covered with a growth of prickly shrubs, upon a dry, barren, gravelly soil. The same character, with trifling variations, belongs to the whole region as far north as the Pecos, where the sterility becomes so great, that even the dwarfed shrubs disappear as the country rises into the great plains.

The coast prairies have large districts of fertile soil, and, if supplied with water, might be available as pastures for rough cattle and sheep; but water is only to be found in gullies and holes, where it is not only muddy and of bad quality, but liable to disappear entirely during the heats of summer, when even the grass withers and dries up.

Mr. Bartlett, who crossed along the northern edge of these prairies in coming from the Rio Grande, at Ringgold-barracks, to

Corpus, describes the country as rising gently from the river for five or six miles, and covered with prickly shrubs. Then for five days, his way lay over slightly-rolling prairies, having clusters of mesquit trees, prickly pear, and some stunted live-oak, until, on the last day, the dead, bare level of the coast prairie was reached, some forty miles from Corpus. About midway, a white sand-hill—the Loma Blanca—was passed, near which was a large tract of dry sand. The first settlements were a starved ranch or two upon the Aguas Dulces, twenty miles from the Nueces.

The valley of the Nueces contains much rich land, but low-lying and malarious. The river is navigable for small steamboats for about forty miles. The bar of Corpus has about six feet of water.

The grassed region below the chaparral wilderness, extending to the coast, is the resort of immense herds of wild horses, as well as of numbers of deer, antelope, and hares. The mustangs are the degenerated progeny of Spanish estrays, now as wild and fully naturalized as the deer themselves. They associate in incredible numbers, like the buffaloes, a single herd sometimes covering a large tract, and, if frightened, rushing to and fro in sweeping lines, with the irresistible force of an army. From their numbers are recruited additions to the stocks of Texan and Mexican herdsmen, and the business of entrapping them has given rise to a class of men called "mustangers," composed of runaway vagabonds, and outlaws of all nations, the legitimate border-ruffians of Texas. While their ostensible employment is this of catching wild horses, they often add the practice of highway robbery, and are, in fact, simply prairie pirates, seizing any property that comes in their way, murdering travelers, and

making descents upon trains and border villages.   Their operations of this sort are carried on under the guise of savages, and,
at the scene of a murder, some "Indian sign," as an arrow-head
or a moccasin, is left to mislead justice.

The wild horses are easily collected, by means of long fences,
called "wings," diverging on either side from the mouth of a
"pen." Having been driven within this, the mares of a herd are
caught with the lasso, and the stallions, which do not repay breaking, turned loose or wantonly shot.   Here and there a "ranch" is
established, forming a temporary home and retreat for the "mustangers."   The herds probably suffer extremely in the dry
season, and have been much injured during generations of exposure and hardship.   They are narrow-chested, weak in haunches,
and of bad disposition, and are worth about one tenth the price
of improved stock, a herd tamed to be driven, selling, delivered
at the settlements, at $8 to $15 per head.   Many stories are
told of the incurable viciousness of tamed mustangs.   An old
animal which you have ridden daily for twenty years, will, when
his opportunity comes at last, suddenly jump upon you, and
stamp you in pieces, his vengeance all the hotter for delay.

No part of the immense remaining territory towards the
North, seems to possess the slightest value.   It is a dry gravelly
desert, supporting only worthless shrubs.   Such was distinctly
its character at the point where we crossed it, and from all the
definite description we could obtain from officers who had led
trains, or scouting parties, here and there over it, or Texans who
had traversed the various routes into Mexico, it nowhere offers
more attractive features.   Should it become desirable to plant
settlements within it, for reasons other than economical, probably a few spots might be selected, where a sufficiently good soil,

with wood and water, exists for such a purpose, and it is also true, that our acquaintance with it is but limited and somewhat vague; for what one calls desert, another calls prairie, and what to one is pure sand or clay, to another is a light or heavy soil— the impression depending much upon the soil the traveler has been accustomed to cultivate, as well as especially upon the season in which his observation is made.

The climate, which, throughout West Texas, begins to approach that of Mexico, has here become absolutely Mexican, and is marked by an extreme dryness—rain so seldom falling during the summer, that ordinary vegetation perishes for lack of moisture, leaving the soil to the occupation of such Bedouin tribes of vegetation as have the necessary powers of endurance. There are here a class of worthless shrubs, whose minute leaves spread as little surface as possible to the dry air, and whose limbs are studded with the sharpest spines, as if to repel all animal life from seeking to share with their own roots this weak shade. They stand in clumps and patches, leaving intervals which may be traversed with more or less difficulty.*

We saw this country in April, probably to the best advantage. Our road lay across a series of elevations, between the beds of insignificant brooks, tributaries of the Nueces. Several of these, dry in later months, contained now running water, and in their valleys, here and there, the gravelly soil was black, and grass was abundant beneath the shrubs, while upon the barren surface of the ridges, even the chaparral growth almost disappeared. The "bottoms" of two or three of these creeks were marked by a thin belt of wood, as hack-berry and elm, and those of the

---

* The principal shrubs are mesquit, rosin-wood, or creosote plant, koeblerinia, and various species of yucca.

Nueces and of Turkey creek, its principal branch on our route, were well shaded by timber. But even at this season, pasturage was the only use that suggested itself for these lands, and this would be impracticable, where sheep would lose their whole fleece in the labyrinths of thorns, and cattle stray instantly out of sight, and beyond possible control.

There is, however, one circumstance which may ultimately lead to important modifications in the fate of this region. It is the fact that a change has recently been gradually manifesting itself in its meteorological conditions toward a steadily increasing amount of moisture. By common Mexican report the commencement of this change is coincident with American occupation. It is certainly, if well attested, a remarkable scientific phenomenon. In the settled districts of Western Texas, the evidence seems to have been so palpable as to have become a matter of common allusion. New springs were repeatedly pointed out to us; upon our route into the hills north of San Antonio, at least three or four such were met with, and we were told of a neighboring farm which, when purchased, had its only water from the river, while since, first one, and, subsequently, four perennial springs had broken out upon it, whose flow was steadily increasing. Around the city, irrigation, which, ten years before, had been indispensable, was almost entirely disused, the canals being suffered to fall out of repair, and all the farmers who have settled the vicinity trust their crops to the skies alone, as in the East. Our guide to the Rio Grande attested the fact, and observed that he had never before this trip found running water in the bed of one of the creeks (I think the Chican) which we crossed.

The volume of water in all the Texan rivers has been observed to be increasing, and a number of streams, whose flow, at intervals, has been subterranean, are said to fill their superficial beds. These facts connect themselves with an increased growth of trees and grass upon the plains. Julius Froebel reports having seen, near the Pecos, an abundant young growth of mesquit trees, beneath millions of old trunks which still stand, though they have been dead no one knows how long, while no intermediate growth exists, and among the present chaparral large stumps are not unfrequently to be found, indicating a former forest. We ourselves noticed a similar young growth of mesquit trees upon open prairies.

These phenomena are thought to be explained by the comparative rarity of *fires* since Americans entered the country. Hundreds of miles, formerly burned over each year by Indians, now escape, and the young seedlings, then destroyed, have had time, where this has occurred, to become strong enough to resist prairie flame. This growth retards evaporation as well as the instant flowing off of rain water, so that freshets are fewer and streams more steady, while the retained water furnishes vapor to the summer atmosphere, for precipitation, upon slighter causes. The theory connects itself with those upon the original formation of prairies, and must be left to the discussion of experts.*

NORTHWESTERN TEXAS.

Northwestern Texas has for its chief feature the Llano Es-

---

* " Not a tree, not a blade of grass, is to be seen in its vicinity, yet, fifty years ago, the whole district was covered with forests, which might have lasted for centuries had not the improvident and wasteful spirit of the first adventurers wantonly destroyed those treasures which to their descendants would have been invaluable. Whole woods were burned in order to clear the ground, and the larger timber required for the mines is now brought from a distance of twenty-two leagues."—WARD, at Catorce.

tacado, or Staked Plain, an immense desolate, barren table-land, stretching from the Canadian to the Pecos. It is a perfectly level desert, more than two thousand feet above the sea, destitute of water, bearing no tree, and, during a great part of the year, only dried grass, supporting no permanent animal life, and probably destined to be of little service to man. Its surface is unbroken by a hill or any projection, but here and there yawn cañons, or horrid chasms, on the brink of which a traveler finds himself without the slightest warning, looking down a dizzy abyss, a thousand feet in depth, and a thousand feet across.

This plain recalls the steppes, the pampas, and the great prairies of Hungary; but, owing to the almost total want of moisture, it has no similar value as a pasture.

From its eastern base, whose edges are as marked and abrupt as the sides of its cañons, flow the rivers which water Texas. On the south, it descends less abruptly into lower table-lands or barren elevated prairies, which subside irregularly into the region of chaparral.

The Pecos forms a western boundary for these plains, but beyond it no characteristic change occurs. It is itself a torrent of muddy drippings, flowing between high banks, and watering no arable soil. For hundreds of miles it furnishes the only supply of water for travelers, and the two roads from San Antonio to El Paso are compelled to unite in following its tedious course.*

Between the Pecos and the Upper Rio Grande rises the rugged

---

* Upon the lower road, by Fort Inge, which is most frequented, a chain of military outposts (Forts Davis, Lancaster, etc.) has been lately established for the purpose of overawing the roving Indians of the plains, and checking their forays upon the Texan settlements. By reports from them we may hope to have a better acquaintance with this region. The distance to El Paso, by this

chain of the Guadalupe mountains. Here vegetation and moisture are found again, forests of pine and oak appearing upon the slopes.

PACIFIC RAILROAD.

It is across this forbidding country that it is proposed to build our southern railroad toward the Pacific. In respect of climate it has a certain advantage over the more northern routes. But impediments more formidable than winter snows are to be met. A principal obstacle occurs at the outset, in the total want of water upon the Staked Plains. Wood or coal might, if necessity demanded, be transported to suitable stations along the road, but a local water supply seems to be indispensable. With the design of removing, if possible, this preliminary objection, a party of engineers have been for two years at work, under orders of the Secretary of War, in ascertaining the practicability of boring artesian wells upon the plains. The results are interesting, but, as yet, afford no practical solution of the difficulty. Upon the parallel of thirty-two degrees, and fifteen miles east of the Pecos, a first tube was sunk in 1855. Water was twice struck, first at three hundred and sixty feet, subsequently at six hundred and forty-one feet, but in neither case did it rise to within two hundred and forty feet of the surface. In 1856, a point, five miles further east, was chosen. The same streams were reached, and, at the depth of eight hundred and sixty feet a third, from which water rose to within one hundred and ten feet of the surface. The appropriation of forty thousand dollars being ex-

road, is six hundred and seventy-five miles. It has been suggested that camels were well adapted to purposes of transportation upon these dry plains, and a ship-load has been lately procured by Government, and landed in good condition upon the Texas coast. At last accounts they were at pasture upon the plantation of Major Howard, near San Antonio.

hausted, operations have been discontinued. Captain Pope, who was in command, describes the geological formation as consisting of alternate strata of indurated clays and cretaceous marls, the latter, apparently, of fertilizing value. He also reports a novel source of fuel in the *roots* of the mesquit, which are found preserved beneath the soil, perfectly sound and hard, extending, sometimes, to the incredible depth of seventy feet.

Should further perseverance succeed in obtaining from this source a permanent and sufficient supply of water, and engineering skill produce a practicable means of crossing the gigantic canons of the plains, there are still the rugged precipices of the Guadalupe mountains to be crossed before reaching the Rio Grande. Nor is the country beyond, though feasible so far as topographical considerations are concerned, better adapted to the support of a costly thoroughfare. In the various journeys through it, connected with his duties as boundary commissioner, Mr. Bartlett became, probably, more familiar with it than any other writer. The following is his appreciation of it:—" At the head-waters of the Concho, therefore, begins that great desert region, which, with no interruption save a limited valley, or bottom-land, along the Rio Grande, and lesser ones near the rivulets of San Pedro and Santa Cruz, extends over a district embracing sixteen degrees of longitude, or about one thousand miles, and is wholly unfit for agriculture. It is a desolate, barren waste, which can never be rendered useful to man or beast, save for a public highway." Upon the Colorado desert, the obstacle of the absence of water again occurs, and the ranges of California mountains offer no trifling obstruction. There is a terminal objection, too, which is by no means insignificant—that the Pacific is reached, at last, at San Diego, which is still five hundred miles from San Francisco, the commercial goal, and that through an almost impassable country.

Whether more advantageous routes can be found further north, it is not pertinent here to inquire; but, with these objections in view, the idea of a railroad, as a commercially economical project, from Texas to the Pacific, may be safely pronounced chimerical. In a military point of view, it may become desirable, and, if necessary, can be built; but the cost, both of construction and preservation, must first be counted.

THE RIO GRANDE.

The Rio Grande flows, for a great part of its course, in a valley so narrow as to be frequently a mere chasm, and receiving few tributaries from the parched region through which it passes, scarcely enlarges its volume for a thousand miles above its mouth. In the neighborhood of El Paso, its banks recede and leave a limited tract of wooded bottom-lands, from a mile to two miles in width and thirty or forty miles in length. In this district has settled a population, almost entirely from the adjacent Mexican territory, of about ten thousand.

From this point to the Pecos the river is bordered by rugged hills, flanking its course sometimes with enormous precipices, the bed of the stream being often so narrowed and obstructed, that furious rapids are occasioned. The immediate vicinity of the mouth of the Pecos, till now unexplored, has recently been visited by an expedition from the military posts upon the El Paso road, against the remnant of the Lipan Indians, who had retreated to its fastnesses. The region is described as almost impenetrable—a wild chaos of rocky heights and gorges.*

* The extermination of the old tribe of Lipans was nearly completed by this

Below the Pecos, the Rio Grande enters the more open chaparral region; but, until the coast prairies are nearly reached, no land of consequence occurs suitable for cultivation. Now and then a narrow meadow is found, and a few short fertile valleys lie upon affluent creeks. These are occupied frequently by old ranches, upon which a little cotton, sugar, and maize are raised by Mexicans. Irrigation is compulsory, no rain sometimes falling for many months. An officer, who had lately been stationed a year or two at Laredo, told me that, at the end of July, no green thing was to be found within a radius of thirty miles from the town. In the neighborhood of Rio Grande city, and thence to the gulf, considerable tracts of arable land border the river. They have hitherto been little occupied by Americans—property of any kind along the river being somewhat insecure, and slaves particularly liable to be lost over the boundary. The necessity of irrigation is a great obstacle, also, to our impatient countrymen.

The river is regularly navigable for small steamboats, as far as Roma. Were there sufficient commercial inducement, it is probable that a class of boats might be constructed to ascend as high as the Pecos, the chief impediment, beside mere shifting shoals, being the Kingsbury Rapids, near Presidio. Through these it is thought a channel might be opened at an expense of one hundred thousand dollars.

The population along the east bank of the Lower Rio Grande

expedition. They were found in several squads, one after another of which was surprised and nearly every man cut off. A very few escaped across the Rio Grande. Greater security seems now to be within reach of the frontier settlements, as, under date of Oct. 14, 1856, it is also stated that the remaining Comanches of the plains have formally consented to come upon the reservation upon the Upper Brazos.

may be estimated at from fifteen to twenty thousand, about half of which is concentrated around the towns of Brownsville and Rio Grande City. The region is the haunt of border outlaws and Mexican refugees, whose presence keeps the frontier society in a continual ferment of fillibusterism.

BEYOND THE RIO GRANDE.

The country adjacent to the Rio Grande, upon the Mexican side, corresponds, in general character, very closely to that just described. The limits of the great chaparral wastes are even further from the river, reaching the mountains of Chihuahua; and the great region from El Paso to the boundaries of Tamaulipas is a barren solitude, scarce trodden by any other foot than that of the Indian. Near Camargo begins the first valuable land, and the delta of the Rio Grande below extends itself wide to the southward, merging into the malarious coast-levels. Here is a soil well adapted to sugar and cotton; but the Mexican occupants have as yet found their profit rather in herds and flocks than in the plow.

Matamoros, the only town of consequence upon the river, supports a population of about twenty thousand by its foreign trade. The population of the villages above depend mainly upon their little household manufactures of wool for a miserable support.

Further inland is the rich and densely populated valley of the Tigre, at whose head stand Monterey and Saltillo. The interval from the Rio Grande is abandoned to hopeless chaparral.

FURTHER ANNEXATION.

There is a general opinion that portions of Mexico, adjoining

Texas, are, sooner or later, "destined" to be annexed to the Union, to add to the number and power of the Slave States. An examination of the character of the country in question serves to materially diminish any such probabilities. If a line be drawn from the mouth of the Rio Grande, due west (along the twenty-sixth parallel) to the Pacific, the remaining territory of Mexico will be divided nearly equally; but, in the northern half, though fine pastures and valuable mines might be acquired, *no cotton lands* are to be found. The only exceptions, of consequence, are those described near the present boundary, and a few sunny valleys along the short, quick rivers of Sonora. The fertile lands of our part of the continent, lying in tracts suitable for the formation of states, are, in short, exhausted, and the prime motive for further extension, disregarding mere political influences, is wanting.

There are other difficulties. We have not yet made the experiment, in our experience of annexations, of absorbing any notable amount of resident foreign population. This territory contains upwards of half a million of Mexicans. The character and numbers of these people, and the physical peculiarities of their occupied lands, are such as to render it improbable that slavery can ever be extensively introduced, or naturalized among them. No country could be selected better adapted to a fugitive and clandestine life, and no people among whom it would be more difficult to enforce the regulations vital to slavery.

The Mexican masses are vaguely considered as degenerate and degraded Spaniards; it is, at least, equally correct to think of them as improved and Christianized Indians. In their tastes and social instincts, they approximate the African. The difference between them and the negro is smaller, and is less felt, I believe, than that between the northern and southern European races.   There are many Mexicans of mixed negro blood, who, in Northern Mexico, bear less suspicion of inferiority than our proletarian naturalized citizens.   There are thousands in respectable social positions whose color and physiognomy would subject them, in Texas, to be sold by the sheriff as negro-estrays who cannot be allowed at large without detriment to the commonwealth.

There is, besides, between our Southern American and the Mexican, an unconquerable antagonism of character, which will prevent any condition of order where the two come together.   The Mexicans, in our little intercourse with them, we found as different as possible from what all Texan reports would have led us to expect.   This was, probably, as much owing to our being able to meet them in a considerate manner, and to their responsive regard, as to any difference in standards of judgment.   People commonly go into Mexico from Texas as if into a country in revolt against them, and return to boast of the insolence with which they have constantly treated the religious and social customs, and the personal self-respect of the inhabitants.   This arrogant disposition is not peculiar to the border class, nor to the old Texans.   Nowhere is it better expressed, than in a book written before the war, by a Virginian who claims to be a friend of President Tyler, and who was appointed by him to a responsible office.   The tone of condescension with which this gentleman patronizes people who are evidently much his superiors in true refinement, education, wealth, and social dignity, is not less absurd than the indignant impatience with which I have heard a ruffian of the frontier describe the politeness, incomprehensible to him, of Mexican hospitality.

The mingled Puritanism and brigandism, which distinguishes the vulgar mind of the South, peculiarly unfits it to harmoniously associate with the bigoted, childish, and passionate Mexicans. They are considered to be heathen; not acknowledged as "white folks." Inevitably they are dealt with insolently and unjustly. They fear and hate the ascendant race, and involuntarily associate and sympathize with the negroes.

Thus, wherever slavery in Texas has been carried in a wholesale way, into the neighborhood of Mexicans, it has been found necessary to treat them as outlaws. Guaranteed, by the treaty of Guadalupe Hidalgo, equal rights with all other citizens of the United States and of Texas, the whole native population of county after county has been driven, by the formal proceedings of substantial planters,* from its homes, and forbidden, on pain of no less punishment than instant death, to return to the vicinity of the plantations.

This is sufficient indication of the nature of the impediments to any further advance of slavery in the southwest. Isolated noisy attempts at conquest will, no doubt, be made by border adventurers, but any permanent establishment of slavery beyond the Rio Grande is intrinsically improbable, unless the real speculators can arrange to have the army of the United States placed at their disposal. For this, it is true, precedent is not

---

* A Southern paper, maintaining the conservative quality of slavery, lately observed : " Public outrages have been committed at the South, mobs have been raised, premises destroyed, persons outraged, and life taken, and all in the name of slavery ; but we have never known an instance in which slaveholders themselves have been members of the mob. The actors have always been lewd fellows, of the baser sort—panderers to position and wealth that they could never aspire to, who thought that they might thus gain favor from slaveholders. But we have never known slaveholders who did not spurn and despise the truckling rowdies thus acting in their name."

A rare confession this, of the real internal relations of the people of the South.

wanting. The population of Tamaulipas and New Leon, first to be encountered, is, however, a long-established one, and too numerous for expulsion; it will have ready resort to malarious jungles, chaparral covers and mountain fastnesses; to perpetual incendiarism and guerrilla descents, nor will it be withheld from resistance to usurpation and tyranny by reverence for the name of Constitution and Law.

20

NOTE UPON FARM PROFITS.

THERE is room for discussion as to some of the items introduced into the agricultural tables at page 205. These are simply given as condensing the results of our own inquiries, and must be taken with due allowance for our prejudices and mistakes. The elements of such calculations are, of course, liable to modification by the market-prices and circumstances of each year. The general conclusion, however, that stock-raising is far more profitable to the individual and to the State, in Western Texas, than cotton-planting, will hold good.

The estimate of the production of cotton to the acre or to the hand, in the tables, may be considered low, when compared with the statements of planters, given in other parts of the volume. Seven bales to the hand have been frequently noted. This may be set down, however, as a " brag crop," or, as mentioned in the interest of land-holding. The same planter in writing to his creditors, or when rallied upon his extreme profits, will deny that in a series of years he can average over three bales to the hand.

In a report to the government upon the cotton capacities of the United States, Mr. Andrews makes four bales, of four hundred pounds, to the hand, the basis of his calculations. In conversation with intelligent and disinterested Texans, I have been assured that what with floods, droughts, worms, and sickness of hands, an average of four bales was more than could be depended upon. A recent elaborate article upon the lands of Texas, in the " *Austin State Gazette*," gives six and a quarter cents as the average net price of Texan cotton. These figures all fall below those introduced in the tables.

A slight difference is allowed for the greater cost of a home to the farmer than to the planter. Probably, in practice this would be more marked, the long-formed habits of the former compelling conformity to a higher standard of comfort.

The price set upon sheep is sufficient to cover their purchase in the Ohio States, and the cost of their transit on foot. They can be purchased, already acclimated, at a slight advance. Sheep, yielding a fair fleece, are every year sold in New York market at less than two dollars, and are quoted at from two and a half to four and a quarter dollars, at New Orleans, November 28, 1856. At the time of our visit to Texas, Mexican sheep might be had at two dollars, delivered in any western county. They cannot now, I understand, be procured from this source.

AN EMIGRANT'S PROSPECTS.

A farmer, on a small scale, arriving in Texas with one thousand dollars, will expend it nearly as follows :

Land, 160 acres—$400.
Cabin and furniture—$150.
Tools, wagon and working cattle—$150.
Cows and pigs—$150.
Temporary subsistence—$150.

He will be able, after putting up his house, to plough and fence a field of twenty acres during the first year. The returns will be about five hundred bushels of corn, worth fifty cents (sometimes 25 cents, sometimes $1 25), and, perhaps, fifty dollars for butter and pork sold, making three hundred dollars. He will require two-thirds of this for improving the condition of his family, and will invest the remainder in the purchase of sheep.

The second year will add ten acres to his field, and the production of corn will be increased upon the land first ploughed, making his crop worth four hundred and twenty-five dollars. Laying aside two hundred dollars for his family, and adding seventy-five for smaller sales, he will have three hundred to invest in sheep, and will have now a flock of seventy.

The third year will see his corn-field in complete cultivation, and yielding, permanently, twelve hundred bushels of corn each year. He will be able to obtain two or three improved bucks, and to number, by purchase and increase, a flock of one hundred and seventy-five sheep.

By an easy calculation, his course, if he retain his industry, and meet with only ordinary losses, may thus be traced for ten years to the possession of a valuable farm, with herds and flocks which will insure him a comfortable subsistence without other personal labor than supervision.

A laboring man, who has not one thousand dollars at command, will probably find his account in first accumulating that sum by working for others. Wages in Texas are a trifle lower than in the Northwestern States, but higher than in the Atlantic States.

Cotton planting, by slave labor, with so small a capital as one thousand dollars, is impossible. A man owning only a negro worth that price must sell him, and become a farmer. Should he invest the first profits of his labor in negroes, a few figures will show that his progress must be far less rapid than that of the corn and sheep-farmer.*

The parts of Texas best adapted to immigrant farmers, are Upper Western and Upper Northeastern Texas. A small planter will choose central Northeastern Texas, a large planter, the river-bottoms of Central Texas, where, with due regard to price of land, the access to market is most convenient.

The cost of passage from New York to Indianola is about thirty dollars, and from the coast to Upper Texas, about fifteen dollars. Freight from New York to San Antonio is usually from one to three dollars per barrel, for light or heavy articles.

The settlement should be fixed, where possible, for early winter, when exposure to sickness is smallest, and when time remains for the erection of a cabin and the preparation of a field before planting-time.

Titles to land, it need hardly be advised, are to be closely scrutinized, before money is paid for them, and none should be accepted which will not bear the thorough investigation of the best local lawyer within reach.

---

* " A St. Augustine paper informs us of the results of one small planter of that county, which is worth recording. On one acre, he raised and sold 450 gallons of syrup at 50 cents, 4 bbls. sugar at 6 cents, and 3,000 canes at 2 cents each, making a total of $433. Besides, he raised 150 bushels of corn, and 200 bushels of sweet potatoes, worth $370, giving a full total of $800. His land was in the piny woods, but he cow-penned it, which makes it the best soil for sugar-cane. With a little industry his family enjoyed all the milk and butter, eggs and bacon they wanted, and this $800 was in his pocket at the end of the year, and with the sum he bought a negro, and will this year go on at compound interest upon the fruits of his small capital. What a lesson this is to lazy people who stand about groceries, and get up an everlasting name for themselves, in our towns, of loafers and trifling fellows. By a little well-directed labor, they might thus secure a good reputation and a sterling reliance for their old age. What is done in Florida can be done, and is done, in Texas."—*Debow's Review.*

APPENDIX.

HISTORICAL TABLE.

THE PRINCIPAL DATA FROM YOAKUM'S HISTORY

1519. Cortes lands in Mexico.

1535. First Viceroy of New Spain.

1581. New Mexico explored.

1590. Mission of Topia.

1595. Monterey founded.

1685. Feb. 18th.—Lasalle lands in Texas, upon the western shore of Matagorda Bay.

1686. Fort St. Louis established upon the Lavaca.
Spanish established at Monclova, in Coahuila.

1687. Lasalle killed, while exploring near the Neches River.
Fort St. Louis destroyed by Indians.

1689. April.—First Spanish expedition from Monclova, under De Leon, into Texas, against the French.

1690. Second expedition of De Leon. Mission of San Francisco established upon the ruins of Fort St. Louis, and the Mission of San Juan Bautista upon the Rio Grande, at Presidio.

1691. Several colonies attempted in Eastern Texas by Teran.

1693. Colonies all abandoned, and Texas left without Europeans.

1714. August.—French trading expedition under St. Denis reaches the Mission of San Juan, upon the Rio Grande.

1715. Re-occupation by Spain. Missions of San Antonio, Dolores, Adaes, and Nacogdoches founded.

1716. Second French trading expedition of St. Denis to the Rio Grande.

1718. War between France and Spain.

1719. Spanish outposts in Eastern Texas driven in by French troops from Natchitoches, to San Antonio. Re-established by De Aguayo.

1721. French expedition to Matagorda Bay. Repulsed by Indians.
Mission of La Bahia established by De Aguayo. Additional missions at San Antonio.

1726. Trade revived between French and Spanish settlements.

1730. San Antonio town founded by immigrants from the Canaries.
1731 Mission of Concepcion founded.
1734. Sandoval Governor of Texas.
1740–50. Colonies languish.
 744. Church of the Alamo founded.
1758. Massacre at Mission San Saba, by the Indians.
1762. Louisiana ceded to Spain.
1765. Europeans in Texas number about 750.
1778. Growth, by immigration, of Nacogdoches.
1794. Texan Missions declared secularized, by Don Pedro de Nava.
1795. Treaty with Spain confirming to Americans the right of navigation of the Mississippi.
 An American trade with Texas springs up.
1800. Nolan's trading expedition attacked and broken up by Spanish troops upon the Brazos.
1801. Louisiana transferred to France.
1803. Louisiana purchased by the United States.
1805. Petty Spanish aggressions along the Sabine. U. S. frontier-posts strengthened. Texan colonies reinforced.
1806. Neutral ground agreed upon between the Arroyo Honda and the Sabine Pike's expedition to New Mexico.
 First American actual settlers in Texas.
 Population of Texas about 7,000.
1807. Burr's expedition.
1809. First revolutionary movements in Mexico.
1810. Revolt of Hidalgo. He is defeated and executed the following year.
1811. Robberies by freebooters of the Neutral Ground.
1812. Expedition of McGee and Gutierres from Red River, for the conquest and republicanization of Texas. Capture of La Bahia.
1813. March.—Battle of Rosalis. Surrender of San Antonio.
 August.—Battle of the Medina. Rout of the Americans. Annihilation of the expedition.
1814. Dispersal of freebooters at Barrataria.
1816. Galveston island occupied by a republican expedition. Aury declared Governor of Texas and Galveston. Perry joins.
 Mina's expedition against Florida. It fails. He joins the forces at Galveston. Great booty in goods and negroes from Spanish prizes. The slaves taken are sold into Louisiana.
1817. Expeditionists sail from Galveston and capture Soto la Marina. Rout and death of Mina. Retreat and death of Perry at La Bahia.
 Occupation of Galveston by Lafitte. His followers number 1,000.
 Temporary settlement by French refugees upon Trinity River.
1819. Feb. 22.—Treaty making the Sabine boundary between United States and Spain.
 Texas invaded from Natchez by a company under Long.
 Provisional independent government established at Nacogdoches.
 First printing-office at Nacogdoches.

1819. Long solicits aid from Lafitte. Appointed Republican Governor of Galveston. The expedition is routed by Spanish forces. Re-assembles at Bolivar Point.

1821. Feb. 24.—Pronunciamento of Iturbide, at Iguala.

Aug. 24.—Plan of Iguala. Regency of six. Iturbide President.

Lafitte's establishment broken up by the United States.

Long goes by sea to West Texas, and captures La Bahia. Is subsequently made prisoner, and killed in the city of Mexico.

Moses Austin (native of Durham, Ct., a speculator in Virginia and Missouri mines) conceives the idea of establishing American settlements, and visits Bexar, 1820. Applies for permission to colonize 300 families. Is robbed and maltreated upon his return to the States, and dies June 10, 1821. His application is granted, and his son, Stephen F. Austin, undertakes the enterprise. The colonists to be Louisianians, of good character, Roman Catholics (or to agree to become so before entering), and to take oath of fidelity to the king and government of Spain.

Aug. 19.—The plan sanctioned in detail by the Governor of Texas. Austin selects lands near the Brazos, and advertises in New Orleans for colonists. In November, first expedition. A few American families settle on the Brazos and Colorado.

1822. Austin proceeds to Mexico. He meets, at Mexico, H. Edwards and other applicants.

Iturbide made Emperor.

1823. Jan. 4.—General colonization law promulgated. Its provisions as above, but colonists may be other than Louisianians.

Sale or purchase of slaves prohibited; all born in the empire are to become free at 14.

Feb. 18.—Austin's grant specially confirmed.

Revolt of Santa Anna. Constituent Congress. Austin's grant re-confirmed. Austin returns to his colony, which has rapidly grown.

1824. Second general colonization law enacted, providing for special laws by the several states.

Federal Constitution proclaimed, 4th October

Texas united with Coahuila, to form a State of the confederacy.

1825. Saucedo appointed "Political Chief" of Texas.

Decree inviting colonists, who are bound to make oath to obey the Constitution, and observe the Catholic religion.

Grants to Robert Leftwich, for 200 families; to Hayden Edwards, for 800; to Austin, for 500 additional; to Green Dewitt, for 300; and to Martin De Leon, for 150.

United States Minister instructed by Mr. Clay to purchase Texas if practicable.

1826. Difficulties in H. Edwards's grant at Nacogdoches. His contract annulled by the Governor. His colonists resist. They style themselves Fredonians, and (Dec. 18) fortify themselves. Saucedo marches against them. Austin takes an adverse part. They are overpowered. The grant of Edwards made over to Burnet & Vehlin

20*

1827. Colonies rapidly advance in population. Gonzales laid out.   Third grant of Austin for 100 families.

United States again offers to purchase Texas.

1828. Fourth grant to Austin, for 300 families.

1829. Power's grant, for 200 families; McMullen & McGloire's grant.

Expulsion of Spaniards from Mexico decreed, March.

Spanish descent at Tampico.

Unlimited powers conferred upon President Guerrero.

Slavery abolished in the Mexican Republic, by a decree of Guerrero.

Guerrero deposed, Dec. 23.

Bustamente usurps the Presidency.   Guerrero shot.

Repeated offers on the part of United States for the purchase of Texas.

1830. April 6.—Decree suspending colony contracts, and forbidding further settlement of Americans.   Further introduction of slaves prohibited.

Custom-houses established at Nacogdoches, San Antonio, Copano, Velasco, and Galveston.

Teran appointed Commandant-general of the Eastern States.

Martial law introduced by Bradburn, Mexican commander at Anahuac (Galveston).

Americans now number 20,000.   Mexican troops in Texas about 800.

1831. Immigration continues, and the new-comers demand titles.

The State Land Commissioner arrested by Teran, and confined at Anahuac.   Petty military tyrannies.   Americans become incensed.

Troops sent to enforce federal measures; to be paid from revenues collected at Texan ports.

Order closing all ports except Anahuac.   Resisted by the Americans, and rescinded under threats of immediate attack upon Anahuac.

Texas divided into two districts by State law, the " political chiefs" having separate jurisdiction.

1832. Travis and Munroe Edwards imprisoned by Bradburn for punishing a soldier's outrage.   Their release demanded.   Two or three hundred armed men appear, ready to invest Anahuac.   Manifesto of adherence to the constitution of 1824, detailing wrongs.   Prisoners released, and Bradburn removed by Piedras.

Revolt of Vera Cruz under Santa Anna.   Resignation and flight of Bustamente.

Texans " pronounce " for Santa Anna and the constitution of 1824, attack and take the military fort at Velasco.   A force from Matamoros arrives under Mexia, with whom they fraternize.   Resolutions expressive of the sentiments of the colonists presented to Col. Mexia, at San Félipe. Col. Piedras holds out at Nacogdoches; attacked and defeated by Texans.

State colonization law modified excluding Americans.

Texans demand a separation from Coahuila; convention for drafting a state constitution.

Sam Houston enters Texas.

1833. Santa Anna elected President.

Adjourned Texan convention prepares a constitution and a memorial to

1833. supreme government. Austin sent delegate to Mexico. He writes advising Texans to take matters into their own hands. He is arrested, and suffers three months' imprisonment.

1834 Texas divided into three departments, having each a " political chief." English language admitted by State law in public affairs. Free land sales established, with provision that no one shall be molested for political or religious opinions. Trial by jury introduced. Subsequent disorganization of the state government by local quarrels. Convention called to consider the necessity for a provisional government.

The Texan memorial heard at Mexico. Decisions unfavorable. Austin released, but detained. Report on Texas by Almonte. He estimates the population at 21,000. (Probably 30,000.)

1835. State land bills passed in the interest of speculators.

Federal law by Santa Anna, disarming the population.

Gen. Cos ordered by Santa Anna to disperse the legislature at Monclova. Legislature adjourns. The Governor retreats toward Bexar, but is arrested. State government dissolved. First " Committee of Safety" at Bastrop, May 17, upon Indian outrages. Troops at Anahuac attacked and driven out by W. B. Travis, the Texans declining to be taxed for the support of a local standing army.

Cos declared Governor by Santa Anna. Public commotion. News of near arrival of an army for "regulating matters" in Texas. A war-party and a peace-party form.

June 22.—Meeting and " address" of the war-party. Militia of Brazos district organized. July 17.—Meeting at San Félipe; peace policy prevails. Resolutions for resistance to Santa Anna on the Navidad. Committee of Safety at Nacogdoches. Order given by the Mexican commandant for sundry arrests of Texans, particularly of Zavala, by Santa Anna. War spirit aroused. Resolutions of the people of San Augustine, led by Houston, in favor of the Constitution of 1824, etc., and organizing the militia. Reinforcements of troops sent to Texas. Austin returns, Sept. 1. Favors a general *Consultation*.

Santa Anna seizes the government.

War appears inevitable. Intelligence that Cos is approaching, to disarm the population, and drive out all colonists introduced since 1830. Austin, as Chairman of Committee of Safety, declares war the only resource, and advises volunteer companies.

Cos lands with 500 troops, and marches toward Bexar. Order from the commandant at Bexar for the surrender of a piece of artillery at Gonzales. Texans refuse compliance. A cavalry force of 100 men sent to enforce the order, attacked by Texans and driven off, Oct. 1.

Texan Revolution begun.

State Legislatures abolished, and central power of Santa Anna confirmed.

Permanent Council of one from each committee of Safety established at San Félipe, Royall President. Austin takes command of the forces gathering at Gonzales. Resolved to drive the Mexicans out of Texas.

Goliad is surprised and taken, with military stores, Oct. 9.

1835. Austin advances toward Bexar with 600 men.

People of the United States called on to assist. Troops sent from New Orleans, 17th and 19th Oct.

Oct. 28.—The Mexican forces engage Austin's advance at the Mission Concepcion, and are routed.

Printing-press and newspaper at San Félipe.

Council at San Félipe assumes the reins of government. It prepares an address to the people of the United States, grants letters of reprisal, and authorizes a loan.

Nov. 3.—Meeting of the *Consultation*, 55 in number ; Branch T. Archer President. Declares in favor of Constitution of 1824. Establishes a Provisional Government of Governor and Council, and elects a Commander-in-chief. Adjourns to 1st March, 1836. Henry Smith elected Governor ; Houston, Commander-in-chief. Bexar besieged. Skirmish, Nov. 26, known as the " Grass-fight."

Dec. 5th.--Bexar assaulted under Milam ; 8th, enemy driven into the Alamo 9th, capitulation. Cos and his army withdraw beyond the Rio Grande

Unfortunate descent on Tampico, under Mexia, from New Orleans.

Regular army decreed ; to be 1,120 strong, enlisted with bounty of 640 acres

Quarrels between the Governor and Council.

Dec. 17.—Demonstration upon Matamoros ordered.

Feeling strong in favor of Declaration of Independence. It is affirmed to be premature by the Council.

Dec. 25.—Volunteers arrive to the number of 200, from Georgia and Alabama.

30th.—Dr. Grant sets out, without orders, from Bexar, with 200 men, for Matamoros.

1836. The Council invade the functions of the Governor ; 11th Jan., they order him to cease his functions.

Jan. 7.—Fannin appointed by the Council *agent* for concentrating at Co pano volunteers against Matamoros.

Jan. 17.—Houston orders the fortifications at Bexar to be demolished, and the artillery to be brought away. Order disobeyed for want of transportation. Travis dispatched with a small force to aid Bexar.

Loans of $250,000 procured in New Orleans.

Feb. 1.—Santa Anna sets out from Saltillo, with 6,000 men.

Urrea, with a smaller force, sent, via Matamoros, to San Patricio.

March 1.—The Convention meets by adjournment.

"   2.—It declares Texas an Independent Republic.

"   4.—Houston appointed Commander-in-chief.

"   6.—He sets out for the West.

"   16.—Constitution adopted, providing a President, and Congress of two houses ; introducing " common-law," and dividing Texas by coun ties. David G. Burnet elected temporary President.

Santa Anna reaches San Antonio, Feb. 23. The Alamo assaulted and carried, March 6. Its defenders massacred.

Urrea, at San Patricio, Feb. 27, routs and slaughters the Texan force.

Battle of the Coleta. Fannin, moving from Goliad to Victoria, is surrounded by Urrea's force, March 19. He capitulates. 26th.—Orders from Santa Anna that the prisoners be shot. 27th.—Massacre of Goliad; Fannin and 330 prisoners shot in cold blood.

Houston reaches Gonzales, March 11. News of fall of the Alamo. His force, 374 men. He burns Gonzales, and falls back. 17th.—Encamps on the Colorado with 600 men. 19th.—Resolved to remove the seat of government to Harrisburg. Two-thirds of the militia called into service. Powder and arms seized. Houston again falls back, 26th. Reaches the Brazos, 28th. Crosses the Brazos, April 13th.

Santa Anna leaves Bexar, March 31—arrives at San Félipe, with the advance, April 7—crosses the Brazos on the 12th, at Fort Bend, and marches to Harrisburg, reaching it, with seven hundred men, on the 15th. Houston follows, and arrives at Harrisburg on the 18th—crosses the bayou, 19th—and follows the Mexicans.

20th.—Advance continued—meets the scouts of the Mexicans returning to Lynch's Ferry. Line of battle formed—skirmishes ensue. Cavalry reconnoissance under Sherman. Mexicans construct a breastwork.

21st, A. M.—Cos joins Santa Anna with reinforcements. Vince's Bridge cut away by Houston, who resolves to give battle. 3 P. M.—Battle of SAN JACINTO. Under a fire of artillery, Texans advance with the cry: "Remember the Alamo," reserving their fire till within pistol-shot. Mexicans give way at all points, and are massacred by the furious Texans, who remain complete masters of the field. Texan Force, 783—Mexican, 1,600. Mexican loss—630 killed, 208 wounded, 730 prisoners; camp-chest taken containing $12,000. Texan loss—8 killed, 25 wounded.

22d.—Santa Anna made prisoner. Signs an armistice, and orders the retreat of his reserves.

14th May.—Treaty signed, at Velasco, by Santa Anna—providing for the withdrawal of Mexican troops. A private treaty binding Santa Anna to acknowledge the independence of Texas. Houston goes to New Orleans. Rusk takes command of the army. Filisola retreats to the Rio Grande. Santa Anna embarks for Vera Cruz, but is brought back.

April 20.—Commissioners sent to Washington, with instructions to propose annexation.

15th July.—An army of four thousand Mexicans, under Urrea, assembles at Matamoros. Texan detachments sent to the Nueces. Santa Anna requests the mediation of General Jackson. American troops sent to Nacogdoches to overawe the neighboring Indians!

September 1.—Houston elected President. Constitution adopted, and annexation demanded by the people. Town of Houston founded.

October 1.—Congress meets. Government organized in detail.

United States claims pressed upon Mexico. Minister demands his passports. Mexican minister leaves Washington. Santa Anna sent by Houston to Washington, whence he returns to Vera Cruz.

1837. March.—Bustamente chosen President of Mexico.
    March 2.—Independence of Texas recognized by the United States. Political convulsions in Mexico. Texas peaceful. Immigration continues. Port of Galveston grows up.
1838. Mexican war with France. Diplomatic relations of Mexico with the United States resumed. Mirabeau B. Lamar elected President of Texas. Quietness continues.
1839. Centralists prevail in Mexico.
    Indians, incited by Mexico, disturb Texas.
    Commercial relations established with England. France recognizes Texan Independence.
    Austin founded, and made capital.
1840. Texas scrip reduced to fourteen cents on the dollar. Twelve newspapers published in Texas. Mexican hostility diverted by intestine troubles England, Holland, and Belgium acknowledge Texan independence.
1841. Great efforts to secure a loan in Europe. Mexico declines negotiations. Yucatan declares independence, and makes a naval alliance with Texas. Skirmishes on the Rio Grande. Santa Fé expedition of about three hundred and twenty-five men, with the object of securing the submission of New Mexico and opening trade. After great suffering on the plains, the party is divided, made prisoners by the Mexicans, and marched, with atrocious cruelties, to Mexico city.
    September.—Sam Houston elected President. Sixth Congress meets The debt and paper issues of the Government extremely embarrassing. Houston recommends a temporary repudiation of all liabilities, the issue of exchequer bills, and the negotiation of a loan. A Belgian loan not accepted by Congress; exchequer bills, redeemable in specie, authorized.
    October 6.—Santa Anna again displaces Bustamente.
1842. Mexican hostilities revived. Seven hundred troops enter Texas, take San Antonio and Refugio, and immediately retire. San Antonio reoccupied by Texan forces. Invasion of Mexico proposed. Recruits assemble at Corpus Christi. They are disorganized by poverty, and, after repulsing a small Mexican attack, are disbanded. Mediation of the United States rejected by Mexico.
    September.—San Antonio again taken by one thousand two hundred Mexicans under Woll. 13th.—Fight on the Salado, and repulse of the Mexicans, who retreat on the 18th toward the Rio Grande. A Texan force of seven hundred and fifty men assembles on the Medina, and marches to Laredo; takes Guerrero, and returns to Bexar. Three hundred men remain, contrary to orders, upon the Rio Grande, attack Mier, meet a Mexican force under Ampudia, and eventually surrender. The prisoners are marched to Mexico. They rise on the guard, 11th February, 1843, and escape. Becoming bewildered in the mountains, they are recaptured, and decimated by order of Santa Anna.
    Increased immigration. Several colony contracts entered into—Peter's, Mercer's, Castro's, Fisher & Miller's.

1843. Irregular propositions for peace, by submission, from Santa Anna. Snively's expedition for the capture of a Mexican caravan to the United States. Through the intervention of the English Chargé at Mexico, Santa Anna proposes an armistice. Accepted and proclaimed, June 15. Continued negotiations through English channels. Strong efforts to hasten annexation by the American Government.

1844. Secret message upon annexation by President Houston to Texan Congress. Commissioners dispatched to Washington with full propositions. French and English Governments protest. Treaty of annexation signed at Washington, 12th April, and sent to the Senate. Parties divide in the United States upon the question. The treaty rejected, 8th June. Armistice with Mexico terminates 18th June.

England and France renew endeavors to secure the complete independence of Texas. Texas prosperous. Immigration continues to flow in. Anson Jones elected President. Remaining Mier prisoners liberated. War of the Regulators and Moderators of the Neutral Ground.

United States election results in the sanction of annexation and the success of Polk.

Herrera made President of Mexico ; federalist and favors peace.

1845. March 1.—Joint resolution of annexation passed Congress, and signed by President Tyler.

Peace offered by Herrera, through the agency of the French and English, on condition of non-annexation. Armistice proclaimed 4th June. Texan Congress, June 23, consents to annexation. The act of annexation accepted, and State Constitution submitted by the Convention, July 4, to the people, by whom it is ratified.

July 25th.—American army arrives at Corpus Christi, under General Taylor.

1846. January 13.—Taylor ordered to advance to the Rio Grande. Hostilities begin, April 24. Battle of Palo Alto, May 8 ; of Resaca, 9th ; of Monterey, September 23. Santa Fé captured, August 24.

1847. Battle of Buena Vista, February 22.

Vera Cruz surrenders, March 29.

Mexico surrenders, September 14.

J. Pinckney Henderson Governor of Texas to December 21.

George T. Wood Governor of Texas from December 21.

Population of Texas, by State census, 143,205.

1848. Peace signed at Guadalupe Hidalgo, February 22. Ratified at Quere taro, May 30. Mexico evacuated, June 12.

1849. Z. Taylor elected President of the United States.

P. H. Bell Governor of Texas from December 21.

1850. Texas boundary-question settled by payment of ten million dollars by the United States, and New Mexico made a territory, September 9.

1851. P. H. Bell re-elected governor.

1853. E. M. Pease, governor.

1855. E. M. Pease re-elected governor

1856. Population of Texas about 425,000

POPULATION.

Population of Texas (Europeans) in the year 1765, about   750
    "   "   "   "   1806,   7,000
    "   '   "   (Americans)   "   1830,   20,000
    "   "   "   "   1834,   30,000

STATE CENSUS OF 1847.

White males,	58,338
White females,	45,503
Total white,	103,841
Free colored,	304
Slaves,	39,060
Population of State,	143,205

U. S. CENSUS OF 1850.

Whites,	154,034
Slaves,	58,161
Free colored,	397
Population of State,	212,592
Adults who cannot read and write, whites,	10,525
" " " free colored,	58
Total,	10,583
Born in foreign countries, whites,	17,620
" " free colored,	61
Total	17,681
Number of slave-owners,	7,747

POPULATION BY COUNTIES—1850.

COUNTIES.	POPULATION.		
	White.	Colored.	Total.
Anderson, ...	2,284	600	2,884
Angelina, ...	945	220	1,165
Austin, ...	2,286	1,555	3,841
Bastrop, ...	2,180	919	3,099
Bexar, ...	5,633	419	6,052
Bowie, ...	1,271	1,641	2,912
Brazoria, ...	1,329	3,512	4,841
Brazos, ...	466	148	614
Burleson, ...	1,213	500	1,713
Caldwell, ...	1,054	275	1,329
Calhoun, ...	867	243	1,110
Cameron, Starr, Webb, . .	8,469	72	8,541
Cass, ...	3,089	1,902	4,991
Cherokee, ...	5,389	1,284	6,673
Collin, ...	1,816	134	1,950
Colorado, ...	1,534	723	2,257
Comal, ...	1,662	61	1,723
Cook, ...	219	1	220
Dallas, ...	2,536	207	2,743
Denton, ...	631	10	641
De Witt, ...	1,148	568	1,716
Ellis, ...	902	87	989
Fannin, ...	3,260	528	3,788
Fayette, ...	2,740	1,016	3,756
Fort Bend, ...	974	1,559	2,533
Galveston, ...	3,785	744	4,529
Guadalupe, ...	1,171	340	1,511
Gillespie, ...	1,235	5	1,240
Goliad, ...	435	213	648
Gonzales, ...	891	601	1,492
Grayson, ...	1,822	186	2,008
Grimes, ...	2,326	1,682	4,008
Harris, ...	3,756	912	4,668
Harrison, ...	5,604	6,218	11,822
Hays, ...	239	128	387
Henderson, ...	1,155	82	1,237
Hopkins, ...	2,469	154	2,623
Houston, ...	2,036	685	2,721
Hunt, ...	1,477	43	1,520
Jackson, ...	627	369	996
Jasper, ...	1,226	541	1,767
Jefferson, ...	1,504	332	1,836
Kaufman, ...	982	65	1,047
Lamar, ...	2,893	1,085	3,978
Lavaca, ...	1,139	432	1,571
Leon, ...	1,325	621	1,946
Liberty, ...	1,623	899	2,522
Limestone, ...	1,990	618	2,608

POPULATION BY COUNTIES—1850.

COUNTIES.	POPULATION.		
	White.	Colored.	Total.
Matagorda, ...	913	1,211	2,124
Medina, ...	881	28	909
Milan, ...	2,469	438	2,907
Montgomery, ...	1,439	945	2,384
Nacogdoches, ...	3,758	1,435	5,193
Navarro, ...	1,943	247	2,190
Newton, ...	1,255	434	1,689
Nueces, ...	650	48	698
Panola, ...	2,676	1,195	3,871
Polk, ...	1,542	806	2,348
Red River, ...	2,493	1,413	3,906
Refugio, ...	269	19	288
Robertson, ...	670	264	934
Rusk, ...	6,012	2,136	8,148
Sabine, ...	1,556	942	2,498
San Augustine, ...	2,087	1,561	3,648
San Patricio, ...	197	3	200
Shelby, ...	3,278	961	4,339
Smith, ...	3,575	717	4,292
Starr, see Cameron, . . .	—	—	—
Tarrant, ...	599	65	664
Titus, ...	3,168	468	3,636
Travis, ...	2,336	802	3,138
Tyler, ...	1,476	418	1,894
Upshur, ...	2,712	682	3,394
Van Zandt, ...	1,308	40	1,348
Victoria, ...	1,396	623	2,019
Walker, ...	2,663	1,301	3,964
Washington, ...	3,166	2,817	5,983
Webb, see Cameron, . . .	—	—	—
Wharton, ...	510	1,242	1,752
Williamson, ...	1,410	158	1,568
Total, ...	154,034	58,558	212,592

POPULATION OF TOWNS—1850.

Galveston, . . .	4,177 (a)	Castroville, . . .	366
San Antonio, . .	3,488 (a)	Rusk, ...	355
Houston, ...	2,396	Richmond, . . .	323
Neu-Braunfels, .	1,298	Lavaca, ...	315 (c)
Marshall, . . .	1,189	Palestine, . . .	212
Victoria, ...	806	Bonham, ...	211
Frederickburg, .	754	McKinney, . . .	192
Austin, ...	629 (b)	Crocket, . . .	150 (d)
Corpus Christi, .	533	Brenham, . . .	— (e)
Nacogdoches, . .	468	Natchitoches, . .	1,261
Indianola, . . .	379	Shrieveport, . .	1,728 (f)

(a) 1853, 7,000. 1856, 10,000.   (d) 1853, 400.
(b) 1855, 3,200.   (e) 1853, 500.
(c) 1853, 1,000.   (f) 1853, 3,000.

LAND AND PRODUCTIONS.

CENSUS OF 1850.

Improved Farm Land	acres,	639,117
Unimproved Farm Land	"	10,759,220
Cash Value of Farms		$16,398,787
Value of Implements and Machinery		$2,133,831
Horses, Asses, and Mules	head,	87,767
Neat Cattle	"	917,524
Sheep	"	99,099
Swine	"	683,604
Value of Live Stock		$10,267,710
Wheat	bush.,	41,729
Indian Corn	"	5,978,590
Oats	"	198,717
Tobacco	lbs.,	66,897
Cotton	bales of 400 "	57,596
Wool	"	131,374
Peas and Beans	bush.,	179,337
Irish Potatoes	"	93,548
Sweet Potatoes	"	1,332,955
Butter	lbs.,	2,308,080
Cheese	"	94,619
Sugar	hhd. 1,000 lbs.,	7,351
Molasses	gall.,	441,638
Beeswax and Honey	lbs.,	380,682
Value of Orchard Products		$12,505
Value of Market Gardens		$12,354
Value of Home Manufactures		$255,724

INCREASE OF SLAVES—1850 TO 1855.

FROM THE REPORT OF THE STATE COMPTROLLER FOR 1855.

Estimated Production of Cotton in 1855, from the " State Gazette."

COUNTIES.	1850. Slaves.	1850. Bales.	1855. Slaves.	1855. Bales.
Anderson . .	600	734	1,917	2,345
Angelina . . .	196	174	291	260
Austin . . .	1,549	3,205	2,353	4,868
Bell . . .	—	—	406	3
Bastrop . .	919	1,478	1,748	2,811
Bosque . . .	—	—	34	—
Bexar . . .	389	—	979	—
Bowie . . .	1,641	1,113	1,866	2,500
Burnet . . .	—	—	150	31
Brazoria . .	3,507	3,531	4,292	4,300
Brazos . . .	148	142	427	420
Burleston . . .	500	1,010	1,047	2,115
Caldwell . .	274	122	1,171	519
Coryell . . .	—	—	139	28
Calhoun . .	234	109	310	144
Cameron* . . .	53	—	15	—
Cass . . .	1,902	1,573	3,518	2,912
Cherokee . . .	1,283	1,083	2,286	1,778
Collin . . .	134	1	432	3
Colorado . .	723	4,771	1,580	9,480
Comal . . .	61	10	126	20
Cook . . .	1	—	123	—
Dallas . . .	207	44	481	100
Denton . .	10	—	74	—
De Witt . . .	568	547	963	1,000
Ellis . . .	77	—	517	—
Fannin . .	528	374	1,019	708
Freestone . . .	—	—	2,167	4,517
Fayette . .	1,016	1,194	2,072	2,473
Fort Bend . .	1,554	2,465	1,746	2,869
Falls . .	—	—	851	633
Galveston . . .	714	—	761	—
Guadalupe . .	333	182	1,637	900
Gillespie . . .	5	—	63	—
Goliad . . .	213	—	416	—
Gonzales . . .	601	1,271	2,136	4,517
Grayson . .	186	5	602	16
Grimes . . .	1,680	2,282	3,124	4,455
Harris . . .	905	11	1,084	—
Hill	—	—	254	13
Harrison . .	6,213	4,581	7,013	5,170
Hays . . .	128	2	517	7
Henderson . .	81	31	411	157
Hopkins . . .	154	8	352	23
Houston . .	673	750	1,595	1,450
Hunt . . .	41	5	198	24
Johnson . . .	—	—	120	19
Jackson . . .	339	290	717	580
Jasper . . .	541	359	991	650

* Including Starr and Webb.

Counties.	1850. Slaves.	1850. Bales.	1855. Slaves.	1855. Bales.
Jefferson . .	269	2	216	2
Kaufman . . .	65	6	329	30
Lamar . . .	1,085	1,055	1,296	1,300
Lavaca . . .	432	526	1,004	1,217
Leon . . .	621	913	1,455	2,047
Liberty . . .	892	253	922	263
Limestone .	618	603	680	670
Matagorda .	1,208	1,613	1,529	1,932
McLennan . .	—	—	1,048	1,217
Medina . .	28	—	25	—
Milam . . .	436	—	713	—
Madison . . .	—	—	429	3
Montgomery . .	945	1,009	1,448	1,688
Nacogdoches . .	1,404	835	1,702	1,026
Navarro . .	246	2	1,135	9
Newton . . .	426	152	602	214
Nueces . . .	4 ?	—	89	—
Orange . . .	—	—	185	174
Panola . :	1,193	887	1,990	1,560
Polk . . .	805	582	1,427	1,100
Red River . .	1,406	579	1,807	826
Refugio . . .	19	—	148	—
Robinson . .	264	429	1,239	2,013
Rusk . . .	2,136	2,659	3,620	4,508
Sabine . . .	942	702	800	596
San Augustine . .	1,561	1,020	1,382	939
San Patricio . .	3	—	21	—
Shelby . . .	961	790	775	637
Smith . . .	717	415	2,414	1,397
Star, see Cameron .	—	—	—	—
Tarrant . .	65	—	280	—
Titus . .	467	292	1,208	755
Trinity . .	—	—	260	122
Travis . . .	791	234	2,068	611
Tyler . . .	418	184	752	331
Upshur . . .	682	673	1,784	1,760
Van Zant . .	40	57	125	179
Victoria . . .	571	270	850	401
Walker . . .	1,301	873	2,758	1,852
Washington . .	2,817	4,008	4,399	6,246
Webb, see Cameron .	—	—	—	—
Wood . . .	—	—	354	290
Wharton . .	1,242	2,892	1,798	4,187
Williamson . .	155	—	757	—
Sum total . .	58,161	58,072	105,974	105,111

ASSESSED VALUES OF PROPERTY FOR TAXATION.*

| Years. | LAND. | | | NEGROES. | | |
	No. Acres assessed.	Value. $	Value Acre.	No. assessed.	Value. $	Value of each, $.
1846 - - - -	31,967,480	17,776,101	55¾	31,099	10,142,198	324
1847 - - - -	30,440,210	17,326,994	57	39,251	12,174,593	310
1848 - - - -	32,160,184	20,777,412	64⅜	40,610	13,398,490	323
1849 - - - -	32,890,887	20,874,641	65	43,534	14,658,837	337
1850 - - - -	32,640,400	21,807,670	66¾	49,197	17,776,500	361
1851 - - - -	37,731,774	31,415,604	83½	59,959	26,246,668	404
1852 - - - -	37,838,792	33,116,772	87½	68,795	28,628,990	416
1853 - - - -	39,175,858	39,256,612	1·00	78,713	35,946,473	456
1854 - - - -	44,580,946	49,961,177	1·12	90,612	46,501,840	513
1855 - - - -	45,893,869	58,671,126	1·28	105,603	53,373,924	505

| Years. | HORSES AND CATTLE. | | | OTHER PROPERTY. |
	Number assessed.	Value. $.	Value per head. $.	Money at interest, goods in stores, etc.
1846 - - - -	411,100	2,929,378	7·12	3,543,501
1847 - - - -	448,971	3,392,784	7·12	4,668,134
1848 - - - -	581,251	4,174,475	7·16	5,461,666
1849 - - - -	631,649	4,419,015	7·00	5,847,516
1850 - - - -	750,352	5,222,270	7·00	6,675,175
1851 - - - -	901,794	6,638,115	7·35	8,639,797
1552 - - - -	1,020,832	7,977,999	7·82	11.030,423
1853 - - - -	1,164,463	10,217,499	8·78	13,734,530
1854 - - - -	1,377,472	13,465,805	9·08	17,052,795
1855 - - - -	1,615,609	16,936,423	10·48	20,539,978

TOTAL VALUE OF PROPERTY.

YEARS.	Aggregate taxable property.	Increase taxable property.	Increase per cent.
1846 - - - -	34,391,175		
1847 - - - -	37,562,505	3,171,330	8⅛
1848 - - - -	43,812,537	6,250,032	16⅝
1849 - - - -	46,241,589	2,429,052	5⅗
1850 - - - -	51,814,615	5,573,026	12⅜
1851 - - - -	69,739,581	17,924,966	33⅞
1852 - - - -	80,754,094		16⅔
1853 - - - -	99,155,114		23
1854 - - - -	126,981,617		28¼
1855 - - - -	149,521,451		17⅞

* COMPARATIVE STATISTICS OF IOWA.—" Permission to settle in this State was first granted to the white man on the 1st June, 1833. The rapidity with

PRODUCTION OF COTTON AND SUGAR.

IMPORTS AND EXPORTS, ETC.

COTTON.

1837, ...	50,000*
1846, cotton shipped, bales, ...	27,000
1849–50, " "	31,000†
1850–51, " "	46,000
1851–52, " "	64,000
1852–53, " "	85,000
1853–54, " "	107,906
1854–55, " "	80,737
1855–56, " "	116,078

SUGAR.—1850.

Counties producing Sugar.	Sugar, hhds. of 1,000 lbs.	Molasses, gallons.
Austin, ...	60	4,195
Brazoria, ...	4,811	314,164
Fort Bend, ...	100	420
Houston, ...	82	340
Liberty, ...	115	4,820
Matagorda, ...	1,394	73,000
Rusk, ...	101	1,090
Victoria, ...	120	6,700
Wharton, ...	317	11,490
	7,100	416,219

Sugar crop of 1852–3, ...	11,023 hhds., of 1,000 lbs.	
" " 1854–5, ...	9,875 " "	
" " 1855–6 (to Sept.), . .	7,513 " "	

which the torrent of immigration poured into this "Western Paradise," as the earlier travelers in this locality designated it, may be inferred from the fact, that the official returns of the territorial census, taken in May, 1838 gave her a population of 22,859; and that of the United States census, taken in 1840, 43,112; showing an average annual increase of over 44 per cent. Since that time, she has bounded forward with an extraordinary rapidity, numbering, by the census returns, taken June, 1850, within her borders, a population of 192,214; exhibiting an average annual increase for the decennial period, ending in 1850, of over 44 per cent.!!!

"With the view of presenting at a glance the increase in the value of property, we have referred to the assessment-rolls of this State, and we find that the total value of all kinds of property, in the year 1852, was $38,427,376; and that of the year 1849, was $18,496,151; showing an increase in the value of property, for three years, of about twenty millions of dollars, or an increase of over 107 per cent.!!!"—*De Bow's Review, Nov.,* '53.

* Yoakum.　　　　　　　　　　　† From Neill Brothers' Cotton Circular, 1856.

EXPORTS AND IMPORTS,

1854.

Exports to foreign countries, ...	$1,314,449
Imports, ...	231,423
Tonnage entered, ...	5,249
" cleared, ...	9,708
" owned in the State, ...	9,698
Steam tonnage owned in the State, ...	2,815
Cotton exported to foreign countries, bales, . . .	18,467

ADJOINING MEXICAN STATES.*

TAMAULIPAS.
Population 100,000; area 30,000 square miles

NUEVO LEON.
Population 133,000; area 16,000 square miles.

COAHUILA.
Population 56,570; area 66,228 square miles.

CHIHUAHUA.
Population 147,000; area 100,000 square miles.

SONORA.
Population 147,000; area 123,000 square miles.

* From *Lippincott's Gazetteer*, 1855.

VOTE OF TEXAS
IN 1855.

DISTRICTS. I.	CONGRESS.		LAND COM. 1855.		PRESIDENT, 1852.	
	K. N. Hancock.	*Dem.* Bell.	*K. N.* Crosby.	*Dem.* Fields.	*Whig.* Scott.	*Dem.* Pierce.
Austin, . . .	230	372	160	436	7	22
Bastrop, . .	305	394	216	458	94	243
Bell, . . .	150	329	111	320	26	157
Bexar, . .	573	1,711	132	2,079	299	804
Bosque, . . .	43	9	27	29	†	†
Brazos, . .	72	29	11	95	9	34
Brazoria, . .	91	258	142	202	43	143
Burleson, . .	124	262	99	249	19	103
Burnett, . . .	115	103	91	128		21
Caldwell, . .	263	315	171	282	84	235
Calhoun, . .	108	160	207	50	94	125
Cameron, . .	*	*	*	*	242	329
Colorado, . .	108	229	232	92	30	92
Comal, . .	13	337	32	308	6	112
Corryell, . . .	125	221	201	144	†	†˙
De Witt, . .	85	248	212	128	0	0
Ellis, . . .	177	147	241	105	43	90
El Paso, . .	116	636	760	0	†	†
Falls, . . .	129	80	187	15	†	†
Fayette, . .	308	504	395	311	165	341
Fort Bend, . .	50	219	122	134	31	86
Freestone, . .	247	27	75	331	8	138
Galveston, . .	251	442	122	496	141	324
Gillespie, . .	51	245	44	220	2	74
Goliad, . . .	126	103	31	201	0	0
Gonzales, . .	411	399	449	334	120	209
Grimes, . . .	428	166	191	204	53	142
Guadalupe, .	255	331	268	307	68	154
Harris, . . .	274	542	352	446	195	468
Hays, . . .	83	60	103	53	21	55
Hidalgo, . . .	0	0	0	0	48	119
Hill, . . .	85	57	117	19	†	†
Jackson, . .	51	105	137	20	33	90
Johnson, . .	64	182	182	55	†	†
Karnes, . . .	68	111	87	85	†	†
Lavaca, . .	175	284	233	201	33	85
Leon, . . .	359	161	29	462	48	124
Limestone, . .	236	127	298	36	38	176
Madison, . . .	117	43	26	123	†	†
Matagorda, . .	10	205	216	6	30	74
McLennan, . .	178	180	231	106	5	45
Medina, . .	7	240	7	235	2	42
Milan, . . .	181	129	127	145	56	119
Montgomery, .	214	163	326	47	74	120
Navarra, . .	310	189	466	30	89	220
Nueces, . .	53	282	274	49	21	52
Refugio, . . .	48	90	89	45	†	†
Robertson, . .	211	34	58	178	53	95
San Patricio, . .	4	51	53	14	0	30
Starr, . . .	8	306	169	137	68	76

NOTE.—Those marked thus * no returns.   Those marked † are new counties.
21

VOTE OF TEXAS IN 1855.

(*Continued.*)

DISTRICTS I.	CONGRESS.		LAND COM. 1855.		PRESIDENT, 1852	
	K. N. Hancock.	Dem. Bell.	K. N. Crosby.	Dem. Fields.	Whig. Scott.	Dem. Pierce.
Tarrant, . .	166	477	613	74	11	61
Travis, . .	491	507	295	690	118	370
Victoria, . .	114	170	109	172	9	96
Walker, . .	316	235	78	476	72	228
Washington, . .	461	483	366	446	121	519
Webb, . .	0	302	132	167	16	117
Wharton, . .	31	106	70	69	17	59
Williamson, .	227	282	217	278	62	143
Total, . .	9,496	14,379	10,389	12,522	2,824	7,561

Majority for Bell, 4,883; majority for Fields, 2,133; majority for Pierce, 4737.

II.	Evans.	Ward.	Crosby.	Fields.	Scott.	Pierce.
Anderson, . .	536	380	676	186	150	412
Angelina, . .	84	13	93	16	28	56
Bowie, . .	39	218	16	189	†	†
Cass, . . .	409	408	420	278	30	75
Cherokee, . .	685	904	797	766	248	696
Collin, . . .	342	246	536	81	58	135
Cooke, . .	67	126	181	2	5	14
Dallas, . . .	205	341	348	186	122	283
Denton, . .	120	112	207	11	0	37
Fannin, . . .	563	204	565	22	68	208
Grayson, . .	442	260	565	68	58	198
Harrison, . .	674	391	67	934	283	402
Henderson, .	219	102	264	12	23	74
Hopkins, . .	387	295	184	344	29	116
Houston, . .	197	339	292	274	46	125
Hunt, . . .	272	231	360	131	19	121
Jasper, . .	78	175	242	2	30	121
Jefferson, . .	0	0	0	0	†	†
Kaufman, . .	208	125	168	106	†	†
Lamar, . .	290	428	363	246	57	189
Liberty, . .	160	131	75	248	40	87
Nacogdoches, .	294	488	642	79	79	312
Newton, . .	77	81	116	3	16	111
Orange, . . .	0	0	0	0	23	39
Panola, . .	277	404	181	398	0	0
Polk, . . .	164	195	130	250	75	157
Red River, .	300	276	279	275	86	233
Rusk, . . .	837	883	862	857	242	590
Sabine, . .	155	68	197	8	13	81
Shelby, . . .	228	314	258	271	19	106

NOTE.—Those marked † are new counties.

VOTE OF TEXAS IN 1855.—(*Continued.*)

DISTRICT II.	Evans.	Ward.	Crosby.	Fields	Scott.	Pierce.
Smith, . . .	548	617	371	719	0	0
St. Augustine, .	122	200	146	160	29	158
Titus, . . .	430	286	641	46	100	240
Trinity, . .	127	56	170	13	3	17
Tyler, . . .	94	247	310	57	5	52
Upshur, .	340	504	310	438	137	361
Van Zandt, . .	143	92	168	0	5	43
Wood, . .	229	171	289	65	15	42
Total, . . .	10,342	10,311	11,489	7,741	2,141	5,891

Majority for Evans, 31 ; majority for Crosby, 3,748 ; majority for Pierce, 3,750.

TOTAL VOTE OF STATE.—Crosby, 21,878 ; Fields, 20,263 ; Scott, 4,965 ; Pierce, 13,452. Majority for Crosby, 1,615 ; majority for Pierce, 8,487.

1856. No exact information has yet been received, from the largest part of Texas, of the vote of the election of November, 1856. (Dec. 24th, 1856.)

TABLE OF ELEVATIONS,

ABOVE THE LEVEL OF THE OCEAN.

Feet

Trespalacios, corner of the stone warehouse, . . . 6½
Galveston, ... 10
Lavaca, ... 24
Guadalupe, at the mouth of Sandies, ... 50
Houston, ... - 60
Austin, ... 200
Columbus, ... 250
Gonzales, ... 270
Cibolo, ... 350
San Antonio, ... 635
Castroville, ... 767
Fort Inge, ... 845
Leona Mountain, near Fort Inge, ... 950
Rio San Pedro, first crossing, ... 859
    "   "   last   "   1,827
Table-lands of Texas, ... 2,091
Howard's Spring, ... 2,075
High table-land beyond, ... 3,008
Live Oak Creek, ... 2,338
Rio Pecos Valley, ... from 2,330 to 2,658
Rio Escondido, first crossing, ... 2,660
Leon Spring, ... 4,240
Limpia, first crossing, ... 3,950
Painted Camp, ... 5,020
Highest point of the road to El Paso, ... 5,765
Providence Creek, ... 5,492
Eagle Spring, ... 4,842
First point on the Rio Grande, ... 3,700
El Paso, ... 3,750
Mouth of Little Wichita, ... 750
    "   Big   " 900
Junction of the south and north forks of Red River, . 1.100
Head of the main or south fork of Red River, . . 2,450
Llano Estacado (Staked Plain), . . . from 2,300 to 2,500

METEOROLOGICAL NOTES.

NEU-BRAUNFELS, LAT. 29° 42'; LON. 21° 14'.—1853.

July.

Ther.—Mean for mo., 7 A. M., 77°
"   "   "   2 P. M., 91°
"   "   "   9 P. M., 77°
Monthly mean,   -   -   -   81·2·3
Highest,   -   -   -   -   101°
Four days,   -   -   -   100°
Lowest,   -   -   -   -   66°
Barometer.—Mean for month, 27·9 7·31

August.

Ther.—Mean for mo., 7 A. M., 77°
"   "   "   2 P. M., 94°
"   "   "   9 P. M., 77°
Monthly mean,   -   -   -   82·2·3
Highest,   -   •   100°
One day only,   -   -   -   100°
Lowest in morning,   -   -   73°
Barometer.—Mean for month, 27·8 7·10

July.—Calm 10 times at 7 A. M.
"   "   0   "   2 P. M.
"   "   0   "   9 P. M.
Prevailing wind, south, 1 to 3.

Aug.—Calm 12 times at 7 A. M.
"   "   0   "   2 P. M.
"   "   1   "   9 P. M.
Prevailing wind, south, 1 to 3.

Sept.—Calm 5 times at 7 A. M.
"   "   0   "   2 P. M.
"   "   0   "   9 P. M.
Prevailing wind, south.

October.

Ther.—Mean for mo., 7 A. M., 59°
"   "   "   2 P. M., 77°
"   "   "   9 P. M., 63°
Monthly mean,   -   -   -   66 1·3
Barometer.—Mean for month, 27·8 3·4
Prevailing wind, north.

November.

Ther.—Mean for mo., 7 A. M., 54°
"   "   "   2 P. M., 70°
"   "   "   9 P. M., 56°
Monthly mean,   -   -   -   60°
Barometer.—Mean for month, 27·9 1·2
Prevailing wind, north.

December.

Ther.—Mean for mo., 7 A. M., 44°
"   "   "   2 P. M., 61°
"   "   "   9 P. M., 47°
Monthly mean,   -   -   -   51°
Barometer.—Mean for month, 27·9 1·7
Prevailing wind, north.

THERMOMETER.   WIND.—DIRECTION AND FORCE.

	7 A.M.	2 P.M.	9 P.M.	7 A.M.	2 P.M.	9 P. M.
1854—Jan. 1	48°	62°	43°	0	S.W. 2	S.S.W. 1
" 2	32	65	45	N. 1	S.S.W. 3	N.W. 1
" 3	41	61	55	0	S. 4	S. 1
" 4	59	75	61	S. 3	N. 3	N. 6
" 5	63	59	33	N. 5	N. 6	N. 5
" 6	23	22	23	N. 4	N. 2	N. 1
" 7	23	49	35	N. 1	N. 1	N. 1
" 8	30	59	48	N. 1	S. 3	0
" 9	51	70	59	0	S.S.W. 2	N. 2
" 10	44	54	41	N 2	N. 3	N. 2
" 11	31	61	49	N. 1	S.S.W. 4	S.S.W. 4
" 12	41	58	43	N. 1	N. 4	N. 2
" 13	34	62	47	0	S.S.E. 1	—
" 14	63	78	70	S. 2	S. 4	S. 4
" 15	67	43	36	0	N. 4	N. 5
" 16	23	48	45	N. 4	N. 2	N. 1
" 17	42	50	50	N.N.E. 1	N.N.E 1	0
" 18	54	70	69	0	S. 1	S. 4
" 19	68	79	33	S. 2	S.E. 2	N. 6
" 20	21	—	—	N. 4	—	—

SISTERDALE, GUADALUPE HILLS.—1852.

Date.	Time.	Lowest Ther.	Time.	Highest Ther.	Prevailing Wind.
Jan. 1	2 A.M.	26·8	2 P.M.	68	Still.
" 2	6 "	30·9	2 "	68·4	"
" 3	7 "	30·4	3 "	71·9	S.
" 4	7 "	34·3	2 "	62·8	N.W.
" 5	7 "	38·3	2 "	63·2	"
" 6	7 "	23·9	2 "	61	S. Still.
" 7	7 "	34·3	2 "	61·4	"
" 8	6 "	28·6	3 "	72·9	W.
" 9	7 "	38·7	2 "	78·8	"
"10	6 "	47·3	12 M.	60·1	N.W.
"11	4 "	27·7	3 P.M.	56	S. Still.
"12	8 P.M.	24·1	7 A.M.	32	Norther.
"13	7 A.M.	10	2 P.M.	38·5	N.W
"14	7 "	20·7	3 "	45·7	W. and S.
"15	7 "	28·2	3 "	57·4	N.W.
"16	7½ "	26·4	2 "	64·7	S. Still.
"17	4 "	54	12 M.	65·8	S.
"18	8 P.M.	23·4	1 P.M.	33·4	N.
"19	7 A.M.	14	3 "	36·5	N. Still.
"20	7 "	18·3	3 "	51·1	Still.
"21	7 "	20·3	3 "	54·5	"
"22	7 "	20·1	3 "	50	"
"23	7 "	36·5	3 "	45·3	"
"24	8 "	41	2 "	51·1	"
"25	7 "	43·7	12 M.	66·6	"
"26	6½ "	33·5	1 P.M.	63·6	W.
"27	7 "	27·5	2 "	69·4	"
"28	7 "	27·8	2 "	—	

NORTHEASTERN TEXAS.

OBSERVATIONS OF MR. SMITH, IN 1849.

Date.	Time.	Ther.	Date.	Time.	Ther.
May 22	12 M.	84	May 29	1.45 P.M.	70
"	3·30 P.M.	88	" 31	3·45 "	82
"	10·30 "	76	June 1	2 "	88
" 23	2·30 "	86	" 2	9·30 A.M.	80
'	7·30 "	78	"	9 P.M.	76
" 24	3 "	86	" 3	2 "	82
" 25	8·15 A.M.	70	" 4	3 "	82
"	12 M.	80	" 5	7 A.M.	74
"	4·45 P.M.	82	" 6	12·30 A.M.	74
" 26	7·45 "	77	" 8	7·30 "	78
" 28	9 "	79	" 10	12 M.	88
" 29	5·15 A.M.	58			

NORTHWESTERN TEXAS.

OBSERVATIONS BY CAPT. MARCY, IN 1852, ON UPPER RED RIVER.

	Date.	Time.	Ther.	Wind.	Rain.	Date.	Time.	Ther.	Wind	Rain.
Ft. Belknap to mouth of Big Witchita.	May 4	4 P.M.	88	S.E.		May 9	7 P.M.	76	S.E.	
	"	9 "	76	"		" 10	5 A.M.	68	"	
	" 5	3 "	77	—	R	"	12 M.	86	"	
	" 7	3 "	80	S.E.		"	7 P.M.	76	"	
	"	7·30 do.	72½	"		" 11	6·30A.M.	68	"	
	"	9 "	70	"	R	"	10·30 "	89	"	
	" 8	5 A.M.	68½	SEbyS	R	"	8·30P.M	71	"	
	"	2 P.M.	84½	S.E		" 12	6 A.M.	68½	"	
	"	8·30 do.	72	"		"	4 P.M.	77	"	R
	" 9	6·30A.M.	68	E.	R	"	7·30 do.	73	SEbyS	R
	"	1 P.M.	86	S.E.						
Cache Creek.	M'y 13	6 A.M.	69	N.W.	R	M'y 16	4·30P.M.	64	NNE.	
	"	7 "	65	"		"	7·30 do.	57½	NNW	
	"	2 P.M.	85	"		" 17	5 A.M.	44½	N.	
	"	9 "	64	"		"	7.45P.M.	51	N.	
	" 14	6·30A.M.	57¼	WNW		" 18	4·30A.M.	40	N.E.	
	"	12 M.	82½	S.		"	3·45P.M.	79	S.	
	"	10 P.M.	69	"		"	8·45 do.	70	S.E.	R
	" 15	5 A.M.	66	S.E.		" 19	5 A.M.	60	E.S.E.	R
	"	3 P.M.	81	"		"	6 "	59	N.N.E	R
	"	9·30 do.	72	"		"	12 M.	61	E.N.E	
	" 16	5 A.M.	66	N.		" 21	6 P.M.	75	N.E.	
Otter Creek.	M'y 22	6.15P.M.	71½	N.E.		M'y 25	2·45P.M.	86	S.	
	" 23	12·45A.M.	64	"		"	7·30 "	67½	WNW	
	"	7 P.M.	58	"	R	" 26	6·15A.M.	62	N.W.	R
	" 24	6 A.M.	62	N.	R	"	1·30P.M.	76	"	
	"	12·30P.M.	80	S.		"	8·30 "	64	N.	
	"	2 P.M.	74	"		" 27	5·30A.M	61½	N.W.	
	"	7·30P.M.	65	"		"	6·15 "	66	N.	
	" 25	6·30A.M.	65	S.E.	R	"	Midnight.	64	"	
Longitude 100°.	M'y 28	7 A.M.	64	N.		June 3	7·30P M.	70	N.	
	"	9 "	76	"		" 4	2·30A.M	60	"	
	"	7·30P.M.	69	N.W.		"	1·30P.M.	76	"	
	" 29	3·30A.M.	61	S.W.		"	7 "	67¾	"	
	"	9 P.M.	—	"		" 5	1·30A.M.	49½	N.W.	
	" 30	9·30 do.	70	"		"	12 M.	77	"	
	" 31	3·30A.M.	—	"		"	7 P.M.	65	S.W.	
	"	10·15P.M.	66	S.E.		" 6	2·30A.M.	54	S.	
	June 1	2·30A.M.	63	S.W.		"	12 M.	73	N.W.	R
	"	2 P.M.	88	"		"	7 P.M.	64	N.	R
	"	7·30 do.	76	S.		" 7	4·30A.M.	58½	"	
	" 2	2·45A.M.	69	"		"	12 M.	83	"	
	"	11·15 "	84	"		"	7 P.M.	67	N.E.	
	"	7 P M.	79	S.E.		" 8	2·30A.M.	46	"	
	" 3	2·15A.M.	70	"	R	"	12 M.	75	S.	
	"	12 M.	86¾	N.E.		"	7·30P.M.	65¾	"	

NORTHWESTERN TEXAS.

OBSERVATIONS BY CAPT. MARCY, IN 1852, ON UPPER RED RIVER.

(*Continued.*)

	Date.	Time.	Ther.	Wind.	Rain.	Date.	Time.	Ther.	Wind.	Rain.
Sweet Water Creek : Lat. 35° 35′, Lon. 101° 55′.	June 9	2·30A.M.	49	S.		Jun.13	5·30A.M.	63	S.	
	"	11·15 "	83	N.E.		"	2·30P.M.	90	"	
	"	7·30P.M.	66	"		"	7·30 do.	77	"	
	" 10	3 A.M.	59	E.		" 14	2·30A.M.	66	"	
	"	11·30 do.	78	S.E.		"	2·30P.M.	84	"	
	"	7·30P.M.	79½	"		"	7·30 "	72	"	
	" 11	2·45A.M.	60	S.		" 15	3·30A.M.	66	"	
	"	12 M.	93	"		"	12 M.	86	"	R
	"	8 P.M.	78½	"		"	9 P.M.	67	SWbyW	
	" 12	3 A.M.	69½	"		" 16	3 A.M.	65	S.W.	R
	"	11 "	85	"		"	1·30P M.	84	"	
	"	7·30P.M.	77	"		"	7·30 "	68	S.	
Canadian River.	Jun.17	4·30A.M.	64	S.	R	Jun.24	1 P.M.	74½	E.N.E	
	"	12 M.	83	"		"	7. "	64	"	
	"	6 P.M.	70	•		" 25	3 A.M.	56	NNE.	
	" 18	4·30A.M.	66	W.		"	2 P.M.	74	S.	
	"	12 M.	87	N.	R	"	7 "	66	"	
	"	6 P.M.	80	S.E.	R	" 26	3 A.M.	56	E.N E	
	" 19	6 A.M.	70	N.	R	"	11 "	79	S.S.E.	
	"	9·30P.M.	66	"		"	7 P.M.	72	S.W.	R
	" 20	2.45A.M.	65	"		" 27	3 A.M.	62	WSW	
	"	11·30 "	77	S.E.		"	12 M.	81	N.	
	"	8.15P.M.	70	S.S.E.		"	6·30P.M.	74	"	
	" 21	3 A.M.	66	"		" 28	3 A.M.	62	N.N.E	R
	"	12 M.	85	S.		"	11·30 do.	83	"	
	"	8 P.M.	72	"		"	10·30P.M.	70	S.W.	
	" 22	2·30A.M	66½	"		" 29	4 A.M.	73	S.E.	
	"	12 M.	89	"		"	12 M.	100	W.	
	"	7 P.M.	80	S.W.	R	"	6 P.M.	86	S.E.	
	" 23	3 A.M.	69½	N.W.	R	" 30	4·30A.M.	80	S.	
	"	1·30P.M.	68	N.E.	R	"	12 M.	103.	S.S.E.	
	"	7 "	63½	"		"	6 P.M.	91	W.	
	" 24	3 A.M.	65	E.N.E						
Main Source Red River.	July 1	4 A.M.	69	W.		July 7	3 A.M.	73	S.	
	"	12 .M.	104	"		"	2 P.M.	92	"	
	"	6 P.M.	91	S.S.E.		"	9 "	82	"	
	" 2	4·30A.M.	66	N.W.		" 8	12·30A.M.	77	"	
	"	12 M.	90	N.E.		"	12 M.	93	"	
	"	6 P.M.	80	S.E.		"	7 P.M.	83	"	
	" 3	4·30A.M.	71	"		" 9	1·30A.M	77	"	
	"	12 M.	89	S.		"	12 M.	91	"	
	"	10 P.M.	74	"		"	8 P.M.	74	"	
	" 4	3 A.M.	66	"		" 10	2·30A.M	62	"	
	"	12 M.	90	"		"	12 M.	94	"	
	"	9 P.M.	72	"		"	7·30P.M.	86	"	
	" 5	1·30A.M.	74	"		" 11	2·30A.M.	73	"	
	"	12 M.	92	"		"	12 M.	99	"	
	"	7·30P.M.	80	"		"	7·30P.M.	82	"	
	" 6	1 A.M.	76	"		" 12	1 A.M.	74	"	
	"	10·30 do.	83	"		"	11·30A.M.	95	"	
	"	7·30P.M.	82½	"		"	7·30P.M.	83½	"	

NORTHWESTERN TEXAS.

OBSERVATIONS BY CAPT. MARCY, IN 1852, ON UPPER RED RIVER.

(*Continued.*)

	Date.	Time.	Ther.	Wind.	Rain.	Date.	Time.	Ther.	Wind.	Rain.
Main Source Red River.	Jul. 13	4 30A.M.	76	S.	R	Jul. 15	9 P.M.	93½	N.E.	
	"	12 M.	84	E.N.E		" 16	2 A.M.	69	E.	
	"	7·30P.M.	74	"		"	11 "	82	S.	
	" 14	3 A.M.	68	"		"	7·30P.M.	76	E.	
	"	11 "	92	N.E.		" 17	3 A.M.	69½	S.	
	"	7·30P.M.	76	"		"	11 "	86	S.E.	
	" 15	1·30A.M.	69½	S.		"	7·30P.M.	74	N.E.	
	"	11 "	100	"						
Cache Creek.	Jul. 18	2·30A.M.	67	E.		Jul. 21	9.30P.M.	68	S.	
	"	12 M.	89	S.S.E.		" 22	1·30A.M.	62	"	
	"	7·30P.M.	73	"		"	1·30P.M.	75	"	
	" 19	3 A.M.	66	"		"	10 "	68	"	
	"	12 M.	81	S.		" 23	5·30A.M.	68	"	R
	"	7·30P.M.	73	"		"	12 M.	94	"	
	" 20	2 A.M.	66	"		"	10·30P.M.	68	"	
	"	12 M.	82½	S.S.W		" 24	3 A.M.	68	"	
	"	7·30P.M.	71	S.		"	1·30P.M.	88	"	
	" 21	2·30A.M.	60	"	R	"	9·30 "	76	"	
	"	12 M.	82	"						
Cross Timbers	Jul. 25	2·30A.M.	72	S.		Jul. 26	4 A.M.	62	S.E.	
	"	2 P.M.	75	"	R	"	2 P.M.	85	E.	R
	"	10 "	68	S.E.		"	9·30P.M.	72	"	
Ft. Arbuckle	Jul. 27	3 A.M.	65	E.		Jul. 27	4·30P.M.	84	S.	
	"	1·30P.M.	88	S.	R					

NORTHWESTERN TEXAS.

EXTREME TEMPERATURES NOTED BY MR. PARKER, ON THE HEADS OF THE BRAZOS, 1854.

July 16	.	.	100°		August 6	.	.	104°	
" 20	.	.	100°		" 11	.	.	105°	9 A.M.
" 21	.	.	102°	10 A.M.	" 12	.	.	106°	
" 22	.	.	102°		" 13	.	.	104°	
" 23	.	.	102°		" 19	.	.	106°	
" 25	.	.	110°		" 20	.	.	105°	
" 26	.		106°		" 26	.	.	106°	

CONSTITUTION OF THE STATE OF TEXAS.

PROVISIONS OF GENERAL INTEREST.

WE the people of the Republic of Texas, acknowledging with gratitude the grace and beneficence of God, in permitting us to make a choice of our form of Government, do, in accordance with the provisions of the joint Resolution for annexing Texas to the United States, approved March first, one thousand eight hundred and forty-five, ordain and establish this Constitution:

Article I.—*Bill of Rights.*

That the general, great, and essential principles of liberty and free government may be recognized and established, we declare that—

SEC. 1. All political power is inherent in the people, and all free governments are founded on their authority, and instituted for their benefit; and they have at all times the unalienable right to alter, reform, or abolish their form of government in such manner as they may think expedient.

SEC. 2. All freemen, when they form a social compact, have equal rights; and no man, or set of men, is entitled to exclusive separate public emoluments or privileges but in consideration of public services.

SEC. 3. No religious test shall ever be required as a qualification to any office or public trust in this State.

SEC. 4. All men have a natural and indefeasible right to worship God according to the dictates of their own consciences. No man shall be compelled to attend, erect, or support any place of worship, or to maintain any ministry against his consent; no human authority ought, in any case whatever, to control or interfere with the rights of conscience in matters of religion; and no preference shall ever be given by law to any religious society or mode of worship. But it shall be the duty of the Legislature to pass such laws as (may) shall be necessary to protect every religious denomination in the peaceable enjoyment of their own mode of public worship.

SEC. 5. Every citizen shall be at liberty to speak, write, or publish his opinion on any subject, being responsible for the abuse of that privilege, and no law shall have the right to control the liberty of speech or of the press.

SEC. 6. In prosecutions for the publication of papers investigating the official conduct of officers or men in public capacity, or when the matter published is proper for public information, the truth thereof may be given in evidence; and in all indictments for libels, the jury shall have the right to determine the law and the facts under the direction of the courts, as in other cases.

SEC. 7. The people shall be secure in their persons, houses, papers, and possessions, from all unreasonable seizures or searches; and no warrant to search any place or to seize any person or thing shall issue without describing them as near as may be, nor without probable cause supported by oath and affirmation.

SEC. 8. In all criminal prosecutions, the accused shall have a speedy public

21*

trial by an impartial jury ; he shall not be compelled to give evidence against himself, he shall have the right of being heard by himself or counsel, or both, shall be confronted with the witnesses against him, and shall have compulsory process for obtaining witnesses in his favor, and no person shall be holden to answer for any criminal charge, but on indictment or information, except in cases arising in the land or naval forces, or offenses against the laws in regulating the militia.

SEC. 9. All prisoners shall be bailable by sufficient sureties, unless for capital offenses, when the proof is evident or the presumption great; but this provision shall not be construed so as to prohibit bail after indictment found upon an examination of the evidence by a Judge of the Supreme or District Court upon the return of the (a) writ of *habeas corpus*, returnable in the county where the offense is committed.

SEC .10. The privileges of the writ of *habeas corpus* shall not be suspended, except when, in case of rebellion, or invasion, the public safety may require it.

SEC. 11. Excessive bail shall not be required nor excessive fines imposed, nor cruel, nor unusual punishment inflicted. All courts shall be open, and every person, for an injury done him in his lands, goods, person, or reputation, shall have remedy by due course of law.

SEC. 12. No person, for the same offense, shall be twice put in jeopardy of life or limb, nor shall a person be again put upon trial for the same offense, after a verdict of not guilty ; and the right of trial by jury shall remain inviolate.

SEC. 13. Every citizen shall have the right to keep and bear arms in the lawful defense of himself or the State.

SEC. 14. No bill of attainder, *ex post facto* law, retroactive laws, or any law impairing the obligations of contracts, shall be made, and no person's property shall be taken or applied to public use without adequate compensation being made, unless by the consent of such person.

SEC. 15. No person shall ever be imprisoned for debt.

SEC. 16. No citizen of the State shall be deprived of life, liberty, property, or privileges, outlawed, exiled, or in any manner disfranchised, except by due course of law of the land.

SEC. 17. The military shall, at all times, be subordinate to the civil authority

SEC. 18. Perpetuities and monopolies are contrary to the genius of a free government, and shall never be allowed ; nor shall the law of primogeniture or entailments ever be in force in this State.

SEC. 19. The citizens shall have the right, in a peaceable manner, to assemble together for their common good, and to apply to those invested with the power of Government, for the redress of grievances, or other purposes, by petition, address, or remonstrance

SEC. 20. No power of suspending laws in this State shall be exercised, except by the Legislature or its authority.

SEC. 21. To guard against transgressions of the higher powers herein designated, we declare that everything in this Bill of Rights is excepted out of the general powers of government, and shall forever remain inviolate, and all laws contrary thereto or the following provisions shall be void.

Articles II -V.—*Division of the Powers, of Government, etc.*

The departments are three—Executive, Legislative, and Judicial—organized as is usual in the other States. To possess the right of suffrage, a person must have attained the age of twenty-one years, have resided one year in the State, and the last six months in his voting district—"Indians not taxed, Africans, and descendants of Africans" are excepted. The sessions of the Legislature are triennial. Members of the House of Representatives are elected for two years; must be citizens, and have been two years inhabitants of the State, and twenty-one years of age. Members of the Senate are chosen for four years; must be citizens, three years inhabitant, and thirty years of age. The doors of each house must be kept open, and neither may adjourn without concurrence for more than three days. Members cannot be ministers of the Gospel or priests. A census is to be taken every eight years from 1850.

The Governor holds office for two years, but is ineligible for more than four years out of six. His qualifications are those of a Senator. He has the power of reprieve and pardon, and of veto; but vetoed bills, repassed by a two-thirds vote, become laws.

The Judicial department is organized into one Supreme Court, District Courts, County Courts, and Justices' Courts.

Article VI.—*Militia.*

SEC. 2. Any person who has conscientious scruples to bear arms, shall not be compelled to do so, but shall pay an equivalent for personal services.

SEC. 3. No licensed minister of the Gospel shall be required to perform military duty, work on roads, or serve on juries in this State.

The control of the militia is given to the Governor.

Article VII.—*General Provisions.*

All officers must take oath that they have not been concerned in any duel.

SEC. 2. Treason against this State shall consist only in levying war against it, or in adhering to its enemies—giving them aid and comfort; and no person shall be convicted of treason unless on the testimony of two witnesses to the same overt act, or his own confession in open court.

SEC. 10. The duration of no office may exceed four years.

SEC. 18. No divorce shall be granted by the Legislature.

SEC. 19. All property, both real and personal, of the wife, owned or claimed by her before marriage, and that acquired afterwards by gift, devise, or descent, shall be her separate property; and laws shall be passed more clearly defining the rights of the wife in relation as well to her separate property as that held in common with her husband. Laws shall also be passed providing for the registration of the wife's separate property.

SEC. 22. Exempts homesteads from forced sale.

SEC. 32. Prohibits paper to circulate as money.

SEC. 35. No soldier in time of peace may be quartered upon any person without his consent.

Mode of Amending the Constitution.

The Legislature, whenever two-thirds of each House shall deem it neces
sary, may propose amendments to this Constitution, which proposed amend
ments shall be duly published in the public prints of the State at least three
months before the next general election of the Representatives, for the consi
deration of the people; and it shall be the duty of the several returning offi
cers, at the next election, which shall thus be holden, to open a poll for, and
make a return to the Secretary of the State of, the names of all those voting for
Representatives who have voted on such proposed amendments, and if, thereupon, it shall appear that a majority of all the citizens of this State, voting for
Representatives, have voted in favor of such proposed amendments, and two-
thirds of each House of the next Legislature shall, after such election, and
before another, ratify the same amendments by yeas and nays, they shall be
valid to all intents and purposes as part of this Constitution, provided that the
said proposed amendments shall, at each of the said sessions, have been read
on three several days in each House.

Article VIII.—*Slaves.*

SEC. 1. The Legislature shall have no power to pass laws for the emancipa
tion of slaves, without the consent of their owners, nor without paying their
owners, previous to such emancipation, a full equivalent in money for the
slaves so emancipated; they shall have no power to prevent emigrants to the
State from bringing with them such persons as are deemed slaves by the laws
of the United States, so long as any person of the same age or description
shall be continued in slavery by the laws of this State; provided that such
slaves be the bona fide property of such emigrants; provided, also, that
laws be passed to inhibit the introduction into this State of slaves who have
committed high crimes in States or Territories; they shall have the right to pass
laws to permit the owners of slaves to emancipate them, saving the rights of
creditors, and preventing them from becoming a public charge; they shall have
full power to pass laws which will oblige the owners of slaves to treat them
with humanity, to provide for their necessary food and clothing, to abstain from
all injuries to them extending to life or limb, and, in case of their neglect or
refusal to comply with the directions of such laws, to have such slave or slaves
taken from such owners and sold for the benefit of such owner or owners;
they may pass laws to prevent slaves from being brought into this State as
merchandise only.

SEC. 2. In the prosecution of slaves for crimes of a higher grade than petit
larceny, the Legislature shall have no power to deprive them of an impartial
trial by a petit jury.

SEC. 3. Any person who shall maliciously dismember or deprive a slave of
life shall suffer such punishment as would be inflicted in case the like offense
had been committed upon a free white person, and on the like proof except
in case of insurrection of such slave.

Article X.—*Education.*

SEC. 1. A general diffusion of knowledge being essential to the preservation of the rights and liberties of the people, it shall be the duty of the Legislature of this State to make suitable provision for the support and maintenance of Public Schools.

SEC. 2. The Legislature shall, as early as practicable, establish free schools throughout the State, and shall furnish means for their support by taxation of property; and it shall be the duty of the Legislature to set apart not less than one-tenth part of the annual revenue of the State, derivable from taxation, as a perpetual fund; which fund shall be appropriated to the support of free public schools, and no law shall ever be made diverting said funds to any other use, and until such time as the Legislature shall provide for the establishment of such schools in the several districts of the State, the fund thus created shall remain as a charge against the State, passed to the credit of the free common school fund.

This Constitution is dated at Austin, August 27, 1845, signed by Thomas J Rusk, President.

TITLES OF LAND.

(From a letter of J. De Cordova to E. Smith.)

Spanish Titles.—Grants.—1. For services.   2. For ecclesiastical purposes.

Mexican Titles.   1. From the Central Government.
  a. Grants on certain conditions, erecting mills, etc.
  b. Sales.
2. From the grants of the States of Coahuila and Texas.
  a. Grants on certain conditions.
  b. Sales.*
  c. Head-rights to actual settlers.

Texan Titles.   1. Grants to settlers.
  a. Who arrived previous to Declaration of In-dependence.
  b. Who arrrived after the Declaration of Inde-pendence, and before the year 1837.
  c. Who arrived after 1st October, 1837, and be-fore 1842.
2. Bounty claims.
  a. For services in the army.
  b. As pensions to those disabled.
  c. For those who served in the battles of San Ja-cinto and Bexar.
3. Land-scrip.
  a. Issued for the support of the army.
  b. Taken in redemption of the promissory notes of the Republic.

COLONIES.

The principal colonies are as follows :—Burnet's, Vehlin's, Robertson's or Nashville, De Witt's, Austin (four colonies), Powers and Hewitson's, Austin and William's, Zavala's, McMullen and McGlone.   All these were empresa-rios who are entitled to premium lands, provided they strictly complied with their contracts.

BOUNTIES.

1. Emigrants who arrived (a.) before Declaration of Independence.   Married men are entitled to one league and one labor; single men to one-third of a league.

* Among these, a sale of forty ten-league grants to John T. Mason, which, with others similar, was declared void by the Republic of Texas.

2. (b.) After Independence, and before 1837. Married men, if enrolled in the army, are entitled to one league and one labor; if single men, to one-third of a league, provided such enrollment was previous to August, 1836.

3. (c.) After 1st October, 1837, and before 1842—640 and 320 acres

Bounty claims, for services in the army, are for 320, 640, 1,280, and 1,920 acres.

For those disabled, one league.

INDIAN COLONIZATION.

[From the Report of Commissioner Moneypenny to the Secretary of the Interior, December, 1856.]

The policy of colonizing the Indians of Texas was commenced early in February, 1855. The reservations for that purpose are in Young county, Texas, one on the Brazos River, and one on the Clear Fork of the Brazos. The Caddoes, Anadahhas, Tahuakleros, Wacos, and Tonkahwas, have been congregated at the former reserve, called the Brazos, and the Comanches at the latter, called the Comanche reserve.

On the 18th of September last, there were nine hundred and forty-eight Indians at the Brazos, and five hundred and fifty-seven at the Comanche reservation. At the former, during the past year, there have been five hundred and forty acres of land fenced in and cultivated, and at the latter two hundred acres. The Indians have made considerable progress in building houses and making other improvements, and have advanced in their moral and social condition. Whisky has, by great vigilance on the part of the agents, and the military and State authorities, been kept entirely away; and, in every point of view, the enterprise, in its present state and future prospects, is more encouraging than its most sanguine friends had anticipated.

The forays and depredations occurring last spring, on the confines of Texas, were not, it is said, to be traced to the indigenous tribes of that State, but were committed entirely by Indians who had not any connection with the reserves. The chastisement of some of these predatory bands, has happily been succeeded by a period of unusual quiet and peace.

The flattering success in Texas gives promise that, by a similar policy, the Southern Comanches, Wichetaws, and other wandering bands, near the northern frontier of that State, may be successfully colonized on the western end of the Choctaw country, for which provision was made by the treaty of June 22, 1855, between the United States and the Choctaws and Chickasaws.

LIST OF WORKS AND AUTHORS.

Texas: its Geography, Natural History, and Topography. By William Kennedy, Esq. (British Consul at Galveston). 8vo. pp. 118. New York: Benjamin & Young, 1844.

Texas: the Rise, Progress, and Prospects of the Republic. By the same.

History of Texas. By David B. Edwards. Cincinnati: 1836. 12mo

History of the Revolution in Texas. By C. Newell. New York: 1838. 12mo.

A Visit to Texas, with a sketch of the late war. By Fiske. New York: Van Nostrand & Dwight, 1836.

A Journey through Northeastern Texas. By Edward Smith. London: 1849. 12mo.

Green's Journal of the Texan Expedition against Mier. New York: 1845. 8vo.

Texas. By Mrs. Mary Austin Holley. 12mo. Baltimore: 1833.

Eagle Pass. By Cora Montgomery. New York: G. P. Putnam. pp. 188.

Letters from Texas. By W. B. Dewees. Louisville: Morton & Griswold, 1852. 12mo., pp. 312.

Notes on Unexplored Texas. By W. B. Parker. Philadelphia: Hayes & Zell, 1855. 12mo., pp. 242.

The Santa Fe Expedition. By G. W. Kendall. New York: Harper & Brothers, 1844. 2 vols., 12mo.

Rambles in Texas.

Personal Narrative. By John R. Bartlett, Commissioner for the Mexican Boundary. New York: D. Appleton & Co., 1854. 2 vols., 8vo.

Texas and the Gulf of Mexico. By Mrs. Houston. Philadelphia. 2 vols., 18mo.

Our Army on the Rio Grande. By T. B. Thorpe. Philadelphia: 1848. 12mo.

A Stray Yankee in Texas. By Philip Paxton.

Wanderings in the Southwest. In the New York "Crayon," 1855-6. By J. D. B. Stillman.

Texas. By L. T. Pease (in Niles's Spanish Republics). Hartford: 1836.

Sam Houston and his Republic. By C. Edwards Lester. New York: Burgess, Stringer & Co. 8vo., pp. 208.

Life of Gen. Sam Houston. New York: Redfield, 1855.

Notes from my Knapsack. Putnam's Monthly, March, 1854.

A trip from Chihuahua to the Sierra Madre. The same, October, 1854.

History of Louisiana. By Gayarré.

Ward's Mexico in 1827. Appendix, Texas. London. 2 vols., 8vo.

History of Texas from its discovery to the present time. By Maillard.

Mexico in 1842. To which is added an account of Texas and Yucatan, and of the Santa Fe Expedition. New York: 1842. 18mo.

Texas and the Texans. By Henry Stewart Foote. 2 vols., 12mo. Philadelphia: 1841.

Notes on the Upper Rio Grande. By Bryan Tilden.

Featherstonaugh, Excursion Through the Slave States. New York: Harper & Brothers.

The Fiscal History of Texas. By W. M. Gouge. Philadelphia: J. P. Lippincott & Co.

Memoir of a Trip to Northern Mexico in 1846 and '47. By A. Wislizenus Senate Doc., Washington, 1848.

Yoakum's History of Texas. 2 vols., 8vo. New York: J. S. Redfield, 1856

SCRAPS OF NEWSPAPER.

☞ To our patrons, who looked for the prompt appearance of our paper this week, with its usual quantity of reading matter, we have to plead, as an excuse, the absence of our printer, the severe affliction of the publisher, and the norther. Our office is a very cold one, and it was almost impossible to work in it on Friday last.

☞ Private parties are getting to be quite common in Bastrop, we understand. Several very creditable candy-pullings are said to have come off during the Christmas week, at which we had not the good fortune to be present. We notice these parties, for they are important to a good state of society in any place. Bastrop has for two years past enjoyed no enviable reputation in this respect, and yet Bastrop has more material than any town of its size in Texas. The substantial and wealthy citizens of a place—the merchants—the church members, whose interest as well as *duty* it is to improve society, should wake up on this matter. Let them give such magnificent entertainments as was given by Mr. and Mrs. C. K. Hall, on the 3rd inst. Liberality is not lost upon the young; and the liberal, social, and generous merchant will always succeed best, other things being equal.

☞ It is true that young people will have amusements, and to this end they will seek some kind of society. If the advantages of good association are denied them they often turn aside to evil practices and bad examples. Christmas week last year was one continual scene of mischief and drunken uproariousness all about town. Plows were perched to roost on the tops of houses. Signs changed their locations, and effigies of good and pious men were posted along the streets. This year all was peaceable, orderly, and quiet.

The reason of this difference is obvious. This year the thoughts have been directed in a civil channel by parties and balls. The Citizens' Ball, given at the Nicholson House, on the 29th, convened an array of beauty and loveliness seldom surpassed. The rough sex, when enjoying such society, forget the moods which would lead to shameful excesses. But speaking of the ball—the supper prepared by Mrs. Beachboard gave perfect satisfaction, the music was excellent, and everything went off harmoniously. But alas, how time flies when shuffled off by nimble feet. The clock struck two, and all were obliged to take note of time "from its loss."

THE party at Col. C———'s, on the 28th ultimo, passed off to the delight of every one present, we believe. The supper-table surpassed all things except the beauty and charms of the ladies around it. Arrangements had been made for dancing, but no fiddler appeared, as was expected. But the Col. informed the boys that dancing had to be done, and no mistake. So a chunk of a fiddler was raked up from the suburbs, who went to work, and kept up that "same old tune" until a late hour.

DURING the past week a Mormon missionary has been holding forth in Gonzales. At his last meeting there, he "pulled off his coat and rolled up his sleeves"—which, alas! caused a stampede of the lady part of his audience. Soon after, he was escorted around the town to the music of tin horns, cow-bells, etc., and told to leave ere the dews of night were kissed by early dawn, and he did nothin' shorter. —*San Antonio Texan.*

AMICABLY ADJUSTED.—We are gratified to learn from the Jefferson *Herald* of the 5th inst., that the pending difficulty between Judge Grinstead, former editor of the *Herald*, and W. H. Parsons, of the Tyler *Telegraph*, has at last been amicably adjusted. The matter was submitted to a Board of Honor, by whose decision both parties agreed to abide. Grinstead selected Hon. W. B. Ochiltree, Parsons selected Col. M. D. Ector, and the referees selected Col. J. C. Robertson. The board agreed upon the following terms of settlement: That all remarks and reflections emanating from either gentleman, tending in any manner to impugn the character for courage, honesty, or integrity of the other, and every remark of a personal character, which has fallen from either of the parties with regard to the other, be withdrawn. This being agreed to by the parties, it was determined by the board that no further cause of difference existed between them, and that they should meet and shake hands as friends. And thus ended a difficulty which at one time threatened to end in mortal combat. We are truly glad that this precedent for the settling of difficulties between editors has been established. We are decidedly opposed to the shooting mode of settling such disputes. It is very apt to derange the nervous system and destroy the appetite.

THE great train for El Paso left San Antonio on the 7th inst. The *Western Texan* states that the train is composed of one hundred and seventy wagons, and two hundred and ten men, besides the escort. Capt. Arthur, 1st infantry, commands the escort.

A SERIOUS AFFAIR.—A fight occurred on last Monday night, at or near the Thomas House, between a hostler and a gentleman who visited the stable. The hostler, who was considerably injured, but who, we are glad to learn, is recovering, hailed the gentleman, and, receiving no answer, made an attack on him, wounding him with a knife. The assailed returned to the hotel, followed by the assailant, where he seized a stick and knocked his adversary down, breaking his ribs, and otherwise injuring him.

SUDDEN DEATH.—A negro woman, the property of Mrs. Lydia J. Cushney, fell dead on Wednesday morning last, it is supposed from a disease of the heart.

Western Texas.

MR. EDITOR:—Perhaps you have come to the conclusion that I have forgotten both you and the *Advocate*, from my protracted silence; but, I can assure you, that both have been and still are the objects of my most tender solicitude. Afflictions and bad weather caused me to be late getting to my work, and have no regular plan of my circuit. The work being very large, and a great portion of the work quite new, it required much time to form such an acquaintance with the country as would enable one to write understandingly. My circuit now embraces a portion of five counties, viz.: Victoria, De Witt, Gonzales, Karnes, and Goliad, and three towns, Clinton, and Yorktown, in De Witt, the former being the county-seat, and Helena in Karnes, is the county-seat. I have twenty-three appointments, at some of which I preach two and sometimes three times per month, and if I meet my engagements, I must preach thirty sermons this (April) month. I have been much afflicted by bad colds, and on one occasion received an injury in the right side by my horse, yet my strength remains as firm as usual. I have a most beautiful country through which to travel, people remarkably kind, and generally anxious to hear preaching. I find in this country many who were once members of some branch of the Christian church, who emigrated without church letters, and failed to make themselves known as professing Christians, until an accumulation of circumstances drove them into a condition which made them ashamed to acknowledge they had ever been church members. This, Mr. Editor, is a great evil under the sun—and I know of no better agent through which to correct that evil than the printing press. Let all Christian editors sound the alarm, and warn all who wish to emigrate.

ARTESIAN WELL.—Captain P. W. Humphreys has a subscription list containing a number of names of those wishing to take shares in a joint-stock company, for sinking an artesian well in Austin. Those favorable to the project should take shares.

☞ "We never played at Poker, nor permitted our negroes to do so.—*State Gazette.*

But, Major! will you have the face to deny that you are not perfectly familiar with all the mysteries of the games of *Bluff* and *Brag*?

R. D. CARR & Co.—The advertisement of these gentlemen will be found in to-day's paper. They have on hand a lot of children's clothing. Notwithstanding Mr. Carr may not have found any need for using these aforesaid garments for small folk, yet we can vouch he shows them to fond mammas with as much gusto and sells them as cheap as "*ary a man*" in Austin.

The Election in Bexar.

The partial returns received from San Antonio, by Wednesday evening's mail, presents to the mind of the true American, and to every lover of his country, reflections of fearful importance. We care not to what party a man may be attached, he cannot be a true patriot who fails to discover in the result of the contest in Bexar and Comal consequences of direful import. He who argues that the unanimity with which the German and Mexican vote was cast *against* the American candidates is an evidence of the purity of the principles of the anti-American party, must also be prepared to reason that the thousands and tens of thou-

sands of European paupers who swarm the land, are more capable of self-government, more deeply imbued with the spirit of republicanism, more competent to perform the duties which the Constitution and laws of the land require at the hands of every citizen, than those to the manner born; either these ignorant, vicious, besotted *greasers*, who have swelled to such an unprecedented extent the majority of the anti-American party in Bexar county, are wrong, or the seventy thousand intellectual, educated, and refined Virginians, who supported the American ticket at the late election in that State, are in error. Both cannot be right.

The worst passions and the silliest fears of the deluded horde of Mexican peons, who populate to such a dangerous extent the county of Bexar, have been appealed to by a squad of black-robed villains, who exercise over the minds of their miserable followers a despotism more absolute than that of any Turkish nobleman over those who people his seraglio.

Into the hands of these priests, fellow-citizens, the ballot-box has been placed in San Antonio. Serpent-like have they entered into the *jacals* of their countrymen, and there hissed into the ears of the inmates the mandates from which a Mexican has no appeal, and the consequence has been, that on election day a horde of political lepers have crawled to the ballot-box, and there nullified the votes of thousands of your countrymen, who had weighed well the principles in controversy. Great God! shall these things always exist? Shall a race of men, many of whom, in knowledge of American institutions, are inferior to the African—men who have proved themselves incapable of self-government under the most favorable auspices—must these men be permitted to wrest from the intelligent American the most sacred and dearest rights which he possesses, at the bidding of a rotten priesthood, and the scarcely less corrupt demagogues who can be always found ready to betray their country, and surrender their birthright for less than a mess of pottage.

We do not, so help us God, envy our enemies the unholy alliance by which they have acquired victory in Bexar. We record the result more in sorrow than in anger. We feel humiliated when we reflect upon the *materiel* by which the votes of so many true Americans have been rendered nugatory.

[For the *State Times*.]

Downfall of the Hocus-Pocus Democracy of Travis County.

Behold! the great Bombshells, in might
   have come down
To organize things in our glorious
   town,—
And to let us know that, in matters of
   State
'Twill take *their* wise-heads, to set
   everything straight;
For how should we AMERICAN men
See aught without light of *their* wits
   and their pen?

With this blustering host cometh, leading the van,
Great JACK, the Big Gun of the Foreigner's clan;
Who, with all his stump thunder, the
   echoes awoke,
Though alack! he but *snapped*, with a
   flash and a smoke!
For though, far and near, they have
   scoured the plain,
Not a single Know-Nothing is found
   to be slain.
     *   *   *   *   *

But hark! what was that?—on a sudden rings out,
From Travis' green hills, a victorious
   shout!
The "Americans" come!—in their
   principles strong,
They have fought a good fight—they.
   have battled with wrong—
They have won!—and the Bombshell
   with meteor light
Has burst! and gone down, in the
   darkness of night!

Then on! ye brave sons of America's
   soil!
With your forefathers, shrink not, for
   freedom to toil!
Let Washington's counsel forever be
   dear,
Keep the reins in your hands, and the
   ballot-box clear!

Protect the adopted; but teach them
   to know.
We yield not our *birth-right*, to friend
   or to foe!
          LITTLE WINDY.

INDIANS. — MAY-BE-SO. — We have been informed that on Monday night last, a party of Indians (so supposed) visited the farm-houses of several of our citizens living on the San Antonio river, some ten or fifteen miles above this place, and drove off from eighty to one hundred head of horses. Thomas Lott, Esq., Capt. Barton Peck, and Colonel John A. Hodges were the sufferers.

This report may be true, but we don't believe the *Indian* story. We feel satisfied that this stampede was made by the *whites*—or, as Jim Burk, an old ranger, would say, if they were not white then, they could be made so by taking them to a water-hole, and use a little soap on them.

Several persons started immediately in pursuit of these rascals, and we hope will soon overtake them. — *Goliad True American, July* 21, 1855.

Excitement in Navarro County, Texas.—A Man Hung and Barbarously Mutilated.—In the *Leon Pioneer* of the 8th November, 1850, we find a long and shocking account of the progress of the excitement in Navarro county, growing out of the supposed theft of a couple of mulatto boys, belonging to Col. Elliot, of that county. Two men in Col. Elliot's employment were suspected, on the statement of a negro. One, named Elliot, was arrested, and a confession of guilt, implicating himself and a man named Wells, forced from him by tying a rope around his neck and threatening to hang him. The man afterward said the statement was untrue, and made to save his life. In his statement, the plan, he said, included the murder of Elliot. After getting this confession, search was immediately made by various parties for Wells, but without, it is said, succeeding in arresting him. On Friday, the 27th ult., his body was found in Chamber's creek, by some persons who were engaged in building a bridge, and who were hunting oxen at the time, and were attracted to the spot by a gang of buzzards. When found, he was floating near the surface of the water, between a forked limb, which had, to all appearance, been placed over him for the purpose of holding the body to the bottom. Around his neck was the print of a rope. His abdomen had been ripped open, and his bowels torn out, thus leaving but little doubt that he was hanged, and afterward his body thrown into the creek for concealment. The body, from appearances, had been in the creek but a short time, probably fourteen or twenty hours. The parties, or some of them, engaged in the search for Wells, are suspected of the murder, and their lives are threatened. One or two of them have gone to Corsicana and demanded a trial, alleging their innocence. Among the nine persons accused of this foul deed are some of the most respectable and prominent men in the county of Navarro; and, as our informant stated that they all stood their trial before an examining court, and were honorably acquitted, we shall omit their names—considering that, if innocent, it will be doing them injustice, and if guilty, it will not forward the ends of justice. The barbarous and shocking mutilation described in the report of the jury, savors more of the fiend than of man; and, unless upon proof the most clear and convincing, we cannot believe that men of the high standing and honorable feeling that we know some of the accused to be, could have consented to such fiendish work, much less, aided and abetted it.

A NEGRO KILLED.—We understand that a negro, the property of Mr. Geo. Smith, of this county, was killed by Capt. Callaghan, at his place on the Blanco, a few days ago. We learn that Capt. Callaghan had been molested several times, for two or three nights, by persons attempting to break into his house. The noise he made in arising scared them away, and each time he found the negro man in question near a woodpile. This probably excited his suspicion. In the mean time he learned that the negro was armed. He therefore ordered him to give up his arms— a six-shooter, and an unearthly, long, sharp steel blade. The negro refused to do so. The Captain then drew his six-shooter, and told him he must give up his arms or be shot. The boy drew his pistol, and told him to shoot, and seemed careless of his life. The Captain then sent his little son to the house for his shot gun, and as the little fellow approached with the gun, the negro broke and ran towards a horse which he had staked out, with a view to mounting him and escaping. The Captain discharged his fowling-piece at him without serious effect, and, the boy still running, he plumped him in the back with his six-shooter, and that was the last of "Poor Old Edward." The Captain's experience with the "Injins" doubtless assisted him in this affair.— *Seguin Mercury.*

A LETTER to a commercial house in Galveston, from a highly respectable citizen of Crockett, dated May 5th, says: An impromptu fight in the woods, near Alabama, between two families, resulted in all three on one side being shot—two dead. The others (peaceable men hitherto) are unhurt. The name of the three brothers shot is Pool; that of the other party, a father and sons, is Click.—*N. O. Pic.*

☞ The value of negroes in this region of country may be judged of to some extent, by the rates at which a lot hired in this city on the 26th ultimo. A lot of nine negro men, one a rough carpenter, hired at the average of $280·92 each per year, the hire to be paid at the expiration of every four months, reaching an aggregate of $2,528·28 per annum for the nine negroes.—*Texas State Gazette, Jan. 3* 1853.

A Free State out of Texas.

From various sources we have come in possession of facts, which go to show that the Germans, French, Swiss, Hungarians, and other foreigners, will, ere long, make a strong demonstration to form a free State out of Western Texas. We have lately conversed with men from that part of the State, and they unhesitatingly aver that the foreigners there to a man are opposed to slavery. There are also men from the North who are insidious leaders in the movement, and are urging the foreigners to take a bold stand in favor of the project. They are busy in the work of drilling them for the contest, and already boast of having ten thousand voters.

The struggle for a division will soon commence and, although natives of the State would like to see a division, yet they fear to test the question. But whether they move or not, the foreigners will move for them, and bring on the issue. The longer the natives of the State delay action on this subject, the worse it will be for them, for their opponents are gathering numerical strength, and will doubtless overwhelm them sooner or later, unless our present patent process of naturalization is speedily arrested.

These patent mills are grinding out voters with astonishing rapidity, and the hopper is kept full of fresh grists from the old world.

Gentlemen who have lately visited that portion of the State, confirm the above statements.

There is food for reflection to Southern men in this matter, and the sooner the issue is promptly met, the better it will be for all parties.

What will our Texas exchanges say to this state of things?—*New Orleans Creole.*

A Free State in Texas!

Some may look upon such a thing as a free State of Western Texas, as improbable, particularly at a time when such strenuous efforts are being made to carry slavery into Kansas, where slavery does not now exist by positive law. Yet there is a strong probability that such an event will occur within the next ten years. Our opinion is based upon the fact that foreign immigration is greater than domestic by at least ten to one; and upon the well-known fact that foreign immigration is opposed to slavery, from principle, prejudice, and education. And there are many of the immigrants from the older States opposed to slavery, who quietly tolerate it so long as it is an institution of the State, but who will vote no slavery when the question comes up whether Western Texas shall be a free or slave State. This fact is not generally known; if so, it is not duly considered. The vote of the

adopted citizens of Texas now numbers at least twelve thousand. In less than ten years it will be increased to three times that number, unless the naturalization laws are changed. This increase will be in a much greater ratio than that of the native-born vote.—*San Antonio Texan.*

MATAGORDA.—The people of Matagorda county have held a meeting and ordered every Mexican to leave the county. To strangers this may seem wrong, but we hold it to be perfectly right and highly necessary; but a word of explanation should be given. In the first place, then, there are none but the lower class or "Peon" Mexicans in the county; secondly, they have no fixed domicile, but hang around the plantations, taking the likeliest negro girls for wives; and, thirdly, they often steal horses, and these girls, too, and endeavor to run them to Mexico. We should rather have anticipated an appeal to Lynch law, than the mild course which has been adopted.

A VOTER.—As an evidence of the capacity of the Mexican population to discriminate in matters of State importance, it may be mentioned that at one of the polls held in this city, a *greaser*, who was challenged, was asked incidentally by a bystander "who he voted for, for Governor?"

"Sublett," was the reply.

"Who for Lieutenant-Governor?"

"Sublett," rejoined the Mexican.

"Who for Representative?"

"Sublett," again muttered this bombshell freeman.

Voters like that swelled the Anti-American majority in Bexar. Boast of your triumphs, gentlemen Bombshells.

A FREE FIGHT IN TEXAS.—*The Palestine American* gives the following extract from a letter, written at Buena Vista, Shelby County, Texas:

"Yesterday, in Buena Vista, William Therman, M. Wheeler, John Yarborough, and Bob McCoy, went to the house of Sam. H. Cooper, for the purpose of raising a row with Stephen S. Runnels, who was at the time in Cooper's house; but Cooper was across the street, opposite the house, in the grocery. Runnels got up and walked out in the piazza, when Therman drew a five-shooter and fired at him. Runnels then returned the fire, without effect upon either party. John Yarborough next shot Runnels from behind (which shot killed him: he only lived three hours). Runnels then shot Yarborough in the thigh, and the next fire he shot Wheeler, breaking his arm; during which time Therman was beating Runnels over the head with a pistol. Runnels then drew another pistol, when Therman retreated, but not in time to save himself, for Runnels shot him just above the hip. I heard, to-day,. that Therman was dead, and I reckon it is so. During the fight, Cooper ran over and exchanged several shots on the side of Runnels, and wounded some of the party. Mrs. Cooper was in the fight also, charging around, and would, doubtless, have done execution, had not the parties retreated. Stephen Runnels fought like a soldier, to the last—he never fell at all, but made all of the opposite party retreat, after he was mortally wounded. I saw him die ; he bid me an affectionate farewell, and was not heard to sigh or groan, because he was too manly. The Wheelers and their company are now in search of Sam Cooper, and they swear vengeance against him. They are here to-day, drinking and swearing around."

We have neither time nor room for comment on the above.

To The Public.

As some contemptible puppy or puppies have taken it upon themselves to intimate that my absence in the battle of " Escondido"* was attributable to motives of fear, I am forced, in justice to myself, to say to all such, they are liars, slanderers, cowards, and sons of liars, and they would not dare to make the charge in my presence. I furthermore state, that at the time myself, with Varnell and Gholson, turned back, it was the general impression that we were going to have no fight, as we were told the Indians had left their camp, and gone to the mountains. Under these circumstances, some of us concluded it would be useless to beat about for weeks through Mexico to no

* Calahan's Expedition, 1855.

purpose; I, for one, knew my business at home would suffer very materially ; therefore, I turned back. I, perhaps, have honored the cowardly insinuator too much by even this short notice of his charge, and should have passed it by with contemptuous silence, were it not that there are those upon whose friendship I place too high an estimate not to disabuse their minds. I furthermore state, that if any of those busybodies desire to test my courage at any time, I will give them the amplest opportunity. Respectfully,
X. B. SANDERS

Contemplated Servile Rising in Texas.

The Galveston *News* publishes the following letter in relation to the late contemplated negro insurrection in Colorado county :

COLUMBUS, Colorado Co., Sept. 9, 1856

The object of this communication is to state to you all the facts of any importance connected with a recent intended insurrection.

Our suspicions were aroused about two weeks ago, when a meeting of the citizens of the county was called, and a committee of investigation appointed to ferret out the whole matter, and lay the facts before the people of the county for their consideration. The committee entered upon their duties, and, in a short time, they were in full possession of the facts of a well-organized and systematized plan for the murder of our entire white population, with the exception of the young ladies, who were to be taken captives, and made the wives of the diabolical murderers of their parents and friends. The committee found in their possession a number of pistols, bowie-knives, guns, and ammunition. Their passwords of organization were adopted, and their motto, " Leave not a shadow behind."

Last Saturday, the 6th inst., was the time agreed upon for the execution of their damning designs. At a late hour at night, all were to make one simultaneous, desperate effort, with from two to ten apportioned to nearly every house in the county, kill all the whites, save the above exception, plunder their homes, take their horses and arms, and fight their way on to a " free State" (Mexico).

Notwithstanding the intense excitement which moved every member of our community, and the desperate measures to which men are liable to be led on by such impending danger to which we have been exposed by our indulgence and lenity to our slaves, we must say the people acted with more caution and deliberation than ever before characterized the action of any people under similar circumstances.

More than two hundred negroes had violated the law, the penalty of which is death. But, by unanimous consent, the law was withheld, and their lives spared, with the exception of three of the ringleaders, who were, on last Friday, the 5th inst., at 2 o'clock P. M., hung, in compliance with the unanimous voice of the citizens of the county.

Without exception, every Mexican in the county was implicated. They were arrested, and ordered to leave the county within five days, and never again to return, under the penalty of death. There is one, however, by the name of Frank, who is proven to be one of the prime movers of the affair, that was not arrested; but we hope that he may yet be, and have meted out to him such reward as his black deed demands.

We are satisfied that the lower class of the Mexican population are incendiaries in any country where slaves are held, and should be dealt with accordingly. And, for the benefit of the Mexican population, we would here state, that a resolution was passed by the unanimous voice of the county, forever forbidding any Mexican from coming within the limits of the county.

Peace, quiet, and good order are again restored, and, by the watchful care of our Vigilance Committee, a well-organized patrol, and good discipline among our planters, we are persuaded that there will never again occur the necessity of a communication of the character of this.

Yours respectfully,
JOHN H. ROBSON, }
H. A. TATUM, } Cor. Com.
J. H. HICKS. }

The Galveston *News*, of the 11th nst., has also the following paragraph:

"We learn, from the Columbian *Planter*, of the 9th, that two of the negroes engaged in the insurrection at Columbus were whipped to death;

three more were hung last Friday, and the Mexicans who were implicated were ordered to leave the country. There was no proof against these last beyond surmises. The band had a deposit of arms and ammunition in the bottom. They had quite a number of guns, and a large lot of knives, manufactured by one of their number. It was their intention to fight their way to Mexico."

[From the *True Issue, Sept. 5.*]

We noticed last week the rumor that a large number of slaves, of Colorado county, had combined and armed themselves for the purpose of fighting their way into Mexico. Developments have since been made of a much more serious nature than our information then indicated. It is ascertained that a secret combination had been formed, embracing most of the negroes of the county, for the purpose of not fleeing to Mexico, but of murdering the inhabitants—men, women, and children promiscuously. To carry out their hellish purposes, they had organized into companies of various sizes, had adopted secret signs and passwords, sworn never to divulge the plot under the penalty of death, and had elected captains and subordinate officers to command the respective companies. They had provided themselves with some fire-arms and home-made bowie-knives, and had appointed the time for a simultaneous movement. Some two hundred, we learn, have been severely punished under the lash, and several are now in jail awaiting the more serious punishment of death, which is to be inflicted to-day. One of the principal instigators of the movement is a free negro, or one who had been permitted to control his own time as a free man.

GALVESTON, Texas, July 10, 1856.

To the Editor of the N. Y. Daily Times:

The inclosed I cut from one of our city papers, and beg you to publish with such comments as you deem necessary.

In explanation, I must tell you that Mr. Sherwood, a Southern man and eminent lawyer, and, at the last session of our Legislature, a member of the House from this city, had to resign before his term expired, because he had the courage to assert, on the floor of the House, that it was his opinion that " *the Congress of the United States had the Constitutional right to legislate on the subject of Slavery in the Territories.*" This is the only so-called Anti-Slavery sentiment Mr. Sherwood, himself a slaveholder, entertains. I underlined some portions of the article I inclose, and ask you, where lies the difference, in regard to Freedom of Speech and Press, between so-called *despotic Austria*, and these Southern Republican States of the great and free (?) North American Republic ?

Yours,   A SOUTHERNER.

Proceedings of a Public Meeting in Galveston, Texas.

[From the *Galveston News*.]

At a meeting of the citizens of Galveston, convened to take into consideration *the propriety of* PERMITTING *Lorenzo Sherwood to address the people in defense of his course in the last Legislature,* Col. Samuel L. Williams was called to the chair, and Alfred F. James appointed Secretary, when, after explaining the object of the meeting, it was

Resolved, That the following letter, prepared and read by Mr. Ballinger, be addressed to Mr. Sherwood, as embracing the views and sentiments of this meeting, in relation to his contemplated address :

GALVESTON, Monday, July 7, 1856.

LORENZO SHERWOOD, ESQ.—*Sir:* At a public meeting of the citizens of Galveston, convened this morning at the Court House, in consequence of your public notice that you would make an address this evening, in defense of your course in the last Legislature, it was unanimously resolved to notify you of the well-considered sentiments and resolute determination of the people of Galveston, as follows :

That your right, in common with every other citizen, to free opinion, free discussion, and the largest liberty of self-defense, is fully recognized, and will be respected. (?)

But there is one subject, connected with your *course in the Legislature— that of Slavery—on which neither you, nor any one entertaining your views,*

22

will be permitted to appear before the community, in a public manner. That *your views on that subject are unsound and dangerous, is the fixed belief of this community, caused by your own speeches, writing, and acts.*

We are aware that, either actually or seemingly, you wholly misapprehended the real views of the people of Texas, and suppose that, *by explanation and argument, you can make your Anti-Slavery theories and plans inoffensive and acceptable.* How far this should be attributed, on your part, to delusion, and how far to design, is not material. *The Slavery subject is not one which is open to you before us.*

You are, therefore, explicitly and peremptorily notified, that, in your speech, you will not be permitted to touch, in any manner, on the subject of Slavery, or your opinions thereon, either directly or indirectly, or by way of explanation, or otherwise. Under the pretext of the personal right of self-defense, you will not be tolerated in any attempt to defend your course in the Legislature on this subject, which was an aggression on the rights, and an outrage on the feelings, of the State of Texas, and much more on those of the people of Galveston, whom you misrepresented, than any other.

The entire subject of Slavery, in all its connections, is forbidden ground, which you shall not invade.

Your introduction of it in any manner, will be the prompt signal FOR CONSEQUENCES TO WHICH WE NEED NOT ALLUDE.

It has been asserted that you have some supporters in this community upon that subject. We trust not. But if so, and if they have sufficient presumption to undertake to sustain you, in any further discussion of this subject before the people, *they will make this evening the occasion for the definite and final settlement of that issue, both as to you and to them.*

We trust, however, that you will confine yourself to matters of legitimate public interest and discussion, and will not, hereafter, *either in public or private,* further abuse the patience of a people with whom, on that question you have no congeniality, and whom you wholly misunderstand.

This communication will be read to the assembled public before you proceed with your speech; and you will clearly understand, is not to be the subject of any animadversion by YOU.

The meeting was addressed by Messrs. Wm. P. Ballinger, P. R. Edwards, Hamilton Stuart, Thomas M. Joseph, B. C. Franklin, Samuel M. Williams, F. H. Merriman, Oscar Farish, M. B. Menard, Noah John, and Joseph J. Hendley.

Col. Samuel M. Williams, Judge B. C. Franklin, Wm. P. Ballinger, Esq., and Col. E. McLean, were appointed a committee to deliver to Mr. Sherwood a copy of the letter addressed to him by this meeting.

On motion of Hamilton Stuart, Esq., *all those opposed to the action taken by this meeting were requested to withdraw, whereupon Messrs. Joseph J. Hendley and Stephen Van Sickle retired.*

The meeting then adjourned, to meet again this evening at the place appointed by Mr. Sherwood to deliver his address.

SAMUEL M. WILLIAMS,
Chairman.
A. F. JAMES, Secretary.

———

[From the *San Antonio Herald, Oct·* 16, 1855.]

Return of Capt. Callahan's Expedition.—Piedras Negras Burnt.—The Citizens taking up arms.

Captain Callahan returned to our city on Saturday last. From him we learn, that, after he had fallen back upon the town of Piedras Negras, the Mexicans stated to him the battle of Escondido was brought on through mistake—that the object of his expedition was not rightly understood. He was given to understand, that if he wished to pursue and chastise the Indians, he could do so unmolested. This was merely to decoy him out of Piedras Negras, so that the Mexicans could carry out their previous design of massacreing his command.

* * * * * * *

Considerable fuss was made at Eagle Pass about the burning of Piedras Negras, and fears were entertained that the Mexicans and Indians would retaliate upon that place. The Mexicans have themselves alone to blame for the burning of their town. Had they not acted in bad faith towards Capt. Callahan, by lavish displays of friendship assisting him to cross the Rio Grande, and proffering to join his ranks, and then joining the force that lay in ambush to fall upon his front and rear and massacre his whole command, their town would not have been destroyed, nor their property taken without rendering a fair equivalent. They even carried off his dead, it is said, for dissection, in San Fernando.

* * * * * *

Already have a number of our citizens taken the field, prepared and determined to carry the war into the enemy's country, if necessary. Captains Callahan, Henry, and Benton, and the brave men of their commands, have set an example worthy the emulation of all who desire the peace and security of the frontier. One hundred and eleven men, most of whom were never in battle before, whipped a force of Indians and Mexicans more than six times greater than their own, upon their own soil. To arms, then, Texans, and avenge your plundered, outraged, and murdered countrymen! Drive back to their vile dens the thieving, murdering hordes that have been laying your country waste, and carrying your wives and daughters into captivity. Then to arms, Texans! *Now is the time for action!*

———

To the People of Texas.

At a meeting of the citizens of Bexar county, the undersigned were appointed a committee to appeal to you, to take this matter into your own hands, as the Federal and State governments have been appealed to in vain. Your fellow-citizens have been cruelly and shamefully murdered almost within view of the capitol of your State, and the head-quarters of the army of the United States. Your women have been violated, and your children carried into captivity. Frontier settlements have been broken up, and their property carried into Mexico. Mexico has violated the letter and spirit of our treaties with her, by aiding and abetting the Indians in their robberies, harboring them within her borders, and fighting their battles when pursued to their camps. Texans, to the rescue and let no repose be taken until victory, complete and triumphant, shall be ours. On the Cibolo, near the mouth of the Santa Clara, will be the point of rendezvous, and the fifteenth day of November is designated as the day when the expedition will move.

Respectfully,
WM. E. JONES,
J. H. CALLAHAN,
J. A. WILCOX,
JNO. SUTHERLAND,
ASA MITCHELL,
S. A. MAVERICK.

San Antonio, Oct. 16, 1855.

[From the *S. A. Sentinel.*]

☞ On the first page of this number we publish the circular of Captain Callahan, who is now with a few men at Piedras Negras, waiting for assistance. Capt. Callahan's position is somewhat a peculiar one, and one out of which more serious difficulties may arise. It might at first be supposed that our men had *violated* the *neutrality* laws in following the Indians into Mexico. But at the present time there is no government really in Mexico. She has just emerged from a revolution form of government, nor does she even recognize your particular man as being really at the head of her governmental affairs.

[From the *San Antonio Zeitung.*]

" *To the Military Commander of the 9th Military Department :*

"Your memorialists would respectfully represent, that on Sunday, the 10th day of December, 1854, Lieut. Jackson was in command of mounted volunteers, in the vicinity of Dhanis; that during the night the property of the citizens was destroyed; two hogs, the property of John Ney, were killed; sign-boards, windows, shutters, and other things was destroyed, and thus destroyed the letter-box and the sign of the post-office, scattering the contents of the letter-box upon the prairie, besides firing their pistols at random in the streets, to the great annoyance and danger of the inhabitants.

"Lieutenant Jackson and some few men who encamped with them, behaved like gentlemen; but, although they possessed the authority, they had not the power to control the conduct of these lawless men. We would like to have the protection of a company of Rangers, but not such as these are—worse than the red Indian himself. They have stolen 52 valuable horses within a few months, within a circle of 20 miles in diameter, have killed our cows and oxen, and occasionally taken the lives of our citizens; but even these we can better endure than the lawlessness of these men, who should be our protectors.

"We would also respectfully request that the citizens may be remunerated for the losses sustained, and that measures may be taken for our protection in future from such outrages.

"We respectfully append an account of damages.

"Dhanis, Dec. 11, 1854."

BOY OUT.

ABOUT the 1st instant, my negro boy, Charles, absconded, and has not since been heard of. Said boy is subject to attacks of "convulsions," and was probably under the influence of that disease when he went away. My chief object in issuing this notice is to warn persons to be on their guard in approaching him while in that condition, as he is then entirely unmanageable and dangerous if force is attempted with him. I will give a reasonable reward for information of the whereabouts of said negro, but will not ask any one to arrest him, as there would be danger in the attempt to do so. Said negro is black, large, and very stout, about 24 years of age, and has an unusually flat nose, particularly so just between the eyes.

Information may be given at the office of Dr. A. J. Lott, or at the *State Gazette* office.

GEORGE S. HUGHES.
Austin, January 4, 1854.

$100 REWARD.

I WILL give the above reward for my boy BILL, who ran away on the 7th instant, from my plantation in Walker County, if taken up by any person west of the San Antonio River; fifty dollars, if taken up west of the Brazos; and twenty-five dollars to any person taking him up east of the Brazos River. The above reward will be paid on delivering said boy into the hands of any jailer convenient to where taken up, and who can securely keep him until I can get him.

BILL is what would be called a bright mulatto, of rather dull expression of countenance; his hair might be called straight, and, when long, very bushy. Was very long when he left home. His age is about 28 years; his height 5 feet 10 inches.

Took with him from home a double-barrel shot-gun.

WM. B. SCOTT.

Huntsville, April 14, 1855.

SEE the advertisement of W. B. Scott for his runaway negro, Bill. The fellow knocked down the overseer, and then ran to the house, got a gun, and put out before the overseer could overhaul him. Gen. Scott is anxious to recover the boy, in order to punish his insubordination.

TAKEN UP

AND committed to the jail of Bexar County, Texas, on the 13th day of March, 1854, a negro man, calling himself MARTIN, or TOM. He says he is a blacksmith, and belongs to John Beal, Attakapas, on Red River. Said negro is about 48 years of age, 5 feet 8 or 9 inches high, and head a little bald. His back is marked with the whip, and marks of cupping on both temples and back of the neck. He speaks Creole French and broken English. The owner of said negro is hereby notified to come forward, prove property, pay charges, and take him away, or he will be dealt with as the law directs.

W. B. KNOX, Sheriff B. C.

By L. SARGENT, Deputy.

$25 REWARD

WILL be given for the apprehension of my boy HENRY, who ran away from Port Lavaca about the 12th inst. Henry is a blacksmith by trade, about 30 or 35 years of age, heavy set, and very black; is very smart, and, when interrogated, will tell a very plausible story. He is acquainted along the road from this place to Lockhart, and he may attemp to go up that way, and then, by the way of San Antonio, to Mexico. The above reward will be given, if lodged in jail, or for such information as will lead to his recovery.   DAVD IRWIN,

per JOHN IRWIN.

Lavaca, Nov. 28th, 1853.

$100 REWARD.

RAN AWAY, or stolen from the subscriber, near Milam, Sabine County, Texas, about the 1st of March last, a negro man named Reuben. Said negro is about forty-five years of age, stout, and well made, inclined to be of a copper color, one or two of his front teeth out, and stammers a little when talking, if bothered.

I will give fifty dollars to have the negro secured in jail, so that I can get him, and fifty dollars for the apprehension of the thief.

J. M. SPEIGHTS.

Nov. 5th, 1853.

Jacks for Sale.

THE undersigned offers for sale a number of the finest young Jacks in the State, from one to two years of age, of a large size and fine stock, sired by the celebrated Black Hawk, purchased of A. T. Nolance, Nashville, Tennessee. The sire is eight years old, and also for sale.

Having recently come to the country, and not being situated so as to take care of said stock, he offers great bargains, and invites those wishing to purchase to call at his ranch, and examine for themselves, near San Marcos.

E. NANCE

June 23d, 1855.

Negroes, Carriage, and Mules.

At the same time, I will sell for cash in hand, two negro women, a fine Rockaway carriage, and two harness mules. One of the women about 40 years old, a good washer and ironer; the other about 25 years old, an excellent cook. Both are stout and healthy, first rate cotton-pickers, and good out-door hands.

WM. P. MILBY.

Indianola, Aug. 23, 1853.

Two Hundred Dollars Reward.

RUN AWAY or was stolen from the subscriber, about the 1st of December last, a negro man named BOSTON, aged about 31 or 32 years, black complexioned, about 5 feet 6 or 8 inches high, weighs about 150 lbs., has a delicate hand and foot for a negro, and is by profession a Methodist preacher—says a great deal about his religion. One hundred dollars reward will be paid for the delivery of said negro to me, or two hundred dollars for the negro and thief, if stolen, with evidence sufficient to convict the thief.

Any information concerning said negro will be thankfully received.

Address,

W. FITZGERALD,
Columbus, Colorado Co., Texas.

$225 REWARD.

STRAYED or stolen from me, about Christmas, 6 head of horses, viz.: 1 bay mare, 7 years old, with a sorrel colt, and four three-year-old horses, two sorrels, one bay, and one dun, all branded on the left shoulder with my brand, except the colt. I will give $25 for their delivery to me, and will give $200 for any information by which I may lay hands upon the thief.

JAS. P. McKINNEY.

Onion Creek, Travis Co., May 3, 1855.

Runaway.

COMMITTED to jail in Bastrop Co., on the 4th of August, 1855, by T. H. Mays, J. P., a negro man, who says his name is Peter, aged about fifty years, dark complexion, 5 feet 8 or 9 inches high, and says he belongs to Horatio Hearn, of Robinson County, Texas. The owner is requested to come forward, prove property, pay charges, and take him away, or he will be dealt with according to law.

JOHN HEARN,
Sheriff B. C.

$10 REWARD.

STRAYED or stolen from the subscriber, one brown mare, about 14 hands high, branded with a Spanish brand on the left hind hip, and the letter D on the left shoulder. She has a long black tail, mane and legs black;

also, star in her forehead, saddle-marks on her right side, and has been fly-blown about the root of the tail; about 7 years old, very skittish, and not easily caught.

CASPER STEUSSEY.

$100 REWARD.

STOP THE HORSE-THIEF!

STOLEN from the undersigned, living in Austin, on the night of the 7th of Aug., a cream-colored American horse, 5 years old, 16 hands high, white mane and tail, with a blaze face, shod all round, paces well, and has some white spots about his breast and shoulders from tick bites. A Texas-rigged saddle, with hair girth, and a brass-plated stiff-bit bridle, with new leather reins, were taken with the horse. I will give the above reward for the apprehension of the thief and recovery of the horse, or twenty-five dollars for the recovery of the horse.

ERNST RAVEN.

CATTLE WANTED.

I HAVE four leagues of land on *Los Pintos* Creek, in Nueces County, fourteen miles from San Patricio, of the finest grazing qualities, the mesquit grass being knee high the year round, one-half of which tract I am willing to exchange for stock cattle, and would be willing to make an arrangement with the purchaser to place an equal number of cattle on the place, to be placed in charge of a competent American family, and the requisite number of Mexican vaqueros.

Those having large stocks of cattle, would do well to communicate with me.

Address me at this place.

WM. H. HOUSTON.

City of Austin, May 31st, 1855.

I. O. of G. S. & D. of S.

CAPITOL UNION LODGE, No. 16, of the Independent Order of Good Samaritans and Daughters of Samaria, meets every Monday evening, at 7 o'clock.

B. F. CARTER,
SEBRON SNEED, W. C. G. S.
W. R. S.
Austin, Dec. 23, 1854.

BY TELEGRAPH!

Important Discovery.

THE reason why Lord Raglan has not stormed Sevastopol, has been mainly owing to the weak and enfeebled condition of the Allied Armies, caused by their unparalleled sufferings in an inhospitable climate. It has now been clearly ascertained to have been produced by the absence of *ROBERTSON'S TONIC BITTERS.*

Notice.

THIS is to notify all persons that they *must not bathe* in the Colorado river anywhere in the vicinity of Swisher's or Grumble's Ferry, after this date, under penalty of being taken before the Hon. J. T. Cleveland, Mayor of the city of Austin, and there undergoing a fine of Ten Dollars for each and every such offense committed against the peace and dignity of this city.

SAM'L C. TAYLOR,
City Marshal.

Austin, July 21, 1855.

Land for Sale.

640 acres, 90 miles north of Austin, the road to Fort Croghan running obliquely through it, part of Gen. Travis's headright, selected, located and surveyed by H. L. Upshur, District Surveyor, who will give particular description. Equal parts mesquit, prairie and post-oak timber—a noted spring and camping-place near the road.

Apply to
HARALSON, FLOURNOY & ROBARDS.

Austin, July 18th, 1855.

LOST.—The dunce Caroline's headright third league land certificate, No. 8, 2d class, issued by Board Land Commissioners for Goliad County, on the 9th day of August, 1838. If not found within the time prescribed by law, application will be made for a duplicate. ENOCH MOORE.

J. DOUGLASS BROWN, Agent.

July 21, 1855.

LOST.—The Discharge of J. T. Wheeler, a Sergeant in Company B, 1st Regiment Texas Army, under Capt. R. Roman. Also, the Headright

---

Certificate of John Swesey for half league of land, No. 41, issued in Harris County. If not heard of within 90 days, application will be made for duplicates of the same. J. W. ISBELL,

July 21, 1855. Agent.

San Saba Land for Sale.

I HAVE 1280 acres of Land on the South bank of the San Saba river, granted to Elijah Gillman, and known as survey No. 34, which I will sell for $1 75 cents per acre.

Apply immediately to
JNO. T. HARCOURT.

Lagrange, Texas, July 26, 1855.

UNION HALL BAR-ROOM
EXCHANGE.

To the Drinking Public.

THE subscriber would say that for their accommodation he has fitted up an establishment second to none *anywhere.* He only solicits such a share of patronage as he may be thought to be entitled to by those who will give him a call.

C. V. SHAFER.

Bastrop, July 16, 1853.

Ecole Primaire.
Française et Anglaise.

MR. A. ROY, professeur de française, a l'honneur d'annoncer aux parents qu'il vient de s'ajoindre au maitre d'anglais qui sera attaché à son école d'une maniere permanente, tous les soins seront donnés aux enfants qui lui seront confiés.

CONDITIONS:

Pour la 1ere. classe, pour le française et l'anglaise, payables par trémestre et d'avance, $24·00
2e. classe 18·00
Français seul 12·50
Anglais seul 12·50

Natchitoches, 3 Septembre, 1853.

Valuable Negroes at Public Auction!

WILL be sold at public auction, to the highest bidder, without reserve, in the town of Natchitoches, on Saturday, the 3d day of December next, 2 valuable Negro men, viz.:

WILLIAM, aged about 32

years, a first rate cotton-picker, good axe-man, smart, sound in every particular, and fully guarantied.

SAM, aged about thirty years, fully guarantied as to health and title. He is inclined to take to the woods when tightly pressed, and has not the resolution or moral firmness to resist the temptation of appropriating to his own use, when hungry, a sack of meal, or other edible—the title to which might be vested in another. He is smart and active, a first rate cotton-picker and axe-man.

Terms:

One-half cash, the other half payable on the 1st of April, 1854—the purchaser or purchasers to give notes with approved security, in solido, bearing interest at the rate of 8 per centum per annum from maturity till paid, payable to the order of the undersigned, auctioneer or bearer, with mortgage and vendor's privilege retained, further to secure the payment of said notes.

The Negroes can be seen at the Saw Mill of W. L. Hains, above Campté.

☞ Will be sold also, at the same time and place, 12 or 15 head of Horned Cattle. The cattle will be sold for cash, as they run in the woods.

D. H. BOULLT,
Nov. 19, 1853.   Auctioneer.

NOTICE!
To Receivers and Shippers of Cotton.

THE proprietors of the *SHIPPER'S COTTON PRESS* are now prepared to receive and store, under cover, 5,500 bales of cotton at one time. Their Storage Shed and Press Building are situated on the Strand, in the west end of the city, and two blocks from any other building, which renders them more secure from fire. Their establishment and its appurtenances cover an entire block—say 260 feet by 300 feet. The Storage Shed extends the whole width (260 feet) of the block to the depth of 60 feet. This structure is of the very best material. The Press Building, which is 60 feet by 40 feet, is built of brick and roofed with tin, rendering it completely fire-proof. The Press Machinery is of Tyler's invention, 48-inch cylinder. All the other machinery employed is of the latest and most improved pattern, while the Press Frame is one of the best, if not the very best, ever built.

All cotton consigned to parties storing at their press will be received on the wharves and drayed to press without giving the parties any trouble, and repairs estimated at the time of receiving the cotton, which will be sampled by an experienced sampler.

☞ The Weighing will always be attended to by experienced weighers. A Watchman will be in attendance day and night to guard against fires and other casualties. The following is their

TARIFF OF CHARGES:

CONSIGNEES' CHARGES.

Drayage to press,	8¾c.	per bale.
Labor,	5	"
Storage,	10	"
Weighing,	8	"
Sampling	3	"
Repairs—Rope,	10	each.
Patches,	15	"
Heads,	30	"
Edges	50	"
Sides	50	"

VESSELS' CHARGES.

Compressing coastwise,	8c.	
Freight 25c. per bale; ⅜c. freight and upwards,	30c. dr. bl.	
Compressing foreign,	40	do.
Extra ropes, each,	8	
Drayage to vessel,	8⅛c pr bl.	

NOTE.—No extra drayage charged on bales that have burst ropes alongside the vessel, if returned to press for repairs.

SHIPPERS' CHARGES.

Storage and labor per mo.,	10c. pr bl	
Classing,	5	"
Weighing,	8	"
Sampling,	3	"
Ship-marking,	3	"
Drayage to vessel,	8⅛	"

NOTE.—No labor or storage charged on any cotton sent to press with orders for compressing and shipment.

L. E. HOOPER & CO.
Galveston, January, 17, 1854.

AVIS.

Michel Anty et al. heirs, vs. Treciny Delouches et al. heirs.   No. 4583.
Cour de District, Natchitoches.

CONFORMEMENT à un ordré de l'hon. Cour de District dans et pour la Paroisse des Natchitoches, rendu dans l'affaire ci-dessus mentionée pour un partage entre les héritiers de la feue Marie Rose Robin, femme de Athanase

Lecour, et les héritiers d'Athanase Lecour, tous les deaux décédás des propriétés appartenant aux successions des dits décédés, en communautè et en propriétés separées, il sera offert en vente publique, à la dernière demeure de la dite defunte, dans la Paroisse de Natchitoches, près de Clouterville, Jeudi le 22 de Décembre, 1853, les propriétés ci-après-décrites appartenant aux successions des dits décédés, savoir : certain meubles consistant de meubles meublans, ustensils, aratoires, bétes à cornes, chevaux, cochons, maïs, et aussi une terre situé dans la Paroisse des Natchitoches, sur la rive gauche de la Rivière, contenant environ deux cents cinquante arpents de superficie, étant la même ou résidait la defunte, bornée en haut par la terre d'Alphonse Sampité, et par en bas par un autre morceau de terre appartenant à la dite Marie Rose, avec toutes les bastisse et améliorations qui s'y trouvent.

Un autre morceau de terre, achetée par la décédée Marie Rose de C. F. Benoist, contenant environ quatre-vingt arpents de superficie, bornée en haut par la précédente, et en bas par la terre de Pierre Lacour, avec toutes les batisses et améliorations dessus.

Aussi, dix-sept esclaves, grands et petits, plus particuliérement décrits dans l'inventaire pris par devant Chas. Sers, Notaire Publique. Les vices et maladies de ces esclaves seront annoncés le jour de la vente, et ils seront vendus comme sujets aux maladies, et vices annoncés.

Conditions de la Vente :

Pour toutes sommes jusqu'à vingt piastres comptant, pour toute somme au-dessus ce montant, payable le premier de Mai, 1854. Pour les terres et les esclaves, le tiers payable le premier de Mai, 1854, un tiers le premier de Mai, 1855, et un tiers le premier de Mai, 1856. Les acheteurs au crédit sus-dit donneront leur billets cautionnés à satisfaction et in solido, à l'ordre de l'officier qui fera la vente ou porteur, avec les intérêts á raison de huit pour cent. par an, de l'échéance jusqu'au paiement, et cautionnés par le privilège du vendeur, et hypothèque spécialé retenus sur les objects vendus, pour lesquelles les billets sont donnés, et les terres et les esclaves seront vendues sujettes à la clause de non alienation au prejudice du privilége du vendeur et

de l'hypothéque retenus pour assurer le paiment des billets. Chaque paiement pour les terre et les esclaves sera divisé en deux portions, pour chacune dequelles les acheteurs donneront leurs billets comme susdits.

J. M. COMPERE,
19 Nov., 1853.   Encanteur.

San Pedro Spring.

Der Unterzeichnete benachrichtigt das Publikum von San Antonio und Umgegend, dass er jetzt vorbereitet ist, allen Anforderungen vorsprechender Gäste in Speisen und Getränken bestmöglichst zu entsprechen, und wünscht ferner die Aufmerksamkeit aller Freunde von Lustbarkeiten darauf zu lenken, dass *jeden Sonntag* HARMONIE- und TANZMUSIK und SCHEIBENSCHIESSEN auf seinem Platze am San Pedro-Spring stattfinden.

WILLIAM MÜLLER.

☞ Der Unterzeichnete wird ferner für geeignete Ambulances Sorge tragen, um das besuchende Publikum dorthin und zurück zu fahren, die Person zu 25 Cts.

EDUARD BRADEN.

Schul-Eroeffnung!

Miss N. E. DAVIS,

ein Zögling des J. O. O. F. Collegiate-Instituts in Rogersville, Tenn., und zuletzt eine Lehrerin in demselben, hat soeben in der Presbyterian-Kirche in San Antonio eine Schule eröffnet, und hofft durch ihre Schule Jedermann zufrieden zu stellen.

Lehr-Bedingungen:
Für die Vorbereitungs-Classen
     pr. Monat -   - $3 00
"   " höheren Classen - $4 00
☞ Keine weiteren Forderungen werden gemacht.

Versiegelte Anerbietungen

wegen Lieferung von *Einhundert und fünfzig Cords* guten gesunden, preiswürdigen MUSKIT-HOLZES, jedes Cord von 128 Fuss Kubik-Inhalt, werden entgegengenommen bei der unterzeichneten Office bis zum 20. d. M., Nachmittags 4 Uhr. Das Holz soll 4 Fuss lang geschnitten sein, in dem Alamo-Hofe gehörig aufgeschichtet, und sämmtlich zwischen dem 27. November 1854 und dem 31. Januar 1855 abgeliefert werden, und jedes Gebot muss von wenigstens zwei guten Bürgen unterstützt sein.

Assist. Qu. Mrs. Office, San Antonio, 9. Novbr. 1854.
JAS. BELGER, ASS. Q. M.

Frank V. D. Stucken,
DEALER IN
DRY GOODS AND GROCERIES, &c.,
Fredericksburg, Texas,

empfiehlt seinen Freunden und dem Publikum überhaupt sein gut assortirtes Lager von DRY GOODS AND GROCERIES, &c., und versichert bei guter und schneller Bedienung die billigsten Preise.

Zwei halbe Acre Lots

(gutes Gartenland) mit Steinhaus und grosser Kuh- und Kälber-Pen, in der Nähe des San Pedro, sind zu verkaufen. Näheres in der Office der San Antonio Zeitung.

COTTON-GIN.

Da wir in Castroville eine Mühle und Cotton-Gin zu errichten beabsichtigen, wozu bereits alle Anstalten getroffen sind, so dass die Maschinen im Herbste dieses Jahres in Thätigkeit treten können; so machen wir die Herren Farmer von Castroville und Medina County hierauf mit dem besonderen Bemerken aufmerksam, dass wir Baumwollen-Saat, den Bushel zu 35 Cents—unserem Einkaufs-Preis—vorräthig halten, und an alle diejenigen ablassen wollen, welche sich auf Erzeugung von Baumwolle dieses Jahr legen wollen.

Castroville und San Antonio, 20. *Feb.*
G. L. HAASS.
LAURENT QUINTLE.

Free Labor and Slave Labor.

We clip an article bearing the above head from Elihu Burritt's "Citizen of the World," and recommend it to our

22*

American readers, not only on account of its truthfulness, but also of the kind and brotherly feelngs with which he treats so delicate a subject.

We believe it is not a premature inference to assume, that many influential and intelligent men, even among the slaveholders of the Southern States, are beginning to balance these two antagonistic economies, with clearer perceptions of their comparative worth and working. We cannot believe it possible that this is not the case. The mighty energies of Free Labor, its inventive capacity and inexhaustible genius, have so filled every vista, and lined every road and lane which they have seen and traveled in their journeyings in the Northern States, that they must have instituted these comparisons between systems so diametrically opposite in their results.

* * * * *

The correctness of the inferences drawn by Mr. Burritt from experiments in English free labor might be denied because the South of the Union is not England, and what in the one country is practicable, may, in the other, be impossible. Therefore, we join the following instances of prices of labor here. Now, a German or Irish farm-laborer can be hired, in Texas, at from $8 to $18 per month, while a negro farm-laborer cannot be hired at less than from $20 to $22 per month [in both cases boarding and lodging included]. A German or Irish maid-servant can be hired at from $8 to $12 per month, while a negro girl of inferior capacity to fill the same place, cannot be got under $15 to $20 per month. Is the free labor so much less worth than the slave labor? By no means; everybody admits the contrary. Why, then, is it that worse work, if done by a slave, is better paid than good work done by free labor? There can scarcely be another cause of this strange state of affairs, than that planters cannot have at hand a ready and abundant supply of white hands on whom they can rely at times when a large force is needed on their crop, while the slave is always at hand, and can be made available at all kinds of work.

If this is the state of things now, and if free labor is really *cheaper* than that of the slave, and only unavailable from its uncertain supply—there is a remedy

Encourage white immigration so as to get an ever fresh and abundant supply of white hands. They can be had at least 25 per cent. cheaper than slave hands, and their work will be much better.

Elecciones Municipales
de SAN ANTONIO.

La Democracia ha obtenido un nuevo triunfo; su boleta entera ha salido de la urna electoral, dando una otra evidencia de que principios prevalecen entre nosotros sobre *consideraciones y amistades personales.* Los Know-Nothings, convencidos de su impotencia, no han aun tratado presentar candidatos de su partido, contentos con fomentar en el Partido Democrata una division de la cual se lizongeaban aprovecharse en la proxima eleccion de Agosto.

Las elecciones pasaron muy quietamente. Solo sentimos ver dos ó tres noches antes una procesion de unos 30 pelados con violin y guitarro, gritando por el candidato batide. La opinion publica deberia hacer justicia de esas bacanales electorales, en que ningun ciudadano honrado condescenderia en figurar.

San Elizario, Diciembre 10, 1855.

Editores del Bejareño.

Señores. Un pobre viejo vecino de esta, que pasa largo de los 60 años, sin recurros ningunos y expuesto á la mendicidad, pasó ha algunos dias á Mejico, donde tiene toda su parentela, allí le obsequiaron con algunas cositas de cariño con que volvió á esta banda el dia 8 del presente, con el contrabando de un piloncillo, una libra de azucar, tres libras de carne aces, dos almudes de orejon, un par de suelas, un pedazo de cordovan, seis tablillas de chocolate y un sombrero de palma gruesa. Al pasar este infeliz por la Isleta (Tejas) uno de los Oficiales de la aduana de los E. U. le decomisó los referidos intereses: cosa muy extravagante á mi parecer, Señores Editores, y que da lugar al refran que dice que " *unos son los de la fama, y otros son los que cargan la lana.*" En Mejico, puede cualquier individuo pasar las provisiones necesarias de boca, sin pagar nada, y menos se le quita nada de eso.

Creyendo que tal acontecimiento es digno de ser puesto en conocimiento del publico, se les comunicó para que le den un lugarcito en los columnas de vuestro apreciable periodico.

Su affmo. amigo,

VERDAD.

(*Comunicado.*)

Pleito concluido.

Adelante *Independientes!*
Tam, taram, arma á diestra!
Apuntan; fuego; turrum . . .
Muchachos, la lancha es nuestra.

Asi anunciaba el *Funeral*
Un pobre Maestro de Escuela,
Que avirtiria este año entrante,
Muchachos, la lancha es nuestra.

Lo sabrás, decia, *Judio,*
Hebreo, veras la muestra,
Requiescant in pace, Amen!
Muchachos, la lancha es nuestra.

Monopolistas de Bejar,
Vereis que es cosa indigesta,
Meterse en esas honduras,
Muchachos, la lancha es nuestra.

¡Oh! *tanquam leones rugientes,*
Latinorum es ma fiesta.
Macti animi. camaradas,
Muchachos, la lancha es nuestra.

Si: como "leones rugientes"
Tenemos boca abierta;
Pero asi vos quedareis,
Muchachos, la lancha es nuestra.

Que ya del Santo *Miguel*
Los *Hurras* forman la Orquestra,
Con narcóticos acentos,
Muchachos, la lancha es nuestra.

Que, el que á buen palo se arrima
Goza sombra y duerme siesta:
Pero si se queda en llano . . .
Muchachos, la lancha es nuestra.

Pues cuando el Juicioso calla,
Y el insensato hace gresca,
Son vehementes las señales;
Muchachos, la lancha es nuestra.

¿ *Requiescant in pace*, dices?
Ved que leccion tan funesta
Para todo entremetido,
Muchachos, la lancha es nuestra.

¡Democratas extraviados!
Que habeis desertado en este.
¡Volved á vuestras banderas!
Muchachos, la lancha es nuestra.

Mas el Pleito ya concluido,
Rindamonos á la ley,
Y al enemigo vencido,
Generosidad con él.

UN VIEJO.

El dia 6 de Enero, se celebrará la ceremonia religiosa del asiento de la primera piedra de la nueva Iglesia Catolica que quedará bajo la invocacion de N. Señora del Alamo.

La banda de los Rifleros, bajo la habil direccion de nuestro amigo Don Rafael Quintana, nos hace oir casi cada noche su suave armonio, cambiando nuestra pobre Plaza Militar, habitualmente tan desierta, en un verdadero Eliseo.

Un periodico Abolicionista propone á las Señoras del Norte que no usen nada de los productos de los Estados que tienen Esclavos.

La causa del pugilista Baker, que fué uno de los que matáron á Bill Poole, el año pasado en Nueva York, causando tanta sensacion, se ha concluido, el juri no pudiendo convenir en el fallo.
La causa servirá mucho para la policia de esa ciudad, pues el testimonio ha sacado á luz los misterios de los cabaretes y casas de alojamiento de la clase de los bravos de Nueva York.

ESCAPE MILAGROSO.—Sabemos que un niño del Sr. W D. Skillman cayó, algunos dias hace, del segundo piso de la Fonda Read, sin recibir mas que contusiones ligeras.

Daguerreotipo.

El Señor McCARTHY tiene el honor de anunciar al publico que sigue tomando retratros daguerreotipos. Confia en que los retratos que hace altienen rivales en la Union y siempre tiene en varios para satisfacer a los incredulos. Oficina en la calle de Comercio.

ante la carrera.—No se aceptarán sino caballos criados en Texas. Pesos segun las regulaciones de la arena de Nueva Orleans, con reduccion de 20 libras.

La inferioridad del tamaño y fondo de los caballos de Texas hacen precisa esta reduccion.

Potros de dos y tres años, 66 libras—de cuatro anos, 80 libras—caballos de cinco años 90 libras—de seis anos, 98 libras—de siete años y por arriba, 104 libras—Reduccion de tres libras para yeguas y caballos caponés.

MARCELLUS FRENCH, } Tesoreros.
A. J. M. McCARTHY, }

CARTAS

En Español y Frances que quedan en la oficina de Correos de San Antonio, el dia 1 de Enero de 1856.

Don José B. Da Camara, 3
" Antonio Peres,
" Eusebio Garcia,

Don Felipe Garza,
" José Maria Gonzales,
" Casimiro Garcia,
" Francisco L. Morales,
" Angel Torres,
" Alberto Locur,
" Francisco Carreño,
" Vicente Soza,
" Jesus Mesa,
Doña Ma. de Jesus Troviño,
Mademoiselle Caroline Grunenwals
Mr. A. Bosigues,
" Emile Raux,
" Odet ——2
" Norville Moreau,
" Jean Raimond Lozes, 2,
" Jean Baptiste Spettel,
" Adolphe Pinçon,
" Louis Keller,
" Laroque Turgeau,
" Reginald de Léon,
" Bénoit Muller,
" Lecomte de Watine.
Sirvanse las personas que pidan estas cartas, decir que han sido anunciadas
El Administrador, J. BROWN.